Photo. J. Russell & Sons

EDWARD ARMSTRONG

ITALIAN STUDIES

BY

EDWARD ARMSTRONG

EDITED BY

CECILIA M. ADY

MACMILLAN AND CO., LIMITED
ST. MARTIN'S STREET, LONDON
1934

COPYRIGHT

PRINTED IN GREAT BRITAIN
BY R. & R. CLARK, LIMITED, EDINBURGH

PREFACE

EDWARD ARMSTRONG was the chief English authority on the history of Italy in the age of Dante and of the Renaissance, yet he wrote only one book on the subject—his monograph on *Lorenzo de' Medici* in the Heroes of the Nations Series. The wealth of his scholarship was lavished upon his pupils, and it lives to-day in the minds of those who were inspired by his teaching. There remain, however, his articles in the *Cambridge Modern History* and the *Cambridge Medieval History*, also a considerable number of essays contributed to various periodicals in the course of over thirty years. Several of these had their origin in papers read before the Oxford Dante Society; others were the outcome of his lecturing and teaching for the Oxford Honour School of Modern History; others again were prompted by travels in Italian byways in which he found unfailing delight. Together, they bear impressive testimony to his intimate and varied knowledge of Italy and the Italians, a knowledge which was won, not only by diligent search in archives, but by studying the countryside and its flowers, by watching the peasants at work in the fields, and by mingling with the citizens as they lounged in the wine-shop or on the piazza. They show, perhaps, more clearly than his larger works the secret of his power as a historian. Wisdom, wit and learning are here enriched by imagination, the gift which enabled him to observe the habits and point of view of the men and women of the past with an interest no less lively and sympathetic than that which marked his intercourse with his contemporaries. As the late Dean of Winchester wrote in the obituary notice which serves as an introduction to the present volume, "his papers well deserve collection". If apology should be made for the publication of this selection from his writings, the fault for which those concerned would plead guilty is that its appearance is long overdue.

Of the fourteen essays collected here, two are published for the first time, and the remainder have appeared in the *Proceedings of the British Academy*, the *Quarterly*, *English Historical*, *Church Quarterly*, and *Modern Language Reviews*, *Macmillan's Magazine*, *History* and the *Pilot*. I have to thank Dr. C. W. Previté-Orton for valuable suggestions with regard to Essay No. III, Mrs. and Miss Armstrong for help without which my task could not have been undertaken, and all those who have given leave for the reproduction of articles: the President and Council of the British Academy, Sir John Murray, Messrs. Longman, Green & Co., the proprietors of the *Church Quarterly* and the Syndics of the Cambridge University Press.

The essays have been reproduced with the minimum of alteration, and this chiefly in the case of the two which the author had not prepared for publication. Such notes and additions as I have made are placed between square brackets.

CECILIA M. ADY

Oxford,
1 *November* 1933

CONTENTS

INTRODUCTION[1]

EDWARD ARMSTRONG (1846–1928)

THERE is a model for anyone who would write in memory of Edward Armstrong, in the words he himself wrote of Edward Moore for the *Proceedings of the British Academy*, of which they both were distinguished members. In the *Proceedings*, vol. vii, is the record of the life and learning of the eminent Dantist: appreciative, sympathetic and candid. Thus should Armstrong be commemorated: the distinction of the subject must excuse the inadequacy of the attempt. He was a many-sided man, the width of whose learning was equalled by the charm of his personal character.

Edward Armstrong was born at Tidenham Vicarage on March 3, 1846, the second son of John Armstrong, then a country parson, afterwards Bishop of Grahamstown. The Bishop died when his son was ten years old, but meanwhile they had travelled together over much of Kafirland, and the boy had been at St. Andrew's College, Grahamstown. He retained vivid memories of South Africa all his life. His mother was Frances Whitmore. She lived till 1908 at Iffley, with her daughter, a delightful artist—a mile or so from her son, who was devoted to her and was never so happy as when presenting to her his friends, who never failed to admire the wisdom and vivacity which she retained till a great age. One of her reminiscences was of a dinner with Sydney Smith, who thus described a personage he had known: "The man's face was like a whole vintage of *clar't*". Bishop Armstrong was an "old-fashioned High Churchman", perhaps not definitely a Tractarian. His son followed him in loyalty to the Church of his baptism. Almost to the last he rarely missed attendance in the College at "morning chapel". Conspicuously a layman himself, he was as much at home with

[1] [Reprinted from *Proceedings of the British Academy*, vol. xiv.]

clergy as with laymen: he was at home with almost all types among them, not least with his neighbour the broad-minded ascetic Richard Meux Benson. What Mr. Humphrey Paul said of John Keble was equally true of him: "There are some men for whom the Church of England is too large and others for whom it is too small. It was exactly the right size for Mr. Keble."

His first wife, a lady of singular beauty, was an ardent worker in charity and religion: he put on her grave the beautiful words, *In simplicitate cordis quaesivit Deum.* His second wife, who made his last years so happy, was a clergyman's daughter.

But a thorough layman was he: mixing freely with all sorts and conditions of men. It is of his learning and scholarship, and his wisdom as a man of affairs, that we are specially to speak; but that would give a very inadequate picture of him which did not recall on what terms of unbroken friendliness he lived with those "in the world's eye" beneath him. You could see in their faces what a pleasure it was to servants to do anything for him, and all those who in different capacities assisted him in his College and those who waited upon him at home, cooks, "scouts", gardeners, housemaids, one always felt, were among his friends, and he would often repeat quaint expressions or wise saws of theirs with pleasure. All these things made his life, in Chaucer's phrase, so "paisible and swete". So he might have lived quietly in college and garden. But this was the part of his life which was least known to the wide world in which he moved as scholar, teacher and man of affairs.

Take the last first. He became Bursar of his College just at the time when Oxford suffered most severely from agricultural depression, and he lived to see it rich and prosperous, a result due not a little to his wise and cautious guidance. He was Pro-Provost, and thus, under the Statutes of that date, head of the College, from 1911 to 1922, ruling with wisdom and geniality, and becoming extremely popular with all Queen's men, young and old.

He became Warden of his old school, Bradfield, at a difficult time, and he guided it to a new success. Similar was the work he did on numerous University Boards and Committees, always prudent, helpful and sagacious.

But it is as an historian that the British Academy will remember him, and here the association is wholly with Oxford. He was elected from Bradfield to a scholarship at Exeter College in 1865, took two first classes, and became Fellow of Queen's in 1869. He began his modern history teaching in 1879 and continued it for more than forty years, instructing not only Queen's men but others by arrangement, and becoming the most popular and influential of all those engaged in the training of the rapidly increasing number of girl students of different colleges. He examined at other Universities, and for two years he was Reader in Foreign History in his own. His lectures were extremely systematic, detailed and exact. But his chief educational work was done with individuals, to whom he devoted an infinity of pains and whose personal friend he almost always became. To read Aristotle's *Politics* with him, says one of his pupils, "was an illumination of all history: the reach of his mind never seemed cramped or hindered by the feeblest of pupils: one was spurred and shamed into endeavouring to keep up with him not only by his mental power but by his whole genial personality". And another speaks of his extraordinarily detailed knowledge of Italian historians "so that we all seemed to be exploring together unfamiliar texts", and adds that he seemed to have lived in medieval Italy, and a visitor to Florence could find her way about from what he had said, and recognise all sorts of delightful details. The amount of care he devoted to personal teaching, criticism, encouragement and advice is indeed almost incredible, and his pupils rewarded his unstinted service with a persisting and devoted loyalty. The College to which he belonged was remarkable for the distinction of its senior members, Magrath, Sayce, Grose, A. C. Clark, E. M. Walker, T. W. Allen conspicuous among them; but no one perhaps was so intimate or so influential in his relation with the undergraduates as was he.

His history teaching led up to his writings, on which his fame as an eminent historian will rest. On the literary side his chief study was devoted to the historical setting of Dante, of which probably no Englishman had so close a knowledge. As a member of the Oxford Dante Society he wrote a number of learned and brilliant papers, notably on Dante's political ideas, on the constitution of Florence in his time, on the sports and pastimes of his age (a particularly vivid and original essay), and, in the very last months of his life, on the Popes of Dante's lifetime.[1] These, and some others of his papers, well deserve collection in a volume. His knowledge of Italian history became wide and exact. It was exemplified in a compact and attractive biography of *Lorenzo de' Medici* (1896). This showed a complete knowledge of all the modern literature of the subject, and, though the author disclaimed original research, it is quite clear that he had studied the original authorities. The style was free and natural, with some such quips as abounded in Armstrong's conversation. "Nothing is easier than to murder one man, few things more difficult than to murder two", is an example. *Elizabeth Farnese* (1892), which combined Spanish with Italian history, was a work of original research, and was based largely on documents which the writer studied in Italy and Spain. More popular again were the brilliant lectures on *The French Wars of Religion*, which were delivered at the summer meeting of the Oxford University Extension in 1892, and then expanded into a book. These were not only the result of long study of the history of the period but were written in a sparkling and attractive style, with the personal touches in which the writer delighted—"Land for nothing and another class to pay the taxes is the invariable programme of rural revolutions"—and masterly analyses of character. The book was important as showing how little

---

[1] [Of the papers mentioned here, two are included in the present volume (III, V), the paper on the constitution of Florence was embodied by the author in his lecture on Dante and Savonarola (VI), while that on the Popes provided material for his article on "Italy in the Time of Dante" (*Cambridge Medieval History*, vol. vii).]

religion really had to do with those religious wars and how deep was the moral corruption of the times, which the Huguenots, immersed in political intrigue, made no real effort to stem. It showed, as Stubbs and S. R. Gardiner had shown, that it was possible for an exact and learned scholar of history in detail to write in summary briefly and brilliantly. It may be that the nature of that Summer Meeting, at which Addington Symonds and Walter Pater also lectured, inspired Armstrong to a greater freedom of style than was usual with him; but though he was personally friendly with many Extension Lecturers he often spoke severely of the encouragement which he believed the system gave to hasty generalisation and inadequate study.

Armstrong's *magnum opus* was his *Charles V* (first edition 1901, second 1910). The biography was an extraordinarily complete one, in spite of the limits which he had set himself. It is true of it, as Freeman would often say of Gibbon, that everything belonging to the time is there, not always discoverable at first, but revealing itself to the student as he knows what to search for, and teaching him more and more in proportion to his knowledge. Armstrong treated Charles primarily from the point of view of a biographer: the times are seen in relation to the man. But this involved no loss of wide survey: on the contrary, it may be doubted if there has ever been given a survey of the age of Charles V which is illuminative over so large a field. And everywhere Armstrong walked with the firm tread of a master. He had no prejudices, or if he had he disguised them well. He had no gaps in his knowledge, or he covered them very adroitly. His description, for example, of the religious attitude of Charles V is eminently clear and judicious; and, the same eulogium may well be passed on his treatment of Luther. The little touches of intimate knowledge with which he delighted to enliven his pages again and again add vividness to our understanding of the position and the men. He admirably summed up Luther's position at Worms, and analysed the nature of Charles's repugnance to him; he sketched the unhappy position of Adrian of Utrecht as Pope with equal force; he was clear and emphatic in tracing the final cause of the *Bauernkrieg* to Luther and his followers: he set Charles in his right place as a missionary sovereign; he showed that in the matter of toleration the Emperor was at least as liberal as the Lutherans; he illustrated to the full Charles's candour and directness, as well as his irresolution, in dealing alike with popes and heretics. This and much more that we might say may be summed up in the conclusion that the book supplied just that perspective which exclusively theological studies of the Reformation history so greatly need.

After the founding of the *English Historical Review* he contributed many careful criticisms to it, chiefly on Italian, German and Spanish books. He disliked the work, but was extraordinarily careful, accurate and patient in it.

Something must be said too of the travels which did so much to give him the topographical knowledge in which so many historians are deficient. He came to know Italy and the Italians intimately, and Spain too, and France, and Germany, though less closely. He loved to walk over little-known country. He began to travel in 1873 and from that time was very frequently abroad. From Italy he went to Greece: later to Spain. Often he was in libraries studying manuscripts: more often on the road, seeing historic sites with his own eyes. Often he made himself known among the humbler folk: it is told how at San Vigilio on the Lago di Garda the people hung out flags to salute him.

Travel brings to memory another aspect of his talent. Of those who thought they had read all he wrote, few probably knew that he could write verse as well as prose; but thirty years ago or so, he told in genuine poetry the story of Venice, and sent it to the little girl of two of his friends. She was christened "Venetia"; and the lines happily mingle the thoughts of the coming of the babe to happy parents and of the city that rose on the stillness of the shore where men's "life lay round them like a wide lagoon", and gradually as the fisher-folk made the approach to their land open to the "friendly craft of outer folk",

A little span of years—there seemed to be
A mirage town afloat 'tween shore and sea,
And none could guess how fishers' humble home
Outshone the splendour of Imperial Rome.

It would not be true perhaps to say that he loved Venice more than any other Italian town, more than Florence which he knew so well: it seemed to those who knew him that he delighted most in the little towns, perched upon hill-tops, or far from the ordinary ways of men. That Venice had a special place in his heart was perhaps due to his friendship with Horatio Brown, who lived there so many years, whom he visited, and whom one often met in the summer in his company at Queen's. Brown received, as he did, the Serena medal: their close study of Italian history linked them together, but still more their common delight in simple human persons and the simple things of life, and their friendship with T. W. Allen, one of the most learned of Armstrong's colleagues and one to whom he was greatly attached. With Brown he once went from Venice to Ravenna, partly by carriage, partly by boat. Armstrong admired Addington Symonds, whose devoted friend and biographer was Horatio Brown, but in the unsentimental exactness of his knowledge of things Italian he resembled the latter much more than the former.

Sometimes he travelled with scholarly friends, Horatio Brown, T. W. Allen, G. McN. Rushforth, R. H. Hodgkin and others: sometimes with his wife, his sister, and in earlier years his mother: quite as often alone. Once he went to Norcia in the Abruzzi, above Spoleto, intending to cross the pass of the Apennines down to the other side: but was stopped there by snow and went round by Macerata, Fermo Ascoli and other out-of-the-way places. Always he was on the look-out for historical sites, examined ancient walls, peered into obscure places which had some historical interest long ago.

In 1908 he represented Oxford at the Tercentenary of the University of Oviedo, and was really the life of the somewhat promiscuous gathering; unfailing in cheeriness and good temper, refusing to be vexed by others' eccentricities, making

Spanish orations with infinite pains in their composition, and always a very prince of travelling companions, eager to help everyone in public and in private. Perhaps that indeed was his most prominent characteristic—his constant helpfulness; certainly all his pupils would say it was; and so too would his friends. His social gifts were very remarkable. He was a most excellent conversationalist: we have rarely met his equal for saving a dull meal, or waking up slow people, or breaking the ice. He liked all kinds of people, and his various experiences (South Africa as a child, and his travels) gave him a choice of topics. The officers quartered in Queen's during the War were amazed at his military knowledge, and the South Africans with his acquaintance with Cape and Natal families. Everyone felt the charm of his "humanity".

He hated anything approaching assumption or self-advertisement. The references in his book carefully understated his research. I think I told him once of the motion of a clever undergraduate at the Union (who, I believe, became a Jesuit), "that in the opinion of this House, sweet are the uses of advertisement", and he regarded it as an assertion of sheer wickedness: one is reminded of a saying of Gladstone's about Disraeli. Parade of learning disgusted him just as much as did hasty generalisation. The sincerity of his historical work was in keeping with the sincerity of his personal life.

I will end by quoting a very vivid picture of him as a teacher which has been given to me by a learned scholar who was at one time his pupil and later his colleague in the History teaching at Oxford. It is written in the very style which Armstrong himself might have used and certainly would greatly have enjoyed.

Once upon a time an insolent undergraduate, wearing an odd combination of a Bullingdon tie and a studious cast of countenance, ascending the steps of a formidable looking building in the Oxford High Street, asked hesitatingly, "Is this a College called Queen's?" There ensued an angry affirmative and then, "Mr. Armstrong is taking his private pupils in lecture-room so and so".

The Society of believers into which the giaour was thus admitted was gathered together to study that limited period of Italian history which is covered by the invasions of the French under Kings Charles VIII and Louis XII. It involved the study in close detail of the works of the philosophical historians Machiavelli and Guicciardini as well as those of statesmen like Commines and soldiers like da Porto. Mr. Armstrong's method was to take each book in turn, threading his way with consummate ease through the bewildering jungle of the politics and constitutions of the different Italian States. If it was a question of geography you were made to see in a flash why, for example, Vicenza was so difficult to defend, "overlooked by a long range of hills something like Shotover": and so with questions of economics and strategy. If the political or historical theories of the authorities were in question there were illuminating incursions into the theory of the historical cycle, the meaning of "Fortuna" or the influence of astrology on contemporary thought. Then the complicated histories and constitutions of Florence and Venice were sorted out, and clarified, while the characters of the party leaders were painted with a vigour which a Lytton Strachey might envy. Even after many many years the hearer feels that he could give a sketch of the complicated manœuvres which preceded the Battle of Ghiara d' Adda, or define the difference between a *pratica* and a *pratica stretta* in the history of Florence. Not less remarkable was the personal interest Mr. Armstrong took in all those who sat at his feet. The writer well remembers complaining that the Constitution of Florence was so intricate that he despaired of ever coming to a comprehension of it. "Well, my friend", said he, "if you don't understand it, neither do I: but take comfort, neither do the Examiners."

It is difficult to imagine a more gracious and tranquillising answer. For there was in it not only the subtly flattering comparison between the state of knowledge of an ignorant undergraduate and that of one who was truly *Maestro di coloro che sanno*, but also an intimation that that grim body of persons—to every candidate for the honour schools Inquisition, Star Chamber and Ku Klux Klan rolled into one—was not after all superhuman. It came to pass in the fulness of time that the recipient of this confidence himself became a member of that body. Then he saw and believed.

Edward Armstrong, Fellow of Queen's College, Oxford, and of the British Academy, died in the house he had built and provided with a beautiful garden which he designed and tended, the Red House, Oxford, on April 11, 1928: full, it may be truly said, of years and honours.

Felix quem veritas per se docet, non per figuras et voces transeuntes, sed sicuti se habet.

W. H. HUTTON,
Dean of Winchester.

PART I

DANTE STUDIES

I

DANTE: IN MEMORIAM[1]

Six hundred years have nearly passed since Dante died. Yet
no writer of medieval or modern times is more alive for us
than he. I wish that I could tell you why, and, perhaps, in
part I could, but for the tyrant Time, my enemy, though for
you the rescuer. In commemorating the death of one whom
we admire or love, we strive to visualise what manner of man
he was. We think of how he lived and where he had his
being, rather than of what he did or what he wrote. Place in
our memory of a man's life is of all elements the most closely
linked to personality. And so it is in history, and above all
in that of Dante. Our thoughts on his memorial day turn
first towards Ravenna, where his bones still lie, hard by the
pine-wood wherein "The South-East wind still rustles its
refrain among the birds, who do not cease to ply their tuneful
task at dawn".[2] Thence they cross the Apennines to Florence,
and, within Florence, to the Baptistery, the holy sheepfold,
where he was received into Christ's flock. The works of
Dante begin and end respectively in the scenes of his birth
and death, and this is rarely so. The *Vita Nuova* has its
setting in Florence, in a very street, and some still say in a
very house, for here, if this was his house, after the first
salute from Beatrice, he had the Vision, which was the theme
of his first sonnet. At Ravenna he wrote, at least, the later
portion of the *Paradiso*, in which he once more saw Beatrice
translucent and enthroned in the empyrean heaven.

What a contrast there is between the Florence of Dante's
early years and Ravenna, his home of rest: Ravenna sleeping
in the marshlands, between the two sluggish streams which

[1] A lecture delivered before the University of Oxford in the Examination Schools in commemoration of the six-hundredth anniversary of the death of Dante (September 14, 1321). [Reprinted from the *Church Quarterly Review*, October 1921.]   [2] [Cf. *Purgatorio*, xxviii, 13-21.]

then enclosed her, the solemn pine-wood stretching nearer
to her walls than now, with unchanging monuments of
Gothic and Byzantine art, with fierce personal passions
possibly, for the Romagnols are *più stomachosi* than other
folk, but accepting passively the gentle sway of a cultured
despot; Ravenna cut off from commerce by land and sea,
marooned between the straight Emilian road, which held her
at a distance, and the sea which had receded from her quays.
Florence revelling in commercial wealth and ostentatious
luxury, pulsating with political passions, spinning Ordinances
of threads so fine that they lasted not from October till mid-
November, restlessly tossing from side to side like a sick
woman finding no comfort on her bed of down; and yet in
the forefront of Italian art and letters, raising in every decade
some famous monument, stirred in mind and body by keen
mountain air from North and East, cleansed by her fast-
flowing river. Yet the Florence and Florentine State which
Dante knew was far other than that of Renaissance days. It
was a city of some 30,000 inhabitants, not nearly so large as
Oxford is. Its territory included none of her later subject
towns, not Prato, less than twelve miles off, not Pistoia,
Arezzo nor Cortona, much less Pisa, Volterra and Leghorn.
Within Florence Dante saw completed none of the buildings
now so familiar, except the Baptistery, and that without its
glorious gates, and the Bargello, though even this was restored after fire a few years later. We must imagine Florence
without two of her three landmarks, the Cathedral Cupola
and Giotto's Tower. There was no Loggia de' Lanzi, no
Or San Michele. San Marco and San Lorenzo were still un-
built, Santa Croce and Santa Maria Novella as yet unfinished.
All the three bridges of Dante's day have since been swept
away or burnt. The great palaces, Riccardi, the Strozzi, the
Pitti and the Rucellai, were much later. Yet in spite of revolutions his was the great building age, and he saw in process of
construction the two churches above mentioned, the new
walls, the Cathedral, while the Palazzo Vecchio was occupied,
though not completed.

Within this Florence there were, between 1265 and 1301,

three Dantes, quite distinct: the Dante of sentiment, the
Dante of sorrow and hard study, the Dante of political
passion, sowing the seed for his epic of Hatred, the *Inferno*.
I shall touch upon his life only just so far as to connect it
with his character and writings. He belonged to an old and
honourable citizen family, probably not noble, certainly not
one of the many families of Grandi, excluded from office by
the recent Ordinances of Justice. They lived in their own
houses in a somewhat aristocratic district, and owned small
properties in the country. Dante's father was a nobody,
perhaps a notary by profession. Of his near relations one
belonged to the Art of Calimala, another to that of Changers.[1]
At this time the term nobility had lost all definite distinction.
It was as hard then to decide whether a citizen was noble as
to determine now whether he is quite a gentleman. Members
of the best families married daughters of rich merchants and
became partners in their firms; wealthy bourgeois bought
up the palaces of needy aristocrats, and lived therein. Of the
two party leaders of Dante's time, Corso Donati the Black
belonged to the former class and Vieri de' Cerchi the White
to the latter. Good society at all events was open to so attractive a young man as Dante. He sent his first sonnet to Guido
Cavalcanti, and so won the lasting friendship of one of the
most prominent personages in Florence, and the reigning
poet until such time as Dante might dethrone him. Cavalcanti it was who made Dante's social and perhaps even
literary fortune. Dante in turn gratefully calls him his first
friend. A less desirable comrade was the glutton Forese
Donati, brother of Corso, by whose sister Piccarda he was
recognised in the First Heaven of the Moon. His future wife
Gemma was a member of the clan. Dante was always carefully dressed, appreciated good cookery, though moderate
in appetite, bought luxurious furniture, was courteous, if
dignified, and reserved, objected to loud and side-shaking
laughter, which in the *Convivio* he terms hen-cackling. He

[1] [*I.e.* L' Arte dei Cambiatori (Bankers). L' Arte di Calimala—named
after the street in which it traded—was concerned in dressing and dyeing
foreign cloth.]

wrote a beautiful hand, with long, fine letters, and was fault-less in orthography. Unfortunately not a syllable survives.

At this time the skies of Florence were relatively clear. The last Hohenstaufen had fallen, papal ambition had not yet developed, the Tuscan Ghibellines had been in 1289 crushed at Campaldino, where Dante had played his part; Florence was the dominant Tuscan power, her frontiers were secure. Class feeling, it is true, was strained; hot-blooded nobles might insult and outrage bourgeois or plebeian. But there was no reason why Dante and Cavalcanti should not apply their fancy to *canzoni* upon their lady-loves, and their subtle brains to elaborate commentaries, to make their meaning more obscure. Dante might pray for a magician to spirit Cavalcanti, himself, and yet a third poet, Lapo Gianni, away to a bark wherein to sail the seas at will, with Cavalcanti's Vanna and Lapo's Lagia, and his own chosen partner from among his selected list of sixty Floren-tine beauties, to complete the crew; doubtless, as he writes, the lovers and their ladies would be well content.

The springtide of Dante's life and love was closed with Beatrice's death in 1290. He took seriously to study, laying the foundations of philosophy and theology on which here-after he was to build. In 1295, being now thirty, he became qualified for political office by enrolment in the Art of Physicians and Druggists. Fortunately a very recent ordin-ance had withdrawn the provision that every member of an Art must exercise his trade. Dante was not a physician, for he is not styled *Magister* in the list of Priors. He would scarcely have had a good bedside manner, and it is im-possible to imagine him as serving out groceries and drugs, or even jewelry, books and artists' colours. From June 15 to August 15, 1300, he was one of the six Priors who with the Gonfalonier formed the chief magistracy of the State. His election does not imply any great political prominence or exceptional statesmanship. His five colleagues were no-nentities. The office was bi-monthly, and in so small a city the choice of capable men to fill it was limited indeed. The working classes were unenfranchised; no fewer than seventy-three families in all their branches had lately been excluded as Grandi, and these would comprise most of those who had experience of government. The Florentine Guelfs had recently split into two factions, the Blacks and Whites. No member of the Black party stood a chance of election, for the Whites, to which Dante belonged, were predominant. Members of the Signoria were disqualified for re-election for two years after laying down their office; thus in two years and two months no fewer than ninety-one distinct individuals would hold the chief office of state. Dante was certainly not a personage because he was elected Prior. He himself states that he was little known at that time, and elsewhere that he was qualified by age and patriotism, but not by prudence. His Priorate, however, fell in eventful times, for on the preceding May-day occurred the first real clash of arms between Blacks and Whites, followed by the exile of the chiefs of both parties. From his Priorate he himself dated all his misfortunes. On the very first day of office it fell to the new Priors to confirm a sentence condemning three Florentine financial agents of the Papacy to have their tongues cut out. This may have been patriotic, but it was scarcely prudent. Even more decisive probably was a motion made by Dante a year later against sending military aid to Pope Boniface. This, after a brisk and adjourned debate, was rejected by 49 to 30 in the Council of 100. That is the solitary occasion on which he is known to have played an independent part, advocating a courageous policy, and leading a substantial minority against the timid, vacillating leaders of his party. This speech doubtless sealed his fate. His last known appearance in public life, or indeed in Florence, was on September 28, 1301. Henceforth there is silence. This may be explained by his alleged embassy to Rome, as to which some historians have doubts, owing to the lack of official documentary evidence and the improbability that for a conciliatory mission a *persona ingratissima* to Boniface should be selected.

On November 1 Charles of Valois with his French lances entered Florence as papal mediator between Blacks and

Whites; the pacification consisted in the wholesale proscription of the Whites. Dante was condemned on January 27, 1302. He was not singled out for vengeance. In all fifteen Priors and Gonfaloniers from December 1299 to November 1301 were condemned. The ferocious sentences fulminated against them were in accordance with the Ordinances of Justice, of which Dante was a pronounced champion. After all, such penalties were mainly a matter of form. Citizens who fled from justice were rarely caught, and in fact Dante and his fellows all escaped. He was excluded from the amnesty of 1311. By this time his political offence had been aggravated by a literary crime. His letters to the Emperor Henry VII and to Florence were a call to battle against the fundamental principles of the Parte Guelfa. This exclusion he shared with between 400 and 500 other families or persons. Among them was Petrarch's father, who had held the post of notary to Dante's Priorate. Dante's giant stature as a statesman was a fanciful reflection cast by his poetic glory. His literary admirers are naturally misled, for men of letters are wont to magnify the political importance of their craft.

Where Dante was when Charles entered Florence, or when his condemnation was announced, is quite unknown. He joined the chiefs of his fellow exiles near Arezzo, but soon broke from that "worthless and vile company",[1] and formed a party consisting of himself. Exiles of all ages and countries are not noted for sympathetic appreciation of their fellows, and Dante not impossibly possessed the gentle art of making enemies. Henceforth until his last refuge at Ravenna Dante was awash among the thousands and thousands of exiles thrown overboard from almost every town in Central or Northern Italy. He drifted, in his own words, "throughout every region to which this tongue of ours extends, a stranger, almost a beggar. Truly I have been a ship without sail and without rudder, wafted to different havens and inlets and shores by the parching wind which poverty exhales. And I have seemed vile in the eyes of many, who, crediting some report, perhaps had pictured me under

---

[1] [*Paradiso*, xvii, 62.]

some other form; in whose eyes not only was my person held cheap, but every work of mine became of less esteem, both that which was already done, and that which was still to do" (*Conv.* I, iii) Dante's fastidious, hypersensitive spirit, the excessive self-esteem, with which Villani debits him, doubtless felt poverty and indifference acutely. Naturally he stored up the hatred, which is the material for his *Inferno*, marking down places visited in his travels as fitting scenes for the terrific drama, the great landslide on the Adige, the boiling stream belched forth at Viterbo, the wild Maremma swarming with snakes among the rough tangled thickets, wherein wild beasts shun the cultivated land, the dark water of the upper Montone booming over its precipitous brink, the boiling, sticky pitch besmearing the banks of the Arsenal at Venice. It is true that the drifting ship chanced at times upon a hospitable port, where the poet found refreshment and due reverence, with the Scala at Verona, the courteous Malaspina of the Lunigiana, the Count Guido da Battifolle in the green, upland basin of the Casentino. Nor were these wander-years intellectually unfruitful. After the death of Beatrice, Dante had learnt from Boethius that philosophy was the best anodyne for sorrow. Close bookwork, assimilated by experience, now took shape in the *Convivio*. It was meant to comprise fifteen books, but the fourth was never quite completed. Dante's moral resolutions and philosophical enterprise were seemingly shattered by a bolt from the Apennine blue in the shape of a beautiful lady who imperilled the sway of Beatrice and countered the Consolations of Boethius. The sudden close of the *Convivio* may on the other hand have resulted from the appearance of the Emperor Henry VII in Italy. Whether to the Apennine lady or to the Emperor posterity owes a debt, for both *Convivio* and *Commedia* could scarcely have been finished within Dante's span of life. It is more probable that Dante himself was discontented with his work. The *Convivio* was in its outer form the continuation of the *Vita Nuova*. Its origin was in the thirty months of study which followed the death of Beatrice, its material was allegorised philosophy as that of the *Vita Nuova* was allegorised love. He probably realised that artistically the *Canzoni* were too slight to bear the weight of the superimposed commentary, and yet that the commentary could not contain the learning, nor perfect the symbolism which underlay it. He must construct a stronger and more comprehensive mould into which he could pour the fused material, not only of all his philosophy and theology, but of the experiences of his political life and exile, and, beyond all, the love which he had never lost. Many men return in later life to the ambitions or affections of their earliest youth. The *Vita Nuova* closes with the resolve that he would speak no more of his blessed one until he could treat of her more worthily. "With that aim I study all I can, as she knows in very truth. And if it be the will of Him, through whom all things live, that my life may last for several years, I hope to say of her what never has been said of any woman." It may well be that from the first he set before himself the *Paradiso* as his ideal. At all events his love was the link between the earliest and latest of his works. The learning of his second stage passes through the *Convivio* to the *Commedia*, wherein also are incorporated the political principles set forth in the *De Monarchia* and his three historical letters.

Dante, as many another exile, set all his hopes on Henry, and gave him all his heart. The composition of the *De Monarchia* has been attributed to dates ranging over a score of years. But in its complete form, at least, it was the outcome of Henry's attempt to revive Imperial rule. It was neither an epitaph nor a prophecy, but a battle-cry. With Henry's death died Dante's hopes. His gorge rose at the insulting conditions of the amnesty proffered in 1315. Never, he wrote, "would he return until he could hide his grey hair under the laurel wreath in the city which he had left with locks still fair".[1]

If Dante's feelings were outraged by the insult of 1315, the material conditions of exile had improved. A victorious

[1] [Eclogue i. *Tutte le opere di Dante Alighieri*, ed. Moore (Oxford, 1904, p. 186).]

Ghibelline reaction had followed close upon Henry's death. Dante could find home and honour in the palace of Can Grande at Verona, where stairs were not so steep, nor bread so bitter, though his last and longest refuge was with the undistinguished Guelfic dynast of Ravenna.

We duly commemorate Dante's birthday and his death. Perhaps above all we should celebrate January 27, 1302, the date of his exile, for to this we unquestionably owe the *Divina Commedia*. It is inconceivable that Dante could have composed this in the feverish activity of political life at Florence. Had the Whites conquered, or had Dante condescended, as did some of his colleagues, to reconciliation with the Blacks, he would have hunted yet more keenly for the paltry spoils of office; he would have been soused in the slough of maladministration. Love sonnets, or some such vulgar verses of occasion as he interchanged with Forese Donati, he might still have written, but never the *Commedia*.

The *Vita Nuova* would indeed have preserved his name in a group with Cavalcanti and Cino da Pistoia, and must always be celebrated as the first real classic in Italian prose, though it is doubtful if such wonderment would have been bestowed upon it, gem as it is, had the Beatrice of the *Vita Nuova* never risen to the *Paradiso*. After all no statesman has ever been a poet of the first rank, unless Bacon was really Shakespeare. It was for his exile, not for his prosperous Florentine life, that Michelangelo envied Dante. And has not Carducci ironically wondered that Florence has never raised a statue of Carrara marble to Conte de' Gabrielli, the ruthless judge to whom Dante owed the inspiration of his exile:

> Were I but he . . .
> Against his exile coupled with his good
> I'd gladly change the world's best heritage.
>
>   J. A. SYMONDS, *Michelangelo*, i, 336.

Men are known, as we are told, by their works; but, if this knowledge were confined to literary works, it would be of very varying degrees. What, for instance, do Shakespeare's works tell us of the man Shakespeare? How rash

it would be to compose a character of any playwright from
his plays. But no great writer has impressed himself upon
his masterpiece as has Dante. Passionate patriotism for both
city and country clashed with righteous indignation and
personal vindictiveness. For him the aim of all government
was peace, justice the means of peace, and discipline of
justice. Yet it was party feeling and the scorn of compromise
that caused his fall. His love for woman could rise to heights
of pure spiritual worship, or could sink to sensuous lapses
with which his earliest biographers charge him, to which he
himself confesses in the *Purgatorio*, and from which in the
last canto of *Paradiso* he beseeches the Virgin that, by the
supplications of Beatrice, he may be restrained. His vehe-
mence could lash itself into violence, so that we may well
believe the story of his later days that he was with difficulty
kept from throwing stones at women whom in his walks he
heard speaking against Ghibellines. Against this may be set
the courtesy and tolerance displayed at times even in the
Inferno, and his gift for hero-worship. The hero may, as the
great Frederick, suffer in Hell, or he may, as Manfred, scrape
into Purgatory. Or he may be the lofty Henry for whom a
high place is reserved in Paradise, or Vergil, who for Dante
had never died.

The whole of Dante's self and of his life was thrown into
the *Commedia*. Visits to Heaven and Hell had before him
been composed for purposes of edification. But it is not a
religious poem, such as a saint or ascetic might have written,
it is fully as much a record of the actual world as a guess at
the unseen. All his earthly love and hate, his political theory
and practical experience, his learning theological, geographical and astronomical, joys, sufferings and wanderings
go to the making of it. His innate naturalism broke through
his fancy for allegory, which was partly a fashion of the
poetry of his age, and partly the product of the super-
sensuous side of his imagination. The framework of the poem
may be thought too mechanical, overloaded with encyclo-
paedic learning, even at times tiresome. Rather than a framework it is a border to the tapestry, more formal it is true,

but woven with it, and not, as a frame, detachable. Within the border, and beneath allegory or doctrine, vitality throbs in every canto. The poem is differentiated from every great epic in the world by being peopled with real men and women actually alive, or recently dead, or so near in time that their deeds or misdeeds were still household words. It is well to remember that Dante was nine in the year in which died St. Thomas Aquinas, the representative Dominican, from whom he drew his Aristotelian philosophy, and St. Bonaventura, the representative Franciscan, through whom he assimilated some measure of Platonic mysticism. Ficino, the greatest Renaissance Platonist, once said of him indeed that he had drunk with Vergil's vessel from the fount of Plato.

The mere mechanism of the *Commedia* might require that the poet should rid himself of all his hate in the *Inferno* of unpardonable sin, that the process of purgation should be regarded with tempered affection, that the full light of spiritual love should be undimmed by any meaner feeling. Yet in the *Inferno* is found the classical example of Dante's love for Brunetto Latini, justly condemned for vile perversion of morality, and the delicate pity for Francesca, the adulteress. On the other hand in the *Paradiso* he still quivers with hot fits of hatred; he presses Clement V yet deeper into Hell by the weight of his successor John XXII, while Dante's ancestor breaks the perfect peace to vituperate the poet's city, the objects of his personal or class dislike, the very dress of the ladies with whom Dante had once dallied.

Vitality and versatility are the characteristics, ingrained in Dante's works, which have so widely spread their influence, and determined their survival. Dante did not write for the poor; there is little evidence that he had active sympathy for the working classes. But love and pity, hatred and revenge, visions of a future life free from labour, sin and sorrow, are the heritage of all classes, and every man could find something in the *Commedia* to meet his needs. If any three readers are asked which of the Canticas they prefer, three different answers may well be given. The mind most refined, we are told, and certainly the most religious, will choose the

Paradiso, repelled by the too fleshly horrors of the *Inferno*; perhaps too the most artistic, if only for the marvellous word-painting of the effects of light. The *Inferno* attracts the less sensitive historian by the vivid delineation of what was in reality a horrible age. The ordinary reader, feeling the mechanism of the *Paradiso* too elaborate, and its mysticism beyond his material power of comprehension, finds in the dignified calm of the *Purgatorio*, with its natural process from repentance to hope, an ideal within the limits of human aspiration.

This all-embracing humanity saved Dante for posterity. The chances seemed against him. No great poet has been exposed to such formidable posthumous rivalry from younger writers, or to such a sweeping revolution in literary fashion as the Renaissance. Petrarch surpassed Dante in the technique of lyrical verse. Prose might easily supplant poetry as the medium for narrative expression; if so, Boccaccio's luscious charm might spoil the taste for the rougher beauty of him whom, above all others, Boccaccio himself admired. Dante had sunk deep the well of poetry, and drawn from the lower strata. New forms of popular song, urban or rural, might displace a style which had become too scientific or too antiquated. Such might be the love songs which Giustiniani popularised from Venice, or the *rispetti*, in which the Tuscan peasant raucously chanted his amours or disappointments. Rhythm is so nearly a mode of thought that change in its fashion might affect the estimate of previous writers. Dante's fortunes might therefore wane as the *octava* displaced the *terzina*. A fresh wave of the romance of chivalry from France and Spain might flood Italy once more, or the drama, long pent up, might burst its bonds, and the playwright overpower the poet. Love is of the very essence of poetry, at all events in Dante's age, and there are fashions in the poetry of love as in the dress of the ladies who inspire it. Not only were Petrarch and Boccaccio in the generation after Dante his conscious or unconscious rivals, but Laura and Fiammetta might easily oust Beatrice from the more material affections of the succeeding age. From almost the first Beatrice was regarded as a mere abstraction for philosophy or religion. Laura might be Laura, or another woman, but woman she unquestionably was, while Fiammetta was veritable flesh and blood. Among Dante's perils was just that which endears him to a more refined modern world, his exquisite spiritual ideal of womanly perfection. Actual hostility to such an ideal there was. It found expression in such a phrase as that of one Sertorio Quattromani: "As for Dante's Bice I doubt if she was ever anything at all nice. I believe that just as he had a perverse judgement in the treatment of poetry, and just as in the choice of words he always fastened on the worst, so too he did in his selection of beauty." But hostility is less dangerous to immortality than is indifference. Of all dangers the greatest was that the Renaissance, with the revival of Latin as the sole Romance language, and its enthusiastic interest in Greek, unparalleled in the history of any other tongue, might drive Dante's prose and verse alike from off the field. Petrarch of course did rely for immortality not on his lyrics but on his Latin epic; even Boccaccio in later life almost deserted the vernacular for Latin. The two great educators of the Quattrocento, Guarino of Verona and Vittorino of Feltre, found no place for Dante, confining education to the classics and the new methods. Dante's greatest claim in the eyes of posterity, that he made out of Italian a literary language, might and did turn with many of the most eminent trecentist and quattrocentist scholars to his disadvantage. It has often been said in fact that the Renaissance killed the interest in Dante.

In spite of all Dante won through. He had fortunately a short start before his chief rival Petrarch was upon him. The love for him was too deeply imbedded in the heart of Italy to be uprooted. Once dead, he became the pride of Florence. Petrarch and Boccaccio might be his rivals within Florence, but together the three glories, the three crowns, were allies for whose fame Florentine humanist Chancellors fought the more hardened humanists of Milan, Decembrio and Loschi, pupils of Guarino. In the long conflict, at once political and literary, between the two states, Dante became the Florentine Carroccio round which the combatants fought. The proofs of

Dante's influence are found in every literary centre and in every class from king to donkey-boy. It is needless to dwell upon the commentaries, which, beginning with Dante's own two sons, continued throughout the centuries, or upon the lectureships established in Bologna, Florence, Pisa, Piacenza, Milan, Ferrara, Venice and, perhaps, Padua and Verona. No poem has been so prolific in imitations as the *Commedia*, imitations doctrinal, moral, geographical and political, with the inevitable guide, Solinus the geographer, Circe, Minerva, the Sibyl and Diana, Savonarola, the prophet Daniel, even Dante himself. Every *capitolo* of poet or poetaster in *terzina* can claim lineal descent from Dante. Lorenzo de' Medici's elder friend, Palmieri, carried the abstract, theological element in the *Commedia* to its extremest limits; Lorenzo himself stooped to vulgar parody in his *Beoni*, "The Boozers"; Machiavelli, who was steeped in Dante, somewhat more seriously adapted it in his *Asino d' Oro*. Lyrical poetry, especially the national and political songs of the late fourteenth and early fifteenth centuries, might in its form be modelled upon Petrarch, but subject and inspiration again and again were drawn from the inexhaustible springs of the *Commedia*. This too took firm hold upon popular fancy; its verses were the common property of the piazza; even some of Dante's lyrics were appropriated by street singers. Legends of hoary antiquity and of fresh invention, serious or comical, gathered round his name. He was a favourite subject for the novelists Sacchetti, Pucci, Sermini. We even owe *Romeo and Juliet* to a misreading of the celebrated line on Montecchi and Cappelletti by Luigi da Porto and Bandello, from whom Shakespeare drew his drama. One curious fact in Dante's life, though founded upon legend, is worth quoting. Either from his supposed intimacy with the powers of evil, or from his association with Vergil, in popular medieval fancy a magician, Dante was credited with a knowledge of the Black Art. Galeazzo Visconti, wishing to procure the death of Pope John XXII, also a foe of Dante, invited the poet a year before his death to Piacenza, or at the least told a rival magician that he had done so. His idea was that Dante should pour poison into the brain cavity of a silver statuette representing the Pope, uttering the while the appropriate incantations.

Trifling incidents, the straws and feathers of history, are often more illustrative than a monolithic commentary or a lumpy lecture. Here are some to prove the wide spread of Dante's influence in space and time. The fashionable humanist schoolmasters might boycott Dante, but a private tutor, Maestro Nolfrio of Siena, advertises in the little hill town of Colle that he is willing to read Dante with anyone who wishes to hear him (1360). In an elaborate syllabus of subjects for a young ladies' college, while Boccaccio's tales are condemned as poisonous reptiles, Petrarch and Dante are beyond measure extolled, Petrarch for embodying pure and honourable love, and Dante Christian philosophy. Among wedding presents bought at a store is a *Dante* complete in red boards. At the end of a treasured volume was a doggerel to the effect, "Oh ! you who take pleasure in this book, keep it from the lamp and from the kids".[1] A scribe is reported as having made 100 copies from the *Commedia*, and dowered his daughter on the profits. Official documents provide examples. A citizen of Pistoia in the assessment of his property declares, in order to preserve his rights, a volume of Dante, which a friend had borrowed and kept for forty years. The Customs tariff at Perugia includes among "heavy articles" the books of Dante, in company with slippers, woollen goods, musical instruments and law books. May I venture on a love story in the uncongenial atmosphere of the Examination Schools? Fortunately it ended badly, and thus is unlikely to leave demoralising germs.

The presumably fair Blandina was expecting her young admirer, Giovanni Gherardi, poet and novelist, Petrarchist and above all Dantist. To show her cultured sympathy she had placed a copy of the *Commedia* upon her table. Her lover entered, the door was closed, the witching hour had come. His eyes travelled from

---

[1] ["Ho! Tu che chun questo libro ti trastuli,
[2] Vardalo da la luzerna e dai fanzuli."

      C. del Balzo, *Poesie di mille autori intorno a Dante Alighieri raccolte*, iii, 476 (Rome, 1890–97).]

Blandina to the book; he took it up and read a canto, and then another, and then a third. When he settled down to a fourth, Blandina lost her temper. She said to herself, "Perhaps he is waiting till I propose to *him*. It seems to me that he has come to hold a Dante class. If so, with his Dante let him stick." With that she left the room, and, as she slammed the door, if she had really read of Paolo and Francesca I can hear her mutter "Accursed be the book and he who wrote it".[1]

Very frequent are the casual references to the religious aspect of the *Commedia*. An artizans' club in Siena used to meet and read authors generally more gay than grave, but in their statutes are these words: "As we are professedly members of the Christian flock, it is our pleasure that at least during the Lenten season we read the elegant and learned *Commedia* of Dante".[2] So too the Town Trumpeter of Pisa in 1488 included it in his catalogue of books for the soul to be read in Lent. Filippo Villani, weary with years and toil, when he prepared to turn with more vigour to his God, could find no fitter study than Dante's *opera angelica*. The poor broken poet Saviozzo, exile and suicide, compares himself to a wide-eyed, trembling boy, standing before the kindly master who helps him with his Latin exercise; so Dante was his master aiding him to win a high and perfect life—Dante, the chosen vessel, who may yet be called alive though he be dead (1404). The fortunate as well as the miserable appreciated Dante. Frederick of Sicily, who had received harsh treatment in his poem, treasured the *Inferno* in his library, and this we know because his Chancellor was convicted of stealing it. Rienzi on his fantastic inauguration as Tribune was presented with six wreaths from different trees; the fourth was of laurel and represented Dante, the other five were those of Greek and Roman poets. Filippo Visconti, most cold-blooded of all Milanese despots, who had himself been taught Dante, made the humanist Barsizza lecture upon him, and induced Filelfo to write the life of St. John the Baptist in *terza rima*. Pius II returning sore and sick from the futile Crusading Conference

---

[1] [C. del Balzo, *op. cit.* iii, 305.]

[2] [C. Mazzi, *La congrega dei Rozzi di Siena nel secolo xvi* (1883), i, 352.]

at Mantua had in his barge passages of the *Commedia* read to him by a young Florentine, more beautifully than anything could be. Ludovico Moro and Beatrice d' Este would discuss Dante in the pleasant gardens of Milan or Pavia, and it pleased that very mundane lady to imagine herself as her Dantesque namesake returned from Paradise. Of these halcyon days Ludovico Moro thought when in his prison at Loches he scribbled on the wall the wail of Francesca: "There is no greater sorrow than to recall in misery the time of happiness". When first taken prisoner he had begged of his captors a copy of *Dante* "per studiare". A very telling picture might be made of fierce old Julius II in the quiet of evening having Dante read to him by his architect, Bramante. It is needless to speak of Dante's better-known admirers: Coluccio Salutati, long Chancellor of Florence; Leo Battista Alberti, champion of the vernacular; Lorenzo de' Medici. Michelangelo is a link in the chain of artists who all drew inspiration from the *Commedia*, Orcagna, Frà Angelico, Gozzoli, Luca Signorelli, Botticelli, and so through Michelangelo down to Blake, and to our own more Dante-loving age.[1]

Dante's own portrait, long after his death, was a not uncommon subject for the decoration of public buildings, and appears again and again in miniature. Two sets of illustrations of the *Commedia* by Botticelli still exist, and one by Michelangelo lies, alas! at the bottom of the Tuscan gulf. A less pleasing use of the *Commedia* was that for the so-called Cartels of Infamy posted under a political enemy hung in effigy. These professed to be spoken by the victim, and lent themselves readily to the vituperative treatment so powerfully applied in the *Inferno*. Had Dante's fame dwindled in the Renaissance period, the *Commedia* and its author would have disappeared from contemporary art. Do fifteenth-century art and legend pay such tribute to Filelfo or Poggio, to Chrysoloras or Aurispa, or even to the well-beloved Coluccio Salutati?

Throughout the dangerous fifteenth century the *Commedia* remained a living force. The conception of love may

---

[1] [For a fuller treatment of this subject cf. the author's "Posthumous Popularity of Dante", *Church Quarterly Review*, 1898.]

have been materialised, the old philosophic theories, the old methods of education exploded. The Church's ideal of the relation of man to the other world may have been dimmed by the scepticism of one and the neo-Platonism of another sect of Hellenists. Political issues had become more confined, more concrete. Popular satire, more personal, if possible, and certainly more vulgar, may seem but the parody of Dante's irony wrought of righteous indignation. Yet for all this whoever wrote of war or politics, of morals or religion, whoever reviled his neighbour or his neighbour's city, whoever hung his fellow citizen in effigy, drew phrase or thought or metre from the never-failing source, which even in the arid tracts of the fifteenth century never ran to waste.

If anything could have killed Dante's fame it would have been the Renaissance. As we all know, it did not, and I have tried to show the reasons why it did not. These reasons are still pledges for his immortality, and may safely be left for the next centenary to confirm. It is time that we should return to the scene where the mortal remains of Dante the man, killed by malaria, still lie. Even for his bones there was little rest. Bertrand de Poyet would fain have burnt them, while Florence would have done penance for his exile by robbing Ravenna of her treasure. Thus it came that they were hidden, and for generations the memory of where they lay was lost.

A dreary sunset after a stormy day. But Dante's sun had only set to rise again. That this would be so, he had been fully conscious in the clouded afternoon of life. The *Commedia* was the realisation of the ideal set before him in the *Convivio*, and the concluding words of the first Treatise are these: "This shall be a new light and a new sun, which shall rise when the old sun has set, and shall shine on those who are in darkness and mist, because of the old sun which gives no light to them". Surely it was this sun, the brightest that ever shone in Italy, which revealed her to herself in the fulness of her powers. And this because the *Divina Commedia* was the most truly national poem ever written, national in language as it is in material, national in the mystical ideal of faith as in its realistic rendering of sin. The soundest of

Dante's early critics, Leonardo Bruni, said that Petrarch was his equal in the *canzone*, his superior in the sonnet, but that the *Commedia* was worth all the works of Petrarch, and, if of Petrarch, of how many poets since? One of these, and he by no means the least, Michelangelo, has written of Dante:

> No tongue can tell of him what should be told.

I must therefore implore my audience to believe that it is Dante's fault not mine that my tongue has proved unequal to its theme.

II

DANTE'S POLITICAL IDEAL[1]

THE authors of political ideals are not to be looked for among the successful statesmen of history. It may even be said that the literary success of a political ideal is usually in inverse proportion to the political success of its author. For its attraction lies in its pathos, in its sharp contrast with the real. Though professing to be a working drawing for the future, it is in reality a fancy portrait of the past. It represents the "should have been" rather than the "is to be". It marks the moment of the passing away of an old system of political thought rather than the birth of a new. And in relation to its author—if he has been a politician at all—it is not the programme, but the apologia of his cause.

Hence it is not surprising that Italy during her period of independence between the fall of the Hohenstaufens and the establishment of Spanish hegemony, while failing, if Venice be excepted, to create any successful political system, should have produced two great political ideals—Dante's *De Monarchia* and the *Principe* of Machiavelli. The circumstances of the authors are so far similar that it may be suggestive to bring them for a moment into connexion. Both were Florentines; both had held high political position; both to some extent had been forced from their original convictions. Both in the prime of life were doomed to political nothingness, and, though after their fall in close communication with the leading statesmen of their day, neither exercised any appreciable influence. Both suffered from the incurable disunion of a single town, and both aspired to a united Italy. To both the temporal power of the Church seemed the chief obstacle to

---

[1] [A paper read before the Oxford Dante Society, November 1884 and February 1885. Reprinted from the *Church Quarterly Review*, April 1890.]

their aspirations. With the one as with the other the realisation of the ideal depended on a definite man. In point of poetry there is the difference between Giuliano or Lorenzo de' Medici and the Emperor Henry VII that there is between Machiavelli and Dante; but the prospects of practical success were perhaps equal on either side.

The *De Monarchia* and the *Principe* are both epitaphs on a dead system, and like epitaphs they deal with what the dead should have been, or what it is hoped they will become hereafter. While the conclusions of the one and the premises of the other are professedly based on history, yet neither is like the *Politics* of Aristotle, the grammar of an actual system. The system that was dead when Machiavelli wrote was indeed a national system, based on the exclusion of the foreigner; the cause of death was the feeble action of internal unity. Machiavelli's ideal was the national system vivified by internal unity. The system with which Dante dealt was a system of unity wasted away from the lack of the vital forces of nationality. Dante, neglecting the cause of disease, would at all costs reintroduce the unity. Hence it is that, while Dante's work is an epitaph only, Machiavelli's was an epitaph with a promise of a future life.

It has been assumed that the *De Monarchia* is a political ideal, and to us at all events it is so. But it is a disadvantage that it is not certainly known under what circumstances or for what end Dante wrote it—whether as a creed on his conversion to theoretic Ghibellinism before the struggle between Boniface VIII and the French crown; or as a political pamphlet intended to give present aid to the cause of Henry VII; or as an apology for and an epitaph on the cause when already lost.[1] Hence, too, there is an uncertainty as to its relation to his other works. The *Commedia*, the *Convivio*, the *Letters* are full of allusions to contemporary life; the *De Monarchia* has probably no single definite allusion. Was the *De Monarchia* the major premise, the general principle, and do his

---

[1] [For a discussion on the date of the *De Monarchia* and the evidence in favour of 1313, as the year of its composition, cf. C. Foligno in *Dante: Essays in Commemoration*, London, 1921.]

other works contain the minor premise and the political conclusion? Is it prior both in order of thought and in order of time? Or is it the abstract result of the actual political experiences which are, as in a diary, jotted down in the other writings?

Fortunately, though there may be divergences on minor points, there is in the different works no discrepancy as to the general theory. If the *De Monarchia* was written in the reign of Albert of Austria, yet it equally represents Dante's political belief as held during and after the reign of Henry VII, and its abstract character and logical method make it the best possible basis for the comparison of the ideal with contemporary political material.

It is noticeable that at the very outset of his work Dante claims to be the discoverer of a new theory of the temporal monarchy. Conclusions have been drawn from this bearing on the date of the work; but all through Dante's political life, and long before, the theory of the universal monarchy was a commonplace. It had been the life-work of many a lawyer and diplomatist. The novelty of Dante's treatment must lie in the fact that he brings it into connexion with metaphysics, and subjects it to a severe logical method. The theory has thus passed out of the hands of the lawyer into those of the philosopher, and in the passage has assumed an entirely fresh aspect. The lawyer has had in view the rights of the empire and the duties of mankind; the philosopher lays stress on the rights of mankind to the attainment of its end, and consequently on the duties of the Emperor. The monarch is only the means by which mankind can realise its full virtue and hold its allotted place in the scheme of the universe. The lawyer has dubbed him "lord of all"; the philosopher appoints him as servant of all. As the Pope is the *Servus Servorum Dei*, so is the Emperor the minister of free humanity.

What, then, is the end, the final cause of the *universalis civilitas* of the human race? "It is", says Dante, "the bringing into activity the fullest potentialities of the passive power of the intellect, firstly in the direction of speculation, secondly by extension, and for its sake in the direction of action."[1] To that end the chief means is peace, and peace depends on justice. Justice between powers that are co-relative is impossible: there must be a single universal judge. He has power and will to be most just; his justice is not blinded by cupidity, for he has nothing to desire; his sway is limited by Oceanus alone. If cupidity blinds justice, so does love enlighten it; and love is inherent in the monarch, for he is nearer to mankind than other princes. His functions, as the *Convivio* tells us, are conterminous with the functions of mankind. He touches man at every point; other rulers only touch in part, and mediately through him.

As justice is a means towards the happiness of mankind, so the monarch is only a minister to help mankind to freedom. He exists for his subjects, not they for him. Under monarchy alone man exists for his own sake and not for another's; he is wholly free. And of this freedom the founthead is the *libertas arbitrii*—the freedom of the judgement from the control of the appetite. This freedom purely intellectual beings possess in its fulness. Freedom and government are bound up together."Evigilate igitur omnes, et assurgite regi vostro, incolae Italiae, non solum sibi ad imperium, sed, ut liberi, ad regimen reservati."[2] It is this which makes us happy here below and as gods above hereafter. This freedom is essential to the realisation of the fulness of the intellectual qualities. Thus *Pax cum libertate* becomes the motto of the Empire.

Here, then, is the philosophical basis of the work. Dante has instructed our ignorance as to principles. But the further question arises, With whom lies the right of empire? Here he has to meet ignorance of facts and dispute as to the inferences from them. Some rebel against the rights of the Roman people. Others are ignorant of its claims.

Right is coincident with the will of God, and if we can prove that Rome won her empire by the will of God she won it of right. Rome has the truest patent of nobility. From her

---

[1] [*De Monarchia*, i, 4, ed. Moore, p. 343.]
[2] [Dante, *Epist.* v, ed. Moore, p. 406.]

founders she has inherited the noblest blood of the three
divisions of the world. All nations have fought for empire.
In each "trial by combat" divine judgement has declared for
Rome. He who aims at the good of the common weal aims
at the end of right, for the end of right is the common weal.
In bringing the world under subjection Rome aimed at the
common weal; her history is one long act of sacrifice. "Omni
cupiditate submota, quae reipublicae semper adversa est, et
universali pace cum libertate dilecta, populus ille sanctus,
pius et gloriosus, propria commoda neglexisse videtur ut pub-
lica pro salute humani generis procuraret. Unde recte illud
scriptum est: 'Romanum Imperium de fonte nascitur pie-
tatis.' "[1] Nature herself has fashioned Rome for empire. For
the law of nature is inseparable from right. Nature, in providing the means for the end of man, designs certain men and
certain nations for command, others for subjection. And what
nation for universal command was ordained but Rome? Others
might lead in art or science. Rome was born to rule.

But granting the title of Rome to be the seat of universal
jurisdiction, is the emperor necessarily the monarch? The
Decretalists say no, and all the proofs that Dante has urged
for the Empire they make to tell for the Papacy. Thus as in
the second book Dante had in the cause of Rome "shaken
asunder the bonds of the kings of the earth", so in the third
he combats the papal lawyers, "men ignorant of theology and
philosophy, who wantonly assert that the traditions of the
Church are the foundation of faith". Here it is not ignorance
that has to be instructed, but counter-claims to be disputed.
Thus as the first book is mainly philosophical, and the second
mainly historical, so the third is eminently polemical. To
modern readers it appears the most real, the most interesting,
and the most able part of the work. At the same time it bears
more resemblance to other apologies of the Empire, whether
previous or subsequent to the *De Monarchia*. But while com-
bating the pretensions of the Papacy Dante does not fail to
deepen his conception of the Empire. He first confutes the
arguments drawn from Scripture for the pre-eminence of the

---

[1] [*De Mon.* ii, 5, p. 354.]

priest over the prince, and the metaphysical arguments for an all-embracing unity which subordinates Emperor to Pope. In vain the Decretalists urge history and charter, the donation of Constantine and subsequent grants. The jurisdiction, says Dante, is prior to the judge, the Empire to the Emperor. Constantine had no more right to grant the possessions of the Empire than the Church to receive them; he could not alienate what was not his own. "Poterat imperator in patrocinium Ecclesiae patrimonium et alia deputare, immoto semper superiori dominio, cujus unitas divisionem non patitur. Poterat et Vicarius Dei recipere, non tanquam possessionem sed tanquam fructum pro Ecclesia, pro Christi pauperibus dispensator."[1] The Emperor could only grant, the Church only receive, the usufruct in trust for the poor.

And so if Charlemagne became the Advocatus and therefore the feoffee of the Church, "Usurpatio juris non facit jus". The Empire is prior to the Church. Christ Himself admitted its temporal power (if Constantine had not possessed this power he could not have made his grant to the Church; its possession by the Church would be abuse). Neither divine nor national law nor universal assent has made it over to the Church. She could not grant it to herself, nor could the Emperor grant it to her. The "virtus auctorizandi imperium nostrae mortalitatis" is contrary to the very nature of the Church.

What, then, is the mutual relation of Church and Empire? Man is a mean between the corruptible and the incorruptible; he has two natures, and each nature has its end—blessedness in this life and blessedness hereafter. The way to the latter lies through spiritual learning, through the theological virtues, and the guide is the Pope. The former is reached through philosophical learning, through the moral and intellectual virtues. The opposing waves of passion are stilled by the peace of the Emperor. This, then, is the end of the Empire: "Ut in areola ista mortalium libere cum pace vivatur".[2] As the order of this world follows that of the heavens, so He who ordered the heavens can alone dispense to the guardian of this world

---

[1] [*De Mon.* iii, 10, p. 372.]   [2] [*Ibid.* 16, p. 376.]

the "utilia documenta libertatis ac pacis". God alone elects, God alone confirms; the so-called electors are only the mouthpiece of God.

The result, then, of the *De Monarchia* is an Emperor whose mission is to produce universal peace by the means of justice. He is the servant of free mankind; other princes are his deputies. He has inherited his right from the Roman people. His jurisdiction is, in the province of secular government and law, to be final, not to be split nor to be trenched upon by the parallel jurisdiction which embraces all government and law in things spiritual.

Such an ideal could have no chance of realisation when the material consisted of such an emperor as Albert of Austria, such princes as Philip le Bel and Charles of Naples, such a Pope as Boniface VIII. But for the accession of Henry VII, and the removal of the Papacy to Avignon, the *De Monarchia* would either not have been written or would have had no bearing upon history. It is only during Henry's reign that Dante's ideal has any relation to the real. The material which history provides consists, on the one hand, of the Emperor himself and of the elements which theoretically should prove pliable—namely, the interests of Ghibellinism and the ambitions of the Roman people; on the other hand, of elements which are likely to resist the superimposition of the ideal, such as the claims of the Papacy resisting unity in the shape of the Empire, and the spirit of nationality rejecting the necessity of unity at all.

If the characteristics of the Empire were ideally its universality—the absence of local and national ties—a position above jarring interests and factions, then the character and the circumstances of the life of Henry of Luxemburg made him an ideal Emperor, and if the *De Monarchia* was written before his accession, Dante was prophet as well as philosopher. Henry had as little definite nationality as Emperor could have. A prince of the German Empire, he was elected unanimously by the German electors. But he came from the borderland between France and Germany; he had been reared at the French Court; his language was French. His election was secured by his brother the Elector of Trier, always the most French of the Electorates, and he owed it to the fact that he was a candidate not unpleasing to the French crown. His interests from the first lay in Italy, and Italy he regarded as the stepping-stone to the Holy Land.

To the Pope his election was agreeable. A French Pope could not but dread the threatened transference of the Empire from the Germans to the French. A certain amount of imperial influence in Italy would check the growth of the Neapolitan dynasty which endangered the independence of the Papal States. And yet the King of the Germans could hardly be dependent upon a French Pope. Henry was in a far better position than the Hapsburgs. In the absence of the Pope from Rome, the *entrée* was open to the Emperor. The possession of a small principality of eight or nine towns hardly constituted a local tie. The grant of Bohèmia to his son did indeed lay the foundation of the great territorial power of the House of Luxemburg, but Henry seems scarcely to have recognised it in that light. At all events his policy, unlike that of the Hapsburgs, his predecessors, and Louis of Bavaria, his successor, was in no way modified by ideas of territorial aggrandisement. Marriage was indeed freely used as a means of attaching powerful princes to himself, but it was rather with the view of older Emperors—that of securing faithful vice-regents of the Empire—than with the later idea of their territories falling in to swell the hereditary possessions of the House of Luxemburg.

In Italy, if Henry had not the positive advantages of Frederick II, yet there were few of the obstacles which for sixty years had closed the Alps to the German kings. Robert of Naples had only just succeeded to his throne, his title was doubtful, and Frederick of Sicily was likely to be at least a match for him. The effect of the tragedy of Boniface VIII cannot be overestimated. It was all the more powerful in that it had befallen one of the strongest of the Popes. Notwithstanding the later expansion of its territory, the Papacy never again assumed the leading position in Italy. The Guelfic theory—if indeed it ever was a theory—of a national federation of municipalities headed by a national Pope was thoroughly discredited. The Pope was no longer national; the municipalities of Lombardy were mostly in the hands of despots; those of Tuscany divided by faction in which it is hopeless to trace a principle.

The lower classes, restless under these noble or *bourgeois* despots, and longing for at least a change of masters, looked to Henry as in 1494 they looked to Charles VIII. "Plebs omnis Italiae, quae novis semper trahi ducibus quaerit, lege fatorum aeterna, venientem Caesarem jam manifestis optabat applausibus."[1] Rome with no court and no trade was ready to welcome an Emperor or a Pope to give back her material prosperity and realise her claims as the world centre. "Fama increbescebat Pop. Rom. praesertimque plebem commodis suarum rerum Regem exoptare."[2]

More than this was the fact that Henry was the one ruler of a very demoralised age who had a high ideal, and this the very ideal which Dante had pictured: a reign of peace, and justice, and freedom from irresponsible tyranny, which, if it could not be universal, should at least be common to the Germany which he had pacified, and to the Italy which he was come to judge. His capital was to be no hereditary possession of his house, but Rome itself. His power was to serve the spiritual, to protect the temporal interests of the Church. Consequently in studying Henry's career, we seem to be reading the *De Monarchia*, book by book. We have the visionary philosophical period, in which he attempts to organise the universal peace; the fanciful historical period, where he sacrifices all to re-establish the connexion of the Empire with Rome; and, lastly and inevitably, the polemical finale, in which he has to combat the rivalry of the Pope and his allies.

The constant references to peace and justice among the chroniclers of Henry's reign are not due to the mere commonplace of royal panegyric. They are to be found among Germans and Italians, among Ghibellines and moderate Guelfs, such as Villani. His rule in Luxemburg was celebrated—

---

[1] Ferretus Vicentinus: Muratori, ix, 1055.
[2] Mussato, v, cap. vii: Muratori, x, 408.

"Quod in eo via justitiae et trames equitatis bases suas fixerit; nam per comitatum Lutzelburgensem mercatoribus et aliis peregrinantibus major fuit securitas quam sit in aliquibus provinciis ecclesiarum immunitas".[1] Peace and justice seem to have been family characteristics. The Chronicler of Baldwin of Trier, after praising the same virtues in him, says of Henry: "Judex justissimus, semper illum gerens animum. Juste judicate, filii hominum".[2] From Luxemburg his reputation spread through Germany; a Salzburg chronicle says of him: "De quo multa bona, et maxime quod pacis amator et justus judex esset quasi per totam Alemaniam dicebatur".[3] And the Annalist of Zwettel believes that "his death was only due to the world's being unworthy of him, for since Charlemagne his like was never found. His zeal for justice, the religious character of his life, equalled any king in the Old or New Testament."

On his descent into Italy the practical form which the reign of peace and justice was to take was a revival of the old network of Imperial Vicars, reintroducing common imperial order into the disintegrated inharmonious mass of tyrannies and commonwealths. Municipal jurisdictions were, indeed, still to exist, but only as a supplement to imperial administration. They had been the tools of faction; they were now to be the subordinate parts of the one great engine of unity. The party names of Guelf and Ghibelline were to be forgotten. This is the burden of his circular letters: "Universos Christicolas sibi cordi esse in pace componendos".[4] This is the text of the royal speech to the Lombards when he sat on his throne in front of St. Ambrogio on the day of his coronation with the iron crown: "Intentionis erat nullam partem tenere, ubique ponere pacem, omnes expulsos introducere".[5] To a loyal exile of Vercelli, who rode in to say that he had suffered for the Empire's party, but would still serve it with all that he had left, Henry answered that he was sorry, but he could not believe that it was for his party that he had suffered: he held no

---

[1] Pertz, xvii, 70: *Annales Worm.*
[2] Baluze, *Misc. Hist.* i, 314.
[3] *Contin. Canonicorum S. Rudberti Salisburgensis*: Pertz, xi, 319.
[4] Letter to Pisans: Mussato, v, cap. v : Muratori, x, 406.
[5] *Nicolai Episc. Botront. Relatio*: Muratori, ix, 894; ed. Heyck, p. 2.

part nor party in Lombardy; he had not come for part nor party, but for all.[1]

The earnest, religious Rhinelander was an astounding contrast to Italian princes of the day. His one pleasure, says Compagni, was peace. "La sua vita non era in sonare, nè in uccellare, nè in sollazzi, ma in continui consigli, in assettando i vicari per le terre, ed a pacificare i discordanti".[2] His was a mission direct from God, he adds, to beat down and chastise the tyrants till every tyranny should be stamped out, and so "Venne qui discendendo di terra in terra mettendo pace come fusse un agnolo di Dio".[3] Clement himself had introduced him as the Messias of Peace. "Vivat rex Salamon. Salamon interpretatus pacificus rex, nam et ipse talis est, pacem enim diligit, pacem quaerit et amplectitur, et pacem procurat, nam Teutoni hoc videntes a bellorum strepitibus quierunt et quiescunt . . . nam ubicumque fuit ita pacem procuravit quod in veritate dicere possumus 'In pace factus est ejus locus'."[4] But more striking than all, when taken in connexion with Dante's philosophical theory, is a passage by the Chronicler of Baldwin of Trier, in which he says of Henry: "Merito illud propheticum ejus debuit auribus insonare 'Specie tua', quoad justitiam humanitatis et ad vitam activam, 'et pulchritudine tua', scil. bonorum operum divinitatis et ad vitam speculativam, 'intende, prospere procede, et regna' ".[5] Dante's first book could certainly find no better exponent than this: "Simplex animus [qui] totaliter aspirabat dare pacem mundo".[6]

Nor was Henry less alive than Dante to the inseparable connexion between peace and the one law and one lawgiver. The universality of the Empire is stamped upon his very seal.

---

[1] *Nicolai Episc. Botront. Relatio* : Muratori, ix, 894 ; ed. Heyck, p. 2. So, too, "Nostro intendimento era di volere i Fiorentini tutti, e non partiti, a buoni fedeli", G. Villani, *Storia*, lib. ix, cap. vii. Villani, ix, 15, says that men's minds were so shaken by his reputation for justice and kindness that but for his delay at Brescia he might have secured Tuscany, Rome and Naples without combat.

[2] Dino Compagni: *Cronica*, lib. iii, cap. xxvi.

[3] *Ibid.* cap. xxiv.   [4] Bonaini, *Acta Henrici VII*, i, 2.

[5] Baluze, *Misc. Hist.* i, 315.

[6] Johannes de Cermenate: Muratori, ix, 1237. [*Historia*, ed. Ferrai (Rome, 1889), p. 39.]

"Ego coronarum corona mundique caput, confirmo principi potestatem sibique subjicio civitates gentiumque nationes. Tueantur aquilae gloriam meam." This universality is impressed alike upon independent commonwealth and papal fief. In his Edict on Treason, of 1313, he speaks of "the Roman Empire in whose peace the order of the whole world reposes, of the divine command that every soul should be subject to the Roman Emperor".[1] Naples is not excluded by virtue of its papal suzerainty. "Regnum Siciliae et specialiter insula Siciliae sicut et ceterae provinciae sunt de Imperio, totus enim mundus imperatoris est."[2]

And of this empire Rome, "with its most loving people, its most dear senate, with whom he comes to spend joyous days", is to be the centre. To us this divine inalienable right of Rome is the most fanciful, unreal part of Dante's ideal and of Henry's ambition. To Henry's practical military advisers it was mere nonsense. Yet in Rome alone was there an ambition and an ideal corresponding to their own, independent alike of time and of party. Not only now, but hereafter whenever the Teutonic overgrowth of noble families was for a season cleared away by a blaze of democracy, along with the weakly growth of municipal liberty, appeared the long hidden flower of universal Empire. It mattered little that the Empire had passed to the Germans; that the right of election was becoming more bound up, not with great imperial offices, but with the possession of certain lands, and those beyond the limits of the old Empire; that the coronation and the popular acclamation conferred little that the Emperor had not before; that it had been dispensed with for sixty years. "Rome", says Gregorovius, "is the one place where the ghosts of the past are never laid." The Emperors, if their titular precedence was to mean anything, could not afford to undervalue the connexion. And if the Pope dreaded the presence of an Emperor in Rome, and hurried his departure, yet in this connexion rested their only practical hold upon the Empire. The last Emperor who was crowned in Rome was the last over whom

[1] Pertz, iv, 544: *Constitutiones Henrici VII.*
[2] Dönniges, *Acta Henrici VII*, ii, 65.

D

the Papacy had any control. With the Hohenstaufens the idea had been subservient to the practical domination of Italy; with Louis of Bavaria it was to be the means of worrying a hostile Pope; with Henry it was the goal of all ambition. He trod in the steps of the Ottos. In vain had the Archbishop of Mainz urged him to give up the idea of crossing the Alps, and to be content with the German kingship.[1] His practical success at Rome depended on points which had little to do with his theory—on the respective strength of the Colonnas and the Orsini, and the associated groups of families; on the power of the German horse to force the Neapolitan barricades; on the speed with which the Florentines could push forward the levies of the Tuscan Parte Guelfa. But of all this abstraction must be made. The real interest lies, not in the street fighting, but in the alliance between the universal monarch and the Roman democracy. The Senate gives him the right of jurisdiction in the city. Beneath the steps of the Capitol he calls a *Parlamento*. Ten thousand citizens represent the theoretical electors of the world. The way to St. Peter's being barred, the papal commission had no authority to crown in the Lateran. But coronation was a matter, not for Pope, but for people. "Ex plebiscito obtentum est Cardinales Reipublicae suasionibus precibusque coronam dare, sin autem coercendos per tribunos populumque Romanum."[2] The coronation was ultimately due to an attack of the people on the Cardinals. Henry firmly believed that the empire of the world depended on the capture of the Roman fortresses. If he could hold his position in Rome, which is the capital of the Roman Empire, he thought, "ceteras terras tanquam appendicias suum veluti caput respectare."[3] Why have I come? he asks the Romans. Only that the Roman people, now scarce known by the outer world, may rule the world under the shield and beneath the title of the majesty of the Caesars. When his German nobles and

---

[1] "Nel primo consiglio fu offeso da' Fiorentini, perchè a' prieghi loro l' Arcivescovo di Maganza lo consigliava, che non passasse, e che gli bastava esser Re della Magna, mettendogli in gran dubbio e pericolo il passare in Italia" (Dino Compagni, iii, 24).

[2] Mussato, viii, cap. vii: Muratori, x, 460.

[3] *Ibid.* 451.

Ghibelline chiefs withdrew, the people would hardly let Henry go—he might stay, indeed, at Tivoli, which was Roman soil.[1] And after his ultimate retreat the sudden rising of the people under Arlotti thrust aside the noble factions and recalled the Emperor. Revolutions in Rome were but reactions. Arlotti was crushed, and Henry died. It was left for Louis of Bavaria to accept the crown from the Roman people.[2] But Petrarch thinks that if Henry had lived, "Romam regnantem et liberrimos Italiae populos ac felicissimos reliquisset".[3]

If Pope and Emperor were to rule two separate kingdoms, it was a pity that they had but one capital between them. Whether monarchy pitched its tents with Henry VII on the Lateran or with Victor Emmanuel on the Quirinal, the Vatican was all too near. The Tiber was an inadequate boundary between the spiritual and the temporal kingdoms. The Bridge of S. Angelo was their recognised battlefield.

An imperial visit to Rome was always the test which parted the Guelfic from the Ghibelline element, the touchstone which showed the alloy in the professed Papal-Imperial friendship. To this Henry's visit was no exception. It tested how far he had been rightly called the Guelfic Emperor, or how far he realised the orthodox Ghibelline conceptions of the relations between Papacy and Empire. All the knotty questions now arise: How far did he consider the two authorities to be independent in origin, distinct in function? What was the bearing of the Donation of Constantine on the Western Empire at large, and on the papal claims in Italy? How far did the coronation of Charlemagne resemble the acceptance of a fief from a suzerain? What was the meaning of the dangerous word Advocatus? had it a feudal technical sense at all, or

---

[1] Ferretus Vicentinus: Muratori, ix, 1106.

[2] "Compertum est, dispositis ad hujus [Arlotti] plebisque ad libitum rebus, praecipue potentioribus fusis, omnia haec parari Caesari, ipsum evocandum in urbem, vehendumque triumphaliter in Capitolium, principatum ab sola plebe recogniturum" (Mussato, xi, cap. xii: Muratori, x, 508).

[3] Petrarch, Letter to Charles IV. [*Ep. Fam.* x, 1, ed. Fracassetti, vol. ii, p. 63 (Florence, 1862).]

was it used in its simple original sense, and used of a single act? Granting the former, that the Emperor stood to the Church at large in the same relation that the Advocatus usually held to the bishopric or abbey, *i.e.* granting that he was the legally constituted protector of the Church, and that he exercised the rights of temporal justice which the Church could not do for herself, what was the effect of this on the tenure of the Empire? Was it a fief granted by the Church for which the Advocate's service was to be the consideration, or was it a possession of the Advocate prior to his office?

Arising from these points comes the more practical question: Was Henry's authority previous or subsequent to coronation? Was he Caesar from the moment of election, or from the moment of coronation, with papal consent? Did the ignorance of the papal conditions invalidate the act of consecration by the papal commission?

Questions such as these were first forced upon Henry by his visit to Rome. With him, as with Dante, theoretical Ghibellinism was probably of comparatively late growth. He had been called the Guelfic Emperor. The Papal Court had no softer name than perjury for his action in Rome.[1] It based this charge on two documents: on Henry's original letter asking for the papal confirmation of his election, and on a document published at Lausanne, which guaranteed the engagements therein contained.[2]

But these prove nothing that is absolutely in contradiction with Dante's theory, with one important exception, as to the papal title to the Roman States. Here the terms are such that the *dominium superius*, as Dante would say, could hardly be said to be reserved. No ordinance is to be issued without papal advice and consent; no territory is to be held, no jurisdiction exercised, by the Emperor or his officers. As Advocatus and Defensor Ecclesiae the Emperor binds himself to defend the papal territories; he engages to make every one of his vicars

---

[1] "Quia multum jam videbatur prosperari Papa Clemens, sumpta occasione ex parte Ruperti regis Siciliae, opposuit se imperatori, imponendo ei perjurium ut habetur in Constitutionibus Clementinis, cap. Romani principis" (Pertz, xiv, 418, *Gesta Arch. Magd.*).

[2] Pertz, iv, 494; *ibid.* 501-3.

in Lombardy and Tuscany swear to do likewise. As a rule the
jurisdiction in ecclesiastical towns reverted to the Emperor
in person when he was within their walls; previous Emperors
had exercised it in Rome without question. This concession
would go to prove that Rome was not an imperial town in the
ordinary sense of the word. But the fact that not only Constantine's Donation is quoted, but the confirmation of his
grant by succeeding Emperors, and that this engagement of
Henry VII is made in the terms of a fresh grant, rather goes
to prove the conception that sovereignty in the last instance
had never been alienated, that the temporalities of the Church
were a fief held of the Empire, though a fief held on different
terms from any other. This was Henry's view. As early as
1311, before there was any breach with the Church in the Ban
of Florence, we read "exemplo Christi, cujus vicem ipsa re-
galis dignitas in terris circa temporalia noscitur obtinere".[1]
Nicolas of Butrinto quotes Henry as saying:

The Emperor and King Robert are not in an equal degree subject to the Church in respect of temporalities, for the one is
Defender and Advocate, holding none of its temporalities of the
Church; the other is subject and vassal, holding his kingdom of
the Church. If he suffered himself to be considered by your
Holiness the vassal of the Church in respect of temporalities he
would be guilty of perjury, since he would be impairing the rights
of the empire, which he had sworn not to impair but to augment.[2]

As the resistance to the Emperor increased, so did the imperial ideas become more definite. If in the letter Henry broke
the engagement of Lausanne, the breach was forced upon him
by the ambiguous conduct of Clement V. The armed occupation of Rome was forced upon him by the armed resistance
of the Neapolitan troops and of the papal feudatories, the
Orsini. The situation was indeed a complex one. Henry was
entering Rome by arrangement with the Pope, accompanied
by the papal commission which was to crown him in St.
Peter's. But the way to St. Peter's was blocked by the troops
of the Pope's own Vicar of Romagna, who had even tried to

[1] Pertz, iv, 519.   [2] Muratori, ix, 921; ed. Heyck, 63.

prevent his passing into Rome over the Ponte Molle. The acceptance of the forbidden jurisdiction in Rome was forced upon him, because the feeling of the people against the papal commission was so strong that it would have been inoperative in their hands; the coronation itself was forced upon him by the danger of delaying until his North Italian and German troops left him; and, moreover, the lives of the commission were threatened by the people. They told the Pope, as indeed was true, that they had consecrated in the Lateran under compulsion. Then after coronation comes a series of conditions of which there had been no word before. The Emperor is never to attack Naples; to make a year's truce with King Robert; to leave Rome on the day of coronation and evacuate the Papal States, never to enter them again without papal permission; to make a declaration that by entering and residence and imprisonment of citizens and occupation of fortresses, he had acquired no new rights.

This it is which calls forth the manifesto of Henry which gives a complete statement of Ghibellinism and is fully in accord with the leading conceptions of the *De Monarchia*.[1] "Nos fuimus et semper esse volumus defensor et pugil sacrosancte Romane Ecclesie in omnibus suis juribus, sed nos non sumus astricti alicui ad juramentum fidelitatis nec unquam juramentum fecimus . . . nec scimus quod antecessores nostri . . . hoc juramentum unquam fecerunt."[2] The Emperor, by election of the electors alone, is put in full possession of his power. This is in accordance with Dante's view, that the voice of the electors is really the declaration of God which alone bestows the temporal power over the world. Lastly, the Pope cannot order the Emperor to leave Rome, which is the head of the Empire and an imperial town.

---

[1] "Quamvis Papa non teneatur inungere fatuum vel hereticum in imperatorem . . . tamen non ideo sequitur quod sola electio Romani Principis ei jus non tribuat imperandi, quemadmodum enim sola Papae electio ei omnem tribuit potestatem et administrationem, quia nemo est eo superior in spiritualibus, ita quidem et Romano principi sola electio ejus omnem tribuit potestatem, quia non eo superior in temporalibus" (Dönniges, *Acta Henrici VII*, ii, 61).

[2] *Ibid*. ii, 54-5 *et seq*.

This is the last word of imperialism, and it is all the more decisive because spoken by the most orthodox, the most pious, the most moral of emperors; by the man on whom Clement, with a process ready prepared against him, was obliged to pronounce a funeral eulogy; the man who, as we are told, communicated monthly—who refused to save his life by getting rid of the poison which to his belief he had taken with the sacrament.[1] Moreover, the declaration was not made in the heat of an actual quarrel, nor was there between Pope and Emperor any personal ill-feeling.[2] With the Hohenstaufens is seen chiefly a struggle of brute force between the two powers. Henry and Clement appear to be fighting with the gloves on; what is lost in excitement is gained in knowledge of the rules of the combat. The career of Henry, who was never brought into actual admitted hostile collision with the Papacy, illustrates the philosophy of the Empire, and so here it is that we seem to be reacting his life through the *De Monarchia*. Henry, unlike his predecessors, at once upon accession proclaims the universality of his designs when unity was most needed; he preaches peace and justice when justice was the tool of party and when peace was found only in the vocabulary of regret. He promises a liberty, which, in theory at all events, was far higher than that enjoyed under the irresponsible rule of a Lombard despot, or the boasted freedom of Florence, which was the privilege of a section, of a faction, of a party. "Si perfidiam Italorum inexpertus agnovisset dolosque vitasset, merito labentes Imperii partes, depressosque tyrannide populos, in salubrem stationis libertatem reformasset."[3] What is this but the analysis of Dante's first book?

Side by side with the second is the Emperor's shadowy unreal period of empire in the capital, which neither "instructs the ignorant" nor "convinces the litigious". There is the high theory of the world-wide rights of the Roman people and its representative, and their inability to walk through their own

---

[1] Pertz, xvi, 423: *Annales Lubicenses*; *Historiens des Gaules et de la France*, xxii, 140: Geoffroi de Paris.

[2] Pertz, xi, 665: *Contin. Zwetlensis Tertia*; Pertz, xvi, 423: *Ann. Lubicenses*.

[3] Ferretus Vicentinus: Muratori, ix, 1059.

streets; a sufficient answer to the charge that "the Roman
Empire was founded on violence and is so maintained".
There is an Emperor above nationality and above party, for
his Germans and his Ghibellines had both deserted him.

And more clear than all is the parallelism to the third book.
The philosophical principles have been controverted, the historical justification ignored. The attacks of the purely litigious
have now to be met, the imperial principles to be proved by
the refutation of the antagonists. Here the task is easier. It is
an equally unpractical theory that has to be demolished. The
arguments all strike home and indeed become the arguments
for the next generation, for Louis of Bavaria and for all time.
The battle was won, if not for the universal Empire, yet
against a universal temporal Church.

Apparently, then, Dante's political system was not a mere
ideal. It was either founded upon the life of Henry VII or
else the book was no sooner written than a monarch arose to
indicate its possibility. But here all reality vanishes. If Dante
was an idealist, so was Henry VII, and their ideals had to be
imposed upon a singularly unimaginative practical generation
—a generation of lawyers and adventurers. What instruments
had Henry to his hand? The Germans? But the youth of the
warrior class, its age of expansion, was over. The spread of
Teutonism in the fourteenth century was to be the mission
of the peasant and the pedlar, not of the knight. And so Henry
had but a small German following. It was useless to tell
the *stolida gens Teutonicorum* that the world empire was their
bride awaiting them; that they had only to accept the principalities of the earth; that the offices, the prefectures, the highest magistracies of the "Senatus Populusque Romanus" were
lying vacant for them.[1] They had no liking for the enterprise;
they said that it was premature to start so big an undertaking.
Even of those who went few seem to have had any political
or territorial ambition. They looked rather to loot than to
land or office. Some of the most distinguished are Germans
only politically, not by nationality. They are Flemings, Bur-
gundians, Dauphinois, Savoyards. Indeed Henry's family had

---

[1] Mussato, i, cap. viii: Muratori, x, 329.

hardly any German colouring: himself a Frenchman; his son a knight-errant of no nationality; Charles IV but the stepfather of the Germans; Wenzel a Czech. Even Sigismond attracted more sympathy abroad than he did in Germany. If, then, Henry could not be the leader of a new Teutonic migration, could he found his sovereignty on the basis of the Italian Ghibellines? If they had been really the party of the rural nobility—of Teutonic origin—fighting the battle of feudalism, of unity, against the Romanesque spirit of municipal separatism, they might have found their place in the ideal. But Ghibellinism was not coincident with the rural nobility any more than Guelfism with the *bourgeois* nobility of the towns. If the Colonnas were of German origin, so were the Orsini. The feudal lords of the Tuscan and Umbrian highlands were chiefly of Teutonic origin, but they were nearly as often Guelf as Ghibelline. The most constant of Guelfs, the Malatestas, were German. The Malaspinas and the Guidos had Guelfic as well as Ghibelline branches. So within the towns, in some the nobility were Guelf and the people Ghibelline, in others the people Guelf and the nobles Ghibelline. Even in Florence the Cerchi represented the party of progress, of prosperous *bourgeoisie*, and yet they allied themselves with the Ghibelline element in the town. There could be no principle in parties which were determined by family feuds and local jealousies. The Ghibelline adventurers used the imperial invasions just as the Guelfic adventurers used the Angevin support, merely for their individual purposes. Titles went for something, and an imperial vicariate was somewhat better than a papal vicariate because the lord was farther off. The Estes made safe by holding both. If we see any principle at all, it is the negation of principle, the purest individualism; what the noble adventurer won he won for his own hand. Nor was this peculiar to the fourteenth century nor to Italy. The Empire had for centuries in vain attempted to create an official class which would keep pace with its expansion and keep touch of the centre. The official never remained an official: he became a lord. Henry made the last attempt to create an all-pervading system of imperial vicars throughout North Italy, to bring municipal justice into connexion with imperial, but the attempt failed as soon as it was made. In many cases the vicars were the lords already, and the office added nothing but the title. This was one of the most frequent causes of revolts. The Cremonese said that Henry was no king, but tyrant—"Cum tyrannides in urbibus exercendas decreverit, antiquatos tyrannos titulis imperialibus approbans".[1] A Paduan orator told his townsfolk that Henry was a destroyer let loose upon the world. "He has foisted on noble towns their ancient tyrants clad with the title of imperial vicars."[2] This was a frequent cause of revolt. The great revolt of all, that of Brescia, was fomented by one of Henry's own vicars. Universal custom and Henry's poverty prompted him to the sale of offices; and the old tyrants had naturally a chance of pre-emption.[3] This is testified to, not only by the critical Mussato, but by the eulogistic Ferreto of Vicenza: "Tum primum Caesar pretio corruptus perfidisque suorum hortatibus fasces magistratusque omnes venum exposuit".[4]

Henry quite recognised the want of principle in the struggle of parties; he saw as well as Dante that "while the Guelfs belled against, the Ghibellines appropriated the imperial power". He saw that the uniformity of imperial power could only be introduced by the extinction of party. He loathed the names of Guelf and Ghibelline, "cuncta absoluto amplectens imperio".[5] The wars of Italy were produced, not only by the factions within the several towns, but by the bands of exiles without, with no employment but war and intrigue. Henry's first object was a general restoration of exiles of both parties, and the same impartiality was at first shown in the appointment of vicars. But one man could not stay the course of party strife in Italy, nor check the tendency towards isolation. The

---

[1] Mussato, ii, cap. x: Muratori, x, 358.

[2] *Ibid.* 416.

[3] G. Villani, ix, 19: "E così tutte l' altre terre di Lombardia lasciò a tiranno, non possendo altro per lo suo male stato, e da ciascuno ebbe moneta assai, e brivilegiolli delle dette signorie".

[4] FerretusVicentinus: Muratori, ix, 1064.

[5] Mussato, i, cap. xiii: Muratori, x, 340.

return of the exiles was the cause of most of the rebellions
which blazed out as soon as Henry turned his back. The
Chronicler of Asti attributes the troubles of North Italy, not
to Henry, but to national faults. "The Lombards were deservedly afflicted with divers plagues, for which the King was
not to blame, for he had come like a kindly monarch to pacify
the Lombards, but could not do so. For the Guelfs could not
live side by side with those over whom they were wont to
lord it, and the Ghibellines wanted to avenge their ancient
wrongs; and so they are very like an eel, which cannot be held
either by its head or by its tail." [1]

Impartiality became impossible, a position above party
meant desertion by both parties. Thus standing in need, as
he did, of support for his operations on Rome, he was forced
to become a party chief, to choose his friends from among the
Ghibelline leaders. Dino Compagni shows us the whole process—the declaration of the Emperor that he had no party; [2]
the Ghibellines complaining that he would see none but
Guelfs, the Guelfs that he would welcome none but Ghibellines; the gradual estrangement of the Guelfs who had not so
much need of his support; then the final stage at Rome, when
Henry, "hearing of the wrongs inflicted on him by the Tuscan
Guelfs, and finding that the Ghibellines took his side with
right good will, changed his policy and drew nearer to them,
gave to them the love which he had first bestowed upon the
Guelfs, decided to follow their lead, to give them his help, to
restore them to their honours; and as for the Guelfs and the
Blacks, to hold them as his enemies and to persecute them". [3]
And these Ghibellines whose lead he followed were not theoretical monarchists like Dante, but men of the stamp of Uguccione della Faggiuola, Can Grande, Matteo Visconti: men
who had no sentimental vision of a universal peace under a
universal Empire; who never looked to an imaginary past for
their model; who were leading Italy into a new phase of life
both natural and national. Rebels against both Church and
Empire, their end was not philosophic contemplation but

[1] *Chron. Astense*, cap. lxi: Muratori, xi, 234.
[2] [*Cronica*, lib. iii, cap. xxvi.]   [3] [*Ibid.* cap. xxxvi.]

material prosperity, to be won indifferently by peace or war; their justice their own will; their liberty extending no farther than themselves. The outcome of the greatest of these creations of Henry, of Matteo Visconti, was the creed of his descendant, "Ego sum et Papa et Imperator et dominus in terris meis". In these fourteenth-century heroes we have, indeed, men who would have delighted Machiavelli, but are far removed from the model ruler of Dante. And yet they were the only tools that Henry had to work with.

Castelar has said that it is impossible to found a republic where there are no republicans. Henry found that he could not establish an empire when there were no imperialists. Moreover, Henry himself was not fitted to be a party chief. His personality and programme were both incompatible with his new position. Neither Henry nor Dante could preach peace, justice and liberty and be partisans. But while Dante was separated from party by scorn and impatience, an excess of pity and a certain irresolution of character prevented Henry from realising the necessities of his case. Nicolas of Butrinto noticed this weakness early in the campaign. A man of Pavia, contrary to his Guelfic bishop's injunctions, left the diocese to join Henry. Count Philippone, the bishop's brother, then with Henry, sent orders that his house and property should be destroyed. Henry found no fault with Philippone, and retained him as his councillor. Nicolas, in his request to the Pope, commenting on this case, says: "In conscientia mea ego ex tunc minus in animo meo ipsum regem reputavi et quod ipse numquam bene faceret justitiam nec de malis hominibus magni studeret facere justitiam, quod supra modum mihi displicebat".[1] A verse of the rhyming Chronicle attributed to Geoffroi de Paris also probably represents the popular opinion:

> Une cóse ot, que trop piteux
> Estoit, e ce li fist damage;
> Car homme de trop grant pitié
> Est souvente foix despitié.[2]

As against this the elements of resistance were most formid-

---

[1] Muratori, ix, 891; ed. Heyck, 7.
[2] *Historiens des Gaules et de la France*, xxii, 126.

able. Every principle of the programme of Dante and of Henry is opposed to some material interest within Italy or without. The municipal separatism of Tuscans and Lombards, the dynastic independence of Naples, were in arms against the champion of imperial unity. The national sense of France revolted against the claims of a Roman Emperor; that of Italy against the presence of a German King. The Papacy employed its spiritual armoury to resist the revolt of the temporal power.

Of the latter point enough almost has been said already. Principle against principle, the struggle was decided. The great importance attributed to the conflict under Louis of Bavaria must not mislead us. The alternations between violence and remorse of a rough superstitious soldier are no real gauge of the watermark of papal supremacy. At the end of the fifteenth century a Vitellozzo Vitelli will pray for absolution from Alexander before being strangled by Alexander's son. The momentary triumphs of John XXII and Benedict XII were due purely to the personal characteristics of Louis and the temporary political necessities of his opponents, not to the realities of papal power.

In this supreme struggle of Henry's for the revival of the Empire the Papacy seems to be the one factor which is inoperative. Clement's temporal influence neither helped at the commencement nor hindered at the conclusion of the campaign. And his spiritual weapons struck harmless against an Emperor strong through the conviction of the righteousness of his cause and the blamelessness of his life. Excommunication had no terrors for the most religious prince of the age. Calmly, without passion or abuse, is the question debated, whether excommunication is binding on an Emperor defending the rights of the Empire. Unequivocally is it stated that it is not. The whole of this debate and the third part of the *De Monarchia* together complete the case for the Empire against the Papacy.

It is more difficult to attribute just weight to the other elements of the opposition. Setting aside France for the moment, as not being formally engaged in the conflict, it is necessary to disentangle the resistance of the municipalities to the monarchy, and the national feeling which on the one side experienced the practical inconveniences of the incursion of the German troopers, but on the other the abiding pressure of municipal tyranny. Again, it is hard to say how far such men as Dante and Compagni or even Villani were in accord with popular feeling as to the theoretical supremacy of Rome. That the theory was alive, and that it was not confined to Rome itself or to merely speculative minds, is proved by the events of Louis's reign, and still further by the attitude of the Italian towns, even of Florence and Venice, towards Rienzi. It may safely be said, however, as to Dante's first book, that the material interests involved in the retention of municipal separatism far outweighed the desire to shake off its burden; and as to the second, that the barbarian development of the Empire was more obvious than its Roman descent.

The want of accord between the ruling families and the populace, the certain fears of the one and the vague hopes of the other, can be well illustrated from a passage from Landulphus de Columna:

Res nova et dura videbatur quibusdam Italicis atque Tuscis, et maxime qui populum regere videbantur, cum sexaginta quinque annis et amplius a deposicione ab imperio ultima Frederici sine imperatoris dominio perstitissent, quod ejus dominio denuo subderentur a quo se existimabant in perpetuum liberatos: sed propter tyrannidis grave jugum, quod in cives suos exercuerant, merebantur ut tyrannidi subderentur, et hoc ipsum minor populus praecipere affectabat.[1]

Whatever may have been the case in the twelfth and thirteenth centuries, there is not much that is admirable in the fourteenth, or rather there was little correspondence between the reality of government and the theory of the constitution. It is hard to see that the tyrant families of the Lombard Guelfic cities or the oligarchical family groups of the Tuscan had any purer love of freedom than those of Ghibelline towns. Before

---

[1] *Historiens des Gaules et de la France*, vol. xxiii: *Breviarium Historicum Landulphi de Columna.*

Henry's death Florence surrenders her constitution to Robert of Naples for five years; in the ensuing year the appointment of her magistrates is vested in his younger brother. Yet there was a real difference between making a bargain for a temporary purpose, and on special terms, and admitting the claims of the Empire, which were independent of time or terms. And these claims were by no means nominal. Henry claimed and exercised the right of appointing the municipal officials—at best selecting one of three elected candidates; of altering the constitution of the town councils; of garrisoning forts. The documents show that the demands for men and money were severe, and not the less irritating because they were not always met. The personal interests of the ruling families were endangered by the return of the exiles. Villani hints that but for this fear the Florentines would have recognised the Emperor. All the more burdensome were the imperial claims from the fact that the municipalities had thought themselves freed from them for ever. Imperial officials had, indeed, been from time to time appointed in Tuscany, *e.g.* in 1281, 1286 and 1296. But their authority did not practically extend to the towns. Even in cities not openly hostile the Emperor found great jealousy. Pisa, indeed, frankly placed her constitution and her customs in his hands, but Genoa grumbled and sometimes resisted. "Henricus novitates plures voluit Januae facere nec potuit, volebat habere castrum Januae et deponere Abbatem Populi nec potuit",[1] says the Chronicler of Asti. The Venetians refused to swear fealty, "Unde nullam bonam causam scio", adds Nicolas of Butrinto, "nisi quia sunt de quinta essentia, nec Deum nec Ecclesiam nec Imperatorem nec mare nec terram volunt recognoscere".[2] Proposals to bribe them by granting the control of the Brenta could not extract any practical aid. Even the fidelity of Ghibelline Verona would not go so far as to admit her Guelfic exiles at the Emperor's bidding.

The difference between Dante and the practical politicians was irreconcilable. He looked at the law; they at the administration of the law. He would admit municipal law as the

---

[1] Muratori, xi, 235.   [2] Muratori, ix, 895; ed. Heyck, 15.

necessary supplement of imperial; they would expel imperial lawmen as necessary supplanters of themselves. Thus family interests, traditional sentiment, pecuniary considerations are combined to set the municipalities actively or passively against a resuscitated Empire. And in Tuscany from being municipal the resistance became almost provincial. The Tuscan Parte Guelfa was more closely knit than the old Lombard League. It began to assume the form of a permanent federation. Moreover, actual experience of the would-be liberators brings popular sentiment into accord with that of the oligarchies.

The Guelfs were not a national party any more than the Ghibellines were a Teutonic party; but the fact that there was an organised party, which in Tuscany was the dominant party, and that it was opposed to the Emperor who was the German king, brought to a head the vague, widely diffused dislike of the Latin races to the Germans. It is noticeable how careful Dante is to conceal the foreign character of the actual Empire; how constantly he harps on its Roman origin. He only mentions incidentally the concession to Charlemagne, and he only introduces the electors to minimise their importance. Contemporary writers are full of remarks pointing to this antagonism, which is found, not so much in the classes to which the Guelfic families belong, but among the lower populace. It is not at all that they have a wish for or an idea of a united Italy; it is simply a dislike for German manners. At the very outset we have the cry of the Milanese populace based on a supposed reconciliation of internal factions for the exclusion of the foreigner. "Moriantur Teutonici omnes; pax est inter Dominum Guidonem et Dominum Matthaeum."[1] John of Cermenate, himself a Ghibelline, talks of "Stolida gens Germaniae nimium praedae avida ac disciplinae militaris ignara".[2] Robert of Naples was really identifying himself with the national feeling when he implored the Pope not to sanction the election of a German Emperor.

Reges Romani consueverunt eligi de lingua Germanica, quae consuevit producere gentem acerbam et intractabilem, quae magis

---

[1] *Nicolai Episc. Butrontini Relatio*: Muratori, ix, 897; ed. Heyck, 18.
[2] Muratori, ix, 1274 [ed. Ferrai, p. 118].

adhaeret barbaricae feritati quam Christianae professioni. . . .
Unde cum Germani cum Gallicis non habeant convenienciam,
immo repugnanciam, et cum Ytalicis non conveniant, cavendum
est quod Germana feritas inter tot reges et naciones non producat
scandala, et dulcedinem Ytaliae in amaritudinem non convertat.[1]

Of this national Italian heartfelt dislike for Germans, the
political Parte Guelfa of Tuscany made itself the mouthpiece,
and the voice was the voice of Florence. "Nunquam nobis
probari potuit Imperator qui in Italiam barbaras copias ducat,
quum id potius cavendum ut hanc nobilissimam provinciam a
barbarorum manibus vindicaret."[2] Dante may be right in his
estimate of the political morality of the Guelfic oligarchy in
Florence; but the pieces given by Bonaini give the highest
idea of its vigour. It binds together the larger and smaller
towns of Tuscany, smoothing down old hostilities; levies
troops from the rural population; stops convoys and Ghibelline parties on their way to join Henry at Pisa. Embassies go
backwards and forwards to Naples and to Avignon; bribes are
not spared to keep these two doubtful allies staunch, to prevent their making their own terms with the Empire. The hand
of the Florentines is to be traced in every revolt that bursts
out in Lombardy, and meanwhile every available man is
pushed on to Rome. And behind Florence stood Naples, the
most, or rather the only, compact power in Italy; and behind
Naples stood France. The resistance of France to the Empire,
and in a degree that of Naples also, was of a very different
quality to the vague indeterminate hostility of Italy generally.
We have here the resistance of a really compact and organised
nation—with its own history and its own system of government and its own definite ambitions—to claims of over-lord-
ships long worn out. It is not only a popular dislike to a foreign
tongue; it has its legal and philosophical justification. France
is on its defence against any infringement on its national
autonomy, whether by Pope or Emperor.

The legal and political writings emanating from Paris at
the beginning of the century belong, indeed, to the contro-

---

[1] Bonaini, *Acta Henrici VII*, i, 237.
[2] Theiner, i, p. 1077: Letter of Florentines to Henry VII.

versy between Philip and Boniface VIII; they are aimed at the
Papacy; but Papacy and Empire are so closely intertwined
that what threatened one endangered the other. The longest
and most methodical of these writings—the treatise of John
of Paris—sometimes marches side by side with the *De Monarchia*, using the same arguments, the same illustrations;
sometimes it is its direct antagonist. It takes the same view
as to Church property being a "trust", and not a *dominium*;
of the precedence of the temporal power in order of thought
and in order of time; of the invalidity of the Donation of
Constantine. If the Pope as Christ's vicar was temporal lord,
Constantine could not give anything; the acts of an Emperor
could not prejudice his successor. The same arguments drawn
by the papal party from Scripture and history are met by the
same answers, but the phraseology of John of Paris is somewhat bolder. "Mystica theologia non est argumentativa nisi
accipiatur ejus probatio ex alia Scriptura."[1] "Where a Pope's
temporal power is questioned, an Emperor's witness goes for
him, but not his own, unless grounded on Scripture."[2] Historical cases of subjection tell as often for Emperor as for
Pope; besides, "Injuria non facit jus". Man has a national and
a supernatural end; the prince helps him to the former, the
priest to the latter. As the latter end is superior in dignity to
the former, so is the Pope superior in dignity to the prince.
Yet the secular power is not less than the spiritual in the sense
of being derived from it. In a family the tutor guides to a
higher end than the doctor, yet the doctor is not subject to
him in ordering physic; the paterfamilias has not subjected
the doctor to the tutor *quoad hoc*.[3]

So, too, John of Paris admits the necessity of monarchy:
"Regnum est regimen multitudinis perfectae ad commune
bonum ordinatum ab uno".[4] Man is born to live together in
such a quantity as to satisfy the needs of his whole nature.
If each sought his own good, society would be dissolved; therefore for the common good it must be regulated by one. One
is more likely to preserve peace, to sacrifice himself to the

---

[1] Goldast, *Monarchia*, ed. 1614, ii, 128.
[2] *Ibid*. 129.	[3] *Ibid*. 113.	[4] *Ibid*. 101.

common weal. Besides, through all nature the law of unity prevails.

But the accord between the two thinkers ceases on the word "perfectae". The circumference of the circles of which monarchy is the centre is quite different. With John of Paris the monarchy is not universal but national. In things spiritual by divine law there must be one supreme head—not so in things temporal. "Faithful laymen are not in things temporal submitted to one supreme monarch by divine law."[1] But by natural instinct, which is of God, they have to live in an ordered social community ("civiliter et in communitate"), and hence, with a view to a happy life, to choose rulers, but rulers differing according to the differences of their communities. They have not either by national tendency or by divine law to be reduced to a single superior hierarchy. Men differ in body more than in soul, and so secular government has more diversity than spiritual. One man cannot rule the world in secular matters as he can in spiritual, for the power of the latter is *spiritualis*, that of the former *manualis*—he cannot reach remote people. Temporal property, unlike Church property, is private and needs no common dispensation; the Emperor can no more tax it than the Pope, except for the common good. The Catholic faith is one, and therefore one head must determine it; but life and polity may differ according to climatic or geographical considerations. There cannot be one law, for what is virtuous in one nature is not in another. Aristotle is with him and so is Augustine. "Melius et magis pacifice regebatur respublica cum uniuscujuscumque vel unumquodque regimen suae patriae terminis finiebatur. . . . Causa destructionis Imp. Rom. fuit ambitio propria dominandi vel provocandi alienas injurias."[2] What, then, is the unity to embrace? The principle of unity is to be ethnological. Even supposing that Constantine gave the Empire to the Pope—which he did not and could not—yet it could not affect the Franks, because, though Gaul was subject to the Empire, the Franks never were. And even granting that they had been, France is free of the Empire by prescription just as Italy is free of

---

[1] Goldast, *Monarchia*, ed. 1614, ii, 111.   [2] *Ibid.* 112.

France, though it once belonged to Frankish emperors. The Western Empire is only by prescription free of the Eastern; why, then, should not other nations plead prescription against it? And all the more as the Roman Empire was founded upon violence. The world had never had such peace under the universal Empire as before and since. "Melius est plures pluribus regibus dominari quam unum toti mundo."[1] The importance of this work is obvious. It appeared within three or four years of Dante's alleged residence at the University of Paris, and unless Witte's theory of the early date of the *De Monarchia* is correct, Dante's work is not improbably partly founded upon and partly intended as an answer to it. It wholly agrees with the third book of the *De Monarchia*, wholly differs from the second, partly agrees with and partly differs from the first. It is true that what similarity there is may be due to identity of source, for in both the influence of St. Thomas Aquinas is apparent. Both differ from the conclusions of the *De Regimine Principum*, but both drew from that storehouse the arguments that tell for their cause. But the treatise of John of Paris was no mere academic exercise. It is far more than the *De Monarchia* an expression of living feeling. The French kings wished to thrust the Empire back into the position of a mere national kingship, or, if it were to be more, to occupy it themselves.[2] The Germans knew this. The annals of Lubeck on Henry's accession say: "Eo tempore [in 1309], quia Reges Alemanniae minus aspirabant post Fredericum imperatorem ad habendum imperium, videbatur Francigenis derisorium quod se scriberent reges Romanorum".[3] And if Dante is challenged by John of Paris, the idealist Henry VII finds his match in the practical statesman, Robert of Naples. His letter quoted above criticises the whole medieval conception of the Empire; it shakes its philosophical basis of uniformity; it finds flaws in its historical pedigree. The Empire was acquired by

---

[1] Goldast, *Monarchia*, ed. 1614, ii, 141.

[2] Cf. two works ascribed to Pierre du Bois. See Dupuy, *Hist. du différend d'entre le Pope Boniface VIII et Philippe le Bel*, and N. de Wailly, *Mémoires de l'Instit. Nat. de France: Académie des Inscriptions et Belles-Lettres*, xviii (2).

[3] Pertz, xvi, 421: *Ann. Lubicenses*.

violent occupation; that which is so acquired cannot be permanent—it is contrary to nature. The Roman-German Empire, then, has no divine origin. The king of the Germans is the natural enemy of France and of Naples. From France he would win back so-called imperial lands from the west of the Saone; the existence of Naples is the bar to his mastery over Italy. The right of dominion changes; the Chaldees, the Egyptians have had it and lost it; Rome has had it, but the dominion of Rome has shrunk to the possession of a few hamlets.

The election of a German is prejudicial to France, to Italy, to Naples; it is a cause of scandal to all princes, "qui sunt in plena et pacifica libertate dominii et potestatis eorum, nec in aliquo subsunt aut obediunt imperatori, excepto rege Boemie". "The Emperors may urge ancient writings, but the Kings can plead prescription."

This is the negation of Dante's first two books, and of the first two chapters of Henry's life; and we feel that Robert, in theory as well as in arms, is on the winning side. Contemporaries did not see this so clearly as we do. Villani tells us that the wiseacres of his day believed that but for Henry's sudden death he would have taken Naples, and then all Italy would have been an easy conquest, and many lands besides; the world was holding its breath, the very Greeks and Saracens were straining their eyes to see the upshot of this enterprise.[1] The chronicler of Baldwin believed that an eclipse and a comet betokened the darkening of the sun of the Catholic faith—a fiery trail of famine and discord—for "Illud gloriosum Rom. Imp. vere fuerat revocatum, coadunatum et in maxima parte restauratum, cujus recuperationis finis imminebat, quod ista mors pessima, toti Catholicae fidei nociva, pessime prohibebat".[2]

But Dante's universal monarchy did not hang on the accident of Henry's life or death. This was but an episode in the faction fight of Guelf and Ghibelline: an episode for which the Aretine Ghibellines might change their armorial horse from white to black, and the Reggian Guelfs compel their

---

[1] G. Villani, ix, 53.   [2] Baluze, *Misc. Hist.* i, 319.

enemies to put candles in the windows; over which the practical Pisans wept as they had never wept before, "for they had spent on the Emperor more than 2000 golden florins, and had done no good with it, and were left in the greatest possible gloom with no money in their pockets".[1]

The causes that left the *De Monarchia* a bare political ideal lay deeper than this episode. If the narrow limits of a Guelfic town were to be no home for Dante, who "could everywhere gaze on the mirrors of the sun and stars, everywhere beneath the roof of heaven meditate on truths most sweet",[2] so Henry's "empire of inviolable right reaching the waves of Amphitrite, scarce deigning to be girt by the vain waters of Oceanus",[3] could not be contained within the bounds of the actual Italy, nor of the actual Europe. The crown and the throne that Dante saw prepared for the lofty Henry were not of this world—not the iron crown that Italy had pawned,[4] nor the Roman throne to which she barred the way.

It may be that our sympathies are at discord with the times. It may be that the criticism of posterity is too severe, wanting in sympathy. Perhaps Dante "per lo suo savere fu alquanto presuntuoso e schivo e isdegnoso, e quasi a guisa di filosofo mal grazioso non bene sapea conversare coi laici"[5]—perhaps he was too apt to "garrire e sclamare a guisa di poeta".[6] Perhaps Henry was after all not "the most fitting physician that could have been chosen to heal the wounds of Italy, if indeed they had been capable of healing".[7] We would fain have ringing in our ears the noble period of Compagni, "huomo savio di nobile sangue, giusto e famoso di gran lealtà, pro d' arme e di nobile schiatta, huomo di grande ingegno e di gran

[1] Baluze, i, 453: *Chron. Pisanum.*

[2] Epist. ix.

[3] *Ibid.* vii.

[4] The iron crown had been pawned by the Della Torre, and Lando of Siena had made a new one for the occasion. It is described by Villani, ix, 9.

[5] G. Villani, ix, 136.

[6] *Ibid.*

[7] "Se i mali straordinarii dell' Italia erano allora capaci di rimedio, non si potea scegliere medico più a proposito di questo" (Muratori, *Annali d' Italia*, viii, 72).

temperanza".[1] But behind it lingers the mocking echo of the Pisan—

Omo di buona vita e di pogo senno.[2]

[1] Dino Compagni: iii, 23.

[2] Sardo, *Cron. Pisana*, lii; *Archiv. Stor. Ital.* vi (2) 94. An interesting and less well-known account of the expedition of Henry VII is to be found in *Documenti di Storia Italiana*, vol. vi: *Cronache dei secoli xiii e xiv* (Firenze, 1876): "Diario di Ser. Giovanni di Lemmo da Comugnori". The writer saw Henry VII during a visit to Pisa.

THE INFLUENCE OF THE "DE MONARCHIA" UPON LATER POLITICAL THOUGHT[1]

THE influence of the *De Monarchia* was hardly likely to expire with the death of the Emperor, in whose service it was almost certainly written, or with that of Dante himself. It may be worth while therefore to trace the imprint of this influence on the political conceptions of the most interesting Italian figures of the succeeding half-century—Marsilius of Padua, Bartolus of Sassoferrato, Rienzi and Petrarch. It should, however, be borne in mind that a knowledge of the *De Monarchia* was probably not confined to Italians. S. Antoninus states that its errors were more widely diffused by Ockham, and, indeed, Ockham's theory of the State does seem to bear the closest relation to the *De Monarchia*. The imperial theory as formulated by the Electors at the Diet of Rense has been directly referred to Dante's work. If the early reputation of Dante be considered and the political position which he held, his book must have been utilised in the renewed struggle between Papacy and Empire.[2] An instrument of party warfare so powerful and so applicable to the new circumstances could not have been neglected. The fact that Dante was a dissident Guelf, that he belonged to what may be termed the Liberal-Unionist party of Italy, would rather have added to the importance of the pamphlet. It must have become, from the first, part and parcel of the stock-in-trade of the Imperialists. If indeed it had been obvious to contemporaries that Henry's failure sealed the fate of the Empire in Italy, the *De Monarchia*, whatever its literary and philo-

---

[1] [The substance of this essay was read before the Oxford Dante Society in two sections, on May 1890 and May 1893.]

[2] [Cf. A. Solmi, *Il pensiero politico di Dante* (Florence, 1922); the author shows that the fame of the *De Monarchia* came at the time of the contest between Louis the Bavarian and the Papacy.]

sophical merits, and whatever its author's reputation, might have been consigned to the limbo of lost causes. But this was far from being the case. The Imperialist party lacked indeed an Emperor, but it was dominant in North Italy, and it was among this party that Dante lived in high consideration. The causes which produced his pamphlet were still at work. The disunion of Italy had been intensified, the *fiera fella* was still untamed and riderless, the widowhood of Rome was yet more desolate,[1] the secular pretensions of the Papacy had increased with the vacancy and the schism in the Empire. The Papacy had become more obviously alien. The presence of a Teutonic Emperor might be preferable to the absence of a Gascon Pope. Henry VII after all had met the fate of Frederick II rather than of Henry IV; if humiliation and failure there were, it was concealed by death. Thus, though Dante perhaps himself, and readers of Dante, might regard this death as the closing scene of the long imperial tragedy, yet this was not the view of the practical statesmen of the day, of Uguccione della Faggiuola, Castruccio Castracani Matteo Visconti and Can Grande della Scala. Louis of Bavaria met with at least as warm a welcome as had Henry. His Luxemburg successor, had he cared to own it, had brighter prospects of success than either. Louis at all events trod in the steps of Henry and his footprints are somewhat deeper. The space after all which separates the campaign of Louis from that of Henry was less than fourteen years, little more than that which divides Solferino (June 1859) from the entrance at the Porta Pia (September 1870). Ten years more, and the Diet of Rense had once and for all proclaimed the independence of the Empire from the Papacy. Yet another ten and the city of Rome was recognised as the arbiter of Italy and was claiming to be the arbiter of Europe. The extinction of faction by imperial unity, the restoration of the Empire to the imperial city, the denial of the secular claims of the Papacy, were still the pass-words for the fifty years succeeding Henry's death.

Rienzi's movement towards Roman supremacy and Italian

[1] [*Purg.* vi, 91-6, 112-14.]

unity, the appeals of the Tribune and of Petrarch to Henry's grandson, the league of the Italian cities to give him welcome, must have attracted attention to Dante's political theory at each successive stage.

Yet for all this it is extremely difficult to trace the direct influence of Dante's work upon succeeding writers. It is rarely if ever possible to lay the finger upon a passage from the *Defensor Pacis* of Marsilius, or from the letters of Rienzi or of Petrarch, and to quote the corresponding passage in the *De Monarchia* or *Convivio* or the *Letters*. This no doubt is partly due to the morbid fear of plagiarism, the craving for a reputation for originality characteristic of this period. Marsilius claimed to be a pioneer in determining the limits of Church and State even as Dante had claimed before him. Petrarch would not even read the *Divina Commedia* for fear lest he should be attracted into imitation. In authors of this period it is rare to find a direct reference to contemporaries or immediate predecessors. They were unworthy to be placed upon a level with the Classics or the Fathers. The roll of authorities is usually closed with S. Thomas Aquinas.

Originality is merely the saying of old things in new order or in other words. Dante and his successors had but a common stock of knowledge and its range was limited. The author's first care was method. How would he rearrange the facts and arguments that others had marshalled before? The syllogism, the dialogue, the letter, the stringing of authorities were utilised in turn. The very identity of argument and quotation gives an appearance of correspondence, but makes the proof of it more difficult. Moreover the methods of defence were conditioned by the methods of attack. The Imperialists, however audacious, were really acting on the defensive. The Papacy had chosen the field of battle. It had launched its claims, and its opponents' retort was in great measure limited by these. When two writers are answering the same arguments, capping the same texts, who shall say that they copy from each other?

Marsilius of Padua

But the difficulty lies yet deeper. The circumstances in each case, however great the apparent similarity, have a distinctive character. Each thinker started from a different post, or was aiming at a different goal. This becomes apparent when the *Defensor Pacis* is compared with the *De Monarchia*. Here there is a measure of external similarity which is probably not accidental. It seems tolerably certain that Marsilius must have read the *De Monarchia* and may even to some extent have been influenced by its method. Both works profess to be founded upon Aristotle's *Politics*, both start with the necessity of Peace. This is the end which determines the organisation and the functions of the state. The *Defensor Pacis* opens with a passage from the *Letters* of Cassiodorus on which Marsilius thus comments : "Cassiodorus . . . tranquillitatis seu pacis civilium regiminum commoditates et fructus expressit, ut per hos tanquam optimos, humanum optimum, ejus vitae scilicet sufficientiam explicans, quam sine pace ac tranquillitate nemo consequi potest, ad pacem habendam invicem et hinc tranquillitatem voluntates hominum excitaret".[1] This closely corresponds with the passage in the *De Monarchia* which is the logical starting-point of Dante: "Patet quod genus humanum in quiete sive tranquillitate pacis ad proprium suum opus . . . liberrime atque facillime se habet. Unde manifestum est quod pax universalis est optimum eorum quae ad nostram beatitudinem ordinantur."[2] The two passages are followed by three identical Scriptural references in the same order in each case.

The method of both books is scholastic, often syllogistic, both are overloaded with quotations in many instances, as above, identical. The first book of the *Defensor Pacis* may be said to correspond with the first of the *De Monarchia*; it discusses the objects and to some extent the form of the State. The second of the *Defensor Pacis* corresponds to the third of

[1] [*Defensor Pacis*, dictio I, cap. i, p. 1; ed. C. W. Prévité-Orton (Cambridge, 1928).]

[2] [*De Mon.* i, cap. iv. Oxford Dante, ed. Dr. E. Moore, p. 343.]

the *De Monarchia*, treating as it does of the relation of Church to State. The third book of the *Defensor Pacis* is merely a summary of conclusions, and the second book of the *De Monarchia* almost drops out of line for reasons which will appear. Yet the object of Marsilius is not identical with that of Dante, and he handles his main authority, Aristotle, to very different purpose. Dante draws his Aristotle as he drew his Vergil into the circle of medieval life and thought. Both poet and philosopher are transformed. They are clad in medieval raiment and speak through medieval masks. Their utterances are adapted or distorted to confirm the preconceptions of contemporary opinion. The relation of Marsilius to Aristotle is completely different. The real renaissance in political thought had with him begun. Pure and abstract Classicism never went farther in political speculation. It is unpolluted by the element of the personal and picturesque so prejudicial to many later manifestos. The clumsy structure of the medieval State is to be swept away, the fabric is to be built up anew on Aristotelian foundations. All materials, all workmanship, that do not satisfy the Aristotelian criteria, are discarded.[1] This fact is all-important because on it depends the relation of Church to State, of Papacy to Empire. The conclusions of the third book of the *De Monarchia* would have been substantially the same if Dante had never read the *Politics*. The *Defensor Pacis* without the *Politics* would dwindle into nothingness. Its originality indeed consists in the application of the principles of the Greek State to the medieval Church. Italy was shortly to be the cradle of the new birth of literature and art, but Classicism in political science was bred if not born in Paris. Paris for a whole century was the hotbed of political revolution, speculative or practical. It was the forcing-house for exotic as for home-grown thought, for Marsilius, and Ockham and Jerome of Prague, as for John of Paris, and Gerson: to Paris was due

---

[1] Albertus Pighius writes: "Fuit homo Aristotelicus magis quam Christianus atque ex illius magis quam Christi institutis novam ecclesiasticae hierarchiae formam conatus effingere" (Raynaldus, *Annales Ecclesiastici*, v, 346 (1327)).

the rebellion at Rome against the Pope, as the rebellion within her own walls against the absolutist monarchy. It has been already hinted that Dante was not improbably indebted to Parisian teaching, and that there is no slight similarity between the *De Monarchia* and the work of John of Paris. But Dante in all his modes of thought was essentially Italian and pre-eminently Florentine. He was to the end a Florentine gentleman, his reputation had been made in Italy and made by the revival of the Italian tongue. Imperialist in name he was nationalist at heart, and particularist in prejudice. Marsilius was a Paduan plebeian, his reputation was due to Paris alone. Here from December 1312 to March 1313 he had been Rector in the University. He lived in its cosmopolitan society. His collaborateur was a Frenchman, John of Jandun. He had no national prejudices. He was trained in principles of universal applicability, attracted by the Franciscan Spiritual movement, of all others the most independent of local ties. Finding for his theories a more favourable field in Germany, he fled to the Imperial Court in the summer of 1326. It was something of an accident that he ever returned to Italy. The greatest Italian publicist of his generation, he left no reputation in Italy. The close of his life was unnoticed, and its date unknown.[1]

Thus Dante and Marsilius start from a different point. Dante is renewing the conflict between the universal Empire and the universal Church. The Luxemburger follows in the path of the Swabian and Franconian Emperors. Marsilius is renewing the conflict between Church and State. Louis of Bavaria is to him Philip le Bel and John XXII is Boniface VIII.[2] The scene is merely shifted. In France the quarrel

[1] Placed by Villani in 1328, but it was clearly much later, either in 1342 or 1343, certainly before April 10, 1343, when Clement VI speaks of him as dead.

[G. Villani, *Historie*, x, cap. civ. It is possible that Villani confused Marsilius's death with that of John of Jandun, who died during Louis the Bavarian's retreat from Rome in the summer of 1328. Cf. C. K. Brampton, "Marsiglio of Padua", Part I, Life, *English Historical Review*. vol. xxxvii (1922).]

[2] Strangely enough in his *De Laudibus Parisius*, written in November 1323, Jean of Jandun holds that universal monarchy belongs to the very

had burnt itself out, but fresh fuel might be found in
Germany. That Louis was Emperor was not an essential
element, it rather invalidated than strengthened the arguments of Marsilius. Again, Henry of Luxemburg entered
upon his Italian campaign with the full consent of the Pope
and was accompanied by papal legates by whom he was
ultimately crowned, though it is true under a certain measure
of compulsion. Louis of Bavaria was from the first the declared enemy of the Pope, not recognised as King of the
Romans, crowned by the people's will in defiance of the
Papacy, and ultimately setting up an anti-Pope. Dante would
possibly have shrunk from Louis, as indeed did many
Ghibellines. Henry VII was to Dante the Salomon, the *rex
pacificus*. Louis of Bavaria came to bring not peace but a
sword, not to reconcile Ghibellines and Guelfs but to ex-
terminate the Guelfs. Thus it is clear from the first that the
great desideratum, Peace, has a different meaning in the
minds of Dante and of Marsilius, and this depends upon a
radically distinct conception of the State. Both writers closely
follow Aristotle in tracing the historical origin of the State.
But while Marsilius progresses one step beyond Aristotle
and makes the "regnum" instead of the "civitas" his final
term, Dante takes yet a further step and regards the imperial
unity as necessary to human felicity because without this
Peace is not perfect.

It was difficult for Marsilius when actually in the service
of the Empire directly to deny its claim to universal dominion.
It is clear, however, that on this subject he is at accord with
John of Paris and not with Dante. As with Dante the idea
of αὐτάρκεια gives place to that of peace, so the peace with
which Marsilius starts is for the moment superseded by
αὐτάρκεια. For this purpose a town State may be indeed too
small, the kingdom is the natural unit. He brushes aside the

---

illustrious Kings of France by right of a natural leaning towards that
which is best—and this in spite of the opinion of Aristotle, the greatest
of philosophers, that it belonged to the Greeks. It was thought that
Charles IV was going to claim the Empire, and indeed John XXII was
eager for his candidature. Jean continues that in due course he would
bring forward arguments to support the claim.

consideration of the world Empire: "Utrum autem universitati civiliter viventium et in orbe totali unicum numero
supremum omnium principatum habere conveniat, aut in
diversis mundi plagis locorum situ quasi necessario separatis,
et praecipue in non communicantibus sermone ac moribus
et consuetudine distantibus plurimum, diversos tales principatus habere conveniat tempore quodam, ad hoc etiam forte
movente causa caelesti, ne hominum superflua propagatio
fiat, rationabilem habet perscrutationem, aliam tamen ab
intentione praesenti".[1] Guarded as this passage is, it states
the principal of nationality based upon language, customs,
and geographical limitations as against that of a world Empire,
and it is on this passage therefore that the difference of view
between Dante and Marsilius mainly depends. The world
Empire is not a Greek idea, and Dante therefore leaves
Aristotle far behind when once he has formulated his leading conception. Dante indeed is mainly interested in the
extension of the State, Marsilius in its intension. Dante's
ruler is necessarily personal, and his right to rule is necessarily divine. The popular elective principle is obviously impossible in a world Empire. God originally elected the sacred
Roman people, and God elects the Emperor. The so-called
Electors are merely the mouthpiece of God. Dante is clearly
hampered by the fact that the divinely elected people had in
his day little to do with the divinely elected Emperor. He
is puzzled also by his generous ideas of popular liberties,
derived partly from his Aristotelian studies, partly from
Aquinas, partly from his national traditions, and he fully
admits that monarchy is rather a *ministerium* than a
dominium. All the explanation that he can give is that a
people is free when it exists for its own sake and not for that
of another, that the monarch above all exists for his people's
sake, "minister omnium procul dubio habendus est".[2] Freedom after all with Aristotle is rather an ethical than a
political term. It is not national freedom of choice of government, or freedom from external control, but the "libertas

---

[1] [*Defensor Pacis*, dictio I, cap. xvii, p. 94.]
[2] [*De Mon.* i, cap. xii, p. 348.]

arbitrii", the freedom of the individual to exercise his judgement without the interference of his own passions, to reach indeed the life of speculation with which passion is incompatible, and which is only possible in the perfect peace which the world ruler can alone secure.

The State with Marsilius is at once more classical and more modern. He is sufficiently orthodox formally to admit that all sovereignty is ultimately derived from God, but immediately it is derived from the people. Unanimity being impossible, the majority of the nation (*pars valentior*) is the source of power.[1] It may indeed delegate its elective rights to a small body of experienced commissioners, and this in matters spiritual as in matters temporal. The Cardinals correspond to the Electors. Thus, while with Dante the Electors are but the mouthpiece of God, whilst with the Papalists they are the nominees of the Pope, with Marsilius they are the representatives of the people. The Empire itself was only transferred to the Germans by the consent of the Roman people, the Pope can but have acted as the people's spokesman. Nor in appointing a ruler has the people permanently divested itself of its sovereignty. All legislation derives its validity from the people's will. The ruler, if he seriously transgresses the conditions of his authority, may be punished or deposed "ut transgressor legis". Thus the great Ghibelline publicist draws his weapons from the disused armoury of the old papal anti-imperial party. He recalls such passages as that of Manegold: "The word king is not a name expressing natural right but is a term for an office. The people does not raise him above itself in such way as to give him a free power of exercising his tyranny thereupon, but that he may defend it from oppression. When the king begins to exercise tyranny is it not clear that he deservedly falls from the dignity that has been granted to him, when it

---

[1] [This is not quite correct; the *pars valentior* is not a mere numerical majority; different weight is attached to different persons according to their position and merit. *Defensor Pacis*, dictio I, cap. xii, p. 49 and note. Cf. also Prévité-Orton, "Marsiglio of Padua", Part II, Doctrines, *English Historical Review*, vol. xxxviii, p. 16 (1923).]

is certain that he has first broken the 'pact' in return for which he was appointed." [1]

But the government which the people has selected must be supreme in all things and over all persons. Thus only can the peace of the State be secured. A single ruler, however, is not essential. At different times or in different places an aristocracy or a democracy may be better suited to the people's needs, but it must speak with a single voice. There is no principle and no person that can be suffered to infringe the unity of the State. Between State and State war, as pestilence, may be a vent which nature has discovered for surplus population, to which the earth would otherwise not suffice. The unity of Marsilius, therefore, is not concerned with a world Empire but with any single State, be it as small as Mainz or as large as the actual Roman Empire.

This internal unity of government the claims of the Papacy have broken up. The Papacy therefore has been the chief cause of discord, the destroyer of peace, and especially within Italy and the Roman Empire where its rights were more anciently and more continuously urged. Here, then, Marsilius is once more on common ground with Dante, but he is soon to leave it, to press forward into the heart of the enemy's country. Dante conceives Papacy and Empire as two separate provinces, as two co-ordinate powers. Each holds its authority immediately from God. Pope and Emperor, in so far as they are Pope and Emperor, cannot be reduced under one common unity or measure. Far different is the view of Marsilius. The clergy is not co-extensive with the Church. The Church is the whole body of Christian men, it is the people in its religious capacity. In the *Defensor Minor* he says that a General Council must include the Greeks; he is not, however, a suffragist like Ockham, who gives the right of session to women.[2] The people is, here too, therefore, the sole source

---

[1] [Manegold to Gebhardus Floto, cap. xxx, *Mon. Ger. Hist. Libelli de Lite*, vol. i, p. 365 (1891).]

[2] "*Disc*. Et dic breviter quare dicitur quod mulieres non sunt simpliciter contra voluntatem earum a generalibus consiliis excludendae.

"*Mag*. Dicitur quod hoc est propter unitatem fidei virorum ac mulierum, quae omnes tangit, et in qua non masculus nec femina secundum

of power, it is the fount of honour, the source of legislation and the supreme judge. The Pope takes precedence but by courtesy. This is a compliment due to the memory of S. Peter and S. Paul, to the traditional importance of the city of Rome and to the wisdom of its early bishops, but it is not an article of faith necessary to salvation. He is at one moment the people's chairman to regulate, but not to summon, its Councils, at another its secretary to draft and circulate its decrees.

The Bishop of Rome has no supremacy over other bishops, nor the bishop over the priest. Steeped as he is in the *Politics*, Marsilius reduces the clergy to the position of the Greek priesthood. It is but a profession in the State—on a level with law and medicine and completely under State control. It is confined to the duty of teaching the Scriptures and administering the sacraments. It is deprived of all legislative, of all judicial, of all executive power. The Pope's decretals have no validity. Where the law of Scripture does not suffice, Councils must supplement by legislation. Thus confession is not a precept of Scripture but an advice—yet if it were prescribed by a Council General or the Universal Church the faithful ought to obey.[1] It is for the government to convoke, for the people to compose the Council. The clergy may well be heard, for they have professional experience. The rights of the Council extend even to apostasy: "If you ask whether, if the whole multitude of the faithful or its greater part or the Prince wished to fall away from the Christian faith, or did in fact fall away, whether, I say, they ought or could be restrained therefrom by the priests or the College of Cardinals, the reply is emphatically No".[2]

Spiritual courts are an anomaly and a misnomer. When the

Apostolum ad Collo. III, 'In novo homine non est masculus et femina'. Et ideo ubi sapientia, bonitas vel potentia mulierum esset tractatui fidei necessaria, non est mulier a generali concilio excludenda.

"*Disc.* Istam assertionem de mulieribus (quae secundum Apostolum docere non debent) tam irrationabilem estimo quod nolo eam amplius pertractari." [*Defensor Minor*, cap. xii, ed. C. K. Brampton (Birmingham, 1922), p. 36. Ockham, *Dialogus*, Part II, lib. vi, cap. lxxxv.]

[1] [*Defensor Minor*, cap. v, p. 16.]   [2] [*Op. cit.* cap. iii, p. 6.]

clergy murder or rob or commit adultery, or buy or sell or mortgage, they are not committing spiritual acts, but those such as a lawyer or a doctor may commit, and by the same courts they must be judged. To inflict temporal penalties the clergy has no power whatever. No man indeed can be temporally punished for his spiritual opinions. If heresy is punished by the State, it must be for a breach of positive State law, not of Divine law. The utmost that lies with the clergy is to point out that it will be well to protect the faithful from contagion, even as the doctor may recommend, though he cannot enforce, the seclusion of a leper. As the doctor, again, the clergy can but point out to the individual the future consequences of his sin, he cannot force him to faith or to repentance. The Pope may not excommunicate nor lay an interdict upon a king or nation without the consent of a general Council. Unjust excommunication has no force. This indeed was no uncommon opinion at the time. It will be remembered that Henry of Luxemburg threatened to disregard an excommunication that was not deserved. So too Dante is on Marsilius' side when he states that absolution and its refusal depend not upon the priest's word but upon the individual's state, which can only be judged by God.

"Assolver non si puo chi non si pente."[1]

"Posset etiam solvere me non poenitentem, quod etiam facere ipse Deus non posset."[2]

The holder of the keys of Peter is not the judge—he merely unlocks and locks the prison door upon the judge's order. The people is the fount of honour. It may delegate its rights to a body of experienced men, but these rights cannot lapse. All appointments to ecclesiastical dignities and benefices depend upon the people. It is for the people to grant licences for teaching, to depose unworthy priests, to give dispensations from marriage, to determine the limits of consanguinity, to legitimise natural children. No Pope nor Bishop can dis-

---

[1] *Inf.* xxvii, 118.

[2] *De Mon.* iii, 8 [p. 369]. See, however, the passage on Manfred [*Purg.* iii, 112-45].

pense from vows: if these concern other persons they must be enforced by Civil law, or if they concern God by punishment hereafter.

Emperors in the past have signified their election to the Pope in order to receive his blessing. They have also allowed him to place the crown upon their heads. But this is a mere ceremony. It confers no more power upon the Pope than does the coronation of the King of France upon the Archbishop of Rheims. A compliment has been distorted into a right of confirmation. The Electors are not the nominees of the Pope but of the people. Were the former true, seven blind men or seven barbers could perform their functions. The Emperor's authority dates from the hour of his election and not from that of its confirmation by the Pope. The scheme for the political subordination of the clergy is rendered complete by the statement of their absolute financial dependence. Here Marsilius, whose prophetic vision has been directed far into the future, is brought back to the actualities of contemporary life. It is here, therefore, that his relation to Dante is the closest. The dispute on the subject of Apostolic Poverty which had long been smouldering broke out at the close of Dante's life into open flame. It spread to the inflammable political material that had been accumulated by the papal action with respect to the schism in the Empire. Louis of Bavaria had indeed been disposed originally to suppress the Spiritual Franciscans. But there was a natural connexion between the Imperialist party and the various sects which denied to the Church the possession of property. Frederick II had at times issued cruel edicts against the Cathari, but the Spiritual Franciscans had looked to his support. The more violent followers of Dolcino had looked towards Frederick of Sicily. He was to be the Emperor, destined to expel the whore of Babylon and to reform the Church. Dante indeed placed Dolcino, who held the same views on Poverty as the Spirituals, in Hell, but the Abbot Joachim is found in Paradise. It is possible that the prophet's works had no small influence upon the poet, as they had later upon Rienzi. The whole purport of the De Monarchia recalls the world's third stage according to the Abbot Joachim, the

reign of Solomon and of perfect peace, and again the third of
another triplet, the stage of contemplation. The Lombard
Ghibellines were always strongly tainted with heresies of the
Spiritual type. During the greater part of Dante's life the
hostility between the Spiritualists and the Papacy was dor-
mant; had the breach been open there is little doubt on which
side Dante would have stood.

It cannot be said, therefore, that Marsilius on this subject
went farther than Dante. He too would hold that Constantine
could not grant what belonged to the ultimate source of power,
the people, and that the Papacy was forbidden by Scriptures
to receive. But the question had now become of greater immediate importance, and Marsilius, whose audacity shrinks
from no conclusions, had scrutinised it to its depths. It cannot be said whether the *De Monarchia* had any direct influence
on his treatment of the subject. It was more probably due to
Parisian influence than to Italian Ghibelline traditions. The
subject, apart from politics, was necessarily the constant
topic of discussion in the schools of Paris. The result is a
curious blending of the Scriptures and the Politics. The Greek
priesthood is reconstituted by the aid of Biblical texts. It is
for the State to determine the number of the clergy. No man
has a right to swell the numbers of this department of the
State without a licence from the State. The payment which
the clergy shall receive is regulated by the State, and the
State shall determine the portion to be allotted to charity.
So-called ecclesiastical benefices belong not to the clergy
but to the donor or the State, and the grants may be recalled
at will. No man may be compelled to pay tithes which have
no warranty in Scripture. The clergy should be content with
bare sustenance—the surplus may be applied to the poor by
the State or may be used for purposes of national defence.
No man can grant property free of burdens which were previously imposed upon it, the revenues of the Church are not
therefore exempt from the burdens of the State. The clergy
may, if necessary, be compelled to labour for their sustenance with their own hands, though the general duty of giving
support to the Church is recognised.

To such conclusions Dante's own principles might have led had they been ruthlessly and logically applied—but Dante in the *De Monarchia* confined himself to a single point and to a defensive attitude. It is therefore rather to the second book of Marsilius' *Defensor Pacis* than to the third of Dante's *De Monarchia* that may be traced the hostility to ecclesiastical jurisdiction, and the scheme for secularisation of Church property, which sporadically made their appearance for the next two centuries until they determined in the great epidemic of the Reformation.

So far it has been possible to draw some comparison only between Marsilius' great work and the first and last books of the *De Monarchia*. Yet the second, if almost missing in Marsilius' book, is to be discovered in his life. Marsilius and Dante were both failures. The one looked too far into the future, the other too fixedly upon the past. The world had outpaced Dante, but Marsilius outpaced the world. He was one of the few theorists who has ever translated his principles into practice, and he failed because they were applied to the wrong place and to the wrong time. The reign of Louis of Bavaria was not the age in which the reconstruction of European life could take its origin, and still less was Rome the place, and yet the attempt was made. In Rome lay the tragic irony of Dante's theory and of Marsilius' career. Dante must have realised that the guild of Roman cow-keepers was no longer the "populus sanctus pius et gloriosus" that by its noble birth and noble deeds and by the verdict of God in the trial of battle had won the eternal mastery of the world. Marsilius sacrificed on a broken altar of the grass-grown capitol his ideal of national αὐτάρκεια and efficient government. Down the Valley of the Tiber danced the miasmatic light that tempted Dante's thought and Marsilius' life into impracticable swamps.

Dante did not indeed, as far as is known, accompany Henry of Luxemburg to Rome, but the coronation of Louis bears much the same relation to that of Henry that is borne by the *Defensor Pacis* to the *De Monarchia*: Louis accepted the senatorial office, and then the imperial crown at the hands of the Roman people. The Bishop of Aleria "(Elleranus ep.) desiderium ejus esse exposuit, ut Senatus populusque Romanus imperii diadema petenti deferret. Ad haec verba secutus est ingens plausus 'vivat Caesar' acclamantium. Fuere qui dubitarent an invito Pontifice haec ita rite agerentur; caeterum Populus Romanus e contra contendebat, suas esse partes Imperium conferre, Pontificis autem consecrare, iisdem auspiciis; Carolum enim Magnum tunc demum coronatum esse, postquam populus Romanus eum imperare jussisset."[1] The manifesto of Louis against the Pope, in all probability written by Marsilius himself, has the true ring of Dante: "In qua urbe divina providentia Caesareo diademate ac sceptro legitime susceptis per nostrum Rom. peculiarem pop. urbi et orbi Dei ac nostra potentia inaestimabili et immutabili praesideamus".[2] Dante has indeed prepared the way for Marsilius; Gregorovius would believe that the *De Monarchia* exercised the most direct influence upon these events. Nay more, that Dante would have recognised in Louis the advent of the *veltro*. But Dante's hero, the lofty Henry, would have scorned to abandon his counsellors, and to pray for absolution on the plea that he could not understand their doctrine of the Empire, being, as Louis called himself, "miles scripturarum et literarum subtilitatis ignarus". It is hard to conceive Dante as drafting the programme of the coronation, in which Sciarra Colonna, the "nuovo ladrone" of Anagni, played the most important part.

---

[1] [Nicolaus Burgundus, *Historia Bavarica sive Ludovicus IV. Imperator*, p. 105. Cf. Gregorovius, *Rome in the Middle Ages*, tr. Hamilton, vol. vi, Part I, p. 142.]

[2] [Cf. Gregorovius, *op. cit.* p. 147.] In the *Defensor Pacis* Marsilius had taken scant notice of the claims of the Roman people, but in the *Defensor Minor*, written it would seem in 1341 or 1342, he finds a theory to justify his Emperor's title: "The supreme legislator is the universality of men to whom the coercive dispositions of the law apply, or the *pars valentior* in each country or province. But as the universality of the provinces has transferred the legislative power to the Roman people on account of its pre-eminent merit, the Roman people has the right to legislate for the whole world. If the Roman people has transferred this to the Prince of the Romans, he has this right, and this must last until the universality of provinces or the *pars valentior*, or the Roman people, has formally withdrawn this power after formal discussion" [*op. cit.* cap. xii, p. 35].

But Marsilius was not content with the realisation of the ideal of Dante. The principle of the second book of the *Defensor Pacis* must be applied to practice. He had been appointed Vicar in Spirituals to the Emperor. He rigorously subjected the clergy to the State. Some were forced to say Mass. Others were put to torture. One was hung over the lions' cage on the Capitol until the beasts could touch the hem of his garment. It was Marsilius that extemporised a council of clergy and of laity that pronounced the Pope to be a heretic. It was Marsilius that drew the Act by which Louis on the Capitol, as protector of the Church and executor of the Council's sentence, deposed the Pope. None other but Marsilius can have suggested the reference to the people of the election of his successor. Pietro of Corbara was selected by the Council of experienced persons, lay and clerical, familiar to readers of the *Defensor Pacis*—the question was then put to a Parliament of the Roman people. It is a strange intellectual process that the study of Aristotle's *Politics* should have led directly to the election of an ignorant Franciscan hermit to the highest Christian office by the most degraded ochlocracy of all Italy.

Dante's Aristotelian studies never led him so far as this, although he supported his appeal to the Italian cardinals by the precepts of the Philosopher who taught that truth was to be preferred to friendship. To Dante the Cardinals were still the "primi praepositi pili Ecclesiae militantis"[1]—let them take up again the standards which "Non emeriti sed immeriti" they had let fall. Cardinals, as Electors, were not the mouthpiece of the populace but of God—*vox Dei* rather than *vox populi*.

BARTOLUS OF SASSOFERRATO[2]

There is a strong contrast between Marsilius, the speculative radical philosopher, and Bartolus, the cautious, con-

---

[1] *Ep*. viii [*op. cit.* p. 412]; cf. *Para*. xxiv, 59.

[2] [Bartolus was born at Sassoferrato, in the duchy of Urbino, in 1314. He studied law at Perugia and at Bologna, taking his doctor's degree at

servative lawyer, the greatest of his day and for many later days. He was no theorist or idealist, and before him lay the difficult task of serving not only one but three masters. As Professor of Civil Law he must uphold the dignity of the Roman code. His chair was in Perugia, and Perugia was in the Papal States, thus he was subject to Canon law alike in temporal and spiritual causes, but she was also a city with many privileges, and clung tenaciously to her own statutes. He must therefore reconcile the theories of the two former with the facts of the latter, and indeed of Italian cities and provinces in general. No wonder that he became the past master of compromise. To him was really due the ultimate entente between Civil and Canon law. But for him, too, there might have been a complete breach or divorce between the old imperial code and later statute or customary law, composed of very various ingredients, and widely differing under local conditions. As it was, owing to Bartolus and his successors, Roman law, far from becoming obsolete, proved its adaptability by spreading from State to State, from the city States of Italy to the principalities and municipalities of Germany, everywhere levelling the ruts and divagations, the awkward corners and steep gradients of the country road into a broad straight Roman highway. Bartolus and his school adapted Roman law to local law, and in time the process was reversed, and local law was bent into Roman law. Even the Code Napoléon has its debt to Bartolus. His system was to distinguish between generalities and particularities. Dante had admitted the existence of both, but with him the particular was submerged by the universal. Bartolus must needs place the main emphasis on the former, and thus, while Dante's main subject was the Empire, and that of Marsilius the Nation, Bartolus' was the City State. To doubt the validity of the universal law of the Empire would, he says, perhaps be heresy, and he has the utmost reverence for

Bologna in 1334. He was professor of law at Pisa (1339–43) and then at Perugia until his death in 1357. [Cf. C. N. S. Woolf, *Bartolus of Sassoferrato: His Position in the History of Medieval Political Thought* (Cambridge, 1913).]

Canon law, and so far he is with Dante, while differing widely from Marsilius. But where the Civil law is not sufficient, the Canon law may supplement it, and, where this too proves inadequate to meet a special case, recourse may be had to custom, or statute. It must be remembered that in Italy there were other elements such as Lombard law, and no small variety of customary law of long standing, and thus ample opportunity for the lawyer's jigsaw puzzle. No thinker of Bartolus' age could escape the consideration of the respective merits of forms of government, and here, too, he refuses to make an absolute rule. On the whole he thinks that democracy, if the lowest classes are excluded, the best government for a secondary city, aristocracy for the more important, such as Venice and Florence, and monarchy for a larger unit. He was fortunate in the time at which his reputation was at its height when there was a direct issue between Pope and Emperor, as in the ages of Henry VII and Louis of Bavaria he could scarcely have avoided taking sides. But Henry's grandson, Charles IV, had been the French candidate for the imperial throne and was on the best of terms with the Avignon Pope. With him, on one of Charles' flying visits to Italy, Bartolus met on friendly terms, and was granted the right to bear arms for himself and such of his heirs as might be lawyers. This was shortly before his death. He could feel safe in having condemned in legal terminology the scornful severance of Italy from the Empire. His Italy, the real Italy, was not that of which Dante dreamed, and Petrarch sang and which Rienzi staged. It was a congeries of independent atoms, some indeed joined in a rough conglomerate by a masterful despot, but most still warring within themselves or against each other. It was for these that Bartolus had to find some mediating, binding formula.

The Emperor being powerless and unrecognised, and the city States practically independent, what common bond could there be to regulate their intermunicipal relations or give some legal shape to their internal governments? The reply of Bartolus was that though the personal lawgiver might be in abeyance, the impersonal law remained, the

Emperor might be unrecognised, but not the Empire. Dante, though from a different point of view, had written that the Empire was prior to the Emperor, the law to the lawgiver. For Bartolus the Populus Romanus was still in being, and embraced not only Rome, but the cities of Italy and all Western Christendom. By the law of the Roman State, the Corpus Iuris, the Universal Law, these cities and their relations could still be guided; the Roman lawyer need not follow the Roman lawgiver into beggary.[1] As in the descending scale the Civil law might, in particularities, be supplemented by statute and custom, so in the ascending scale it could appeal in generalities to Divine law, Natural law or the law of Nations. What powers under such circumstances, with the superior lord unrecognised, devolved upon the city State? Practically all, replied Bartolus; it had acquired them by concession, by long prescription, by mere exercise. The revenue, once imperial, reverted to the city, so did the highest jurisdiction, and the legislation, so long as this latter was not in contradiction to the Civil and Canon law, to the laws of God, of Nature and of Nations. The city State had become a sovereign State. It was even justified in waging war against another State, though both were members of the Populus Romanus, provided that such State also rejected imperial supremacy.

So far the path of the city and of its legal adviser seemed smooth enough: the sovereignty with Bartolus, as with Marsilius, lay with the people, for, though conservative in his reverence for Roman law, he was radical in politics. The people merely delegated its executive power to the aristocratic or democratic government. But what if, over and above both people and government, there loomed the figure of a tyrant? And Bartolus in Dante's very words was forced to admit that all Italy was full of tyrants. He gives an admirable analysis of the several types which actually held supreme

[1] [For the conception of *Populus Romanus* as applied to the Italian city State, and the adaptation of theories of the Roman Empire to the political requirements of their day by Bartolus and other jurists of the Bolognese School, cf. F. Ercole, *Dal Comune al Principato*, saggio iii (Florence, 1929).]

power in Italy, and asks whether statutes framed, or ordinances issued, or executive acts performed under their orders, were within the law. He is frankly puzzled, and is forced to hedge. Tyranny being in its very definition not founded upon law, was repellent to his legal mind, and yet it was there *de facto* and with facts the practical lawyer had to deal. He could but say that if such acts were performed for the people's good and by their will, and if they would have been performed in the absence of a tyranny, then they might pass for legal, but he preferred to shelve the question with the pious wish that tyranny was only an interruption, a passing phase. Meanwhile he jumped eagerly at a solution of the problem which satisfied his legal mind, if not the feelings of the tyrants' subjects. Both Emperors and Popes had been in the custom of conferring vicariates on tyrants. Thus Henry VII was accused of legalising the despotism of the great Lombard Ghibelline lords, and now, in Bartolus' own time, Cardinal Albornoz, in the service of the Papacy, had recovered the shadow of recognition by granting the title of vicar to the actual ruling lords of the papal cities. Bartolus had reason for feeling uncomfortable on this subject, for the tyrant beat the lawyer, as he beat Pope and Emperor. He was no passing phase, but had come to stay. "Ego sum et Papa et Imperator et dominus in terris meis", said a great Visconti despot, the ruler of half Italy and more.

RIENZI

Rienzi and Petrarch, though farther removed from Dante in point of time, have a closer spiritual kinship to him than has Marsilius. It would be possible indeed to introduce a fourth term into the equation, to show that Petrarch is to Rienzi what Dante was to Henry VII, Petrarch inheriting in part the literary traditions of the apostle of the Empire, and Rienzi the political aims of its chivalrous champion. There is in the relation of poet to poet, and tribune to Emperor, a connexion of sentiment not without its practical consequences. On the self-same day Dante and Petrarch's father were exiled from Florence; the families had been intimate; the elder Petrarch had kindred tastes, pursued the same studies; domestic cares alone postponed for a generation the literary eminence of the house. Petrarch himself in boyhood had met Dante. The connexion between Henry VII and Rienzi is indeed founded on fable, but the fable had its foundation in a spiritual if not a fleshly relationship. Rienzi claimed to be the Emperor's son, the one living result of the romantic Roman visit. Such was the tale which Rienzi told to Henry's grandson Charles. The claim is a proof of Rienzi's conscious realisation that his aims were inherited from the Emperor; Dante's political ideal was thus still applicable to practical politics, and Petrarch was its modern mouthpiece.[1]

If Dante served his political apprenticeship in the great Guelf republic, Rienzi entered the lists as protector of the commons against a nobility mainly Ghibelline. The life of the tribune, as of the poet, may be divided into two main portions, the day of exile forming the dividing line. Both were driven by ineradicable faction and papal partiality from the championship of communal independence to that of imperial government. Yet the parallel is, perhaps, accidental and not essential, due to circumstance and not to character. If the letters of Rienzi be compared with the *De Monarchia* and the political letters ascribed to Dante, a characteristic distinction will at once be found. Dante fills his foreground with the figure of the universal judge or peacemaker, whilst the imperial city is left somewhat in shadow. Of Rienzi's composition the rock of the Capitol is the centre. In other words, Rienzi opens the *De Monarchia* at the second book, there to find the philosophical foundation of his political fabric. He does, indeed, gradually formulate the conception of the universal peacemaker "ut vigeat pax ubique", but this is subordinate to that of the prescriptive rule of the Roman people. The Empire must be reinvigorated from its heart. Rome must first be restored to herself, her own people freed from

---

[1] [A recent biographer of Rienzi maintains that belief in his descent from Henry VII is the key to the understanding of Rienzi's career. P. Piur, *Cola di Rienzo* (Vienna, 1931).]

the oligarchic factions, the foes of peace and justice and popular election. This necessity is emphasised by the fact that Rienzi's nobles were not even Romans. The barbarous hordes which had for centuries settled on the hill fortresses of Latium must be burnt out, or forced to recognise the title of the people. Rome restored to herself will bring again into cultivation Italy, the garden, the *pomarium* of the Emperor. Rome will enforce peace upon Italy and the tribune is the peacemaker; Rome will throw her citizenship open to all Italians, she will be once more the *communis patria*. It was in realisation of this ideal that the deputies of the Italian cities met at the festival of Italian unity and took their standards from the tribune's hands. Rienzi would at this time have scorned the imputation that he was following in the steps of Henry of Luxemburg. Yet his programme was almost identical. The end was *libertas, pax et justitia*, the means the abolition of faction within the walls of every town in Italy, the return of exiles, the extinction of the very names of Guelf and Ghibelline "quod nemo detestabilia nomina Guelfum et Ghibellinum tanti iam, proh dolor! christiani sanguinis effusiva, audeat per totam Italian nominare" (xxii, 36).[1] Henceforth Rome was in a position to reassert her claims upon the world. "Even as everything", the tribune wrote to Petrarch, "easily returns to its own nature, so the city will again stand forth as the 'caput et principium libertatis'" (xv, 24).[2] The Kings of France and England were summoned to make peace at Rome's behest; the King of Hungary and the Queen of Naples voluntarily submitted their claims to Rienzi's arbitration. Above all, to the citizens in Rome alone belonged the decision of the disputed succession to the Empire. Hence the bold mandate to the rival candidates, Louis of Bavaria and Charles of Luxemburg, and to the six electors and the princes, to appear in person and submit their claims

---

[1] [To Pope Clement VI, August 15–31, 1347. The references in the text are to A. Gabrielli, *Epistolario di Cola di Rienzo* (Rome, 1890). For a more complete and critical version cf. K. Burdach and P. Piur, *Briefwechsel des Cola di Rienzo*, Part 3 (Berlin, 1912–29). In this the above letter is No. 35, p. 130.]

[2] [To Francesco Petrarca, July 28, 1347. Burdach, No. 25, p. 86.]

to the tribune and the papal vicar: "Dicimus, confitemur et etiam declaramus Romani imperii electionem, iurisdictionem et monarchiam totius sacri imperii ad ipsam almam Urbem et eius populum, nec non ad universam sacram Italiam pertinere".[1]

The imperial prerogative of the Germans had been but lately threatened by the French; it was now restored to Italy. As Italy sighed for an Italian Pope, so Rienzi wrought for an Italian Emperor, and this could be no other than himself. His intention is made clear in the letter of September 19, 1347, to the Florentines : "We intend that after the term of Pentecost has expired that some Italian worthily inspired to zeal for Italy, by the feeling of unity or race, and by national consciousness (*proprietas*) should be promoted to the Empire" (xxiv, 86).[2] The Roman Empire was, in short, to be reconstituted anew, and thus Rienzi gained the goal of Dante, but from another side, for Rome is reached by many roads.

The third book of the *De Monarchia* has as yet little importance for Rienzi; though the hostility of the Papacy caused the tribune's fall, the conflicting claims of temporal and spiritual authority presented no difficulties to him. Nevertheless Rienzi was careful always to safeguard the rights of the Church. He professed, and probably without hypocrisy, that he was but the servant of the Church. No foreigner should enter Italy but by the Pope's licence, no scutcheon should be seen on the nobles' houses but the papal keys. From the tribune's present point of view he had but realised and glorified the Guelfic ideal of a federation of Italian cities under the protectorate of the Church, he shared with the Guelfic opponents of Henry of Luxemburg and of Louis of Bavaria the hatred of Germans; he later confessed to Charles IV that he had railed against the Alamanni.

Whether during the earlier stage of his career Rienzi was directly influenced by the writings of Dante it is impossible

---

[1] [August 1, 1347. Gabrielli, xvii, 42. Burdach, No. 27, p. 103.]
[2] [To the Commune of Florence, September 19, 1347. Burdach, No. 41, p. 155.]

to decide. There is something essentially Dantesque in the pictures on the walls by which the popular imagination was excited, the allegorical figures, the ship without her helmsman sinking in the storm—"Nave senza nocchiero in gran tempesto" (*Purg*. vi, 77)—the widow with her dishevelled hair. But it would be rash to press parallels too far; such rude frescoes for purposes of popular instruction or admonition were not uncommon. Petrarch some few years later said that Rienzi was acquainted with all the poets who were ordinarily read, and it is impossible that Dante should have been excluded from this roll.[1]

If the notice which Dante's *De Monarchia* attracted during the invasion of Louis be considered, it seems hardly probable that the pamphlet should have remained unread; yet it has been believed that Rienzi first became acquainted with the political literature of the imperial party after his fall, and during his retirement among the Fraticelli of Monte Maiella. It is with this seclusion that the second stage of Rienzi's career begins, and in this he is unquestionably brought into far closer connexion with the political ideas of Dante. This accord in the case of Rienzi, as of Marsilius, has its origin in the question of Apostolic Poverty. The views of the Spiritual Franciscans had an irresistible fascination for such imaginations as those of Dante and Rienzi when once they were

---

[1] There has indeed latterly appeared some direct evidence bearing upon this subject, for Signor Gabrielli has published in an appendix to the *Epistolario* a curious document giving the signification of the six crowns and the apple which Rienzi received. In the programme of the tribune's coronation the symbolism of the six is thus explained—"Quarta corona fuit de lauro: unde Dantes in principio secunde partis sue comedie:

<blockquote>

Triumphantis moes.

O divina virtù, se mi ti presti
Tanto che l' ombra del beato regno
Segnata nel mio capo manifesti,
Venir vedram al tuo diletto legno,
E coronarmi allor di quelle foglie,
Che la materia e tu mi farai degno.
Sì rade volte, Padre, se ne coglie
Per trionfare o Cesare o poeta,
Colpa e vergogna dell' umane voglie."

</blockquote>

[*Par*. i, 22, Gabrielli, *op. cit.* App. v, p. 247.]

forced to face the problems. There is a rough general line of demarcation between Rienzi as the practical dramatic Guelf and as the mystic speculative Ghibelline. Yet on closer examination both are phases of a not inconsistent character.

The principles of the Fraticelli may thus be summarised. They carried to its extreme and logical lengths the doctrine of Apostolic Poverty, and thus, while insisting on Papal Infallibility, they held that the Papacy was forfeited by its present occupant. They believed in the direct and constant inspiration of the Holy Ghost, and in its imminent manifestation upon earth. Their sacred books consisted in a collection of prophets, among whom the names of Merlin, Cyrillus and Joachim da Fiore are prominent. This was in the case of the individual supplemented by visions, dreams and ecstasies. Rienzi had throughout his tribunitian career believed in the direct interposition of the Holy Ghost; of this his very title "Candidatus Spiritus Sancti" is an outward sign. His references to the Second Person of the Trinity are purely formal. Christ was, in the language of the Piagnoni, the King of Florence, but, to the tribune, the Holy Ghost was the lord of Rome. Nor is this all. More than once had Rienzi been influenced by visions. One such had postponed his coronation as tribune, the appearance of Boniface VIII had encouraged him in his final triumph over the Colonnas. The very details of this victory had been prophesied, and the prophecies before the event had been registered in the records. The tribune, moreover, had a remarkable readiness in mystical interpretation. When informed that four Colonnas had fallen, he clearly saw the correspondence with the four saints who had championed him to victory. When a revised report represented that the dead and dying numbered seven, he at once interpreted the number by his own six crowns and apple. To this it may be added that he had long been subject to fits of fainting or epilepsy, no uncommon accompaniment of religious mania. It must be confessed, therefore, that Rienzi was a proselyte formed by nature for the visionary hermits of the Abruzzi, and the rapid change from his sumptuous life at Rome to the rigid asceticism of Monte

G

Maiella may have developed his physical and mental tendencies.

To us it is more essential that Rienzi was now forced to examine the justification of the temporal power and jurisdiction of the Papacy which he had hitherto taken for granted. He himself has picturesquely drawn out in detail the contrast between the unbridled licence of the Court of Avignon and the Apostolic life of the brethren of the Abruzzi, many of them originally men of birth and wealth. The contrast may well have inflamed his private wrongs. Rienzi realised at length that it was the French Papacy and not the German Emperor that had wrecked his schemes for the restoration of Rome and the unity of Italy. It had been debated in the Papal Consistory "utrum unitas urbis et Italiae Romanae ecclesiae expediat". The Pope's temporal claims were now found to have their origin in heresy, to be the unfailing source of sin, the perennial fount of discord. It is to the Pope that the persistence of the Guelf and Ghibelline factions is due; it is he that has placed in the hands of each the sword of extermination. The proof is found in the fact that faction rages in the provinces which once were imperial and now are papal. Here Guelf and Ghibelline cannot live together in the same town, nor may they intermarry; the parties of the Church lay interdicts on those who will not bow their necks to the Guelfic yoke. "Is this", he cries, "the planting and the fostering of the Church? Is this the giving root to love and unity, as is due, in Christ? or is it extirpation anew of all that has hitherto been planted and taken root?" With each fresh tyrant of Italy the Pope has struck his bargain, from Christ's flock the pastor exacts not only the milk but his share of the blood.[1]

Neither Rienzi, nor Rome, nor Italy could as yet stand alone. If the ex-tribune, therefore, could not be the minister of the Papacy, he would be the lieutenant of the Emperor, he would prepare the way to Rome, but without the bloodshed which had stained the march of Charles' predecessors. In

---

[1] [To the Archbishop of Prague, August 1350. Gabrielli, xxxv, 144. Burdach, No. 57, p. 236.]

changing his political colours Rienzi did not altogether desert his former platform; the salvation of Italy was to be earned by Italians, and pre-eminently by himself, he still had the Guelfic dread of foreigners. Above all, Italy must be united from her centre and not from her extremities: "A Jerusalem Christus incipit, et sic a Roma, capite mundi, incipiendum est, et non Lombardis" (*Ep.* xxxv, 682).[1] It was unworthy of Caesar to go on begging the opening of the mountain passes from the Lombard tyrants. Rienzi before the coming Pentecost would win for Caesar the whole of the provinces comprised in the brazen tablet of the *pomarium* of the Empire, with the exception of Sicily, Sardinia, Corsica and Provence. At that date Caesar should enter his Jerusalem not with bloodshed, not with the clash of arms, and German savagery, but to the sound of cymbal and psaltery, peaceful and secure beyond Solomon himself. Rienzi represents Dante's self calling upon the Luxemburger to restore the glory of Rome, and the purity of the Church. He even recognises the translations of the Empire to the Germans, and the rights of the Electors who, as with Dante, are the mouthpiece of the Holy Spirit. He even recognises that Rome depends upon the Emperor rather than the Emperor on Rome, all power exercised over Romans without the Emperor's licence is adulterine (xxx. 120).[2]

But however nearly Rienzi approaches to Dante in his political theory, the difference in their character and aims is fundamental. Rienzi is at once the less courageous and the more adventurous. Whether the visit to Charles IV was the result of spiritual inspiration or of personal ambitions, it was a bold step, and with any Luxemburg but Charles or Wenzel, might have had practical results. His physical courage was, however, doubted even on the day of his triumph. Dante proudly bewails the bitterness of another's bread, the hard path of another's stair; Rienzi plaintively appeals for a fire in his room, which even in Italy his tendency to fainting fits had rendered necessary, and how much more therefore in

---

[1] [To Archbishop of Prague cit.]
[2] [To Charles IV, July 1350. Burdach, No. 49, p. 197.]

the bitter cold of Prague. It is the Roman and not the Florentine who cries for the "aer apertus, letus et liber, prout medici suggerunt" (xxxi, 75).[1] Rienzi himself confesses to physical timidity, which was in great measure the cause of his superstition, and therefore an all-important factor in his life. "If", he writes, "a small boy were to tell me in the street that I should die to-morrow, I would at once prepare for death."[2] Yet with all this Rienzi was one who was never content with a mere conception or a theory, it must perforce be translated into practice. He was in both senses an actor; political ideas must be converted into facts, poetical conceptions must be dramatised and put upon the stage. Thus not content, as were Dante and Petrarch, with calling upon the Emperor to fulfil his mission, he himself must play the leading part therein. He meant to be not merely the harbinger of the Emperor's recall, he was to rule in Rome while the Emperor was relegated to the dominion of the East. Thus exile, which was possible to Dante, for thought was free, was impossible to Rienzi for whom thought was inseparable from action, and hence the surrender of his earlier principles to the Emperor, and of his later principles to the Pope. There was but one spot on which the great poet would receive his crown, the great actor would play on any stage and in any company rather than not play at all. Rienzi mounted the piece which Dante had composed. With whom lay the responsibility of failure? Perhaps with neither or with both. Neither author nor actor could wring success from a worn-out *motif*. The play was magnificent, the actor superb, but contemporaries denied a call.

PETRARCH

Petrarch was no professed political thinker, he has nowhere formulated a complete philosophical theory, his one political treatise is sentimental rather than speculative. A statement of his political creed must needs be a *cento*, a

[1] [To Charles IV, August 1350. Burdach, No. 50, p. 200.]

[2] [To the Archbishop of Prague, November 1350. Gabrielli, xxxvii, 110. Burdach, No. 63, p. 347.]

collection of passages scattered throughout his letters. Yet
Petrarch fills an important place in the series of Italian
publicists of the fourteenth century. His passionate love for
the past of Rome, his patriot yearning for the future of Italy,
shape themselves well-nigh into a theory; they link him at all
events to the two extremities of Italian political thought, to
Machiavelli and to Dante. The letters of Petrarch raise
many an echo of the *De Monarchia*. The third book indeed
has little interest for one who was too far a dependent of the
Papacy to be an aggressive champion of the Empire. The
limits of civil and ecclesiastical government were no longer
the burning questions of the day, nor was Petrarch dia-
lectical by nature. The first two books he, as Rienzi, would
transpose both in their logical order and importance. The
revival of the Empire is to him a mere instrument to the
restoration of Rome's glories. There might, indeed, be divers
means to this great end. He had welcomed a republican Rome,
ruling a federal Italy, under the guidance of Rienzi. But on
the tribune's failure he turned to the natural lord of Rome,
the Caesar. Charles IV must tread in the footprints of his
grandsire. If Rienzi could effect so much, how much more
the Emperor, whom no one in his senses could resist. Of
practical difficulties he saw none. At no time, he urged, had
Italy been so eager to welcome her lord. There was no need
to search for alien examples, to hunt in ancient annals. One
precedent would suffice for all, Henry VII of eternal memory.
If to him life had been granted to complete the scheme which
in his holy mind he had conceived, the world's fortunes
would have changed, he would have left Rome's enemies in
sorrow, Rome in full sway, and the States of Italy in all
freedom and content.[1] The whole of Italy was calling to
him: "Tua te, inquam, Italia, Caesar, vocat: Caesar, Caesar,
Caesar meus ubi es? Cur me deseris? Quid cunctaris?"[2]

Rome to Petrarch was unquestionably more real than she
was to Dante. Four times in ten years he had revisited the
Eternal City. He was a Roman citizen, crowned at Rome

---

[1] [*Ep. Fam.* x, 1, ed. Fracassetti, vol. ii, p. 63 (Florence, 1859–63.]
[2] [*Ibid.*, xxiii, 15, *op. cit.* vol. iii, p. 230.]

with the poet's wreath. The revival of Rome was the burden
of every letter whether to Pope or Caesar. These letters are
indeed an amplification of Dante's words. "More than to
any other city", he writes to Urban, "are you bound to
Rome. All other cities have their spouses, which, though
subject to you, take thought for them; Rome has you alone,
you alone are Rome's pontiff, you her only spouse. And yet
she is left poor, feeble, wretched, deserted, clad in the raiment
of widowhood,[1] weeping day and night, mournfully singing
with the prophet, see how lonely sits the city, thronged of
yore, ruler once of all nations, now widowed and abandoned,
mistress of old of provinces, now tributary and slave."[2] The
Pope's true seat could be nowhere but at Rome, the spot
accepted by God, worshipped by men. Rome that is built
of the blood and the bones of the martyrs. If the Pope would
not return, let him at least withdraw his veto from her other
spouse the Emperor.

Despairing of the Pope, Petrarch would turn to Caesar.
"Though you have here no abiding city, yet if anywhere in
the world you have a fatherland that is your own, Rome
is the home of the Caesars and their true fatherland; nay
more, it is the common fatherland of all, *rerum caput, orbis
atque urbium regina.*"[3] If the Roman Empire were not at
Rome where else could it be? If elsewhere it was no longer
the Empire of the Romans, but of those with whom a fleeting
fortune had placed it in deposit. The Emperor in the service
of the State might indeed journey north or south or east or
west. "Imperatores vagi esse possunt; stabile fixumque
semper Imperium est." The Roman Empire, however
bruised and crushed by the wrongs of fortune, though seized
by Spaniards, Africans, Greeks, Gauls and Turks, however
small it had become, still had its seat at Rome, and there

---

[1] *Purg.* vi, 112: Viene a veder la tua Roma che piagne,
Vedova, sola, e dì e notte chiama;
Cesare mio, perchè non m' accompagne?
Cf. also Dante, *Ep.* viii, which opens "quomodo sola sedet civitas plena
populo; facta est quasi vidua domina gentium!"
[2] [*Ep. Sen.* vii, 1, tr. Fracassetti (Florence, 1869), vol. i, p. 391.]
[3] [*Ep. Fam.* xxiii, 2, *op. cit.* vol. iii, p. 193.]

would stay, though nought of so great a city were left but the bare rock of her Capitol. What greater happiness could Petrarch know than to go Romewards with his Emperor? what greater grief than to see his Emperor leave it with a vow that he would never make it his abiding resting-place?

It is needless to point out the close parallel between some of these expressions of Petrarch and the earlier utterances of Dante. The younger poet seems at times to be the interpreter of the elder to the new generation, the prolix scholiast on the fragmentary text, the ornate preacher on the plain gospel of Ghibellinism. And if the ideas were similar or the same, the outward circumstances bore a close resemblance. The grandeur of Charles might even enlarge upon his grandfather's actions, even as Petrarch dilated on the ideals of Dante. Yet between the two poets, as indeed between the Emperors, lies one of the great gulfs of the world's intellectual history. Dante is essentially medieval, Petrarch preeminently modern. The very proof of his modernism is his antiquarianism. He realises that the classical world is ancient, he consciously regards it from outside itself. He is absorbed indeed in the history and the literature of antiquity, but it is the absorption of a passionate connoisseur, or an enthusiastic copyist. He retreats a step from time to time to obtain a better light, a correcter view. The poem upon which he hoped to found his fame is an imitation of Statius. His letters are not the product of the traditional "Ars dictatoria", elaborated for medieval use from the rules of Rhetoric; they are immediately inspired by the epistolary art of Rome, by Cicero, Seneca and the younger Pliny. Dante, it is true, was no less influenced by the study of antiquity. Yet he does not consciously live in another world; there is no hard and fast line between the present and the past; the heroes of the preceding generation, nay even of his own, are of the same flesh and blood as Scipio, as Cato and as Caesar. Dante, had he written the history of illustrious men, could never have stayed his hand at Caesar, or at Titus. His Roman heroes sit upon medieval thrones, they talk a medieval tongue, and are decked in medieval garb. Petrarch, on the other hand, will

convert his noble friends of modern Rome into the characters of Livy; he will console his niece on the pains of her
confinement by the similar sufferings of Greek or Roman.
Without the study of antiquity both Dante and Petrarch
would have been far other than what they are; but its influence upon Dante is chemical, upon Petrarch it is purely
mechanical. Cincinnatus and Brutus are to Petrarch what
they were to the political revivalists of the French Revolution.
Napoleon, in his dream of universal Empire of which Rome
was capital, was more akin to Dante. The figures of Dante
are as those of the Pisani; without antique models they would
have been impossible; yet they are not antiques, there is no
absolute breach with the actual world, they are Italians as
the eye trained by study of the antique really saw them.
Petrarch's letters may be compared to a picture by Mantegna;
they are not affected, love and reverence are too genuine
for affectation, yet all the apparatus of the studio is introduced. The modernism and antiquarianism of Petrarch find
perhaps their fullest expression in a letter to Giovanni
Colonna: "Tired by the vast size of the city around which
we had rambled, we were wont full often to come to a stand-
still at the Baths of Diocletian, sometimes in sooth to climb
above the dome of that once most sumptuous palace, for
there the air was healthful, the view was open, and silence
and religious solitude as nowhere else. There of business
never a word we spoke, nor yet of home, nor yet anent the
State, enough that we have wept it once for all! What then
was our theme? Long was our talk on history which we
seemed so to share that you in modern, I in ancient history
appeared the wider read. Ancient let all be called before
the name of Christ was received with rite and reverence by
Roman Emperors at Rome, and modern all from that date
to this our age." While talking thus Petrarch and Colonna
might seem two students in two branches of the Oxford Final
Schools, whose periods parted company at the victory of
the Milvian Bridge.[1] Petrarch was fully conscious of his own

---

[1] [*Ep. Fam.* vi, 2, *op. cit.* vol. i, p. 314.] Cf. also Petrarch's *Itinerarium*,
which Koerting compares to a guide-book by Baedeker or Gsellfels.

antiquarian spirit; he was, he urged, so ill at ease in the world in which he was born, that he deliberately tried to live among the ancients. His real passion for Rome is antiquarian; he visits it with all the feelings of an intelligent tourist; he is delighted to find that he is not disappointed, as he feared might be the case; he gives days to the pagan and Christian antiquities in turn, and keeps them sedulously apart. His friends might, he wrote, have expected some great work now that he had reached his goal, but his feelings and his curiosity overwhelmed him, and he could not write as yet. Petrarch was busy in the past, and the past can wait for the literary mood. Dante must write perforce while his pulse is throbbing with the passions of the present. On Dante's retina the passing crowd of pilgrims on S. Angelo's Bridge had made an abiding impression. Petrarch wrote to his friend that he was glad that he did not join him at the Jubilee of 1350, for that their thoughts, as usual, would not have turned upon religion but upon the antiquities of Rome. The crowded bridge had no poetic side for him.

Petrarch has been called the first modern man; he was perhaps the first modern Italian. If his love for Rome was antiquarian, his love for Italy was conscious and sensitive as those of a nineteenth-century champion of *Italia irredenta*. Examples of this may be multiplied. His sonnet "Italia" has, with the epilogue of Machiavelli's "Prince" which quotes it at its close, been always on the lips of the patriots of Italy until her liberation. But in Petrarch's letters can be traced more clearly the sensitiveness to criticism from abroad, and this he seems to have shared with the small Italian circle in which he habitually moved.

Dante undoubtedly drew no such sharp a line between foreigner and Italian as did Petrarch. The latter would have shuddered at the barbarian host of Henry VII which Dante welcomed. He is in fact at accord rather with the national antipathy which thwarted Henry's enterprise. An invocation to German Albert would have been impossible. Once and again he will persuade himself that Charles is an Italian. If he was born abroad, he was bred in Italy, "illic natus, hic nutritus". "The Germans, if it pleases them, may claim you for their own, but we regard you as Italian." [1] When at length Charles paid his fleeting visit he saw Italy with Petrarch's eyes, he needed Petrarch's guidance in the Tuscan towns of which he spoke in such enthusiastic terms "ut Italicum hominem et Italicum credere posses ingenium".

Italy indeed had its special place in Dante's scheme as being the garden of the Empire, but he is steeped in traditional particularism, he realises all provincial and municipal distinctions. It is upon civil war within the walls of a single town that he pours out the vials of his wrath. But to Petrarch the war of Venice and Genoa is fratricidal. They are the two eyes of Italy that keep watch over the upper and the lower sea, the one looking toward north and east, the other to the south and west. Their strife is imperilling the maritime supremacy of the world which Italy had at such infinite pains acquired. "Adhuc enim", he writes to Stefano Colonna, "Januenses et Veneti in armis sunt; sic, ne quid ex nostro more depereat, rodimus rodimurque vicissim, et nos ipsos mutuo laceramus." [2] It is interesting to compare and to contrast with this the phrase of Dante, of which at first sound it seems an echo:

> Ed ora in te non stanno senza guerra
> Li vivi tuoi, e l' un l' altro si rode
> Di quei, che un muro ed una fossa serra.
>
> *Purg.* vi, 82.

Petrarch had glimpses of Italy as a united Mediterranean State with Rome as capital of an Italian federation. But the breach with the past could not be complete. He, as Rienzi, was brought to realise that Italy could not yet stand alone, the revival of the Empire was still the panacea for her woes. He was believed, and believed himself, to be still preaching the doctrines of Dante. Peace was still the end of man, and peace could only be attained by justice. Freedom was still bound up with government. "Pax cum libertate" was still the motto of the Empire. Notwithstanding his passing enthusi-

---

[1] [*Ep. Fam.* x, 1, *op. cit.* vol. ii, p. 59.]
[2] [*Ibid.* xv, 7, *op. cit.* vol. ii, p. 33.]

asm for Rienzi, Petrarch was no republican; he would rather
endure the yoke of the hardest ruler than that of a tyrannical
people.

Thus it is that the efforts of Petrarch and Rienzi were
the last serious struggles to realise the medieval conception
of unity whether in the Ghibelline or Guelfic sense. The
unity of the world Empire was long since a memory of the
past, the unity of Italy a daydream for a distant future. The
Papacy was even now, as in the days of Machiavelli, a cause
not of union but disruption, too feeble to unite Italy itself,
too strong to allow its union at the hands of another power.
The most that the Emperor could do was to legalise titles
which were in reality the symbols of particularism. The house
of Luxemburg, it is true, by no means surrendered its claims
to Rome and Italy. Sigismund had a far higher ideal of his
position than had his father. The heritage of Henry was passed
on by marriage to the Hapsburgs. If Frederick III was the
feeble counterpart of Charles IV, Maximilian was the adventurous parody of Henry VII. Maximilian, if he could not
reign at Rome as Emperor, would reign as Pope. But the
yearning for reconnexion was now rather from the German
than from the Italian side. The semi-conscious national feeling that had resisted Henry of Luxemburg and Louis of
Bavaria was now wide-awake, and in this awakening Dante
had some, Petrarch and Rienzi yet a larger, share. Italy's
next effort was to expel the foreign mercenary hordes, to
create a *condottiere* system of her own. It was better to fight
at home than to be bullied from abroad. There was still
indeed a cry that the material interest of Rome, the sunken
capital, should be revived by the return of the Papacy, and
louder still that the ruler of the Papacy's Italian State must
be Italian born. But Italian patriots no longer looked to a
foreign ruler "in things temporal supreme". It is to the
"Italia mia" rather than to the Empire that Machiavelli
turned. Henceforth "Italia farà da sè" for better or for worse.
The loss of the great medieval ideals was greater to the twin
medieval powers than to Italy herself. Petrarch proudly recognised that "Italia stabit inter Alpes et duo maria, ut ab

initio rerum stetit, et si terreni regis auxilium desit, imperatoris aeterni misericordiam implorabit. Crede autem mihi,
pater, magnum est in sede Petri, magnum in solio Caesaris
sedere."[1]

It was this hopefulness of Petrarch for the future of Italy
which won for him among later generations of Italians the
love which the pessimism of Dante repelled. The graves of
the two poets, as their birthplaces, scarce fifty miles apart,
would seem to be characteristic of their respective creeds.
Both born with faces set towards the Tuscan sea, their dying
eyes were turned towards the sea of Adria. And yet how
different Arquà from Ravenna. Petrarch, the prophet of
modern Italy, "Euganeo augur colle sedens", rests on the
slope of "everlasting hills". The very vines and olives of
to-day were his as they were those that Martial sang, the
"picta pampineis arva iugis". It was Petrarch who stored the
stream for peasants of to-day to draw. In no spot of Italy,
perhaps, are antiquity and modern life so near. But Ravenna's
monuments are neither of modern nor of ancient times.
Dante died clinging to the wreck of an Empire that was not
Roman, of a monarchy that was not Italian, a derelict,
stranded by the receding sea upon a shore malarious with the
decay of dead ideals.

[1] [*Ep. Fam.* xv, 5, *op. cit.* vol. ii, p. 325.]

IV

DANTE IN RELATION TO THE SPORTS AND PASTIMES OF HIS AGE[1]

I

FROM the outset it must be confessed that Dante is an inadequate exponent of the sports and pastimes of his age. His references are so scanty that they may be considered barely worth collecting. Yet this very scarcity has an interest, because it sets his reader thinking how it was that Dante, who sings and writes of so many sides of Italian life, should almost pass by in silence those amusements which for the majority of his countrymen made life worth living. It is true that contemporary poets provide even less illustrative material than does Dante, but then Cavalcanti, Guinicelli, Cino and the like, in their sonnets, ballads and *canzoni* bearing mainly upon love, would draw upon sport for the merest commonplace of metaphor, the stock-in-trade of love poets throughout all ages. Fazio Uberti in his *Dittamondo* had better opportunities, especially as in Italy sport like everything else had its peculiar local colouring; but he is too severely geographical to be instructive, though he does supply one of the very few references to quintain. A more promising source might seem to be Francesco da Barberino's *Del reggimento e de' costumi delle donne*.[2] He was an exact contemporary of Dante, and his subject is eminently social. But he is unfortunately too prudish and domestic for our purpose. He even warns his lady pupil that a love for balls is a sign of vanity, of the desire for the praise of strangers, and though he allows her to ride abroad during the Quinquagesima, with or without her husband, she

[1] [Papers read before the Oxford Dante Society, February and June 1905. Reprinted from the *Modern Language Review*, vol. i, 1906.]

[2] [Ed. C. Baudi di Vesme. Bologna, 1875.]

must allow no strange gentlemen to annex themselves to her cavalcade. Above all, she is warned, if a nun, to shun peeping from the windows at the games in the square, and it is precisely these games which we are seeking. In years long later Santa Maddalena de' Pazzi was praised for such avoidance in her early youth, although the too liberal Lasca had expressly recommended peeping. It is possible that if the popular sermons of the thirteenth and fourteenth centuries at all resemble those of S. Bernardino in the fifteenth, they might repay the sieve. Chroniclers, of course, are a main resource, but save such born gossips as Salimbene, they say little on social amusements, unless they have, as many indeed did have, a direct connexion with public municipal events. The last places, perhaps, where details upon sport would be naturally sought, are the statutes of the several cities, and yet for one important sport, and that the one which most nearly touches Dante, they prove to be the happiest hunting-ground.

Other sources being so defective, it may seem unfair to expect more from Dante than we get. But his own versatility is to blame for our disappointment. If his poetry and prose are storehouses of theology and philosophy, astronomy, history and geography—if we resort to him for the politics, the personalities, the hatreds, the social abuses of his time—if he has a feeling for natural scenery and for certain forms of animal life that few medieval writers possessed, why may we not also turn to him as an Encyclopaedia of Sport?

The forms of sport or amusement for which illustration might be sought fall under several heads: (1) the natural country sports, fishing, fowling and hunting; (2) artificial competitive sports, racing on horse or foot, or in boats; football and other games of ball; jousting, quintain, and the mimic combats common to many Italian towns; (3) non-competitive amusements of a semi-public character, theatricals grave or gay, and the pastimes provided by professional purveyors, who, like modern merry-go-round proprietors, followed the annual cycle of feasts and fairs from town to town; (4) private pastimes, such as singing, dancing, chess, draughts, and the very numerous and obscure games of chance.

The latter two classes must here be lightly treated. The *Paradiso* is resonant with song, and the spirit dancers throng the heavens. But the dancing, at all events, is too super-sensuous for historical earthly use: the solitary human touch is that which describes the movement of a lady's feet:

> Come si volge con le piante strette
> A terra ed intra sè donna che balli,
> E piede innanzi piede a pena mette.
> *Purg.* xxviii, 52.

Dante's intimate knowledge of the music of his time is beyond all doubt.[1] The *Convivio* (ii, 14) may be said to contain his theory, and moreover admirably describes the absorption of all the sensitive faculties in that of sound. This absorption finds its practical illustration in *Purgatorio*, ii, 112, where Dante and his master were so content with the dulcet notes of Casella's song that nought else could affect their minds. And as they stood in rapt attention to the strain, the strain which, as Dante confesses, never after left his ears, stern Cato, as many a tutor since, was forced to chide them for their neglect in not following the steep path before them, which was that of duty.

In the *Paradiso*, vii, viii and x, are to be found passages quite modern on the relation between light and sound, and so the reader is taken back again to the *Convivio*, to the parallel between music and the qualities of heat in the planet Mars. The *Commedia* contains almost every variety of music then known: the songs of Casella, of Matilda and Arnaut, the duet of Peter of Aragon and Charles of Provence, the solo and choir in the *Te lucis ante*, the unison of a hundred voices in the *In Exitu Israel*. In the *Agnus Dei*,

> Una parola in tutte era ed un modo
> Sì che parea tra esse ogni concordia.
> *Purg.* xvi, 20.

The glory of the *Paradiso* culminates with the *Ave Maria*,

[1] For a recent work on this subject see *Dante e la musica* by Arnald Bonaventura (Leghorn, 1904), and a review by C. Bellaigue in *Journal des Savants*, May 1905.

which all the company of the Blessed takes up in chorus. Concerted instrumental music was probably unknown to Dante's age, except perhaps as an adjunct of the dance, but he fully appreciated the accompaniment to the voice, as in *Paradiso*, xx, 142:

> E come a buon cantor buon citarista
> Fa seguitar lo guizzo della corda,
> In che più di piacer lo canto acquista,

and in *Purgatorio*, ix, 140:

> E *Te Deum laudamus* mi parea
> Udir in voce mista al dolce suono.
> Tale immagine appunto mi rendea
> Ciò ch' io udiva, qual prender si suole
> Quando a cantar con organi si stea.

Thus Dante is a faithful exponent of the highest musical knowledge of his time. And yet to ascertain the place which music held in life of every day, its domestic graces and its social humours, it might be well to turn to an authority less exalted. Salimbene, the friar chronicler of Parma, brings home the realities of music as a pastime in the ordinary Italian home. Examples of this are his few lines on the domestic concert in the courtyard of a noble Pisan house which he visited while begging for his Order, and again, Frà Vita's light, sweet tenor, so gladly heard by bishops, arch-bishops, cardinals and the very Pope—a voice which put to shame the most persistent talker, for at once the phrase of Ecclesiastes went round the room, "Do not disturb the music". Very real is this Frà Vita, so courteous about singing that he never refused on the plea of sore throat and cold, and belied the long current verses:

> Omnibus hoc vitium est cantoribus, inter amicos
> Ut nunquam inducant animum cantare rogati.

Then again there was Frà Henry, whose voice was better suited for the chamber than the choir, and who upon a time sang so deliciously that a certain nun who heard him threw herself out of the window to follow, but could not, because in the fall she broke her leg, so that as Aegidius of Perugia well said, "It is a great gift not to possess gifts" ("Magna gratia est non habere gratiam").[1]

Chess, draughts, ninepins, knucklebones, dice and various games of chance wherein money was won and lost played a large part in Italian life of Dante's day. Chess and draughts were lawful and might be played in public: Sacchetti has several references to this. But many a man was ruined by dicing. Long before Savonarola religious revivals were marked by the destruction of the devil's playthings. Brunetto Latini warns his readers beyond all things to shun dice: he will have none of the man who throws himself away on that perverting and destructive art. Yet he admits occasional compromise: if you are asked to play as a favour to a friend or a lord, play high, and do not say "I cannot" ("'i' non posso"); if you lose, look as if it did not cost you anything, and above all do not use bad language. More serious is Orcagna's lament that a hundred tongues could not tell the tale of his troubles and the ruin of his soul, and of all the cause was that foul hazard ("n' è cagione la brutta zara").

Meanwhile statutes prohibited name by name the various forms of gambling. Those of Pisa in Dante's time strove at least to save from such profanation the Campo Santo, the Cathedral and its steps. Florentine statutes were most explicit: "Nullus in civitate, comitatu vel districtu Florentiae aliquo tempore, etiam ultima die Aprilis et prima die Maii et qualibet die totius anni ad ludum zarae sive zardi cum taxillis" (then follow a number of other varieties) "ludere audeat nec stare ad videndum ludentes ad aliquem ludum zardi".[2] The penalty was imprisonment, and before release the culprit must "cum aqua baptisari et aqua totus perfundi". Such precautions were of course in vain, and even in women a knowledge of games was, as now, regarded as an accomplishment, an asset in the matrimonial market. It tempted, among other attractions, Pino de Gente of Parma in 1285 to

---

[1] [Frà Salimbene de Adam, *Cronica*, pp. 181-4, ed. Holder Egger, *Mon. Ger. Hist. Scriptorum*, xxxii.]

[2] *Statuta Populi et Communis Florentiae*, vol. ii, lib. iv, 28.

H

lure away his father's fiancée. Her name was Beatrix, an Apulian who lived in Ancona, and who "thesaurum habebat et erat pulchra domina, et alacris, et solatiosa et liberalis et curialis, et de ludo scaccorum et alearum optime noverat".[1] So Pino married her, though it is true that he afterwards employed a man to smother her with a bolster. Chess, again, is mentioned by Salimbene as on a level with the legal, ecclesiastical and administrative qualifications of Bishop Opizo of Parma, nephew of Innocent IV. "Hic fuit litteratus homo maxime in jure Canonico et in ecclesiastico officio valde expertus. Et de ludo scaccorum noverat, et clericos seculares multos tenebat sub baculo."[2] Yet to all such vices and virtues Dante, I think, makes but one reference—that in *Purgatorio*, vi, 1: "Quando si parte il giuoco della zara". Here, however, there is no lack of realism in his description of the winner and the loser, the latter going over his throws again and learning experience by misfortune; the former with his train of parasites, one marching in front, another plucking his robe behind, a third jogging his memory at his side, and he, never stopping, listening to this suitor and to that, defending himself from crushing by stretching out a generous hand so that the recipient may lessen the attendant throng. If Dante did not have a throw himself, he at least brought himself within the arm of the law and incurred the penalty of total perfusion by looking on.

The amusements included in the third class were incidents of the annual feasts in the greater cities, and of the jousting days held on special occasions. The miracle plays or similar performances were an inveterate custom in every town, and might have lent themselves to such a theme as Dante's. It is known that the Florentine company, which in 1304 performed the Day of Judgement with such disastrously premature consequences to the spectators on the Carraia Bridge, was not a travelling but a stock company, and must have in one year or another reckoned Dante among its onlookers. But of such representations there seems to be no trace in the *Commedia*. Every great festival was attended by professional

---

[1] [Salimbene, *op. cit.* p. 606.]   [2] [*Ibid.* p. 62.]

mimes, mountebanks and musicians in their hundreds. They received rewards almost as high as those reputed to fall until lately to their amateur brethren in Anglo-Indian circles. Brunetto Latini preaches against the waste of money on such triflers. Florentine statutes forbade their entering the Palazzo Publico.[1] These *joculatores* comprised street-singers of the tales of Roland and Oliver, destined long afterwards to give the death-blow to Dante's popularity, tight-rope dancers, tumblers, jugglers, owners of dogs with a spirit of divination or miraculous insight into character, and performing bears. To the attractions of the latter Dante at least was not blind, for in *Canzone*, xii, 71, is to be found the comparison of the "Orso quando scherza". It is possible too that the *bos ephippiatus* and the *porcus balteatus* of the *De Vulgari Eloquentia*[2] may be reminiscences of these rollicking Court-days, for the riding of a caparisoned ox was no uncommon feature, and the pig also at times played a serio-comic part, as when in the piazza at Venice twelve pigs were annually beheaded with much ceremonial in lieu of the twelve canons of Aquileia.

Another popular frolic was some form of sport with bulls. This was apparently at Rome a bull-fight proper, but elsewhere it was less developed. At Venice the bull was baited by dogs. At Brescia the animal was let loose by a gang of crapulous butchers among the crowd of worshippers during the most solemn procession of the year, a source of exquisite amusement to the lower classes and of righteous disgust to the sober-minded. A *ludus tauri* was, as early as 1276, subsidised by the city of Perugia, while the nuns of Santa Mustiola in Chiusi were bound to supply the bull. There was, of course, much cruelty to the bull and some danger to the passers-by. To some such scenes Dante perhaps refers in the pathetic lines on the fatal wound of the tethered bull in *Inferno*, xii, 22:

> Qual è quel toro che si slaccia in quella
> Che ha ricevuto già 'l colpo mortale,
> Che gir non sa, ma qua e là saltella,

---

[1] *Op. cit.* vol. ii, lib. iii, 106.
[2] [Lib. ii, cap. i, ed. Moore, p. 391.]

Vid' io lo Minotauro far cotale.
E quegli accorto gridò: Corre al varco;
Mentre ch' è in furia, è buon che tu ti cale.

The practice of masquerading at these festivals, also forbidden by the Florentine statutes, finds one slight reference in *Paradiso*, xxx, 91:

Poi come gente stata sotto larve
Che pare altro che prima, se si sveste
La sembianza non sua in che disparve.

No doubt, moreover, the triumphal car drawn by the Griffin (*Purgatorio*, xxix), which through Petrarch's *Trionfi* has exercised such an extraordinary influence upon poetry and art, was a glorification of the allegorical chariots which early formed the leading feature of the festival of S. Giovanni at Florence, reaching its artistic climax under the imaginative care of Lorenzo de' Medici.

A delightful paper by Mr. H. F. Tozer illustrates Dante's close knowledge of the art of mountaineering.[1] Yet though in his wandering life he gained much experience in breasting the flanks of Alps or Apennines, it may be doubted whether he regarded them as his playground. Climbing was probably rather a painful necessity than a pastime or a sport. Nor can his line on a man swimming in the Lambro be taken as a proof that he was fond of bathing. It is, however, far more strange that he should show so little feeling for sport proper, for hunting, that is, and fowling, tastes so universal in his age. Almost all Florentine families, noble or bourgeois, had their estates or little farms in the *contado*, where brake and stream made haunts for beast and fowl, where hunting, fowling and fishing were features of everyday life. Metaphors from these were so imbedded in the national speech that it would be impossible to avoid them. In Dante, therefore, they are necessarily found, but they are not frequent, though most of the characters whom he introduces must have been constant, if not mighty, hunters and fowlers. Of the two hunting scenes one is the dream of Ugolino, wherein he saw Archbishop

---

[1] See *Modern Language Quarterly*, i. 274 ff.

Ruggieri as a master of hounds chasing the wolf and its cubs with his lean eager dogs (*Inferno*, xxxiii, 28). The other is the graphic description (*Inferno*, xiii, 112) of Lano and Giacomo della Cappella fleeing from the demons. Here is real hunting life—the rush of the boars and the swish of branches as they burst through the barriers of the wood, behind them the forest full of black hounds breaking away from the confinement of the leash, and fixing their teeth in their prey just as it sought shelter in the brushwood. These references are really all, though the dilemma of the dog between two equidistant does in *Paradiso*, iv, may just be mentioned. The theme would be the richer if we could only quote as Dante's the vivid lines in the Vatican MS. ascribed to him by Mario Pelaez:

> Sonar bracchetti e chacciator nizzare
> Lepri levare ed isgridar le genti
> E di guinzagli uscir veltri correnti
> Per belle piaggie volger o' nboccone
> Assai credo
> Ke deggia dilectare
> Libero core
> E van d' intendimenti.[1]

Here is proof of the real hunting spirit, and the making of a true hunting song. This leads forward to the fine dithyramb of Niccolò Soldanieri, *I cacciatori della volpe*, printed in Perticari's *Difesa di Dante*,[2] and to a very similar fourteenth-century poem on stag-hunting of unknown authorship, published by Trucchi, with equally spirited lines on fowling and fishing—the latter curiously modern in character and a rare example. Direct from such parentage spring the verses of Lorenzo de' Medici, *La caccia di falcone*, which are the sunniest reflection of golden sporting days in Tuscany.

Dante's references to fowling are more numerous than those accorded to hunting. "In vain," he writes, in *Purgatorio*, xxxi, "in the sight of full-fledged birds is the net spread or the arrow aimed." Geryon, in *Inferno* xvii, is compared to the

---

[1] *Rime antiche italiane*, p. 143 (*Collezione di opere inedite o rare di scrittori italiani dal xiii al xvi secolo*, ed. G. Carducci, 1895).

[2] *Opere*, i, 317.

falcon descending sulkily without its prey, while in xxii is the
elaborate comparison of the Navarrese jobber with a duck
which plunges as the falcon stoops, and then the fight between the demons in which Alichino fixes his claws, like a
sparrow-hawk, in his fellow devil. *Paradiso*, xix, contributes
the pretty simile of the falcon, when its hood is withdrawn,
moving its head and clapping its wings, pruning itself and
showing its readiness for flight. This, however, is rather to be
classed with passages illustrating Dante's wonderful feeling
for bird life—the lark rising and the rooks, the bird waiting
for the dawn, the stork circling round its nest, the low flight
of the swallows, and the soaring of the kite. But we must not
forget the picture where Dante compares himself as he gazed
through the green foliage to the man who wastes his time in
pursuit of small birds (*Purgatorio*, xxii), nor the comparison
of the whirling spheres to the falconer's lure, followed by the
lines of the falcon looking to earth, then turning at the
master's cry, extending itself in flight after its quarry (*Purgatorio*, xix), nor again the bird netted by the snarer's call
(*Inferno*, iii). These examples suffice to show that the poet, if
no keen sportsman, was not untouched by the most picturesque of sports. Yet we could wish for more, and poets contemporary, or earlier, give us more. As instances may be
cited the spirited sonnets of Folgore da San Gemignano on
hunting and hawking for the months of February, September and October, and better still, perhaps, those for Friday
and Saturday in his sonnets for the week. And even Dante in
his love for bird life can hardly outdo the song of the anonymous lady who lost her falcon, the pathos of which is quite
Catullian:

> Tapina me che amavo uno sparviero,
>   Amavol' tanto, ch' io me ne moria
>   A lo richiamo ben m' era maniero
>   Ed unque troppo pascer no 'l dovía.
> Or è montato e salito sí altero
>   Ed è assiso dentro a un verziero,
>   E un' altra donna l' averà in balía.
> I sparvier mio ch' io t' avea nodrito
>   Sonaglio d' oro ti facea portare
>   Perchè nel uccellar fussi più ardito.

Or sei salito siccome lo mare
Ed ai volto li geti e sei fuggito
Quando eri fermo nel tuo uccellare.

                    E. Levi, *Lirica antica italiana* (1905)

It is noticeable that in these few references to hunting and
fowling there is no mention of a horse. This animal apparently did not appeal to Dante. When mentioned at all it is
almost always in metaphor, and is then represented as a vicious, troublesome brute. There are no touches, such as might
be expected from his love of animal life, on the turn of the
head, the prick of the ears, the sleekness of skin and the grace
of movement. The very name occurs perhaps not more than
some ten times in the whole of Dante's poetry and prose, and
this is extraordinary if the importance of the horse in medieval
economy be considered. The three most elaborate passages
relate to the fractious character which requires governance.
In the celebrated lines on German Albert, Italy is the *fiera
fella* which has not been tamed by the spur, an idea which is
repeated in *Convivio*, iv, where the Emperor is figured as the
"Cavalcatore della umana volontà, lo qual cavallo come vada
sanza il cavalcatore per lo campo assai è manifesto, e spezial-
mente nella misera Italia che sanza mezzo alcuno alla sua
governazione è rimasa".[1] So also in *Convivio*, iii, the man is
more praiseworthy who curbs a naturally bad character
against the impulses of nature, just as he is the finer rider who
controls a vicious horse, while in *Convivio*, iv, 26, is found
the comparison of appetite to a riderless horse, which, even
if it be of noble nature, goes ill without the guidance of the
fine rider with rein and spur. Among mere mentions of the
horse may be cited from *Convivio*, iv, those who spend ill-
gotten gains on banquets, horses and arms; the children who
desire first an apple, then a bird, then fine raiment, then a
horse, and finally a lady-love; the ecclesiastics whose flowing
mantles cover their palfreys so that two beasts jog along under
a single skin. We might suspect that Dante never possessed a
horse, or even rode one, unless we are to take as fact the line

----

[1] [*Convivio*, iv, 9, ed. Moore, p. 307.]

in the *Vita Nuova*,[1] : "Cavalcando l' altr' ier per un cam-
mino", or as real regret the cry against "inopina paupertas",
which "velut effera persecutrix, equis armisque vacantem,
jam suae captivitatis me detrusit in antrum" (Letter ii, to the
Counts of Romena).

It may be thought marvellous that there does not seem to
be a single reference in all Dante to any of the games of ball
for which Italy became famous. Homer has proved that the
theme is not unpoetic, but Dante's Beatrice was no Nausicaa.
It is difficult, however, to find an honest test of Dante's deficiencies, because his contemporaries are equally silent.
Statutes forbid the playing of ball against this or that monastery wall, but there is no evidence to show the stage of evolution which the game had reached. A century later there are
frequent references, and by yet another century differentia-
tion had produced numerous forms. Rinuccini mentions
several kinds of fives or racquets played along the blind walls
of Florence. Only gradually had the great triad of Italian
ball-games, *calcio*, *pallone* and *palla maglia*, emerged. Mr.
Heywood in his recent book, *Palio and Ponte*, states his belief
that *calcio* and *pallone*, utterly distinct as they became, were
developed from a common simple type into the highly elaborate games of the seventeenth and eighteenth centuries.
This might account for several peculiarities in the two games.
The wall on one side of the ground or court remained a
feature in both. In Italian football the whole end of the
ground was, as in the Winchester game, the goal, while in
pallone the most successful stroke is one that clears the back
line—which may possibly have kinship with the "shy" in
the Eton wall-game. In both *calcio* and *pallone* the ball was
bounced into the ground by a neutral, as in the old English
game of "hurling". Moreover, the ball in *calcio* was known by
the names *pallone*, *palla grossa*, *palla gonfiata*—our balloon
or wind-ball. That now used in *pallone* is quite unlike those
of tennis or racquets, for it is made of leather, distended by
pneumatic pressure, and is of considerable size, some fifteen
inches in diameter. Again, *pallone* in the fifteenth century was

---

[1] [*Sonetto quinto*, ed. Moore, p. 209.]

not played, as now, by three a side, but by considerable numbers, and speed was highly valued. In *calcio* apparently the
ball might be "dribbled", carried, and above all, hit with the
fist. Venice, however, peculiar in this as in all else, is said to
have played a strict "Association" game, the use of hands and
arms being disallowed. It is certain that *calcio* was an old
game in Italy, and that is all that can be said of early days.
S. Bernardino advised ladies to withdraw from the windows
when it was played, not as might be prudishly recommended
now, because the players wore shorts, but because they did
not. In Dante's own city football has quite an interesting
history. S. Antonino broke his arm at it, "dum luderet ludo
pilae inflatae quae dicitur palla grossa fregerat sibi brac-
chium". Young Piero de' Medici shocked graver opinion by
playing it in the streets when he should have been attending
to affairs of state, and this contributed to his fall. A few years
later ill-starred Filippo Strozzi, one of the leading young
bloods of the day, describes a game at Naples, twenty-three
a side, grey and rose stripes against yellow and white, in
which Antonio Gondi broke his ankle. Filippo's sons were
later taken up by the police for playing a disorderly game
through the streets of Florence on Christmas Eve, in the
course of which they spoiled a large quantity of Christmas
goods displayed for show, and finally kicked the muddy ball
against a choleric member of the Ministry of Justice. Their
half-brother, the afterwards celebrated Leone Strozzi, made
an ineffectual attempt to rescue them from the constables.
During the siege of Florence in 1527 the youth played
twenty-five a side in full costume on the Piazza Sta. Croce,
with a band on an adjoining house to call the enemy's attention to their bravado. A parallel to this was a game of *pallone*
which two bands of young men played at Siena during the
siege of 1555 for two hours or more, while the French officers
looking on, "si stupivano delle nostre pazzie". This was
followed by a game of *pugna* at which Monluc nearly wept
for joy to see such spirit, but of this sport more hereafter.

Football then was no mere vulgar amusement, and in comparatively early times stood high in Florentine affections,

though Alamanno Rinuccini states that in the middle of the seventeenth century it was only played by boys, whereas he could remember bearded men taking part therein.[1] The farther it went back, the rougher it probably was, resembling the games still played at Dorking or Derby or Corfe Castle on Shrove Tuesday, and doubtless the *rageries de grosses pelotes* of Dante's own age in London, against which Edward II in 1314 legislated with small effect.[2] Yet of all this Dante is completely silent! Surely a writer who descanted upon Hell without a solitary mention of football can scarcely be acquitted of wasted opportunity.

Even more violent and perhaps more picturesque than football were the mimic combats of immemorial antiquity in several Italian cities.[3] These were battles deliberately fought on stated festivals between different quarters of a town. The combatants commonly used staves or else their shields as offensive weapons, while the light-armed were employed as stone-throwers. The defensive armour was often elaborately composed of wicker and padding, but casualties were invariable, and fatal accidents not uncommon. The battle of the Bridge of Pisa was the most celebrated survival of this game. In Dante's time this was played, not on the bridge, but in the piazza, and he must probably have seen it, for it was a usual day out for Florentine holiday-makers, at least for blind beggars and their dogs. Ungratefully enough when Pisa was forced to surrender in 1406, the Florentines even disarmed these innocent, if brutal, athletes of their clubs and shields.

---

[1] Bologna, still the chief centre of *pallone*, can boast respectable antiquity for its "wall-game", *ludus pallae coreae ad spondam muri*, which was always played along a particular line of houses. This is incidentally mentioned in a law-suit of 1435, while on August 5, 1480, Giovanni Bentivoglio patronised a match of Greens versus Yellows, fifty a side. Just a century later football was forbidden, as provoking quarrels and fights among the gentry. L. Frati, *La vita privata di Bologna dal secolo xiii al xvii*, 1900. [Cf. C. Ghirardacci, *Historia di Bologna*, Muratori, new ed., vol. xxxiii, Part I, p. 222, for a description of the match; he and other chroniclers describe the teams as dressed in green and red.]

[2] Quoted by Mr. Shearman in his *History of Football*.

[3] On this subject little can be added to Mr. Heywood's admirable account in his *Palio and Ponte* (1904).

The revival of the sport, and its transference from the piazza to the bridge, has been attributed to Lorenzo de' Medici, who did his utmost to quicken Pisa into new social and economic life. The game was also played at Gubbio, at Orvieto, where it was known as *prelium de lapidibus* and lasted from All Saints' Day to the beginning of Lent, and at Perugia, where it was singularly persistent under the name of *battaglia de' sassi*. Here in 1372, writes Mr. Heywood, the Papal Vicar strove to suppress it, and this was actually effected by S. Bernardino, though only for a time. It is noticeable that the first game of the year was played on the feast of the local saint, S. Ercolano, at government expense. At Perugia, and probably elsewhere, it became an incident in the serious fight between Guelfs and Ghibellines. This was natural enough, because the two factions here, as at Brescia and elsewhere, predominated in separate quarters.

At Bologna a similar game, the *ludus graticulorum*, in which one party was armed with sticks and the other with baskets of eggs as missiles, was prohibited as early as 1306. The Sienese Statutes of 1309–10 mention this combat under the name of *Elmora*, and documentary evidence of its existence goes back to 1253. A peculiarly bloodthirsty fight took place in Dante's age, in 1318. The custom was apparently continued without much interruption, for a game was played in honour of Charles V in 1536, while another delighted the French garrison in the last agonies of the siege. At Florence the game was very old, but few details are known of it. The statutes of 1415 strenuously forbid citizens, of whatever condition, either to play at, or be spectators of, the *bellum de mazzis*, or to join in the stone-throwing which accompanied it.[1] But survivals are found in the organised stone-throwing by boys, especially at certain seasons. Even Savonarola only succeeded in suppressing them for a season, by substituting raids on their neighbour's fineries. The custom was not confined to Tuscany and Umbria. At Venice two districts long fought each other on the bridges, originally with stout bamboos, and

---

[1] *Statuta Populi et Communis Florentiae . . . anno salutis MCCCCXV.* lib. iv, 39.

since 1292 with sticks.[1] One of these combats was held in honour of Henry III's passage through the town on his way from Poland to France.

Salimbene mentions as a landmark the open ground outside the gates, where the fight was habitually held at Parma. By far the most elaborate of the early accounts is that contained in the *De laudibus Paviae*, written about 1330; this describes in some detail the *Battiolae* between North and South, which lasted from New Year's Day to Lent.[2] Yet of these games once so common, and so frequently mentioned alike in law and history, I have found no mention in Dante, nor, indeed, in any *litterae humaniores* at all contemporary. The absence of all reference is the stranger, as these combats were closely connected with the chief religious festivals of the city, often with that of the patron Saint: they were frequently subsidised by the municipal government, and the opening game of the season was as integral a part of the festival as the procession and the offerings of tapers and *palii* on the part of subject communes and feudatory nobles. And when the festival was over, these games were continued for some months, so that they formed no inconsiderable feature in medieval Italian life.

Far otherwise is it with the more aristocratic jousts and tournaments, and the graceful evolutions on horseback included under the term *hastiludia*. Every Italian dynasty on occasion of a marriage, a birth, or some social or political event, held a *Corte bandita* to which were invited nobles from all parts of Italy, and invariably associated with this *Corte* was the ceremony of conferring knighthood. Even the republics—Florence, for instance, and in Dante's day—held similar festivals, though there were not the same frequent occasions provided by birth or marriage: in republican Italy the wives and daughters of temporary presidents did not pose as princesses. Chief among the entertainments were of course the tournament and joust. It is needless to say that these were not characteristically Italian. An early case is mentioned at Bologna in 1147, when it is stated that the sport was intro-

---

[1] P. Molmenti, *Storia di Venezia nella vita privata* (ed. 1905), i, 204.

[2] Muratori, *Rerum Italicarum scriptores*, xi, 22.

duced from Saxony. It is certain that the fashion was greatly
stimulated in the second half of the thirteenth century by
Charles of Anjou. More specifically Italian, perhaps, were the
hastiludia, a phrase which sometimes comprised the others,
but more strictly connoted the display of horsemanship and
skill in handling arms, recalling the celebrated scene in
Virgil, and known to much later times as Troy game. The
hastiludia occasionally degenerated into buffoonery, as when
at Parma the young gentry, dressed as women, skirmished on
horseback through the town the whole night long, their faces
covered with whitened masks. This, however, Salimbene,
though no prude, regarded as indelicate, and, indeed, the
men of Parma, as he tells us, spent all their time and substance on variety entertainers, actors and the like. More frequently these evolutions were performed in compliment, as
when in 1282 the Bolognese knights manœuvred round the
carroccio of Parma on the piazza of Cremona, thinking to do
the Parmesans a pleasure.

Most chroniclers have references to these high festivals,
the most celebrated of which in Dante's time was given in
honour of the marriage of Beatrice d' Este to Galeazzo Visconti. Dante regarded this as a *mésalliance* for the widowed
lady, but her late husband, the Judge of Gallura, could not
have bettered this splendid festival, the sensation of the day,
the talk of all Italy. So deeply imbedded in the thought and
language of upper-class Italy were the ceremony of knighthood and the feats of arms connected with it, that even in the
lightest love poetry metaphors from the lists are frequent.
For the nearest approach to actual description recourse must
again be had to Folgore da San Gemignano in his verses on
May, thus translated by Rossetti:

> I give you horses for your games in May,
>   And all of them well train'd unto the course,—
>   Each docile, swift, erect, a goodly horse;
> With armour on their chests, and bells at play
> Between their brows, and pennons fair and gay;
>   Fine nets and housings meet for warriors,
>   Emblazon'd with the shields ye claim for yours,
> Gules, argent, or, all dizzy at noon-day.

And spears shall split, and fruit go flying up
In merry counterchange for wreaths that drop
From balconies and casements far above;
And tender damsels with young men and youths
Shall kiss together on the cheeks and mouths;
And every day be glad with joyful love.[1]

Probably every gentleman that Dante knew, and most of his acquaintances in *Inferno*, *Purgatorio* and *Paradiso*, belonged to this class, must have taken part in these contests or displays. Yet his references are few. The most distinct which I can recall is in *Inferno*, xxii, 9, a curious passage, because it seems to confound real acts of war in the territory of hostile Arezzo with the *ferir torneamenti e correr giostra*, which were their mimic representatives. In *Inferno*, vii, 34-5, the shock of the avaricious and the prodigal is a metaphor taken from the lists:

> Poi si volgea ciascun, quand' era giunto,
> Per lo suo mezzo cerchio all' altra giostra.

Aquarone in his *Dante in Siena* believes that the *giostre del Toppo*, which are thrown in Lano's teeth, contain a reference to the tournaments of the *brigata spendeveccia* in Siena, extravagance in which led to Lano's self-sought death at Piere al Toppo. A passage in *Convivio*, iv, 27, supplies a hint that Dante disapproved of the extravagance of these despots' Court-days, wherein the money wrung from the poor is squandered on banquets, gifts of horses, arms, raiment and largess—a passage recalled a little later by Coluccio Salutati's reproof to Petrarch for his presence at Violante Visconti's wedding-feast in the midst of a starving Lombardy, a reproof emphasised by its conclusion that the gout from which the poet was suffering served him right.

It may be due to this indignation with the abuses of his age, from this want of sympathy with its pleasures, that Dante fails to leave any impression of Court life, to which, after all, he was no stranger. No dynasty was more lavish in its Court-days that than of Scala, and even that of Polenta

---

[1] [*The Early Italian Poets*, translated by D. G. Rossetti, p. 108. London, 1861.]

did not shrink from wasting the substance of others in the glorification of itself. The whole works of Dante, poetic or prosaic, give no such picture of a great Italian Court as the single short phonographic description of the hum and buzz, the jangle and the babel of the palace of Can Grande, in the *Bisbidis* of Dante's friend, Manuel the Jew.[1]

II

THE RACE FOR THE "PALIO"

Of all Italian sports in and after Dante's age the most universal and characteristic was the racing for the *palio*. This was a long strip, or sometimes two strips laced together, of valuable cloth, silk or rich brocade, resembling in shape the banners now used at school feasts and in the processions of benefit societies. The chief uses of these banners were two, and it will be seen that they had some connexion. Firstly, they were carried in procession and presented annually to a ruling city on the great municipal festival by subject communes or noble feudatories as a recognition of her sovereignty. Thereafter they were hung in the principal church. Thus at Florence S. Giovanni's was hung round with *palii*. Secondly, they were suspended on poles and hoisted at the winning-post of race-courses as the first prize. Hence the *palio* came to mean the race itself, much as we use the phrases Ascot Cup or Middle Park Plate. To give an example. Just as the War of the League of Cambrai was breaking out, young Luigi da Porto wrote from Vicenza to his Uncle in the Friuli, "If I don't send my Barbary horse to run the *palio* at Udine this St. George's day, it is because I think that throughout all the Venetian territory there is bound to be something else to do this year than running the usual *palii*".[2] So universal were these two practices that the manufacture of *palii* was quite an important industry, *e.g.* at Venice, and the prices paid for the race prizes were,

---

[1] Mario Pelaez, *Rime antiche italiane*, p. 356.
[2] [*Lettere storiche*, Ep. 2, ed. Bressan, p. 25.]

even according to the earlier statutes, very high, and then continually rose. Thus the *palio* of Piacenza, which in 1372 was won by Bernabò Visconti's horse, had for three years past cost 112 gold ducats, whereas *in temporibus retroactis* the value was 15.[1]

In the second half of the fourteenth century and in the fifteenth the chief race meetings were events as fashionable as they were in England in the nineteenth. Horses were sent from all over Italy, and no prince's or great nobleman's establishment was complete without its stud. There were professional training stables kept sometimes by the lesser members of well-known families. The companion of Pico della Mirandola's voluntary or involuntary elopement was the wife of a Medici, a horse-trainer at Arezzo, which no doubt accounted for the skill with which she leapt on the croup of the attractive philosopher's horse. We know for certain that, immediately after Dante's death, to win the *palio* was the ambition of the most prominent bloods of Lombardy. That of Milan was carried off in 1339 by Bruzio Visconti, *podestà* of Lodi, the handsome gallant bastard of Luchino Visconti, and it cost 40 gold florins—at least £160 in modern values. Twice afterwards the same prize fell to him, and his stable was equally successful at other meetings.

I have found notices of these races throughout Northern and Central Italy, from Vercelli to Udine, from Milan to Rome. Nevertheless their origin is totally obscure. Muratori could not trace it beyond the thirteenth century.[2] Yet it is improbable that it then had a mushroom growth all over Italy. The absence of earlier mention may be accounted for by the balder and more formal character of the chronicles, and more particularly by the absence of codified statutes, our best authority, for which the classical age is the latter part of the century. The earliest notice is, I believe, that recently quoted in Mr. Heywood's *Palio and Ponte* from the *Libri de' pretori* of Siena, when in 1238, the loser of the race— *colui che perde* in Dante's phrase—was heavily fined for refus-

---

[1] *Chron. Plac. Agazzari*, p. 50.
[2] *Dissertazioni sopra le antichità italiane*, xxix.

ing to carry his consolation prize publicly into the city. This chance notice carries back this curious custom, to which I shall again refer hereafter, quite as a matter of course beyond any mention of the *palio* in chronicle or statute. Not far behind, however, are the statutes of Bologna of 1250, which provide for a change in the course for the *palio* of S. Pietro, the existing one being too short and inconvenient.[1] Very old also was the *palio* of S. Bartholomew at Bologna, which is said to have originated in 1249, and of which there is documentary evidence in 1269.[2]

It is possible that the races were introduced from the East or from Africa during the Crusading period, but I can find no evidence for this. The horses certainly seem to have had Arab blood. The term *Barberi* is said in Della Crusca to have been confined exclusively to horses run for the *palio*. This is the word used in Da Porto's letter already quoted, while the large pictures of the Duke of Ferrara's horses in the Schifanoia Palace supply evidence of half a century earlier.

The older races were invariably connected with a religious festival, and were often named after the patron saint of the city, *e.g* after S. Eusebius at Vercelli, after S. Syrus at Pavia, and yet another race after S. Petronius at Bologna. S. Mary of August was, however, the most usual public holiday. To the present day the horses are blest and sprinkled with holy water in church before the race, for which ceremony there is a special office with prayers for their preservation from all harm. Mr. Heywood believes this practice at Siena to be not earlier than the eighteenth century, but its alleged existence in small Tuscan townlets, where life is extremely conservative, may point to longer custom. The races were not only an essential feature of a religious but of a patriotic festival, for they were usually founded in honour of a national deliverance or victory. Thus at Padua the race celebrated the death of Eccelino da Romano. The Florentine legend is as instructive as it is false—that the *palio* and the Church of S. Reparata were both founded in honour of Stilicho's victory over the Goths. The *palio* of S. Barnabas

---

[1] *Statuti del Comune di Bologna*, ed. Frati, ii. 128.   [2] *Ibid.* 29.

did actually commemorate Campaldino, that of S. Anne the expulsion of the Duke of Athens, that of S. Victor a defeat of the Pisans in 1364. The Sienese honoured the exorcism of demons by S. Ambrogio Sansedoni, and similarly the overthrow of the faction of the Twelve and the Milanese protectorate after Gian Galeazzo Visconti's death. The defeat of Bernabò Visconti at S. Ruffillo in 1361 was the excuse for yet another meeting at Bologna, for which the prize was a *palio* of striped velvet with the Saint's picture on the pennon which sometimes surmounts the banner.[1] Connected with these sporting displays of patriotism or party-feeling was the custom of running the *palio* outside an enemy's town when its troops had been driven within the walls. At the same time it was usual to coin gold money. This latter was a symbol of sovereignty, and it is possible that the *palio* was also regarded as a proof of occupation. An interesting early statute at Parma orders that if the *podestà* should be away with the army on the stated day for the national *palio*, it should be run wherever he, the representative of the state, and the army, that is the nation in arms, should chance to be. This, no doubt, was also the meaning of the *palio* run by the Florentines outside Arezzo on S. Giovanni's Day in 1289, which is often erroneously described as the origin of the race. But in Italy jest and earnest go in pairs, and in this practice there was an element of jibe, as when at Arezzo in 1335 the Perugians gave a *palio* for a prostitutes' race. Earlier than this, in 1325, the Florentines had suffered a similar insult from Castruccio Castracane, who on S. Francis' Day gave three *palii* for horses, men and prostitutes outside the city from the Ponte alle Mosse to Peretola.[2] Yet, as will be seen hereafter, this was merely the extension of not uncommon domestic customs to the national army in the field. These very Atalantas of the camp were no novices on the track: they had received their training on the recreation grounds or through the streets of their native cities. Regarded, however, merely as a jibe, these patriotic indiscretions would fall into line with the hanging of asses with the

---

[1] L. Frati, *Vita privata di Bologna*, p. 151.   [2] G. Villani, ix, 316.

names of the enemy's most eminent citizens round their necks: at Arezzo, indeed, on another occasion, the poor donkey's head was crowned with the mitre of the fighting bishop of the city. Also in 1325 the two aspects of this custom, the patriotic and the opprobrious, are illustrated at Bologna, which was besieged by the Cremonese, Mantuans and Modenese: each State ran its *palio* "ad aeternam memoriam praemissorum, et ipsorum Bononensium scandalum et opprobrium". Sercambi of Lucca has an interesting passage in this connexion. The Florentines in 1357 were besieging Pisa, of which Lucca was a somewhat forced ally. They ran three *palii* outside the city, and this is the chronicler's comment: "The Commune of Lucca in its power ordained the running of these three *palii* in sign of victory. And therefore the Commune of Florence ought not to wish by way of scorn to have these races run which the Commune of Lucca annually held by way of exaltation. And in this Florence showed little love towards Lucca." [1] Sercambi gives us probably the first two pictures of this opprobrious racing— one of the Pisans outside Florence, the other of the Florentines outside Pisa.[2] The horses are seen racing towards the *palio*, which is held aloft on a staff at the goal.

The banner which formed the first prize for these races was always of some shade of red, so that *correre il scarleto* was almost as common a phrase as *correre il palio*. This, for instance, occurs in the thirteenth-century Paduan statute, and so too at Parma in 1324 the reconciliation of the factions of Rossi and Corrigeschi took place on the race-course, "quando currebatur scarlattus extra portam Novam de mense Augusti in festo beatae Mariae". Sometimes the prize was fortified by a more material gift, as at Ferrara and Bologna by a horse. The second and third prizes gave more scope for imagination: they included hawks, hounds, pairs of gloves or spurs, cocks with or without cages, sucking pigs, hams, owls, and not uncommonly geese with a sympathetic

[1] Sercambi, i, 116. [*Le croniche di Giovanni Sercambi*, 3 vols., ed. Bonghi, *Fonti per la storia d' Italia*, 1892).]

[2] *Ibid.* 122, 125.

bunch of garlic, suggestive of their coming fate. The winner of the last prize was something of a butt, though in the thirteenth-century statutes, *e.g.* at Verona and Padua, precautions were taken that the horses must be thoroughly sound and of considerable value. The *colui che perde* was often required, as has been seen at Siena, to carry his trophy attached to his horse into the city.

It has been hinted that not only horses raced. At Pisa boat-racing was in vogue as early as the thirteenth century, and the head of the river received an ox with scarlet housings. The thoroughly Dantesque date, 1300, marks the first notice of the far-famed Venetian regattas. There were also races in several towns for men, women, donkeys, and Jews, the latter at all events in Rome under the patronage of Paul II, while in 1490 Jews ran from the Campo de' Fiori to the Piazza of S. Peter, where the winning Hebrew received a red cloth *palio* in the gracious presence of Alexander VI— himself dubbed Marano. Races for men are mentioned at Ferrara, Verona, Brescia, Pisa and Lucca, and were probably universal. Those of women and donkeys added a coarse, comic zest, thoroughly Italian, to the solemn religious patriotic festivals. Yet they were not uncriticised. At Brescia, time after time, the authorities, especially in periods of religious revival, strove to suppress the women's races as demoralising and irreverent, but they were what the lower classes really cared for, and conservative or argumentative people urged that it was a good means of distinguishing disreputable from reputable womankind. At Brescia, it may just be noticed that the prize for the horse-race was of scarlet of England, that for men of *drappo verde*, and that for girls of blue: at Ferrara the *panno verde* was the prize for boys. The donkeys must be content with linen or canvas *palii*. The very curious fresco in the Schifanoia Palace shows horses, mares, donkeys, men and women all racing one behind the other, while Borso d' Este and his Court look on. Donkey-riders, then as now, sat on the nethermost end of their mounts.

The best early account of races perhaps occurs in the *De*

laudibus Paviae, written about 1330, but describing customs of long standing. On the feast of the Translation of S. Syrus the horses ran very early in the morning on a long course outside the city for a silken or gold-embroidered *palio*, a roast sucking-pig and a live white cock. After lunch, varlets and women ran in another place for salt and fresh meat. The writer gives the only account with which I am acquainted of the ultimate destination of the *palio*. The winner offered it to S. Syrus, or any other church, or did what he liked with it.

If Paul II enjoyed the races down the Corso at Rome, his predecessor, Pius II, encouraged them in his little native hill-town of Corsignano, and has left a most graphic description in his *Commentaries*.[1] The people here had always held races on S. Matthias's Day, but the ceremony of the opening of Pius II's new Cathedral and the surrounding group of build-ings, domestic and municipal, was celebrated with unusual splendour at his expense. A fair was held in booths outside the town, whole oxen straight from the plough were roasted, and then towards evening came the races. The horses were assigned their stations, the signal given for the start, but "inequality of speed and an uncontested victory rendered the spectacle somewhat poor", the horse of one Alexander leaving the field nowhere. The donkeys, however, made amends by their spirited competition, for under the stimulus of a shower of blows first one and then the other forged ahead. So also the races for men and boys on the chalky soil greased by rain caused much excitement and amusement, for none could keep their feet, the last frequently became first, and the naked runners coated with mud became unrecognisable by their backers. The feature of the meeting was the race for small boys who ran round the course to the city gate, sticking and stumbling, losing their wind and getting up again, while their

---

[1] Book ix, p. 433 (Rome, 1584). [The editor has falsified the text to make it appear that Pius II was engaged on graver matters than watching races, but the original text runs: "Haec Pontifex rex altissima fenestra cum Cardinalibus non sine jucunditate spectavit, quamvis interea de publicis negotiis auscultaret" (Cugnoni, *Aeneas Silvius, Opera inedita*, p. 222).]

parents and brothers shouted exhortations. Victory wavered
between several to the very last. The success of young Piensis
was deservedly popular: he was carried shoulder-high to his
home to the great delight of all his quarter. If Dante had
only been as human as Aeneas Sylvius, how much more
social history his admirers would have known!

The first actual description of the *palio* in verse belongs to
the early years of the quattrocento: the poem gives an elaborate account of the festival of S. Giovanni. The unknown
poet celebrates the *carroccio* drawn by horses draped in red
and white, with the *marzocco* at each corner—and then he
writes:

> Nel mezzo al carro è fitto un alto stile,
> Dov' è il palio gentile
> E tutto steso, di color vermiglio,
> E 'n su la cima d' oro è posto un giglio . . .
> I corsier senza resta
> Furon condotti poi a ventun' ora,
> Che, per giungere ad ora,
> Qual grida, quale isferza, qual vien meno
> A qual si rompe il freno.
> Pure alla fin l' ebbe quel di Ferrara
> Trascorrendo ciascun per forza e gara.
>
> E. Levi, *Lirica italiana*, p. 46

This poem provides one proof among several that in the
earlier races the horses were ridden, as now at Siena, by
jockeys, *raggazzini* as they were called in the fourteenth
century. In later days riderless races were far more common.
Those at Rome down the Corso, which men still living may
remember, are said to have been originated by Paul II, by
whose palace, the Palazzo Venezia, was the goal. But the
drawings of Sercambi of the fourteenth century, the frescoes
of the Schifanoia Palace, and an illumination of Basinio Parmense's Argonauts, 1454 (engraved in Yriarte's *Rimini*), show
jockeys riding their horses bare-backed. In the latter they
are seen racing through the town gate towards the front of
Sigismund Malatesta's *Tempio*.

Here then, setting aside the races for women and donkeys,
we have a more or less dignified form of sport, which in each

city was the great event of the year, which was instituted in honour of some notable victory, paid for by government, and associated with the name of the chief civic saints. A custom so universal, combining elements of religion, of national pride and scorn, could scarcely pass wholly unnoticed by Dante, if he were really to tell the story of his age. Year by year, he must have seen these races in Florence or without. He does, indeed, make no less than four distinct references to the *palio*. In a previous paper I called attention to Dante's apparent lack of interest in the horse. It is noticeable that in none of these four passages does he directly refer to horses as being engaged in the races, while three bear exclusively on the far less important foot-races. The first and slightest reference is in *Convivio*, iv, 22, where in quoting Corinthians i, 9, he translates *Qui in stadio currunt* by *Che corrono al palio*. This is important so far as showing that the very idea of a race was by Dante's time inseparably connected with the *palio*. Otherwise the passage is disappointing, because in enlarging on his text he describes, not the competition of runners upon a single track, but the competition of tracks, only one of which leads to the right goal. The use of the simile is, it must be confessed, singularly clumsy and inept.

More apposite to our purpose is the passage in *De Monarchia*, ii, §§ 8-9, where Dante speaks of different nations either fighting or racing for the prize of Empire: of the latter contest he writes—"sicut fit per pugnam athletorum currentium ad bravium", which Ficino translates "come avviene a quelli atleti che corrono al palio". *Bravium* and *pallium* were, indeed, employed as synonyms, *e.g.* in the statutes of Vercelli, "Ordinatum est quod unum palium sive bravium sufficiens et idoneum et omnia alia pertinentia dicto palio ementur per comune Vercellarum". Then after referring to the race of Atalanta in Ovid's *Metamorphoses*, x, Dante quotes Cicero, *De Officiis*, "Qui stadium currit eniti et contendere debet quam maxime possit ut vincat: supplantare eum, quicum certet, nullo modo debet"—translated by Ficino, "Chi corre al palio deve sforzarsi quanto più può di vincere, ma dare gambetto a colui che con lui combatte non debbe".

This absence of fouling is here stated as the essential distinction between fighting and racing. The modern race for the *palio* at Siena is one continuous foul, and a foretaste of the practice is found in the more comic races even in the fourteenth century. But in purer times and more serious racing it is sternly forbidden by the statutes of several cities, for instance that of Florence on the *palio* of S. Reparata, "et nullus cursorum ipsos seu eorum equos, nec ipsi cursores inter se impedire debeant", and a similar statute applies to the race on S. Barnabas' Day.

We now come to the two references to racing which have a distinct local interest. In *Paradiso*, xvi, 40, Cacciaguida says:

> Gli antichi miei ed io nacqui nel loco
> Dove si trova pria l' ultimo sesto
> Da quel che corre il vostro annual gioco.

"My ancestors and I were born in the place where the last of the six districts is first reached by him who runs in your annual sport." This site is known to have been near the junction of the Mercato Vecchio and the Corso, probably the angle of the Via Speziali and the Via Calzaioli. Here Dante gives a real piece of information, for the statute only prescribes the course through the Borgo Ognissanti and the Via della Vigna: "Palium sive bravium praedictum curratur . . . per burgum Omnium Sanctorum et per viam della Vigna et alicunde non". Dante therefore marks it a stage farther on, on the farther side, that is, of the Mercato Vecchio, on the way towards the Corso and the Porta S. Piero, which was the goal, for the anonymous poem already quoted states definitely that the race was run from the Prato on the west to this gate.

And now at last we reach the most distinct of all Dante's allusions to sport:

> Poi si rivolse, e parve di coloro
> Che corrono a Verona 'l drappo verde
> Per la campagna; e parve di costoro
> Quegli che vince, e non colui che perde.
>
> *Inf.* xv, 121

In this case the Florentine poet and the Veronese statutes supplement each other. Most fortunately the statute, the celebrated Albertina, compiled between 1271 and 1278, under the provisions of which the Veronese races were run in Dante's time, still exists, as does the next issue of Can Grande in 1323. It seems worth while to quote the text as bearing so directly upon Dante's lines and the sport from which he draws his graphic illustration:[1]

Ad honorem dei patris omnipotentis filii et spiritus sancti et gloriosae beatae Virginis Mariae et beati Zenonis cujus patrocinio gaudemus et ad honorem et letitiam et bonum statum partis regentis Veronam quae est commune Veronae et erit in seculorum secula Deo dante statuimus et ordinamus quod potestas communis Verone teneatur quolibet anno in die dominica tocius populi ponere seu poni facere pro communi Veronae duo bravia in loco ubi utilius ei videbitur. Ad unum quorum curratur equester ad alterum curratur pedester et illud ad quod current ad equum sit unum palium et una baffa de qua licitum sit cuilibet accipere et prius currenti detur palium et ultimo currenti detur baffa de qua licitum sit cuilibet incidere et tollere postquam currens habuerit ad collum equi ligatam. Aliud vero ad quod curratur ad pedes sit unum palium et unus gallus quae palam portare debeat usque in civitatem. Ad quae bravia non debeat aliquis currere cum aliqua equa nec etiam cum aliquo equo quod (*sic*) non sit integer omnibus suis membris et potestas habeat liberum arbitrium in ordinatione bannorum ponendorum circa constitutionem et ordinationem dicti ludi et leticiae in his quae videretur (*sic*) utilia circa ea et in puniendo quemlibet facientem contra ea quae per potestatem in predictis et circa predicta fuerint ordinata non obstante aliquo statuto generali vel speciali in contrarium loquenti quae omnia praesenti statuto sint penitus abrogata. Et potestas teneatur exclamari facere per civitatem et burgos uno mense ante predictum terminum quod quilibet volens currere ad dicta bravia seu curri facere debeat se parari ad predicta.

In this statute it is noticeable that nothing is said of the

---

[1] Since copying the statute from the MS. of the Albertina at Verona I have found that this, together with the statutes of Can Grande and Gian Galeazzo Visconti relating to the *palio*, were printed by Gaetano da Re, *I tre primi Statuti sulle corse de' Palii di Verona*, in the now defunct *Rivista critica della letteratura italiana*, vii, 80-87.

colour of either of the *palii*, which is unusual: nor is there any hint as to a definite race-course, for this is left to the pleasure of the *podestà*. The former deficiency is supplied by the next statute, that of Can Grande in 1323, for after the words *duo bravia* is the addition *unum de scarleto et aliud de panno viridi*. Here then is Dante's *drappo verde*, which by a few years anticipates the information given in the statutes. His lines also help to settle a long controversy as to the customary course. The races in later days were unquestionably run through the streets of Verona, and it has been argued that this was the immemorial course, and in accordance with the usual practice at other cities. It is certain, however, that at Siena the race through the city was later, and that at Parma and Pavia the statutable course was a stadium outside the town. The two statutes of Verona imply that the course was external, for the loser, *colui che perde*, had to carry his consolation prize *usque in civitatem*. Dante clinches the matter by definitely stating that the foot-race at all events was run *in campo*, the meadows outside the city. In these respects then, and in his precise notice of a point in the Florentine race-course, Dante has actually contributed to our knowledge of contemporary sport. Apart from this we should know as much had he never put pen to paper. Is it possible to account for our disappointment, for his almost complete silence on the pastimes of his countrymen, when on all else he was so eloquent? It may be due in part to his character, *schifo e disdegnoso a guisa di filosofo*, as Villani complained.[1] He had little sympathy with the pleasures of his fellow-gentry, less with those of the vulgar. His mind was too serious for sport, too indignant for amusement. But this is not nearly all. Such amusements were too quotidian to find mention in graver writers, and even in those of lighter vein they only intrude by accident. It may be suggested moreover that in the literature of most ages there is a gap in narrative poetry, that the taste for narrative is either early or comparatively late, and it is of course narrative that offers the best opportunity for the setting out of prominent customs. In such a gap Dante wrote,

---

[1] Lib. ix, cap. 136.

for in spite of appearance he is not really narrative, and, when the taste for narrative revived, he retired for the nonce to limbo. After all, in modern England football absorbs more of the thought of the lower classes and golf of the higher than any one other subject grave or gay. Yet they will leave little mark upon our literature, save for an obscure line of Mr. Rudyard Kipling's. Our inquisitive successors will be as much at fault as to our amusements as we find ourselves when we ransack Dante. He tells us little of sport in his poetry or prose, mainly because the poets and prose-writers of all ages rarely tell posterity what at the moment it wants to know.

V

TWO FLORENTINE TRAGEDIES : DANTE AND SAVONAROLA

IF anyone were asked what two events have cast the most eternal disgrace upon Florence, the inevitable reply would be the exile of Dante and the burning of Savonarola. These therefore I have called the two Florentine Tragedies—tragedies which still move many who have never seen Florence, how much more those who have reverently wandered through the cells of San Marco, or down the narrow street where the Alighieri had their home. Other tragedies of course there were, such as the murder of young Buondelmonte which stained the Ponte Vecchio, and that of Lorenzo de' Medici's popular brother Giuliano which polluted the Cathedral. But these were acts of personal vengeance, whereas Dante was exiled and Savonarola burnt by the official Florentine government, which had apparently the weight of public feeling behind it. Both decisions were deliberate and unrepented.

The two tragedies were not isolated accidents in Florentine history: they are illustrations of the character of a people, the inevitable results of permanent causes acting on an uncompromising type of personality. Such were, above all, the unceasing prevalence of family faction, the weakness of government and want of discipline, the fickleness of Florentine democracy. On both cases the intervention of the Papacy, sentence of excommunication and threat of interdict, exercised an immediate and sinister influence, and the characters of the Popes concerned, of Boniface VIII and Alexander VI, provoke comparison. The short time within which both tragedies develop is very remarkable when contrasted with the permanence of the chief causes. Dante's fate was decided within the period between June 1300 and January 1302, that of Savonarola between the spring of 1494 and that of 1498.

Dante's public career followed closely upon the democratic Ordinances of Justice, that is, the overthrow of oligarchy, Savonarola's upon the expulsion of Piero de' Medici, the overthrow of monarchy. Both fell upon moments of peculiar unsettlement. The very agents of the two tragedies bear some small resemblance. Doffo Spini, the most open and persistent of Savonarola's foes, the leader of the aristocratic bloods, is a decadent travesty of Carlo Donati, the fierce, unscrupulous head of the old Florentine nobility whose audacity caused Dante's fall. Charles of Valois is the forerunner of the equally unstable Charles VIII. Certain similarities of character between the poet and the preacher may just be treated. Dante was no saint, yet there is in him a strong element of asceticism; his perpetual references to spiritual poverty anticipate Savonarola; his puritanism, as shown in his diatribe on the decolletage of the dress of Florentine women in the *Purgatorio*,[1] finds its repetition in Savonarola's scathing criticisms on feminine fashions at the close of the quattrocento. If Dante never claimed to be a prophet, yet prophecy is a constantly recurring feature in his art. Both failed in politics, perhaps from a constitutional incapacity for compromise, or from lack of the sense of measure; both possessed the gift of fierce denunciation. Both had a high opinion of their own importance. Yet whatever similarities there may be between the causes of the fall of these two men, and whatever the correspondence between their characters, their respective fates were tragedies in very different degrees. The end of the preacher was dramatic in the extreme; the curtain falls at the intensest moment. But to call Dante's fate a tragedy seems almost a contradiction of terms, for there was nothing dramatic in its incidents or in his exit; in fact throughout the last act he had never been on the stage. For all that a tragedy it was, a drawn-out tragedy without a climax.

DANTE

The fall of Dante, as that of Savonarola, was directly due to the conflict of families, and less directly to that of classes,

[1] *Purg.* xxiii, 97-102.

the two combining to produce the clash of parties. Guicciardini later wrote that the Florentines possessed two opposite characteristics, the passion for equality and the ambition of every family to be first, the jealousy, that is, of a democracy and the greed of an oligarchy. This is a summary of all Florentine history.

It is the fashion to speak of the interest of Italian history as consisting in individuality. But to those who look deeper the real unit of importance is the family. Family faction, the curse of every city in Northern and Central Italy with the glorious exception of Venice, is traced to the successive settlements of Teutonic military families. In Germany their feuds took for centuries the form of private wars, but in Italy, where the nobility adapted themselves to urban life, they became civic wars, fought in the narrow streets from massive towers, while the cavalry dashed down the roadway till checked by chains and barricades.

Meanwhile a lower class was pushing into prominence owing to the rise of trade and manufacture. Thus a new conflict arose, really one of principle between class and class, between the nobles who had previously ruled the city and the *popolo*. Yet soon an alliance would take place between one section of the nobles and the *popolo*. Then the other section would gain allies among the people, often among the lower classes who enjoyed none of the privileges wrung from the nobles by the upper middle class. The two parties were known by family names or nicknames, of which Dante gives an example in his lines:

> Montecchi e Cappelletti.
> Monaldi e Filippeschi.[1]

Often these local parties became merged in the great divisions between Guelfs and Ghibellines, which gave an outward appearance of principle, frequently not more, to old and meaningless family feuds. Gradually the group of families would be led by a single family, and that by its ablest member. Then came, especially in Lombardy, the despotism. This was not

---

[1] *Purg.* vi, 106.

generally the result of violence: the rule of one man was voluntarily and statutably accepted as the only remedy for chronic anarchy. His sway would spread to neighbouring cities, which would not have brooked the rule of a rival municipality, but could endure that of a personal lord. Thus arose the vast aggregate of territories ruled by the Scala and Visconti, which, when complete, ensured a relative amount of peace over a considerable area.

Even in Tuscany a leaning towards tyranny is seen in Dante's time in Pisa, Lucca and Arezzo, and later in Florence itself. But the development here is more like that of ancient Greece: the tyrannies are short-lived; there seems a real principle of opposition between despot and people, though the need for peace was quite as crying, the factions quite as violent. The Florentine was no braver than the Milanese or Brescian, the Paduan or Parmesan, but, as Savonarola later said, his temperament was more restless, more critical, more impatient of control.

Open violence between factions at Florence is dated by Dante and others from the murder of young Buondelmonti in 1215.[1] This illustrates the saying of Aristotle that oligarchies generally split over succession to property or marriages. When the fickle youth transferred his affections from an Amidei to Gualdrada Donati the great family of Uberti took up the injured lady's cause. Thenceforward there was a hammer-and-tongs fight between the rival parties under the guise of Guelfs and Ghibellines. The Guelfs at last secured their powers by the victory of Campaldino in 1289, in which Dante took part when twenty-four. Henceforth Florence was a Guelfic city for ever. This, however, helped little towards peace, for as early as 1280, that is, nine years before the battle, the rivalry of two chief Guelfic houses was becoming obvious. These were, first, the old noble house of Donati, headed by its brilliant leader, Corso, eloquent in speech as he was valorous in battle, highly cultured and wholly unscrupulous, championing the cause of the old nobility and the unrepresented classes against the wealthy parvenus and

[1] *Par.* xvi, 140-47.

the bourgeoisie; secondly, the house of Cerchi, more recently settled in Florence, but which had bought the palaces of the Guidi in the immediate neighbourhood of the Donati. Their leader, Vieri, was rich, somewhat vulgar and inarticulate, capable, but too moderate for an age of revolution. Both, and particularly Corso Donati, had distinguished themselves at Campaldino, and this gave them a higher idea of their importance. It was the violence of Corso, and, as Dante thought, the betrayal of Vieri, which was the immediate cause of his exile.

Not only was Dante's fate involved in the clash of family factions, but, less directly, in that of classes, and here we must needs dive into the constitution of Florence if Dante's political position is in the least degree to be understood; for Dante was exiled, not as a poet, but as a recent Prior of the Arts. At the time of his Priorate in 1300, the qualifications for office were three, locality, class and profession, the two latter intermingling but not being identical. Florence was divided into six districts, each of which had an equal share in offices of state. Before 1250 these offices were confined to the old nobility having their houses in the several sixths, each of which would be controlled by groups of noble families jostling for power. The constitution was the simple form of most early Italian towns, at the head a foreign noble as annual *podestà* to ensure the impartiality of justice, and under him a greater and a lesser Council. To this was added, by a series of measures culminating in 1250, the constitution of the Popolo, also with a foreign noble as Captain, and its two Councils. Unless these two sections were to be actively hostile they must co-mingle, and this was done by simply adding one constitution to the other, so that there was both a *podestà* and a Captain and Four Councils.

The third element in the formation of the Constitution were the Arts or guilds. These powerful organisations had long exercised a predominant influence in the Popolo, but the Arts and Popolo were by no means conterminous. The bulk of the people was outside the twenty-one Arts which alone had any representative privileges, while these Arts did not entirely exclude nobles who were actually engaged in trade, or who were enrolled for political purposes. At this time the Greater Arts were reckoned sometimes as seven, sometimes as twelve, and the Lesser at fourteen or nine. The seven were professional or mercantile, comprising, apart from noble members, the upper middle class. The fourteen were essentially tradesmen's Arts. The fifty-one others which did the manual work of Florence were constitutionally out in the cold, but in a State where there was no standing army and few police, artisan opinion could not always be neglected. In 1282, when Dante was seventeen, a magistracy called the Priors of the Arts was formed to exercise a stricter control over finance. They soon shouldered out the existing chief magistracy, the fourteen *Buonuomini*, and became the government or ministry. Their numbers were then fixed at six, one for each district; the term of office was for two months only. This was a change in the basis of government, and gave the Arts the leading position in the State. Shortly afterwards, in 1289, an old Council, the Hundred, was revived for financial and other urgent matters, and at once became the most important council of the city. Henceforth every legislative proposal had to be initiated by the Priors and then to pass the Hundred, the two Councils of the Captain and the two of the *podestà*. Even to one who is not a single-chamber man, a ministry and five councils might seem excessive for a city of fifty-five thousand inhabitants.[1]

The object of all these measures had been to curb the violence and corruption of the great nobles, but they were too competent and too traditionally powerful to be easily beaten. The Arts had captured the constitution, but the *Grandi* manipulated the Arts. Thus it was that Giano della Bella, himself a man of good family, carried in 1293 the Ordinances of Justice. According to their provisions all magnates were excluded from offices of state; they could only sit in the Councils of the *podestà* and no magnate could be head of any

---

[1] [Writing some years later, the author estimated the population of Florence at 30,000. Cf. above, p. 4. No figure can, however, be cited with any degree of accuracy. Cf. R. Caggese, *Cam. Med. Hist.* vol. vii, p. 65.]

K

guild. All magnates had to give security for themselves and their relations. Penalties for breaches of the peace on the part of a magnate were very severe. The Priors were strengthened by the addition of the Gonfalonier of Justice, who became the chief political officer of the State. A citizen army of two thousand foot was created; there were five hundred more in the suburbs and six thousand in the territory, all to help the Gonfalonier in bringing the nobles to justice and destroying their towers. Giano was noble, honest and patriotic. He was backed by the lesser guilds and populace and by a large party in the upper guilds. With his reforms power had passed definitely, it appeared, to the middle classes and the guilds.[1]

It had not been easy to decide who was or was not of the *Grandi*, because the old line of demarcation between noble and *popolano* had almost worn away. *Popolani*, who had mostly come from outside Florence, had invested their gains in land, bought old noble palaces, and intermarried with old feudal families. On the other hand, nobles engaged in trade, and nobles and *popolani* were partners of the same woollen or banking firms. The Cerchi are an example of the former class, the Donati of the latter. The rough-and-ready test adopted was the rather accidental possession of a knighthood by any branch of the family. Thus some of the best-known families, even of those days, escaped exclusion from office by the accident that they had no knight. Such were the Medici, Albizzi, Pitti, Strozzi, Peruzzi. Knighthood, it must be remembered, was then a purely social distinction, much as it is now, conferred by very different authorities for very different reasons. The results of the Ordinances of Justice were doubtless as curious as if all the branches of the family of every modern knight were given the sole right to the titles of gentleman or esquire.

Though the *Grandi* were excluded from the official government, they controlled an organisation which often

---

[1] [For Giano della Bella and the Ordinances of Justice see G. Villari, *Historie Firentine*, viii, caps. i and viii; Dino Compagni, *Cronica*, i, caps. xi-xvi; R. Caggese, *Firenze della decadenza di Roma al Risorgimento d' Italia*, vol. i (Florence, 1912).]

overshadowed it—that of the Parte Guelfa. This was administered by three Captains and a Special and a General Council. It had ample means, arising from the confiscation of Ghibelline estates; its punitive powers were very large, and it in great measure dominated the foreign policy of the State. In this its oligarchical exclusiveness and its longer terms of office made it far more efficient than the rapidly changing magistrates of the official State. Magnates and knights here had a free field for their ambitions. The skill with which they organised Guelfic interests throughout Central Italy is in marked contrast with the inefficiency of the *bourgeois* government, which wholly failed to secure the internal peace which was the professed object of the much vaunted reforms.

The new ruling class was not only inefficient but corrupt. The bribery, with which we shall fine Dante charged, was confessedly rampant, and the lawyers and notaries are said usually to have been the medium. The Priors, short as was their term of office, were very powerful. The assessment of the individual tax-payer was at their mercy, and their patronage was extensive. They played the chief part in the election of their successors, who were interested in protecting them from prosecution. Thus the Priorate was sought by everyone who had a personal or party axe to grind, or the interests of his guild to push, and the avenue to it was often not service or capacity but log-rolling and corruption.

Not only did family faction and class cleavage play their parts in Dante's fall, as later in that of Savonarola: foreign politics must needs complicate the issue. The connexion of Florence, as the chief Guelfic city of Tuscany, with Rome was extremely close. Though the Pope had no legal claim to suzerainty, yet as head of the Guelfs he had a pretext for meddling in Florentine internal politics, especially if there were any danger of a revival of Ghibellinism, or if the value of the city's alliance was weakened by divisions among the Guelfs. Boniface VIII was the last Pope to neglect such a chance. Violent and vicious, yet subtle and competent, he had an insatiable greed for power and territory. His aim was to establish his authority over Tuscany under pretext of mediation. Looking around for a tool, he hit upon Charles of Valois, brother of the French king, greedy, faithless and incapable, ever seeking for a State, but destined, as his brother said, to inherit wind. Charles should be the agent in pacifying Florence, and so in 1301 Charles came to Italy. The question remained—Would Florence tamely submit to what every statesman knew to be the virtual sovereignty of the Pope?

And now at last we come to Dante. He was thirty when he first entered public life. At that age he was qualified for admission to an Art, and the Art selected was that of doctors and druggists. This at once brings us into the debatable question of his social position. It is usually assumed that he was a noble, but it has been seen that this term, like that of gentleman or esquire to-day, had lost all meaning. Villari describes his family by the vague phrase *antico ed onorevole*.[1] Dante himself was proud of his origin: he regarded himself as belonging to the old Florentine stock which claimed to be descended from the Romans, distinct from the beasts of Fiesole,[2] or the boors of Campi, Certaldo and Figline, who had flooded the city since the good old days.[3] Two cantos of the *Paradiso* are devoted to his great-great-grandfather Cacciaguida, from the family of whose wife, the Alighieri probably of Ferrara, Dante derived his name. Nothing, however, apart from Dante, is known of Cacciaguida except the fact of his existence. The Alighieri certainly did not belong to the *Grandi* who were excluded from office. It has indeed been supposed that they were one of the harmless *Grandi* families admitted to office under a modification of the Ordinances, but this is pure assumption. The Alighieri are never mentioned among the great Guelfic families either Black or White. Ammirato, who lived much later but whose sources of information were excellent, definitely places them among the *popolani*. Dante did not enter a trade in 1295 because the modification of the Ordinances had just been passed, but because he was of the proper age.

---

[1] [Villari, ix, cap. 136.]

[2] [*Inf.* xv, 61-73. Cf. *Epist.* vi, "Miserrima Fesulanorum propago", ed. Moore, p. 409.]   [3] [*Par.* xvi. 49-57.]

But whatever his parentage, Dante lived in good society, at all events in good literary society. He was a close friend of Corso Donati's brother, Forese the Glutton, with whom he exchanged vulgar—not to say disgusting—sonnets. His wife Gemma was of the Donati clan, though how nearly connected with its chiefs is not known. One of Corso's capital enemies, Guido Cavalcanti, a Guelfic leader of high distinction apart from his poems, was another of Dante's friends. Society, indeed, in Florence was democratic up to a certain point. At all events, the family lived on its own somewhat scanty means in its own houses in the aristocratic if not respectable Sesto Porta S. Piero, the Sesto dello Scandalo, the quarter of the quarrelsome families where the rows which ruined Florence germinated. Dante must enter public life, not only as a member of a class or an Art, but of a party. He belonged to that of the Cerchi afterwards called Whites, in favour, therefore, of a peace policy and conciliatory towards the Ghibellines, leaning rather towards the *bourgeoisie* than the nobles and the Parte Guelfa, though the party quarrel between Blacks and Whites divided all these classes—the *Grandi*, the *popolo grasso* and the *popolo minuto*.

Dante's first public office was in the Captain's Council of Thirty-Six, from November 1, 1295, to April 30, 1296. He was at present shy and does not seem to have spoken, but in a smaller body on December 14, 1295, he found his voice. He was then on a committee which decided on the method of electing the incoming Priors. His proposal was not carried, but his selection proves that he was a safe party man. In 1296 he was a member of the important Hundred, and spoke on June 5. The only external honour which fell to his lot previous to his election to the Priorate was a mission to S. Gimignano, a very trifling distinction. Dante then, at the time of his election to the Priorate (June 15 to August 15, 1300), seems to have been a serviceable and perhaps ambitious citizen, *vaghissimo*, as Boccaccio says, *d' onore e di pompa*,[1] well thought of by his party. But it is unreasonable to think that

---

[1] G. Boccaccio, *Vita di Dante. Il comento alla divina Commedia e gli altri scritti intorno a Dante*, vol. i, p. 35, ed. Guerri (Bari, 1918).]

he was elected for peculiar merits, any more than were the
five nonentities who were his colleagues. Had he won high
distinction he would have served in more than one Priorate
in his six years of official life.

The Priorate was in fact an honour which fell to the lot of
any average citizen qualified by a mediocre social position
and membership of an Art. Dante, who cannot be accused of
undue modesty, himself confesses that in 1300 his renown
had not reached far.[1] As Dantists have exaggerated the importance of the poet's office, so they have multiplied the
events which took place during its two months. They have
placed in it the temporary ostracism of the heads of the two
parties, and have dwelt on the justice and strength of this
salutary measure, but in truth this sentence was passed by
Dante's immediate predecessors, and was the direct outcome
of the sudden, furious fight on May Day.[2] All that Dante and
his colleagues did in this connexion was to recall some of the
White leaders, among them Dante's personal friend Guido
Cavalcanti, on the singularly modern ground that the completion of his sentence at so unhealthy a place as Sarzana
would have been dangerous to health. Not unnaturally this
favouritism towards the Whites aggravated the hostility of
the Blacks. Another event wrongly placed in Dante's Priorate
was the final breach with Cardinal Acquasparta, whom the
Pope had sent as mediator. During Dante's Priorate negotiations with the Cardinal still continued in spite of an attempt
to shoot him through his window. It was in the succeeding
Priorate that Acquasparta left in dudgeon, shaking the dust
from his sandals against the rebellious city, and excom-
municating the members of its government. For all this

---

[1] ["Chè il nome mio ancor molto non suona," *Purg.* xiv, 21.]

[2] [This is not quite accurate. The leaders of the Black and White
parties were placed under bounds after the assault of the magnates on
the guilds, as they went in procession to the Cathedral on St. John's Eve
(June 23), that is during Dante's Priorate. Yet the affray between Cerchi
and Donati at the May Day ball on the Piazza di S. Trinità had already
prompted a movement in the Councils for the defence of the Ordinances
of Justice. Thus the policy of ostracism was prepared, although not
executed, without Dante's participation. Cf. Dino Compagni, i, caps.
xxi-xxiii; Villani, viii, caps. xxxix-xl.]

Dante's priorate was a most important moment in his life: from this he dates all his future misfortunes, and his attitude towards parties was the direct cause of his exile. He also probably refers mainly to this in his justification for writing the *De Monarchia*.

For six months after the expiry of his Priorate Dante does not again appear, but from April to September 1301 he is frequently in evidence. On April 14 he again sat on the committee for the election of Priors at a very critical moment, and his action was one of the grounds of his sentence. In May as a member of the Hundred he must have been partly responsible for action which made the breach between the two parties inevitable. All that these parties needed was a nickname, and that came to them from Pistoia. Here a bloodthirsty feud had broken out between the branches of the house of Cancellieri, who called themselves respectively Blacks and Whites. In 1296 the friendly government of Florence had been invited to undertake the administration for five years, till July 1301. It sent a *podestà* and Captain, and engaged to treat both parties with impartiality, giving to each an equal share in the offices. Several of the leaders were made to take up their residence in Florence, and with the true Pistoian fighting spirit they stimulated the feud between Cerchi and Donati. At a not very clearly ascertained moment the two houses took up the Pistoian colours, and the Cerchi, or most of them, for there was a branch of Black Cerchi, became Whites, and the Donati Blacks. In May 1301 the Whites wished to make sure of the support of Pistoia, as the other Tuscan Guelfic cities, Siena and Lucca, were of the Donati party. The Florentine *podestà* betrayed his trust and excluded the Pistoian Blacks from office, and then initiated a proscription of the most brutal character. The Blacks were entirely expelled, save the large number who suffered execution after the most cruel torture. The wretched exiles were denied entrance to Florence. This was a direct menace to the Florentine Blacks, who were justified in taking extreme measures for self-protection. In June Dante set himself in direct opposition to the demands of the Papacy. Boniface had asked for a renewal of the aid which Florence had given him in his war against the great house of Aldobrandeschi in the extreme south of Tuscany. Dante proposed in the Hundred that, with respect to sending aid to the Pope, nothing should be done. The discussion was apparently so brisk that the debate was adjourned, and on resumption Dante's proposal was lost by 49 to 32. This is the solitary occasion on which Dante is known to have played an independent and important part. He advocated a courageous, patriotic policy, and led a substantial minority against the timid vacillating leaders of his party. This speech doubtless sealed his fate. On September 13 he spoke in an assembly of all the Councils of the City on the means of upholding the Ordinances of Justice, which were being endangered by the growing lawlessness of the nobles. Unfortunately the secretary omitted to take down his speech, and in the minutes there is a blank, truly an *hiatus valde deflendus*. On two later occasions he spoke in the Hundred on general business, and his last appearance in public life was on September 26. There is an old tradition that, in October, Dante was nominated with others for an embassy to Rome, and that he proudly said, "If I go, who stays? If I stay, who goes?" Dante was certainly not of sufficient importance at the time to use such boastful words. The story rests on the unsatisfactory evidence of Boccaccio,[1] but Dino Compagni in his solitary reference to Dante, which has no connexion with the Embassy, adds the words "who was ambassador at Rome".[2] This is thought to be a late interpolation, for there is no contemporary copy of Compagni's *Chronicle*. It seems unlikely that Dante after his speech of June should have been selected as a *persona grata* to the Pope, or that Boniface, who had already decided on the fall of the Whites, should have given so militant a party man the chance of escaping just as Charles of Valois was about to enter Florence. Still the tradition cannot safely be brushed aside, though it is unsupported by any documentary evidence either at Rome or Florence. It is noticeable that Compagni in his very detailed account of this crisis only mentions Dante once, and that in a list of those sentenced

---

[1] [*Vita, op. cit.* p. 46.]   [2] [*Cronica*, lib. ii, cap. xxv.]

to exile. Villani never speaks of him until his death in 1321, when he had become famous as a poet. Stefani only gives his name in his two-monthly schedule of the Priors.[1] On the whole it would appear that Dante was not a statesman of high importance at this moment, though he had attracted attention by his advocacy of a resolute policy against the Pope, and against the grandees who dominated the Parte Guelfa.

The shadow of Dante's fate now falls upon us. Charles of Valois sent his Chancellor from Siena to announce his mission as mediator. The government dared not deny him entrance; they had made no preparations for resistance. Merchants as their leaders were, they trusted to bargaining and haggling. "They took", says Compagni, "great pains to defend the city from their designing enemies, but nothing served them, for they employed peaceful measures, whereas those that were needed were strong and swift: humility is worthless when pitted against great craft."[2] The Priors made a feeble attempt to propitiate the Blacks by forming a committee of both parties to advise them: they nervously turned for counsel to the Parte Guelfa, whose sympathies were against them; they even made the admission of Charles the subject of a referendum to all the seventy-two guilds, and this was probably the only occasion on which the fifty-one lower working-class guilds were ever consulted. Seventy-one voted for admission; the gallant bakers alone opposed it, saying that Charles should neither be received nor honoured for he was coming to destroy the city.[3] In view of coming events the precautions for public order taken by the worthy Priors seem ludicrous—abusive language was to be punished by excision of the tongue: in front of the Palazzo Pubblico, now rising from its foundations, stood the executioner with axe and block prepared for customers: Charles was warned of the imprudence of entering on All Saints Day, when the lower classes would be full of new wine.

---

[1] [Marchionne di Coffo Stefani, *Cronaca Fiorentina*, ed. Rodolico N. Muratori, new ed. vol. xxx, Part I, p. 82.]

[2] [*Op. cit.* ii, cap. 13.]   [3] [*Ibid.* ii, cap. 7.]

Charles risked the new wine, and entered on November 1 by the Porta S. Piero Gattolino, unarmed save with the lance of treachery with which Judas tilted, with whose point he was to burst asunder the bowels of Florence (*Purg.* xx, 73). Of course there were omens of disaster. The comet which we now know as Halley's was in the sky, and on one of the first nights of November, as Dante says in the *Convivio*, there was seen in the heavens the beginning of destruction, a cross formed by the fiery vapours which follow the course of Mars, and which are well known to portend the death of kings and the revolution of States, because such are the effects of the lordship of Mars.[1] Charles thought it unsafe to stay in the heart of Florence. So he made the Frescobaldi palaces at the southern end of the Ponte Sta. Trinità his headquarters, while his suite occupied the Spini palace on the northern bank. At first he was courtesy itself, inviting the Priors to dinner, with the knowledge perhaps that it was against the law for Priors to dine out, and attending the sermon of the then celebrated Friar Remigio Girolami, who, as Savonarola afterwards, discoursed on the evils of tyranny. A great Parliament of Peace was summoned to S. Maria Novella for November 5. Charles here received full powers to act as mediator, and took the solemn oath that he would faithfully perform his task, but his agents had already concerted the revolution with the Blacks. Even on the night before, the Medici had grievously wounded Orlanduccio Orlandi, who had lately been Gonfalonier of Justice. Though the citizens gathered round the Priorate ready to take vengeance, the cowardly Priors refrained. A few individual Whites and Ghibellines began to arm their towers, and in the narrower streets barricades were being raised.

The villain of the piece now takes the stage. Corso Donati, who had been lurking in the neighbourhood, tried one after another of the gates of Florence, and finally with aid from within he forced an entry by the postern da Pinti. The adjoining nunnery of S. Piero Maggiore was seized and its campanile fortified. The feeling of the populace was already veer-

---

[1] [*Convivio*, Tract. ii, cap. xiv. Dino Compagni, ii, cap. 19.]

ing with the breeze of audacity, and there arose the well-known cries of *Viva Messer Corso il barone*. All his noble confederates from without were slipping into Florence, and many of the upper *bourgeoisie* openly joined him. Corso first plundered the houses of the citizens who as Priors had exiled him, and then threw the prisons open. An orgy of blood and lust and fire began. But the worst of the crimes were not committed by the rabble or the gaol-birds, but by the noblest or wealthiest families of Florence, the Donati, Tornaquinci, Tosinghi, Rossi, and Medici, and they were committed against the persons and property of near neighbours of their own standing, with whom they had lived on terms of intimacy until the recent split in the Guelfic ranks. In the Ghibelline house of the Stimati the children had been left behind in perfect confidence; two noble families in succession looted the palace, the second stripping the very shirts from the children's backs. The warehouses of the merchants and tradesmen were ransacked. Money was extorted under promise of protection which was never given, heiresses were married by force and their shivering fathers compelled to sign and seal the marriage settlements. In vain the great bell of the Priorate clanged to arms. The few faithful citizens who rallied to its call found no leaders and few followers. Charles of Valois threatened to hang Corso, but never stirred a finger; when a palace was blazing he would ask what that fire was, and was content on hearing that it was a cottage. The populace was panic-stricken, and no wonder when the Cerchi were hiding in their palaces. Corso put the finishing touch to the revolution by invading the palace of the *podestà* and expelling him and his suite, and then he turned the Priors out of office. The sole executive magistrate who was left was the Captain of the People. Yet even in the flush of triumph the Guelfic nobles had a wholesome fear of a popular reaction; they dared not touch the constitution, nor the chief object of their hatred, the Ordinances of Justice. They were content with the nomination of new Priors on November 7. These received absolute power for restoring order; but they were at the beck and call of the Black nobles, to whom they

submitted every measure before it was formally proposed.
On November 9 the new *podestà* was appointed, that Cante
de' Gabrielli of Gubbio to whom Dante was to owe his exile.
Some sort of order was now restored. Cardinal Acquasparta,
who had returned, nominally succeeded in reconciling hostile
families, even the Donati with the Cerchi, but the futility
of such friendship was shown by the tragedy which ensued.
Young Simone Donati, most brilliant of the bloods of
Florence and his father's darling, while hearing a Franciscan
preach on the Piazza Santa Croce, saw old Niccolo de' Cerchi,
his own uncle, pass through the piazza on his way to his
country house. He followed him beyond the gate, fell upon
him unawares, and murdered him. One of the servants before
flying plunged his sword into Simone's side, and the bloodthirsty youngster died on the following day.

Meanwhile what had become of Dante in the turmoil of
party hatred? It has never been known where he was when
Charles of Valois entered Florence. Tradition, founded on his
supposed embassy to Rome, states that he never returned to
Florence, but joined the White and Ghibelline exiles in the
neighbourhood of Arezzo. But there is no real evidence for
this, and he may have been in Florence until shortly before
his exile. As long as there was any hope of compromise
judicial processes were delayed, but in January the trials, or
rather the sentences, began. Much has been written of the in-
distinguishable hatred borne by the Blacks towards Dante. I
am sceptical as to this. I believe it to be the creation of the
preconceived idea of his high importance. He was not included in the first batch of three victims condemned on
January 18, 1302, and he shared his fate with three others on
January 27. In all, fifteen of the Priors or Gonfaloniers from
December 1299 to November 1301 were condemned, and
most of them on the same charges. These were *baratteria*, *i.e.*
corrupt influence in elections and peculation, resistance to
Boniface VIII and Charles of Valois, and the expulsion of the
Blacks from Pistoia. The sentence was a fine to the State and
restitution of goods extorted during the term of office. If the
condemned paid he would be exiled from Florentine terri-

tory for two years, he would be disqualified for office, and his name would be inscribed in the register as a deceiver and peculator: if he did not pay, his property would be destroyed. Dante had not stood his trial, and the atrocious sentence against him and the other fourteen was that they should be burnt for contumacy. This was in accordance with law and practice; it was indeed formulated in Giano della Bella's Ordinances of Justice, of which Dante was a champion. He had in fact no reason to complain. Had not his first act as Prior been to confirm the sentence passed by his predecessors on three prominent Florentine agents of the Papacy that they should have their tongues cut out? He had certainly been in part responsible for the cruel treatment of the Pistoian Blacks. It is thought inconceivable that he should have been guilty of corruption, but he was probably just as innocent, or as guilty, as his fellow victims. If poets take to politics they run the risk of soiling their hands as do other men. After all, these penalties were mainly a matter of form. Citizens who fled from justice were rarely caught. A good horse, or even a sturdy pair of legs, would soon put the culprit beyond the reach of Florentine jurisdiction. Dante and his fourteen fellows all escaped. Possibly the government felt a measure of relief at their being beyond the jurisdiction of the court. Dante was excluded from the amnesty drafted in 1311 by Aguglione, the malodorous boor whom he has pilloried in the *Paradiso* (xvi, 56). By this time his political offence had been aggravated by a literary crime, for his letters to the Emperor and to Florence were a call to battle against the fundamental principles of the Parte Guelfa. But after all he shared this exclusion with from four to five hundred families or individuals. Among these were his colleague in the Priorate Ricco Falconetti, the armourer, who alone had shared Dante's courageous views, and Petrarch's father, who had been notary to the same Priorate. In September 1315 an amnesty was at length granted to Dante and many other exiles, but under such humiliating conditions that no man of spirit could accept it, and once more Dante was condemned to death. A is well known, he never again saw the *bello ovile* where as a lamb he slept.[1] He was one of those exiles to whom he refers who only revisit their country in their dreams.[2]

Wherein, then, lay the tragedy of Dante's exile? The answer is not easy. It was a tragedy shared by many hundreds of worthy citizens, even less guilty of the civic troubles than Dante's self. At each recurring outbreak of faction hundreds trod the paths of exile to be scattered throughout France and Italy, they too finding how bitter the bread and how hard the stairs of a stranger's home. Few of these had the honourable welcome accorded to Dante in Verona and Ravenna. Dante had but met the common fate of most Florentines who engaged in party politics. Seven years more and his very victor, Corso Donati, when on the point of making himself despot, was driven headlong from the city, caught at a mile from the gates, dragged by the stirrup of his frightened charger, pierced to death by a Catalan mercenary and humbly buried with ceremonies most unbefitting *il Barone*, whose brilliant surprise of the city in 1301 had been acclaimed by the hoarse throats of the applauding mob. For posterity certainly Dante's exile was no tragedy, for to this it owes the *Divina Commedia*. It is inconceivable that Dante should have composed this in the feverish activity of political life in Florence. Had the Whites conquered, or had Dante condescended to reconciliation with the Blacks, he would have hunted even more keenly for the paltry spoils of office; he would have been soused in the slough of maladministrations. Love sonnets he might still have written, but never the *Commedia*. No statesman has been a poet of the foremost rank—unless Bacon was really Shakespeare.

And yet as one reads the *Commedia* it is impossible not to feel that tragedy is printed deep into its pages, the tragedy of a noble nature instinct with pure and delicate affection, yet charged by circumstances with vitriolic hatred and contempt, hatred for the foes who had routed him and for the friends whose exile he had shared, hatred for the Pope who had caused his ruin and for the French king who had avenged it, hatred for his city of Florence, which yet he never ceased to

---

[1] [*Par.* xxv, 5.]   [2] *Epist.* ix.

love, hatred for his province of Tuscany—hatred indeed for Italy at large, for Dante, the champion of Florentine independence from shadowy papal suzerainty, called upon the German to make his empire over Italy real. If this stock of hatred were stored only in the *Inferno* it might be attributed to the technique of his art, but it is imbedded even in the *Paradiso*. The tragedy is indeed that of a poisoned heart.

And what of the tragedy of Florence, which did nothing but exile and try to burn its noblest poet—Florence which can lay small claim to the greatest of Italian poems, not a line of which was written within her walls—Florence which caused Dante to be buried, as Petrarch to be born, in foreign lands, which in later years had to beg for Dante's bones from a petty Romagnol despot, and beg in vain, which pulled down his house stone by stone and then had to invent another to attract generations of foreign worshippers? Did not Boccaccio in his first lecture upon Dante rightly upbraid his countrymen, "Se a tutte le altre iniquità fiorentine fosse possibile il nascondersi agli occhi di Dio, che veggono tutto, non dovrebbe quest' una bastare a provocare sopra di sè la sua vià? Certo sì".[1]

SAVONAROLA

It is unlikely that Savonarola would have become a tragical figure in history but for the premature death of Lorenzo de' Medici. Lorenzo would almost certainly have averted the French invasion of 1494 which gave Savonarola his opportunity. His name might have come down to us as that of an effective missioner, such as his immediate predecessor Frà Bernardino of Feltre, who also stirred the soul of Florence, who made bonfires of women's vanities, who advocated State pawnbroking to assist the poor, and who was ejected by the government for inspiring attacks upon the Jews. Or else, mellowed by years, listening to the voice of sympathy rather than to that of righteous indignation—for both qualities he possessed in full measure—he might

---

[1] ["If all the other sins of Florence could be hidden from the eyes of God, who sees all, would not this alone suffice to call down His wrath upon her? Most surely, yes" (*Vita di Dante, op. cit.* p. 4).]

have ripened into a second St. Antoninus, the gentle, saintly Archbishop of half a century before. In either case he would have been a subject for the hagiologist, or at most the ecclesiastical historian, and not for the student of general Italian politics. Lorenzo was generous and considerate towards Savonarola, the Prior of the family convent. The utmost step he took against him was to send five friends to advise him, as from themselves, not to prophesy so freely. The statesman knew that prophecies are apt to force their own fulfilment.

Lorenzo had always displayed the velvet sleeve. His son Piero, a youth of twenty, thumped the mailed fist. He was the Florentine Rehoboam and brought the revolution on himself. He disgusted the staider Florentines by playing football and *pallone* in the streets, alienated the leading men of the Medicean party, his near connexions, by rejecting their counsels of moderation, quarrelled with his popular young cousins of the junior line, even threatening them with death. Yet to Savonarola he showed favour. The object which the Friar had most at heart was the separation of the Tuscan from the laxer Lombard congregation of the Dominican Order: this was pushed through by Piero in opposition to the wishes of the King of Naples and the Duke of Milan, and against the better judgement of the Pope, who was induced to sign the deed of separation by a trick. Savonarola wrote a grateful letter. He later inveighed against the Medici, but most surely they would not have burnt him.

Foreign politics produced the crisis which brought Savonarola to political power. The old triple alliance of Naples, Milan and Florence broke up. The two former quarrelled, Ludovico il Moro called in the French, and Piero chose the wrong side, the side of Naples and the Pope. The Florentine aristocracy resented the breach with Milan, the keystone of the Medicean dynasty; the populace hated the Neapolitans; all classes were interested in the trade with France, the best customer of Florence. Had Piero fought it out he might have saved himself, but no sooner did the French king approach the new and strong fortress of Sarzana than he left Florence to make his peace, and surrendered all the chief fortresses.

On his return the gate of the Palazzo Pubblico was shut in his face. As he rode home the crowd shook their caps at him, the boys pelted him with stones and insulted him with cat-calls. Piero lost his nerve and fled: the dynasty of four generations fell without drawing sword.

Even before Piero's return, when the news of the surrender of the fortresses arrived, Savonarola's political career began. He was sent as a member of an embassy to Charles VIII, who was now at Pisa. Almost from that moment (November 5, 1494) till the day of his death he was the first man in Florence. How had he made the reputation which justified his choice as envoy, and how did he use it? He had preached himself into prominence. His first success ten years before had been at S. Gimignano, the scene also of Dante's first embassy, but it seemed unlikely that he would ever please the taste of the fastidious capital of the Renaissance. Yet, since his final settlement in Florence in 1490, his fame was always rising. You will ask the secret of his preaching. He combined in a remarkable degree the gifts of persuasion and denuncia-tion; in the code of life which he set forth, especially in the upbringing of children, he was extremely practical, while the allegorical embroidery which makes his sermons hard read-ing to us now, was then attractive. His voice was rough to the Tuscan ear but undeniably effective, and he preached with the eye as well as with the lips. Just as Dante was the chief exponent of the *dolce stil nuovo* in poetry, so was Savonarola the first to introduce at Florence a new style of pulpit oratory, not forced and artificial, as Guicciardini, who heard his sermons, tells us, but easy and natural. He had hit the happy mean between the grotesque familiar style common in Franciscan preaching and the over ornate diction and gesture of Frà Agostino, his rival fashionable preacher. Savonarola was, moreover, no mere fluent revivalist, but a man of real learning and an admirable teacher. His convent was admittedly at once the strictest and most highly educated in Italy. But above all it was the prophecy of the chastise-ment to come, that was to purge Italy of sin and then renew the world, that affected the masses who gloat on horrors till

L

they come. Men shuddered at his references to the terrible
French artillery, which was the Zeppelin of to-day. And now
the terror from the North which he had predicted: the sword
that should strike the earth and that quickly, was actually
there: the guns had knocked to pieces the one little Apennine
castle against which they had been trained. Who could avert
the doom but he who had foretold it? Who could propitiate
the French king but he who had set him up on high as the
instrument of God?

Within a year Savonarola had revolutionised the political
and social state of Florence. He had rescued the Medicean
extremists, with one solitary exception, from the vengeance of
the people; he had tided over the economic crisis by organised
charity, and had persuaded the restless, dangerous artisans
to return to work. Mainly owing to his preaching the Florentines had overthrown, not only the Councils which the Medici
had introduced, but the two surviving Councils of long before
Dante's day, and even the sign of the original sovereignty of
the assembled people, the Parlamento; they had set up what is
called a popular constitution modelled upon Venice.[1] Savonarola was a single taxer: he had introduced a People's Budget:
taxation should be confined to ten per cent on the profits derived from land, to be levied only once a year. He had devised
a sweeping judicial reform, which was, indeed, never carried
out; one of his devotees had anticipated Machiavelli in forming a scheme for national service. Greater still was the change
in the moral aspect of the city. It is true that Savonarola's
success in Florence was not due to her wickedness, but to her
comparative righteousness; she was fit to be the chosen city:
there was in the upper and lower middle classes a large body
of opinion, serious, moral and religious. Still she was a city
of pleasure with her gross Carnival festivities, and her horse-
races. Gambling and sexual vices had been open and un-
ashamed, dress was not always modest nor literature decent.
Now virtue was the fashion and vice was forced to hide itself.
Everyone knows how Savonarola converted the boys of

---

[1] [The constitution was based on a Grand Council of some 3000
citizens, drawn exclusively from the Arts, and in which the Greater Arts
preponderated by about three to one.]

Florence from hordes of dangerous hooligans into spiritual
boy-scouts, whose function it was to track out vice even
behind the closed doors of private palaces. Chanting processions took the place of horse-races, and burning of the
vanities that of the Carnival pageants. The churches were
crowded, and in the home Savonarola had insisted that the
day should begin with family prayer. Abroad all, of course,
had not been success. Charles VIII had broken faith, Pisa
and Sarzana had been lost, only Leghorn had been restored.
But then Charles lost his children, the penalty which the
prophet had predicted. The Emperor Maximilian had crossed
the Alps and besieged Leghorn; his success meant the strang-
ling of the State, but Savonarola had preached that God would
arise and His enemies be scattered, and the winds and the waves
had obeyed Him and dispersed the Emperor's fleet. God was
indeed the king of Florence and Savonarola was His prophet.

In the spring of 1496 Savonarola was all prophet; in the
spring of 1497 he held his ground though the signs of hostility were not wanting. On March 14, 1498, the Eighty,[1]
together with all the magistrates of the city, other than the
Signoria, debated whether to obey the Papal Brief and forbid
his preaching, or to allow him to continue in the face of his
excommunication. Opinions were very equally divided, but
almost all the speakers recognised his great services to the
State. On May 22 he was executed amid the very general
applause of the city. Sudden as this change seems, the causes
had really been long at work. First among these came party
politics. It has often been debated whether Savonarola did
wisely in entering into politics, whether his religious influence
would not have been more permanent had he stood aloof.
Certain it is that at Florence it was impossible at once to
enter politics and to escape from parties. From the very outset three parties appear: the aristocrats who had expelled
the Medici and who are called Whites; the popular party,
the Blacks, who, resting on the new constitution, dispute
their claim to power; and the old Mediceans, who at present
had to lie low, but who possessed all the real experience of

---

[1] [*I.e.* the Senate of the Savonarolist constitution.]

government in the State. The leaders of the aristocracy were, as always, jealous of each other, and they would strive to enlist the favour of Savonarola, which brought with it that of the city at large. From the earliest days there were men who believed that Capponi or Soderini or Valori were using him as a tool. Inevitably, if unwillingly and almost unconsciously, he was dragged into the vortex of party, insomuch that the original names were soon changed into those of *Arrabbiati* and *Frateschi*. The religious reformer had become a political fugleman. The *Frateschi*, it is true, had attracted aristocratic supporters from the original Whites, while the *Bigi* or *Palleschi*, whose experience was now giving them a large share of State offices, was divided between the parties. Nothing could have been more fatal to the permanence of religious influence. The absurdity of the Florentine constitution aggravated the evil. Every two months the Grand Council was agitated by the choice between *Arrabbiati* or *Frateschi* candidates, and the same trouble was involved in the recurring elections to the Ten of War, the Eight of Justice, or even less important bodies. In the election for January and February 1497 Savonarola seemed to have won a conclusive triumph. His chief supporter, Francesco Valori, was elected Gonfalonier of Justice, and ruthlessly used his power in the *Frateschi* cause, even expelling the rival Franciscan preachers from Florence. Yet perhaps nothing so directly contributed to Savonarola's death. No citizen, says Guicciardini, who disliked Valori, had cleaner hands or was a more zealous patriot than he,[1] but he was rough, eccentric, uncompromising and unpopular. Henceforth everyone who disliked Valori was at heart an enemy to the Friar. In the very next election Valori was succeeded by Bernardo del Nero, a thorough Medicean whom the *Arrabbiàti* had been forced to make their leader as the only man who could cope with Valori. In the following Signoria the parties were so evenly divided that five were in favour of dismissing Savonarola from Florence and four against. A majority of two-thirds was needed, and one more vote would have rid Florence of her immediate trouble and

---

[1] [*Storia fiorentina*, p. 173, *Opere inedite*, vol. iii (Florence, 1859).]

her later shame.[1] In August Valori won a signal victory: he
intimidated the Signoria into condemning to death, without
the constitutional appeal to the Grand Council, Bernardo del
Nero and four other leading citizens, for a Medicean con-
spiracy. Savonarola did not stir a finger in favour of the
appeal, the feature of the new constitution on which he had
most insisted. Bernardo was his enemy, but his inaction
alienated important friends, and the populace, which had
welcomed the execution, regretted the victims a few months
after death, and this reacted not a little on Valori and Savonarola. And thus the see-saw of parties went on with no rest
and no chance of a settled policy until the fatal April and
May of 1498 when the Signoria on the whole was unfavour-
able to Savonarola. Faction caused the burning of Savonarola
as it had caused the exile of Dante. And yet it is more than
doubtful if Savonarola was personally involved in party
politics. In his sermons on Ruth and Amos, he implored his
hearers not to pester himself and his friars with legislative
proposals, or with this or that man's candidature; he was no
politician, he had no finger in their government, nor yet in
their foreign relations. The daily or weekly visits of the party
leaders to San Marco gave colour to the accusations. His
enemies naturally believed that the midnight meetings on
the eve of elections in Medicean days had been transferred
from the Medici palace to the parlour of San Marco. It would
indeed appear that Frà Salvestro, one of Savonarola's chief
lieutenants, was a busybody, and it is possible that he acted
as the Piagnoni agent without his Prior's precise knowledge.

Foreign politics certainly contributed to Savonarola's
failure. The Italian powers, Venice, Milan and the Papacy,
backed by the Catholic kings and the Emperor, had combined
to drive Charles from Italy. They were resolved to protect
Italy from another French invasion, and yet Florence under
Savonarola's influence was ever beckoning to Charles. The
German Maximilian and the Spaniard Alexander VI vainly
implored the Florentines to be *buoni Italiani*. But at Florence
territorial interests outweighed national: she believed, per-

[1] [*Ibid.* p. 151.]

haps rightly, that she would only recover Pisa through
French aid. Savonarola's clinging to French loyalty would
have been pathetic if it had not been so pitiably unfounded.
The *Arrabbiati* had from the first condemned Piero's breach
with Milan: reconciliation would also serve their party prospects, for the Duke did not wish for Piero's restoration, but
for an oligarchy with which he could contrive measures
with speed and secrecy. Savonarola had no more persistent
enemies than Ludovico il Moro and Somenzi, his ambassador
at Florence.

The Pope's hostility to Savonarola was rather political
than personal, in spite of the Friar's violent and scarcely
veiled abuse. Alexander VI was a healthy animal with an
equable temper: he was not easily irritated by personalities;
men who live in habitual sin are not sensitive to scandal.
Sinners are not so hard on saints as saints on sinners. But
Alexander knew that another French invasion would mean
his deposition: the refusal of Florence to join the league
made such an invasion possible, and Savonarola was ever
urging it. Considering the provocation, Alexander was extremely patient, and Savonarola would have met with shorter
shrift had he come into conflict with one of the virtuous
Popes of the Catholic Revival. Alexander's complaints turned
chiefly on the abuse of prophecy, the public invectives by which
the Papacy was brought into contempt, and the trickery
by which the separation of the Tuscan congregation had
been obtained. The Pope's remonstrances opened with a
Brief of July 21, 1495, summoning Savonarola to Rome, but
his excuses were tacitly accepted. In November 1496 he
united all the Tuscan Dominican convents under a new
Tusco-Roman Congregation. To this Brief Savonarola's reply
from the pulpit was almost a declaration of war: there were
limits to obedience, and if a Brief of Excommunication were
brought into the city on a spearhead he should know how to
reply, and his answer would make many a face turn pale. At
length, on June 18, 1497, the excommunication was published in the Florentine churches. Yet the Pope hesitated, for
Savonarola had ceased from preaching, and wrote a humble

letter seeking absolution. But on Christmas day he celebrated
Mass in San Marco and on February 11, 1498, he at length
broke silence. He preached in San Marco on the invalidity
of the excommunication, declaring that whosoever believed
in it was a heretic. "If, oh Lord," he cried, "I should seek to
be absolved from this excommunication, let me be sent to
Hell: I should shrink from absolution as from mortal sin."[1]
These utterances, followed by others fully as audacious,
forced Alexander to a resolution. He demanded under pain
of interdict that either the government must place Savonarola
in his custody, subject to a promise that he should not be
hurt, or at least prevent his preaching. After much debate
Savonarola was ordered not to preach, whereon he delivered
his farewell sermon:[2] he was willing to obey the State, for he
could not force virtue on the city against its will. It was time,
he cried, to appeal from the Pope to Christ: the ecclesiastical
power was ruining the Church, it was therefore no longer
power ecclesiatic but power infernal, power of Satan. Henceforth Savonarola was silent but not idle. He prepared an
appeal to a General Council calling upon European princes
to depose the Pope, who was no Pope, for his election was
simoniacal, he was a heretic and unbeliever, for he disbelieved
in the existence of God, the deepest depth of unbelief. Had
Savonarola's cause been quite as strong in Florence as of
yore, or had succeeding Signorie been as bold in his defence
as that of January 1498, a formal schism must have followed,
and who can say that revolt would have been limited to
Florence, and that it would not have overstepped the frontier
between discipline and doctrine? There were dangerous possibilities in the gift of prophecy, in the claim to direct inspiration. More than once Savonarola had gone perilously
near to an appeal to private judgement. Schism will always
strive to find a theoretical justification by distorting doctrine.
It is certain that Savonarola's excommunication, his dis-

[1] [*Prediche sopra l' Exodo*, No. 1 (preached on Septuagesima Sunday,
1498) (Venice, 1520).]
[2] [*Ibid., op. cit.* (preached on the 3rd Sunday in Lent, March 18,
1498.]

obedience and the threat of an interdict shook the faith of
many of his adherents in all classes, and among them some
of the very best, moderate men who had welcomed his moral
reforms, who had regretted his oratorical excesses, and who
were unprepared for a revolution alike in Church and State.

Among Savonarola's enemies from the first are mentioned
the sceptics and the evil-livers. The former would include
not merely atheists and pagans, who would be a negligible
quantity, but men of the fifteenth-century renaissance, who
had a contempt for the *Frateschi* of whatever order. They
would either profess a decent, formal religion, or else they
would be imbued with that delicate and even spiritual Christo-
Platonism which had appealed so strongly to the better side
of the Medicean circle. Both classes would dislike the perpetual prophecy, the constant reference to old-fashioned,
grossly material representations of Heaven and Hell. The
Florentines, like all subtle spirits, were very sensitive, and
many ordinary citizens would share this feeling that they
were being laughed at by all cultivated Italy. The processions
of children, three or five abreast, with red crosses on their
white robes, and garlands of olive leaves on their heads, were
in good taste and might tend to edification; even an occasional
bonfire of vanities might pass. But when it came, as in 1498,
to a dance in three circles, the first of novices each attended
by a child dressed as an angel, the second of students each
with a lay youth for a companion, and the third of older
friars partnered by grave and reverend citizens, all dancing
presumably in very elementary one-step time, the result was
ridicule. The asceticism inculcated by Savonarola was probably
exaggerated outside Florence, but it must have been galling
to hear the Florentines described as a city of teetotallers
at the bidding of a Friar. There was, among the women devotees and occasionally among the men, an element of hys-
teria in the religious exaltation. Women would rush at night
to the Cathedral to struggle with Savonarola's opponents;
they saw in him the true light that was to come into the world.
At the convent of Santa Lucia there was an outbreak of religious
mania among nuns of good family. Perhaps the only occasion

on which Savonarola is spoken of as smiling was when during
his trial he described how an hysterical nun so belaboured
him that he could scarce escape from her. Of course he discouraged this; in his confession he said, "At first I used to
converse with women, and learned things from them, which
I afterwards put forth as revelations. But of late I avoided all
converse with them. One of them", whom he named, "seemed
to me to be mad."[1] Yet he naturally had to bear the blame
for these extravagances. Home life, at first sanctified by
family prayer, was made uncomfortable by divisions, or by
inconsiderate devotion, and it is difficult to condone the
encouragement given to children and servants to denounce the
private misdoings of the heads of the family. These grievances were doubtless swelling month by month the effective
ranks of the silent voter.

Anything but silent were the evil livers who formed the
nucleus of the party called the *Compagnacci*. The lusts of the
flesh were reinforced by the pride of life, by gilded youths
who wanted life in all its richest colours, who gambled and
raced not always in moderation, who in their dances must
have partners having nothing in common with Savonarola's
Friars. It is difficult to exaggerate the importance of this
group: they had little weight in the Grand Council but much
outside: they came from the best families, were well horsed
and well armed, good customers to the tradesmen, favourites
with the large class of half-employed who live on tips. It may
be noticed that their leader, Doffo Spini, was a member of the
house which was among Dante's deadliest foes—had he not
sentenced one of them to have his tongue cut out? From early
days the *Compagnacci* terrorised the feeble government. They
caused the disgraceful tumult in the Cathedral in May 1497,
when Savonarola had to stop his sermon and to be escorted
home by armed citizens. For this they were never punished.
They were prepared to fall upon the *Piagnoni* at the time of
the Ordeal, and they led the mob to the attack upon the
convent.

[1] [P. Villari, *Life and Times of Savonarola*, Appendix to Italian edition,
doc. 50.]

The new constitution, though always popular with the middle class, proved quite incompetent to deal with war without and faction within. The Florentines loved to play with constitutions, as children do with a box of bricks. The new toy was a travesty of its proposed Venetian model. It had taken as its basis the Grand Council, which at Venice had long been the declining partner, had become little more than the Electorate, and that but partially. At Florence it was all-powerful, leaving little authority to the Senate, which at Venice was the effective governing power. Above all Florence rejected the strong and expert Venetian executive, and retained its ridiculous two months' Priorate, as fatal to Savonarola as to Dante. Savonarola's budget had been a failure from the first: the lower Arno valley, the granary of Florence, was scoured by Venetian light horse from Pisa: eleven months of rain had soaked the land. The Florentines discovered that to tax the land is not the means to cheaper food. The single tax had failed, and others soon were added: State salaries were mulcted of one-half, and Savonarola preached that the holders of State securities should patriotically forgo their dividends, but this was not so popular as taxing landlords.

A talent for prophecy is a dangerous gift. It is possible that a highly spiritualised nature may possess a prophetic instinct, but only possible when this is spontaneous and unsought. Without profanity it may perhaps be called a religious form of betting, and like betting it is apt to grow upon the character. Savonarola relied more and more upon his prophecies. He would publicly boast of their success—he had foretold the death of Lorenzo, of Innocent VIII, the arrival and triumph of the French king, his punishment for not performing his pledges in the death of his children, the failure of Maximilian at Leghorn. Critics might say that in some of these cases he was prophesying on certainties, at least on generalities, but they were sufficient to inspire awe even in so cool a statesman as Philip de Commynes. But the great prophecy of all, the prophecy which was to affect the fortunes of every man in Florence, had signally failed. Italy at large, and more particularly Rome, was to be scourged, but Florence, the chosen city, after a short chastisement was to recover Pisa and much more besides, and be more glorious than ever. But God's instrument had come and gone, the Pope was unhurt and unabashed, other Italian powers were left unscathed. The chosen city alone was shorn of her trade and her possessions, decimated by plague and famine. He could not confess failure; like the gambler he must double and redouble his stake. He lost the spontaneous instinct—he was reduced to forcing, even borrowing his prophecies. There seems little doubt that in his exhaustion he turned to the somnambulist Frà Salvestro, dreamer of dreams real or invented, which his Prior took for inspiration. As belief had been strongest in the lower classes, so was the disillusion bitterest—it was they who felt the stress of plague and hunger, they whose wives were crushed to death in the crowd round the relief office.

In the poor quarters of Florence, the east end, the Medici had been very popular. Here was the great Franciscan Church of Santa Croce, where the Friars, essentially the Order of the poor, incessantly denounced Savonarola as an impostor. The great piazza outside the church had been the scene of the historic jousts and junketings of the golden Medicean age. Now it was left deserted, popular interest had shifted to the religious centres, the Cathedral and San Marco. The loss of Medicean charities was sure to be missed in the long run, and, after the first excitement, bonfires of vanities were a mild substitute for the pageants of Carnival or St. John's Day, and the wild race of horses through the streets. In June 1497 the Signoria revived the races, saying, "Let us cheer the people up a little: we can't all be pious". A private Venetian letter even as early as 1497 describes the populace as Medicean. What was the great reform, the Grand Council, to artisans and unemployed or half-employed? They had no vote nor lot therein; they had been robbed by Savonarola of their time-dishonoured Parlamento, which gave them a show of power, some amusement and probably much liquor. The people, wrote Machiavelli, are by nature changeable: it is easy to persuade them of a thing, but difficult to fix them in that persuasion, and so the organisation must be such that when they no longer believe one may be able to make them believe by force. Savonarola fell, he concludes, because unlike Moses (and he might have added Mahomet) he was an unarmed prophet: he could neither hold the believers to their faith, or force the disbelievers to believe.[1]

It is possible that but for the accident of the Ordeal of Fire Savonarola might have held his own. Charles VIII died upon that very day, April 7. The accession of Louis XII, bent upon immediate war with Savonarola's capital enemy, Ludovico il Moro, would soon have brought his own party to the top, and shattered the chances of the hostile aristocrats who had pinned their faith on the Italian League. Louis XII did indeed write to the Signoria to spare him when he was in prison, but it was too late. The accident of the Ordeal was the more cruel as Savonarola's right-hand man, Frà Domenico, took up the Franciscan challenge without his Prior's knowledge, and entirely against his wish. More than once Savonarola had been challenged to the fire ordeal by members of the rival orders. But he would not force a miracle upon God to suit the fancy of a Franciscan friar. He rightly felt, however, that Frà Domenico had carried the matter too far for retreat, and he could only preach and pray, and perhaps believe, that Heaven would defend his cause.

Only after long debate did the government consent to this extraordinary solution of the faction which rent the city. Some thought that it would make Florence the laughing-stock of Italy, others that it would rid the city of both parties of prating friars, some wished a less dangerous ordeal than fire: let the two champions walk through the Arno without getting wet; let them even be put in a tub and the water warmed to make the trial more comfortable. The feeling, however, prevailed that any chance of relieving the intolerable strain of the last few months would be worth the taking. If the Dominican champion survived, Savonarola's authority must be accepted; if he died it would fall with a crash; if there were any fiasco it would be discredited. Only one or

---

[1] [*Il Principe*, cap. vi.]

two of these statesmen believed in a miracle. The Signoria, on the whole unfriendly to Savonarola, authorised the trial.

April 7 was a great public holiday, far more exciting than the mere burning of the vanities. The gates of the city were guarded, the streets patrolled, foreigners sent away, all entrances to the piazza but three barricaded and these strongly held. The armed guards of the government were present in force, and their captain was, it seems, a partisan of Savonarola, but at one end of the square sat on their horses a troop of *Compagnacci* under Doffo Spini, an omen of disturbance. The Signoria sat in the Palazzo to supervise the scene. The Loggia de' Lanzi, then unadorned by master-pieces of art, was divided into two compartments for the rival friars. The Franciscans arrived first without formality and took their places. Then followed the last of the great processions from San Marco which have become so famous. In the middle of the files of friars walked Frà Domenico with the red *pianeta*, the robe of martyrs, upon his shoulders, bearing the Crucifix with the Christ turned towards him; in front of him the Prior himself, carrying the Host, and on either side and behind a company of zealous *Piagnoni* with lighted torches, and bringing up the train some hundreds of women wailing and weeping, most pitiful to behold. The Signoria, however, forbade the women to enter the piazza so as not to give occasion for scandal in view of their feeble and ignorant sex. The women might weep but they were brave enough, for when Frà Domenico had called in the Church of San Marco for champions, three hundred had risen and shouted "Sì." The rest of the procession, all singing, "Let the Lord arise and let his enemies be scattered", accompanied the Friars across the piazza to the Loggia. The long lanes of fire were ready laid upon a plat-form covered with earth and unbaked bricks, and on the top of these great logs, and bundles of brushwood and faggots, most purpose-like for a fine fire. Then began the tiresome wrangles while all the public was yearning for the show. The Franciscans insisted that Domenico should change his robes, since they might have been rendered fireproof by magic.

Domenico at length consented, and then after receiving the
Prior's blessing prepared to start for the fire with the Host
in hand. This was by Savonarola's express order, but it
raised a fierce outcry—it was to imperil the faith of Christ
that His Holy Body should be burnt. As no agreement could
be reached, both parties were dismissed to their respective
convents. To render the fiasco more depressing for the
onlookers, a fierce April storm had swept across the piazza
with hail and lightning, had soaked the lane of brushwood,
and soaked the shivering crowd. The *Frateschi* claimed that
God had given a sign of the friar's holiness, his adversaries
that the impostor by magic had unchained the devils of hell
to stop the ordeal and so conceal his lies. The people only
knew that they were drenched to the skin and cheated of a
horror.

Savonarola preached that evening in San Marco on his
victory, but he must have known that he was beaten. He
had confessed as much by asking for a State escort home.
His bedraggled procession had been the butt of every kind
of insult. Doffo Spini's troop had made a set at him, but had
been roughly beaten off by the State guards. The Franciscans
from the first had held the stronger ground—they knew that
their champion would be burnt, but it was worth the sacrifice
to be rid of this mischief and division in the State. This was
a common-sense view, and when the tension of expectancy
was relaxed common sense was likely to resume its sway.
Nevertheless the air was electric, and anything might happen
at any moment, especially as the lower classes had turned
distinctly against Savonarola. It only needed one of the
Compagnacci to hammer at the pulpit at vespers in the
Cathedral,[1] and to tell the women to go home for there would
be no sermon, to produce the riot and the end. The mob of
boys and hooligans was hounded towards San Marco. Valori
escaped to defend his own house whither the mob was now
diverted. His wife was killed by an arrow through the head
as she remonstrated with the crowd from an upper window.
Valori himself hid in the roof, but surrendered to police

[1] [On Palm Sunday, April 8.]

officers who were sent to rescue him. On the way he was hacked down by Vincenzo Ridolfi and Simone Tornabuoni in revenge for the death of their relations in the Medicean plot. Thus died, unshriven, the honest, violent leader of the popular party, absolute master of Florence for a time. His body, stripped to the shirt, was saved from further outrage by his old Franciscan foes, who bore it safely to Santa Croce. The *Compagnacci* then led the mob away to San Marco, where wood was piled against the doors and fired. Here for some six hours prayer and fight went on together, Savonarola and the worshippers awaiting death in supplication, the more militant making a gallant defence with tiles and stones and heavy crucifixes, against such invaders as had found entrance. At length the mob rushed the big gates and poured into the church. The last stand was made on the altar steps. The Signoria had done nothing to stop the riot. At length, after midnight, a written order was sent that Savonarola with Frà Domenico and Frà Salvestro should be brought to the Palace. The two former surrendered, and the officers led them out into the street, through the surging, howling mob, spitting, kicking and striking at its victims. Next day Frà Salvestro came out of hiding and was given up.

The trial of the three friars was undertaken with a view to condemnation, and the method of examination was the invariable one of torture. It is usual nowadays to regard evidence obtained under torture as valueless, but that is because we have no experience. The rack may be no more trying to certain nervous systems than examination in a modern court by an impudent young barrister who is "on the make". There were good witnesses under torture and bad witnesses, just as there are now. The simple, brave Frà Domenico was a good witness, and his deposition is usually accepted as entirely truthful. Savonarola was a bad witness. He had, as he confessed, more fear than most men of the cord. He had never played among other boys: never been brought into contact with physical pain. The idea that he was the constant object of plots of assassination by agents of the Duke of Milan, of Piero de' Medici or the League was almost an obsession. At this time his bodily strength was exhausted by anxiety, by the Lenten fast, by the terrible night's watching in San Marco. His examination at the hands, first of the Florentine commissioners and then of the papal, lasted almost without intermission from April 9 to May 22. It is small wonder if he confessed and retracted and confessed again. Moreover, the rascally secretary, Ser Ceccone, is known to have garbled the depositions. On the main counts on which he was condemned there could be no question. He had disobeyed the Pope, declared that he was no true Pope, and had called upon foreign powers to summon a General Council. This was sufficient to constitute schism and constructive heresy. But the Florentine commissioners were anxious to extort an avowal that his gift of prophecy was an imposture, the result of ambition, of a desire to appear wise and holy. On this head Savonarola wavered again and again. In his agony he cried out that the spirit had departed from him. He was probably at war within himself on this mysterious subject, on which indeed his utterances had never been quite consistent. But he stoutly denied that they had been based on confessions made to Frà Salvestro. Whatever the truth, the falsified deposition read in the Grand Council destroyed the faith of devoted supporters among the laity, and even of the friars of his own convent. On the subject of political intrigue little information was extracted, and this is probably what was desired, for the party which was prompting the government was anxious above all things to divert popular fury from a general political proscription to the persons of the friars. At the most his confessions, garbled as they were, showed, as Guicciardini states, no fault except ambition.[1] And who can say that in his last agony Savonarola himself may not have been conscious of past ambition, the parasite which clings most closely to monastic walls. Pride was the fault which Alexander VI had from the first fixed upon his future enemy, while he yet had admiration for his saintliness.

It is needless to dwell upon the end. Most of you know it

[1] [*Storia fiorentina*, p. 175.]

from the pages of Romola, and as you stand on the west of the great piazza and look towards the Palazzo Vecchio, it is only too easy to reset the scene—the piazza crowded with onlookers, every window a frame for clustered heads, barrels of wine broached at municipal expense, as for a high holiday. In front of the Palazzo the platform projecting from the building, the scene of so many royal receptions, of so many constitutions promulgated, so many victories acclaimed. And thereon three groups of judges before which in turn the three friars were led. From among the first the Archbishop's suffragan stripped the victims of their religious robe; the papal commissaires then declared them guilty of heresy and schism, and passed them on to the Gonfalonier and Priors who condemned them to death by hanging, their bodies thereafter to be burnt. The friars then traversed the raised gangway to the platform where was the gibbet and beneath it the fire laid for sacrifice. As the bodies hung and the fire blazed up, the boys of Florence stoned the corpses, even as they had stoned Piero de' Medici when he turned back from the Palazzo through this very square, as in their more re-generate days they had stoned notorious sinners, and as a few years later they stoned the executioner who was now amusing the crowd with clownish jokes. A few brave women rushed in to collect the sacred ashes, but the police pushed them back, and the boys broke the vessels. The remains were carefully collected and thrown into the Arno. There should be no miracle of resurrection, no relics to be hoarded against the day of reaction inevitable in this fickle populace. The fire went out, the onlookers dispersed. But such was Savonarola's personality that the tragedy is still poignant and the fire still burning. Thirty-two years more and the old passions once more blazed up into life. The *Piagnoni* revolutionists held the city against Pope and Emperor, against Mediceans without and aristocrats within. Far higher was their courage than that of those who let Savonarola die.[1] And to this very day Catholics and Protestants, Dominicans and Jesuits, men

---

[1] [For the Savonarolist tradition as an animating force in the defence of Florence in 1530, cf. C. Roth, *The Last Florentine Republic* (1925).]

of secular and men of spiritual temperament, fight over his memory with all the zest of those who had crowded to the piazza on the morning of the ill-fated ordeal.

As to the tragedy of Savonarola's fate there can be no doubt. For him it came quickly and was quickly over. But what of the tragedy for the State? Florence had killed the alien guest who loved her far more deeply than ever Dante did, and she must always bear the stain. The only word of blame that ever escaped his lips in the last agony were these, "I did not think that the people would change so soon".[1] He was not charged with any definite offence against the State: he was hung and burnt for disobedience to the Pope, the Pope whom half Florence had disobeyed, and whom every decent Florentine execrated for his simoniacal election and his evil life. So, too, Dante had been exiled because Florence had lacked the courage to withstand another evil-living Pope. The guilt of Florence in burning Savonarola was far greater than in banishing Dante. She could not know that Dante was to be her greatest poet: he had done little for Florence, except once to urge her to a brave and patriotic policy. It was not the act of banishing Dante that brought shame, but the system which produced such acts. In Savonarola's case the act was yet more blameworthy than the system. Granted that he had become a focus of dissension, it might have been wise to remove him to another sphere of usefulness. But his fault, if any, was so totally incommensurate with its punishment. He, moreover, had been the idol of Florence, her greatest teacher for many generations. He was, in Mrs. Oliphant's phrase, a maker of the very Florence which destroyed him. None had had the courage to defend Dante's cause, which a full half of the city had shared, and none stirred a finger for Savonarola, save the little band who fought for him at San Marco. Only one man, Agnolo Niccolini, had dared to suggest in the Council that Savonarola should be imprisoned instead of killed, so that the world might benefit by the sermons which he would write in gaol.

---

[1] [Frà Benedetto, *Cedrus Libani*, cap. ix. Cf. P. Villari, *Life and Times of Savonarola*, iv, cap. viii.]

The answer was an unconscious satire on the weathercock constitution of the State—"It would not be safe, for any one of the frequent changes of government at Florence might result in his liberation".[1] A man must be killed at once, because two months hence he might be the people's hero.

One of the most pitiful features of the tragedy is the greatness of the man when compared with the littleness of all around him. It has often been said that the French Revolution can boast of no single man of any greatness with the possible exception of Mirabeau. Certainly the Florentine republican experiment was fruitful of nothing but littleness. From the first, it was noted, small men were chosen for the Signoria, because the people wished it so. The people rejoiced at the death of Piero Capponi, who had withstood the French king and died fighting against the Pisans, because he had some sign of greatness. The only other good republican fighting man, Giacomini, was allowed to die in poverty and neglect. Here and there a clever lawyer such as Guidantonio Vespucci, a citizen of piety and impartiality such as Gian Battista Ridolfi, or a rough-handed party leader like Valori, raise their heads a little above the crowd, but what the people wanted were *spicciolati*, nonentities, and it was what they got. But this was nothing new: it was inevitable that in the condition of perpetual strife, when the victory of one party meant the exile or death of all the leading members of the other, Florence must lose one after another all the men of spirit among her citizens.

It was thought that Savonarola had been the one cause of dissension, and that with his removal peace would return. So it had been thought when in 1302 Dante was banished and the Whites expelled. But what was the actual result? In Savonarola's revivalist movement there had, it may be confessed, been an element of exaggeration, and a measure of reaction must always follow when its author disappears. But now the official government had deliberately turned the city back to sin, and that mainly at the bidding of the chief sinners, the *Compagnacci*. Their licence now was such as

---

[1] [P. Burlamacchi, *Vita di Girolamo Savonarola*, p. 161 (Lucca, 1761).]

had never been known before; to lust and play they added the wildest sacrilege, chasing a tortured horse round the Cathedral, masquerading as women in S. Maria Novella, stinking the congregation out of the Annunziata. And none were punished. The chronicler Parenti,[1] once a zealous adherent and afterwards one of Savonarola's judges, continues this account: "There was little good to be seen and less to be hoped for. Everyone confessed that the city was in such disorder that it could scarce be worse. There was no reverence for any citizen whatever—magistrates were not obeyed, justice was not administered—almost every Signoria brought a change of government. Nothing was secure, everything unstable and dissolving. It seemed that only God could lay his hands upon us and save us from our peril, since we by our own deeds were heading straight for ruin." Florence was not heading for ruin but for despotism. The troubles which followed Dante's exile culminated in disgraceful submission to a foreign military adventurer, the Duke of Athens. After Savonarola's death it was soon certain that Florence could only find peace by the restoration of the one native family which, among all those who jostled for power, was able to secure and hold it. It was the people, whose cause Dante had championed, who banished him: it was the tyrants whom he had denounced who gave him welcome and an honoured grave. It was Savonarola's own republic, his own creation, his chosen people, which tore him from the convent which the Medici had founded and protected, and threw his ashes to the Arno. And all this because, as Dante wrote, the Florentines had justice always on their lips and nowhere else, because those who talk best about liberty are usually those least fitted to enjoy it, because when the fairy godmother bestowed upon the city her generous gifts, and above all the love of liberty, she withheld the art of discipline, without which the tree of liberty bears only Dead Sea fruit.

[1] [P. Parenti, *Storia fiorentina*, MS. Biblioteca Nazionale Florence.]

VI

MONTAGUES AND CAPULETS [1]

BURKE vowed that he would sooner sleep in the southern corner of a little country churchyard than in the family vault of all the Capulets. In this he showed his usual good sense. Had his bones lain with all the Capulets, they would have been singularly scattered, whilst the Capulets' only vault was often that of heaven, freezing or scorching the corpses of stricken fugitives. Burke was no medievalist, and probably no fact in medieval history has been so universally accepted as that Montagues and Capulets were two noble houses of Verona. Yet this is not a fact, nor even a mere fiction, but a falsity. The Capulets were not a house, and in Verona they had neither sac nor soc. For all this they were real people with a real history, and their home, when they had one, was Cremona. This is why the historian must condemn the legend as a falsity, and not condone it as a fable. The popular belief can, indeed, claim plenty of prescription, for history and literature have been at disaccord for more than five hundred years, almost since Dante, at once historian and man of letters, inveighed against the German Albert:

> Vieni a veder Montecchi e Cappelletti,
> Monaldi e Filippeschi, uom senza cura,
> Color già tristi e questi con sospetti.
> *Purg.* vi, 106-108.

The long duration of the schism makes it of interest to ascertain the point of time at which the two Muses parted company, and it may be convenient if I retrace the steps of my own investigations. While reading early Veronese history without any knowledge of Dante's commentators, and with-

[1] [Communicated to the Oxford Dante Society, November 1902. Reprinted from *The Pilot*, May 16 and June 27, 1903.]

out, for the moment, much thought of himself, I became aware that no mention of Cappelletti ever occurred, whereas references to the Montecchi were frequent. The latter were, in fact, the leaders at Verona of the faction which may roughly be classed as Ghibelline. Their Guelfic opponents are always dubbed the *Pars Comitum*, the party, that is, of the famous Counts of San Bonifazio, the remnants of whose stronghold may be seen half-way between Verona and Vicenza in the state of ruin to which Eccelino da Romano brought it. Nearer to Vicenza is the village of Montecchio or Monticoli, the original home of the Montecchi, although they had become also a great urban family, fighting the party of the Counts for the municipal loaves and fishes which the dominant faction could multiply to its own profit and pleasure.

Although both under Eccelino and his successors of the house of Scala the Ghibellines had the upper hand at Verona, the Montecchi seem to have dwindled by Dante's time. One branch, indeed, was still of sufficient importance to be exiled by Dante's patron, Can Grande, a few years after the poet's death. This family retired to Udine in the Friuli—of which a few words hereafter. Thus, then, the Montagues make their exits and their entrances on the stage of Verona, but of the Capulets there is never a glimpse, not even in the *coulisses*. It is practically impossible that the name of any leading family should remain without mention in the annals of a great city in Dante's age. There are lists of proscribed or returning exiles, lists of members of Councils and Committees, lists of witnesses to public treaties or private contracts. Every Lombard or Tuscan city appointed annually or half-yearly a foreign *podestà* as chief magistrate, and this always from the noble families of another town. Of such magistrates tables still exist for several cities, while the various chronicles usually give their names under the year of their office. There are, above all, two early schedules of the best old families of Verona, some thirty in all, to Dante's age and upwards. Yet nowhere is the house of Capulet to be found. It is true that a laborious student unearthed the will of a Cappello, dated 1427, whose subsequent genealogy could boast three Giulias.

But what Italian family could not do as much? At all events it seems impossible that the Cappelletti should have been a Veronese family of such importance that Dante should match them with the famous Montecchi.

From Veronese history I happened to pass to the annals of Parma and Piacenza, and first came upon the Capulets in the prince of medieval gossip, Salimbene. Enumerating the factions by which Italian cities were divided, he writes that in Cremona the Church party were called Cappellini or Cappelletti, and the Imperialists Barbarasi.[1] Here, then, the explanation seemed to lie. It is well known that Ghibellines and Guelfs took pride in distinguishing themselves from their opponents by peculiarities in gait, in their manners at table, in their clothes, in the dressing of their hair, just as Oxford and Cambridge men were once distinguishable by their respective methods of arriving at the interior of an egg. Cappelletti was the nickname for the long-haired party, the Guelfs of Cremona, and Barbarasi for the short-haired Imperialists, "the shavers". Such nicknames were usual. At Parma, for instance, Ghibellines were called Malafucini, "jerry-built".

There was, however, just a possibility that the Capulets might also be a Cremonese family, and so far therefore in line with the Montagues. I could find none such sufficiently important to christen a party. There was, indeed, a family named Cappellini, but only one member, Leonardo, was of any dignity, being one of the Consuls in 1212, and in 1217 a member of the Lesser Council. A Martino appears shortly afterwards, but the only member mentioned within measurable distance of Dante's age was Abramino, who held the modest post of notary to the Customs. Such are the sole references to a family name in the hundreds of Cremonese documents collected by Astigiano. Nor in the lists of Cremonese *podestà* in other towns does the name appear, whereas those of the really leading families, the Doara, the Sommi, the Cavalcabò, occur repeatedly. On the other hand there are frequent references to the Cappelletti as a Cremonese

---

[1] [*Cronica*, p. 371, ed. O. Holder-Egger, *Mon. Ger. Hist.* vol. xxxii.]

political party. The Annals of Piacenza, for instance, relate
that in 1250 the Marquis Pellavicino, being *podestà* of
Cremona, and seeing the Cappelletti likely to get the upper
hand, banished thirty of them.[1] In 1266 the same annals
mention their restoration, but in 1277 a quarrel arose between them and Bosio da Doara, chief of the Barbarasi. A
document printed by Astigiano proves that in 1311 the
Cappelletti were in power, but the Ghibellines were re-
instated, the former being headed by the house of Cavalcabò,
while the latter, now called Tronca-ciuffi, "clip-locks" or
"round heads", by that of Doara. In conclusion, the statutes
of 1313 speak of the faction officially as the Pars Capella-
torum.[2]

Thus, then, when Dante wrote, there was no family of
Cappelletti of any distinction in either Verona or Cremona,
whereas it was a party nickname denoting the Guelfic half
of a prominent Lombard city, a name which must have been
as familiar to Dante as to Salimbene. In the three lines which
summarise the factions of Italy he could not possibly have
applied this notorious party name to some undistinguished
household. Dante, be it observed, never said that the Cappelletti were a family, nor that they were Veronese. The two
errors are assumptions deduced from the undoubted fact that
the Monaldi and Filippeschi were two family parties, whom
Giovanni Villani describes as fighting for supremacy in
Orvieto when the Emperor Henry VII was on the march to
Rome in 1312.[3] Because both these were families belonging
to a single city, and because the Montecchi were a family
connected with Verona, therefore, it has been concluded,
the Cappelletti were a family and Verona was their home.
Dante, no doubt, chose the two names as representing a
Ghibelline and a Guelfic party, each under a cloud owing to
political faction, though the moment of which he writes is
far from clear. He is not blameless, for his clumsiness led to

[1] [*Annales Placentini Gibelini*, 1154–1284, ed. Pertz, *Mon. Ger. Hist.*
vol. xviii.]
[2] [L. Astigiano, *Codex diplomaticus Cremonae*, vol. ii, No. 170.]
[3] [*Historie*, ix, cap. xxxix.]

error; he ought to have made his two pairs balance. It is fair
to remember that family names early became nicknames,
denoting, not only the members of a house, but the whole
political party which clustered round it. Frequently the use
of the name survived the importance of the family; thus
the notorious factions of Pistoia were called Panciatichi and
Cancellieri long after these two families had sunk to poverty
and insignificance. So, too, the Montecchi were rather a
party than a family. It is possible to be a Gladstonian without
being a son or nephew or third cousin of the lost Liberal
leader. Nevertheless, a Liberal Unionist poet describing—
after Dante—the sorry state alike of Jingoes and Gladstonians
might easily mislead posterity, and future commentators
might explain either that Gladstonian was an abusive nickname or that Jingo was the eponymous hero of a once
mighty party. To the latter belief the obscurity of the facts
of Jingo's life would contribute; as a small boy I once asked
the village schoolmaster who Jingo was. "I don't rightly
know, sir," was the reply, "but I've every reason to believe
he was a very wicked man."

Dante, then, did not sin against historic truth, but his
literary workmanship was clumsy; with all his merit he had
not the finish of—let us say—Mr. Austin Dobson.

If Dante was not directly responsible for the false parentage ascribed to the impossibly existent Juliet, who was the
culprit? In the hope of detecting him I turned to the literary
genealogy of the Capulet legend, working backwards from
the comparatively known to the totally—to me—unknown.
Shakespeare and the earlier Elizabethans, together with Lope
de Vega, all probably borrowed the story from Bandello,
whose novels were published in 1554. Just before this date
the tale was told in *ottava rima* under the pseudonym of
"Clizia, dama Veronese". More than a quarter of a century
earlier Luigi da Porto, of Vicenza, had written his novel,
La Giuletta or *Giuletta e Romeo*.[1] The date of its composition
is not certain, but he died, comparatively young, in 1529.

---

[1] [Cf. *Lettere storiche*, ed. Bressan (Florence, 1857), which contains in
appendix "La celebre novella di Giulietta e Romeo".]

On him it is worth while to linger, for he first presented the story in its quite modern shape, though Shakespeare transfused it with most of its tenderness and all its humour. At all events Da Porto gave to the legend its local habitation and its name, the historical setting, that is, which is the source of all deception. The tale itself may have been borrowed from Masuccio, some half-century further back, who gives a Sienese drop-scene to the drama. In its crude form it was probably a tragical Joe Miller, easily adapting itself to unfortunate domestic incidents in any city of faction-riven Italy.

Luigi da Porto was a young noble of Vicenza, who must have known Verona almost as well as his own city. He confesses to frequently boating on Lake Garda, which is beyond Verona, and during the War of Cambrai he fought over every inch of the ground between Vicenza and the ruins of San Bonifazio. Familiar to him were the twin castles on the hillside, which tradition converts into the country residences of Montagues and Capulets. He was no mere novelist. His letters are the best authority for the war of 1509, but he is an historian with a literary vein, determining from the first to utilise his military experiences for "copy". He was, moreover, and this is important, an enthusiastic Dantist. In this he showed much literary independence, for Dante was not in fashion at that moment, and least of all in Da Porto's own environment. Bembo, his very particular friend, was then and there the autocrat of literary criticism, and Bembo was a staunch pro-Petrarchist, if not a bitter anti-Dantist. Nevertheless his youthful admirer quotes *il gran Dante* at least thrice, while pebbles from the *Commedia* are frequently found imbedded in the conglomerate of his letters. As Dante was poet and historian, so was Da Porto, to compare small—not very small—men with great, historian and novelist. The novelist peeps out of his professedly historical letters, while he seems forced to give to his one formal novel a plausible historical setting.

During a campaign in the Friuli Da Porto was dangerously wounded in the throat by a German, and in the heart by a lady. The former thrust incapacitated him for service, the latter reduced him to sentimental literature, for his was a true passion, and she married another, as, indeed, she usually does. In an artistic introduction to his novel Da Porto ascribes the tale to his archer Pellegrino, a Veronese—like all his countrymen, a famous *raconteur*, and in spite of his fifty years always in love, and making of love his favourite theme. While the young soldier was moodily riding ahead of three troopers from Gradisca to Udine, brooding on the cruel fair, the archer drew up to him, and, on the plea that those give the best advice who cannot follow it, warned his captain of the mournful fate to which love leads its prisoners. Then to allay the tedium of the war-scorched road, he told him of the two noble lovers of Verona, guided by love to a piteous death. On this follows the well-known tragedy, in the setting of which one or two small points are noticeable. Reference is made in the opening to the descent of Da Porto's courteous friends the Monticoli of Udine from the Montecchi of Verona, which may well have drawn the novelist's attention to the line of his favourite poet which he made his text. Again, a very precise date is given to the tale, for it is ascribed to the reign of Bartolomeo della Scala, which only lasted from 1301 to 1304. Yet, for the Dantist this short-lived and not distinguished lord had a special significance, for early commentators claimed him as the *gran Lombardo* of Cacciaguida's prophecy and the first host of Dante at Verona.

Having once resolved to transfer Masuccio's story from Siena to Verona, and having chosen Dante's line as his text, Da Porto would turn for information to one or more of the well-known commentaries on the *Commedia*. Of these several place both Capulets and Montagues at Cremona. Thus Buti, towards the end of the fourteenth century, wrote: "These were two parties, which lived in Lombardy at Cremona, and whose hostilities reduced them to ruin. The Monaldi and Filippeschi were two parties in the March, that is in Ancona, which in Dante's day lived in suspicion of each other."[1] Buti

---

[1] [Francesco da Buti, *Commento sopra la Divina Comedia*, vol. ii, p. 138 (Pisa, 1858–62).]

and the so-called Ottimo do but repeat these statements from the commentary of Jacopo della Lana, written only a few years after Dante's death. The published text both of the Ottimo and of Jacopo gives not Cremona but Verona, the editors in each case explaining in a note that Cremona, the reading of all the MSS., is an obvious error. So case-hardened had become the belief that both Montagues and Capulets were Veronese! This group of commentators then was right as to the Capulets, but wrong as to everything else, unless it is possible to accept the March of Ancona as meaning the Papal States in contradistinction to Lombardy. These, however, were not Da Porto's sources. He turned perhaps to Landino, perhaps direct to Benvenuto da Imola or the Anonymo Fiorentino, who wrote nearly a century earlier, at the close of the *trecento*. Benvenuto places the Monaldi and Filippeschi at Civita Vecchia, but this is a medieval synonym for the Orvieto (*urbs vetus*) of Landino. On the point at issue here are Benvenuto's words: "Istae fuerint duae clarae familiae Veronae . . . quae habuerunt diu bellum cum alia nobilissima familia, scilicet cum comitibus de Sancto Bonifacio. Nam Monticuli comites cum favore Eccelini de Romano ejecerunt Azonem II, marchionem estensem, rectorem illius civitatis. Sed ipse in manu forti cum Comite Huberto Sancti Bonifacii, Monticulis acie debellatis, reintravit Veronam, ubi finem vitae feliciter terminavit."[1] Benvenuto knew this much, that the rival faction to the Montecchi were the Counts of San Bonifazio. He therefore grouped the Cappelletti with the Montecchi as belonging to the same Ghibelline party and involved in the same ruin. He is wrong as to the Cappelletti, and wrong in ascribing the downfall of the Montecchi to the events related, for these occurred just a century before Dante wrote, and after them the Montecchi returned in triumph with the notorious Eccelino, whom Benvenuto probably confused with his father, as also their respective enemies, the earlier and the later Azzo d' Este. In Benvenuto's story there is a distinct reminiscence of the tragedy

---

[1] [Benvenuti de Rambaldis de Imola, *Commentum super Dantis Aldigherii Comoediam*, vol. iii, p. 185 (Florence, 1887).]

named *Ecerinis* by the Paduan historian-poet Mussato, to which in other connexions he twice refers, and on which an elaborate commentary had been written by the Bolognese Guizzardo, familiar no doubt to the Bolognese professor Benvenuto. Mussato had deliberately for the purposes of the great Lombard tragedy fused the two Eccelini and the two Marquises of Este, and had left the impression that the Montecchi fell on the overthrow of their tyrant ally. Mussato's authorities would naturally be the Vicentine historian Gerardus Maurisius, the Paduan Rolandinus, and the *Chronicon Monachi Patavini*. Benvenuto, perhaps, read the latter, for otherwise he would have scarcely known that Azzo d' Este II did actually rule in Verona until his death in that very town. The tale was flattering to the Court of Ferrara in which, after trouble at Bologna, Benvenuto found a refuge.

Benvenuto, as far as I can judge, first established the Capulets at Verona, but makes no mention of their quarrel with the Montagues. For Da Porto this quarrel is essential, but his obligation to Benvenuto seems certain from the archer's statement that he had read in old chronicles that the two families united expelled Azzo from Verona, but that he afterwards returned by favour of the San Bonifazi. The archer thus perpetuated the historical blunders and confusions of Benvenuto. Is it just possible that Da Porto also harked back to the ancient chronicles, and that Bartholomaeus de Palatio, whom Gerardus Maurisius describes as *podestà* of Verona in those early troubles, was the original of Bartolomeo della Scala of the novel, the good Prince Escalus of Shakespeare?

In this condition I must leave the puzzle

> Till we can clear these ambiguities,
> And know their head, their spring and true descent.

The strange thing is that one commentator was in every particular correct, and yet none of his earlier or later brethren have followed him. This is none less than Dante's own son Pietro, who tells a very different tale to them: "From this [*i.e.* from the Emperor Albert's neglect] it followed that in Verona arose the party of the Montecchi and the party of the

Counts, in Cremona the Cappelletti and Tronca-ciuffi, in Orvieto the party of the Monaldi and the Filippeschi".[1] The other commentators above mentioned hailed from Tuscany or Bologna and its neighbourhood. But on a matter of Veronese history it was most improbable that Pietro di Dante should be wrong, for Verona was his home, he was a member of the Greater Council and Vicar of the College of Judges. He had, therefore, every means of knowing the story of the chief Veronese families. That Pietro was right makes it the more certain that Dante was not wrong; the poet's character for historical accuracy is cleared at the expense of his artistic workmanship. The moral is a warning to historians that by clumsiness of expression they may lead five centuries of their weaker literary brethren into grievous error, for error it is to give a setting, not merely imaginary but historically false, to a tale that professes to be a history. Sceptical tourists have long passed Juliet's house and Juliet's tomb tearless and unmoved. Now they have the further solace that, though Romeo may well have lived and died, his Juliet was born not, neither did she die. The impatient reader may testily exclaim with Escalus, "A plague o' both your houses". Not so the historian Dryasdust who, sitting in judgement on the numerous offenders, will borrow the prince's more judicial phrase, "Some shall be punish'd and some pardon'd". Benvenuto will suffer the extreme penalty of whatever the law may be. The jurymen of letters will doubtless recommend to mercy Shakespeare and Bandello, but shall I plead in vain for love-lorn Da Porto and his amorous archer? for, after all,

> At lovers' perjuries,
> They say, Jove laughs.

[1] [Pietro Alighieri, *Super Dantis ipsius genitoris comoediam commentarium* (Florence, 1845), p. 332.]

* Mercutio. The historian also may err --

PART II

OTHER ITALIAN STUDIES

VII

HISTORY AND ART IN THE QUATTROCENTO [1]

MEDIEVAL pictorial art was, in the well-worn phrase, the handmaid of religion. The phrase is true enough of the art of Duccio, Cimabue and Giotto; it is true in the main, at a much later date, of Frà Angelico. But already in his day art was looking wistfully towards the temple door or the cloister gate. She was feeling her once willing work monotonous, was yearning for more liberty in secular, even in domestic, service. Henceforth, until the end of the fifteenth century and a little later, she served two mistresses, but the freshest of her work was perhaps given to the newer. Thus then she became the servant, the lady-help, if you will, of the Muse of History.

Centuries are even less satisfactory than reigns as lines of demarcation. A reign's beginning, or its end, may really cause or emphasise a change in national literature or art, whereas there is no personality in a year. Few artists have been, as was Cellini, considerately born in the first year of a century, and few have died in the last year. The trecento overlaps the quattrocento, and that, in compensation, poaches upon its successor. Masolino and Masaccio have been called the last of the Giotteschi, and the pioneers of the quattrocento. In their subjects and their feeling towards them they were indeed successors of Giotto, but in science they might claim to be the first modernists, the founders of the new scientific school. Frà Angelico is deliberately trecentist in his devoted service to religion, but he is a realist in his landscape and his study of the most modern Renaissance architecture, as is shown, for instance, in the Preaching of S. Stephen. Perugino, whose character was as commercial as that of Angelico was spiritual, retained to the end, except in his landscape, the traditional

[1] [Annual Italian Lecture, read before the British Academy, May 31, 1923. Reprinted from *Proceedings of the British Academy*, vol. x.]

N

conventions of the religious painters. There were, indeed, few of the quattrocentists who could wholly break away from these, because then and long after there was in churches and monasteries a constant conservative demand. At the other end several unquestioned quattrocentists lived well into the cinquecento, while Leonardo and Michelangelo did no insignificant part of their work in its predecessor. Yet it is impossible not to feel that a strong difference exists, and it may be worth while to search for some guiding dates or personalities. Pintoricchio and Filippino Lippi have been, I think, justly called the last of the quattrocentists, while in political history there were events which did have a real influence upon the fortunes of art. The captivity of Ludovico Sforza in 1500 deprived Italy of one of her chief patrons. This was the more decisive because the death of Lorenzo de' Medici had led to the expulsion of his family in 1494 and to the predominance of Savonarola, who had denounced the secularisation of art, and had drawn Botticelli, Lorenzo di Credi and Frà Bartolommeo into the exclusive service of religion. Another determining factor was the accession of Julius II in 1503, because this involved the destruction of quattrocento masterpieces in favour of Rafael and Michelangelo.

In no other century has the connexion between Italian art and contemporary history been quite so close. This was the result of a change of feeling, almost unconscious, of more settled political conditions, of a higher standard of comfort or luxury. The home was becoming the rival of the Church, and, indeed, within the Church the family chapel was little more than an annexe of the home. This new direction is often attributed to the individualism of the Renaissance. I should ascribe it rather to the secularism, of which the political causes were more potent than the personal, and which gave free play to the pride of family and state, so marked a feature of Italian life.

The second half of the fifteenth century was a time of comparative peace. Even the invasion of Charles VIII, in 1494, hardly affected artistic life in general. The very divisions of Italy, so fatal to its future, were stimulants for its art. The

monarchies of Naples and Milan, the elective rulers of the
Papacy and Venice, the personal predominance of the
Medici, found imitation, or even initiative, in the lesser
dynasties of Ferrara and Mantua, Urbino and Rimini. All
these were closely associated with each other, and vied in
architecture, sculpture and painting as they did in policy. The
smaller republic of Siena had its own important school, while
cities once free but now absorbed, such as Verona, Vicenza
and Brescia, preserved their independent schools of art. Never
had artists so wide a range of service; never was the association between artists and rulers, whether personal or communal, so intimate. Great works of art were intensely personal; each succeeding Pope and Doge must have his portrait
and his monument. The chief buildings all recall important
personalities, the Certosa of Pavia, just before our century,
that of Gian Galeazzo Visconti; the splendid hospital of
Milan that of Francesco Sforza; the decoration of its castle
Ludovico Moro; the Riccardi Palace testifies to the civic
modesty of the Medici; the Triumphal Arch at Naples to the
bravado of Alfonso the Magnanimous; Sixtus IV has left his
name to the Sistine Chapel; Pius II to a sanctuary of Renaissance architecture, the tiny city of Pienza, complete with
its cathedral, its family palace of the Piccolomini, its town
hall and loggia, its graceful public well; even to Alexander VI
we have to render gratitude for the Borgia Apartments. Unquestionably humanity, individual or corporate, was becoming more interesting to itself, and artists, who, after all, were
tradesmen, were keen to encourage and supply the new
demand.

This interest in humanity and its immediate material
atmosphere may, on its artistic side, be styled realism, but
to it classicism is sometimes so closely related as to be almost
interchangeable, the reason being that the artists of the early
quattrocento rediscovered nature through the medium of
such classical masterpieces as were known to them. Antiques
were frequently brought to light, just as were the classical
MSS. which were revolutionising letters. These discoveries,
it is true, were as yet confined to sculpture, but they speedily

had influence on painting. Masolino and Masaccio are in a manner the counterparts of Poggio Bracciolini and Leonardo Bruni. Fortunately for the historian classicism and realism, though connected, are not conterminous; had they so been, the art of the fifteenth century would have been as uninstructive to him as is much of the corresponding Latinist literature, then so highly prized. The artists, with few exceptions, lagged behind the humanists; their classicism was nearly half a century in arrear; few of them were so highly educated as to have an intimate knowledge of classical history or archaeology. From the classical models they learnt much in technique and acquired a wider range of subjects, but they retained much of the simplicity of the primitives; they were not so noticeably affected by the artificiality of the Renaissance as were the writers. As soon as classical knowledge filtered through to their educational level, it might make painting as artificial in point of subject matter as it had made literature in point of style. There was an early presage of this impending loss to the historians in the work of Mantegna. He had to paint to order several subjects of absolutely contemporary life, and here he furnishes illustrations most valuable for my purpose. His own bent, however, was towards an exaggerated classicism. He was himself an enthusiastic collector of antiques; he would overload sacred subjects with classical detail. Consequently, in the works which he loved best, such as the Triumphs of Caesar or of Scipio, he interests the historian only as showing the stage which a knowledge of antiquity had reached. Very different are the Petrarchesque *Trionfi* of Filippino Lippi and others, which do, indeed, idealise, but modern Italian rather than old Latin life.

Apart from classicism the introduction even of realism might result in diverting art from contemporary history. The study of the nude would in time inevitably loosen their connexion, for the nude belongs to all nations and to all centuries. Its worship would dwarf, limit or entirely alter the range of subjects. Thus, even in religious pictures, the Marriage of the Virgin and the Visitation of the Magi, so full of opportunities for illustrative art, would wane in popularity before Flagellations, Depositions, S. Sebastians and the limb-twisting horrors of hell. The foremost example of this both in time and talent is the devotion of Signorelli to the undraped human figure, which allies him more closely to his successors than to his contemporaries.

The study of drapery for its own sake would have the same tendency as that of undrapery, since the short jackets and tunics and long, tight stockings of contemporary life, however picturesque to the historical eye, did not lend themselves to the treatment of drapery finely conceived as a work of art. This is true also of the well-fitting bodices and stiff, upstanding skirts of brocade, which Ghirlandaio exhibits in his fashion plates on Florentine church walls, to the despair of modern dressmakers and the delight of modern historians of both sexes. The Philistine historian can have no lively interest in the graceful folds by which Rafael, Correggio or Andrea del Sarto represent the traditional conventions of religious costumes.

There was, however, a form of realism of which quattrocento art fortunately became enamoured; the realism of contemporary life in all its aspects; men, women, children and animals, natural scenery and flowers, armour and dress, architecture and furniture. A distinguished critic has complained that the fault of Florentine artists from Uccello to Michelangelo was a tendency to illustration; for the historian that is just their virtue. But this fault or virtue is quite as prominent in the Venetians or the Umbrians, in Gentile Bellini and Carpaccio, in Gentile da Fabriano and Pintoricchio. It is a question rather of period than of province. The quattrocento was the hey-day of Italy. In its latter half, at all events, she could enjoy herself, and, what is more, be proud of herself— of her civilisation, her wealth, her independence. A very few years later the barbarian had trampled pride and pleasure underfoot; there could be little joy in the illustration of contemporary life. Art must fall back on the glories of antiquity, the consolations of religion, or absorb herself in the elaboration of technique, or the presentation of mere physical beauty.

In Venice alone does this illustration continue almost without a check down to Veronese and Tintoretto, because Venice, except for her short, sharp seven years' war from 1509 to 1516, was almost untouched by the cataclysm of barbarian invasion. Venice had certainly a full half-century more of self-esteem.

It would be wrong to regard quattrocento art as being illustrative of external events and material life alone. The literary taste, the poetic fancy, the theological doctrines, all find expression therein. We should not understand the more poetic side of the Medicean age without the Spring and the Venus of Botticelli, while his Assumption of the Virgin, if, as I still believe, his it is, gives an insight into its doctrinal fancies, and the embrace of the three friars with the angels in the Nativity illustrates the highly strung mystical phase not only of his own later days under Savonarola's influence, but of the tarnished years of Italy's golden age. Next in importance, perhaps, would come Piero di Cosimo with his romantic, unclassical rendering of classical legend, his Death of Procris and his Hylas, his idealisation of Tuscan country life, his attempts to peer into the secrets of nature, of animal and plant life. It is enough, however, to call attention to this aspect of illustrative art, for my immediate purpose is its relation to history proper, and the external features of social life.

The art of the fifteenth century is a reflection of its history in several different ways, and, as an attempt to make this clearer, I am classifying the subject under five heads, though these several heads are apt to knock against each other. These are illustrations of (1) actual historical events, (2) actual family groups, professing to be such, (3) real individuals or groups appearing as characters in religious pictures, (4) individual portraits, (5) actual political or social life represented in religious, classical or legendary subjects. The surviving pictures of actual historical events are not so very numerous, though probably more so than is often imagined, for public buildings have not been so carefully ransacked for their frescoes as have the churches. Some have been destroyed by fire, as the pictures of Gentile Bellini and others in the great hall of the Doge's Palace in 1577. These, it is true, represented scenes in early Venetian history, but Gentile's other pictures prove that they would have been true to quattrocento life, as, indeed, is evident from the solitary sketch which still exists. At Rome Julius II sacrificed the frescoes of Signorelli and Bramantino or Melozzo to make room for those of Rafael. A yet more grievous loss for the historian was that of Pintoricchio's work in the garden house of S. Angelo, relating to the meeting between Charles VIII and Alexander VI, and giving a large number of portraits of the chief participants in the fateful invasion of 1494. Ferrara once possessed frescoes of the council at which Eugenius IV met the Greek Emperor and the Patriarch. These have been destroyed, but the visit has left many traces of Oriental magnificence, especially in remarkable headgear. Examples of this are Frà Angelico's picture of S. Cosmas and S. Damianus pleading before Lysias, and, above all, the Finding of the True Cross, painted by Piero della Francesca at Arezzo. At Belluno a series of historical pictures were destroyed in the last century by a town council. Many others painted in the open or in half-open loggias have suffered from exposure. Such has been the fate of a fresco in the castle of Bracciano showing the welcome given to its Orsini master on his return from a victorious campaign. The courtyard of the *condottiere* Colleone's castle of Malpaga near Bergamo is surrounded by similar pictures. These, indeed, were the work of Romanino, who is rather a cinquecento than a quattrocento artist, but faithfully represent incidents in the general's life, especially the visit of Christian I of Denmark. Here are seen not only Colleone himself and the king with the long white beard, which attracted much attention in clean-shaven Italy, but a view of Italian scenery, so very different then from now, and of a day's hunting and fowling in the golden times. Siena has been particularly fortunate in preserving treasures of this kind. The Piccolomini Library has the series setting forth the whole life of Aeneas Sylvius, from his leaving Siena for the Council of Bâle to his death at Ancona, where the sick Pope had wearily waited for the Venetian fleet on which he was to have shipped for the Crusade. His reception by James of

Scotland, his coronation as poet by the Emperor Frederick III, the Emperor's betrothal to his Portuguese bride, his own accession to the Papacy, the futile Diet of Mantua, which wrecked his Crusading hopes, all form, with other incidents, a pictorial biography which can scarcely have its equal. These paintings again are not quite contemporary, for they were a commission to Pintoricchio from the Pope's nephew, Pius III, in 1502, thirty-eight years after his uncle's death. Absolutely contemporary is the Defeat of the Florentines at Poggibonsi in 1479, a joint work of Giovanni di Cristoforo and Francesco d' Andrea (1480). Here the Dukes of Calabria and Urbino are charging the Florentines, whose general, Costanzo Sforza, is in full flight, while along the ridge run the light-armed infantry, making for the Florentine tents. In the Pitti Palace is an allegorical picture by Botticelli of Pallas, wreathed with olive branches, taming a centaur.[1] This is believed to celebrate Lorenzo de' Medici's return from his hazardous visit to Naples which led to a reconciliation, and to signify the triumph of civilisation and peace over anarchy and war. Of an earlier date, 1455, is a mystical treatment by Sano di Pietro of a military event, the protection of Siena from Piccinino's attack by the agency of Calixtus III. Beneath the figure of the Borgia Pope is seen the city, with mules laden with grain sent by him approaching its walls.

Of high importance are three out of four battle scenes by Uccello, one of which is in the National Gallery, another in the Louvre, and a third in the Uffizi. These portray a real Italian battle, either that of S. Egidio or another, in real Italian landscape, full of spirit and truth in spite of the rocking-horse action of the chargers, one of which has turned turtle. Here are seen the elaborate contemporary costumes, the clumsy, brittle, painted lances, criticised at a later date by Commines, and the tendency to run away to fight another day. There is far more force in these battle pictures than in the representation in the *Mer des Histoires* of Charles VIII's victory over Venetians and Milanese at Fornovo in 1495. On the other hand it is profitable to compare them with a cavalry

[1] [Now in the Uffizi.]

skirmish in the National Gallery by an unknown artist of the early sixteenth century. The atmosphere of art has completely changed; no battle like this was ever fought in fifteenth-century Italy. The artistic essentials have become the human and equine figure, the drapery and armour, and for subject the mêlée of ideal classical heroes. A series of illustrations of combined military and naval operations exists in the MS. of Basinio Parmense's *Hesperides and Argonauts*. This celebrates the exploits of Sigismondo Malatesta, his troop of horse marching against Alfonso of Naples, the revictualling of the Neapolitan camp by galleys, the capitulation of Piombino, and Sigismondo's triumphal entrance into Rimini, the latter being celebrated by a horse-race, the course leading, as was usual, up to and through the city gates.

Interspersed with military events are diplomatic, religious and pestilential incidents. A very interesting contemporary scene is the reception of a Venetian ambassador at Cairo, by Gentile Bellini, so exactly true to life that, in its care for detail, it is a document of Egyptian history of the highest value. Less striking, but of local interest, is the entrance of Charles VIII's embassy to Siena in 1496, illuminated on the cover of one of the Sienese Exchequer Books. At Siena, indeed, history must be looked for underfoot as well as on the walls, for the Emperor Sigismund's visit to the city is immortalised on the Cathedral pavement among other narrative *graffiti*. Sigismund's head indeed is not his own, for, owing to forgetfulness of his features, it was copied from that of a Sienese gentleman who was traditionally believed to have resembled him. Siena also provides two pictures by Sano di Pietro of S. Bernardino's famous revivalist sermons, one of which inspired Aeneas Sylvius with the somewhat transitory resolution to don the cowl. The Taylor Gallery has a very similar picture of a Dominican preaching,[1] and an engraving, virtually contemporary, well displays the impassioned action of Savonarola. Strictly historical is the fresco by Francesco di Vito of Francesco Sforza opening his magnificent hospital at Milan with Pius II's Bull of Foundation.

---

[1] [By Domenico Morone, Ashmolean Museum, Oxford.]

Hospitals did not avert plagues, as Milan herself was to testify by that of 1630, made famous by Manzoni's *Promessi Sposi*. The large *lazzarretto* built to supplement the hospital has only been destroyed in quite recent times. On this subject Dr. Raymond Crawfurd's book, *Plague and Pestilence*, shows the importance of the quattrocento in this long and doleful story. The striking picture in S. Pietro in Vincoli at Rome, attributed to the Pollaiuoli, represents indeed the plague of 680 in a fifteenth-century setting, but other pictures or banners are contemporary historical documents. Foremost among these is Bonfigli's *Gonfalone* at Perugia, which is dated 1464, and gives a vivid picture of the town with a citizen, child and wife on horseback escaping from the gates. Another of his banners records the plague of 1486, while several are found in neighbouring towns. Sinibaldo Ibi has also left a fine example, the Madonna del Soccorso at Mentone, dated 1482. Gozzoli, too, commemorates the plague years, 1464 and 1465, by frescoes in the Collegiata and S. Francesco at S. Gimignano. The plague indeed helped to make the fortune of hagiographical art in the fifteenth and sixteenth centuries, as being responsible for the figures of S. Sebastian and S. Rocco.

Among notable family groups must be mentioned in the forefront Melozzo's picture of Sixtus IV and four of his *nipoti*, representing the grant of the keys of the Vatican to Platina. The setting is a perfect specimen of the new Renaissance architecture, just at its hey-day, while the two great pilasters which enclose the foreground are arabesqued with the holm oak and its acorns, the emblem of the Della Rovere, to be seen also on the family tombs in S. Maria del Popolo. Mantegna dropped for the moment his classical studies, and painted for the house of the Gonzaga the very naturalistic groups in the Camera de' Sposi at Mantua. The Marquis, his plain Hohenzollern wife, children and dwarf appear in all their ugliness, the pages, horses and dogs in all their beauty. Very similar is a larger and earlier series in the Schifanoia Palace at Ferrara, giving scenes from the Court life of Borso de' Este. In these the Duke renders justice or receives envoys, gives money to his dwarf, rides out hunting or watches the races of horses, donkeys, men, boys and women, the very best representation of these universal races in Italian art. These historical groups, not very common, may be said to have secularised themselves, to have broken loose from a type of religious picture usual in the century, or rather from two types. In the one, the donor and his family are professedly portraits, and they naturally enough step out of their subordinate and suppliant position in the religious picture into one of greater self-importance. Excellent examples of this type are the large and unlucky family, thirteen children and a wife, of Giovanni Bentivoglio, at Bologna, and the portraits of Ludovico Moro, Beatrice d' Este and their two sons, afterwards Dukes of Milan. A votive picture commemorating an important historical event is the Madonna della Vittoria, where the Marquis of Mantua and Isabella d' Este[1] kneel to return thanks for what was really not his victory but defeat at Fornovo by Charles VIII. Much less known is the admirable portrait of Louis XII in the little Cappella della Vittoria, built to commemorate his very real victory over Venice at Agnadello. Of a more private character is Ghirlandaio's lovely group of the Vespucci family beneath the sheltering arms of Mercy. But perhaps of more interest than all is the portrait of Alexander VI adoring the risen Saviour, by Pintoricchio, in the Borgia Apartments.

In the second type the religious subject is merely a peg for contemporary portrait groups. The Adoration of the Magi, the Marriage of the Virgin, or scenes from the Old Testament, lent themselves readily to this purpose. A brilliant specimen of the first in the Riccardi Palace is the procession of the Medici riding down a mountain path in the guise of the Three Kings, as they may often have ridden from their estates in the Mugello. Equally famous is Gozzoli's group, at Pisa, of the same family witnessing the building of the Tower

---

[1] [The kneeling woman opposite the Marquis represents S. Elizabeth, Isabella d' Este's patron saint; this venerable figure is certainly not a portrait of Isabella, who was thirty-one when the picture was painted, although it may be that of her Dominican friend the Beata Osanna. Cf. Cartwright, *Isabella d' Este*, vol. i, p. 125.]

of Babel, and Botticelli's later picture of the Adoration of the Magi, under the forms of Piero and his sons. But the most prolific source of all is Ghirlandaio. His Call of the First Disciples in the Sistine Chapel introduces the leading members of the Florentine colony at Rome. The story of S. Francis in Santa Trinità presents the ladies and gentlemen of the wealthy banking family of Sassetti. Above all, the long series of frescoes in Santa Maria Novella contains group after group of the Tornabuoni, an unequalled representation of Florentine family life. Among them are the handsome young Lorenzo Tornabuoni, destined to a shameful death, and his beautiful bride, Giovanna Albizzi, the choicest flower of the city. In all Florence there were no such perfect subjects for the painter as this young couple. Botticelli characteristically used allegorical subjects to depict them in the decoration of their own new home, the so-called Villa Lemmi, whence the pictures have been removed to the Louvre. Not content with family portraits, Ghirlandaio painted in Santa Maria a group of the four chief humanists of the day, Landino, Ficino, Pico and Gentile Becchi. Against this misuse of family chapels Savonarola thundered: "Young men go about saying of this lady and that—'here is a Virgin, here is a Magdalen, here a S. John'. Ye paint their faces in the Churches, a great profanation of things divine. Ye painters do very ill, ye fill the Churches with vain things. Think ye the Virgin should be painted as ye paint her? I tell ye, she went clothed as a beggar."[1] Pintoricchio is more excusable when he paints the lawyer Bufalini and his son as present at S. Bernardino's funeral, an excellent picture, by the way, as representing child life in all its stages, including a baby at the breast, and a *bambino* in a basket. In rural Italy within the last month I have seen two chubby children with heads projecting from the long basket carried on the back of a labouring woman. Of more historical interest is his *Disputa* of S. Catherine, where the young saint with fair long hair is believed to be Lucrezia Borgia, and the youth on horseback her bridegroom,

---

[1] [*Prediche sopra Amos e Zaccaria*, Lent 1496. Cf. Villari, *Life*, iii, cap. vi.]

Giovanni Sforza, while Andrea Paleologo, heir of the Eastern Empire, and Djem, the refugee brother of Sultan Bajazet, are among the audience. Even Frà Angelico did not shrink from portraiture, for in his fresco of S. Laurence in the Vatican, the Pope, nominally Sixtus II, is really Nicholas V, and his friend, the architect Michelozzo, is one of the figures in his Deposition. In many religious pictures bystanders are undoubtedly portraits. An example is the Marriage of the Virgin by Lorenzo di Viterbo, while comedy is touched by the brothers San Severini, who make a youthful Baptist in camel's hair preach to a congregation of fat, well-clad citizens, while an elegant young noble riding by politely touches his cap to the Saint.

This secularisation of religious art is usual in widely different schools—Tuscan, Umbrian and Venetian—but they have a common origin in Gentile da Fabriano, the teacher of Jacopo Bellini, father of Gentile and Giovanni and father-in-law of Mantegna. In Venice it was very permanent, passing through Bonifazio and the Bassani to Veronese and Tintoretto. Veronese's Marriage of Cana is merely a gorgeous Venetian banquet with all the accessories of decadent, voluptuous life. Yet it is the direct descendant of the refined and not unspiritual Adoration of the Magi by Gentile Fabriano, a century and a half before.

The development of the individual portrait is, perhaps, somewhat distinct from that of the portrait groups, which were a natural outcome of religious pictures. With extraordinary rapidity portraiture reached in the quattrocento a high stage in its history. Its sources were more than one. In the German, Netherland and French Schools it may have been the product of the art of illumination, *miniatura*, as it was called in Italy, a name which has clung to one branch of the art. In Italy, on the other hand, perhaps its chief source was the medal. This is of particular interest to my subject, because the medal is, of course, a glorified form of numismatics, and coins and medals are strictly historical documents. It is impossible to exaggerate the importance of the fifteenth century in the history of the medal. It witnessed virtually its origin, it gave birth to the greatest medallists, Pisanello, Pasti, Sperandio, Filarete, Francia and many others. Within the first half-century of the cinquecento the decline of the art began. From the advent of the first and greatest of all medallists, the Veronese Pisanello, the fashion spread rapidly. Every ruling house had its series, nor were princes alone immortalised, for there are medals of friars and doctors, even of the chief of schoolmasters, Guarino and Vittorino. Wealthy people collected medals, much as in these days they specialise in postage stamps. In 1492 Lorenzo de' Medici's collection numbered 1844 bronze medals and one of gold.

The popularity of the medal at once affected sculpture, producing a vogue for profile portraits in very low relief. Architecture became dotted with decorative medallions. Even the original della Robbia ware shows an application of this fashion. Illumination itself underwent its influence, for in Italian MSS. of the fifteenth century the faces are more frequently in profile, and in medallist form let into the arabesque framework of the page. Necessarily, then, the individual painted portrait favours profile. This may be noticed especially in those ascribed to Piero della Francesca and to Pisanello himself. They are largely, though not exclusively, followed by Botticelli, whose profiles outnumber his full-face or three-quarter portraits. Ghirlandaio is eclectic; he has two pictures in which he consciously contrasts the full-face and the profile, the one of Sassetti and his son, the other of an old man, said to be himself, and a boy's head in profile. But perhaps Ghirlandaio's schoolmistress was not fashion but nature, for the story goes that, while still a goldsmith, he spent his time in drawing the faces of those who entered the shop or passed it.

Yet another important source of the portrait was sculpture. In 1400 sculpture was far in advance of painting, and the latter borrowed its forms. This may be seen in equestrian portraits. A fresco dating from 1328 of the Sienese captain, Guido Riccio Fogliani, is sculpturesque and admirably realistic; it might well belong to a much later date. The early fifteenth century exhibits those of Hawkwood and Niccolò da

Tolentino, painted by Uccello and Castagno respectively on the walls of the Cathedral at Florence in professed imitation of sculpture. The fourteenth century had provided admirable models, the Scaliger Monuments at Verona, the figure of Bernabò Visconti at Milan, and that of Robert of Naples, earlier and still finer than this latter. To the first two decades of the quattrocento belongs the splendid figure of Ladislas of Naples. The profile type in the portraits above mentioned may have been partly due to the difficulty of foreshortening a horse, after which Uccello so gallantly strives in his battle pieces, but partly it was caused by the position of the sculptured statues as seen against a church wall, and this would apply also to kneeling figures; the architecture did not admit of strong projections.

In the fifteenth and sixteenth centuries, however, the more important monuments began to detach themselves from the lines of the architecture, becoming more individual, and therefore more obviously historical. This reaches its climax in the kneeling figure of the Emperor Maximilian in the very centre of the nave at Innsbruck, while its sides are lined by huge isolated figures of heroes of the house. The completion of the monument belongs indeed to the late sixteenth century, but the design was the Emperor's own, and is a natural development of the tendency of the fifteenth century. Sometimes sculpture left the Church for the piazza, and in so doing became yet more essentially historical, because then it was exclusively devoted to the greater heroes of the State. Such are those magnificent martial horsemen—Donatello's Gattamelata at Padua and Verrocchio's Colleone at Venice. But there was no hard and fast line, for the statues erected by the State to the Count of Pitigliano and Frà Leonardo of Prato still ride along the interior of church walls. That of the faithful, dashing knight of Malta, Frà Leonardo, is a touching illustration of the close relation between Venetian art and history. This master of light horse, after many a time beating up the enemy, was himself surprised and killed before he could don his helmet. So there he rides in full body armour, but with bare head, and his brave, kindly face turned towards us.

Another Venetian general, Roberto San Severino, is to be seen in the porch of Trent Cathedral. He was killed by the Austrians in the Adige valley, and was given stately burial by the enemy, but he is unmounted, and the Venetian banner which he grasps is sculptured flag downwards. Leonardo da Vinci's incapacity for finishing his tasks has deprived us of a statue of the greatest soldier-statesman of the century, Francesco Sforza, and only the studies for it in the Royal Library at Windsor give an idea of the loss. A spirited statue in relief is that of Anibale Bentivoglio by Niccolò dell' Arca (1458) in S. Giacomo Maggiore at Bologna.

Before the middle of the quattrocento the rage set in for portrait busts, in marble, bronze or, more frequently, clay. Masks were often taken from the face immediately after death. These terra-cotta busts were peculiarly common among great Florentine families, precisely as was the case in ancient Rome. To this custom we owe those of Niccolò Uzzano, Piero and Lorenzo de' Medici and many others. In this century oil and fresco, bronze and marble, wood, clay and wax combine in forming a range of portraiture perhaps unequalled in any other age. In the following century there are pictures and monuments in abundance; in the Venetian and Ferrarese schools the realistic tradition survived; nor are the Florentine and Umbrian without examples. But to show how great is the change it is enough to compare the *chef-d'œuvre* of the greatest Tuscan artist with the sculpture of his predecessors, the mock heroics of Michelangelo's second-rate Medici in the sacristy of San Lorenzo with the simple, dignified figures of the earlier age. In the fifteenth century we can be sure that we have the likeness. Nobody would have limned the strong, plain faces of Medici and Montefeltri, Sforza and Gonzaga, unless they had been really as ugly as we see them. It was no want of art; the portraits of those who were painted for their beauty, men or women, would satisfy the most exacting taste. Moreover, the gallery is so complete. There is scarcely an Italian of note in the second half of the fifteenth century whom we cannot know by sight. The century produced no portrait painter as fine as Titian or Velasquez or Rembrandt, but Ghirlandaio, Piero della Francesca, Melozzo, Giovanni Bellini, Ambrogio de Predis, Botticelli and Lorenzo di Credi form a strong combination. I doubt if Ghirlandaio has ever received full justice; for the texture of skin and hair, and for mobility of expression his superiors would be few. Higher still must we rank the sculptors. No century since Athens fell can boast so powerful a group as Donatello, Verrocchio, Della Quercia, Benedetto da Maiano, Desiderio da Settignano, Mino da Fiesole and Luca della Robbia, and to these may be added the first works of Michelangelo.

No age can claim a monopoly in the art of representing everyday life, for even the most artistic imagination has environment. The trecento contributes some lively examples of this art, and that too without the aid of scriptural or classical subject-matter. Almost at haphazard may be mentioned the scenes in the corn-market and the excise at the gates of Florence given by Guido Biagi in "Men and Manners in Old Florence" from the MS. named the *Biadajolo* in the Laurentian Library, and the better-known frescoes by Ambrogio Lorenzetti in the Sala della Pace at Siena, representing good and bad government and their results. These closely touch my subject, because they were painted expressly to celebrate the accession of the bourgeois party, the *Monte de' Nove*, to political power, and contrast scenes in the streets of Siena under the previous government with those (as it was hoped) under its own sway. Both of these instances are Tuscan: on the other hand Mr. Heywood in his *History of Perugia* laments that no such aid is given by art to history in his own favourite medieval period, for "unfortunately the Umbrian School is the product of the fifteenth century".

This conclusion is in general true of Italian art and history at large. The illustrative character of quattrocento art is to the historian of inestimable value, and this on account of the simplicity or curiosity of the artists, of their resolve, whatever their subject, to paint life exactly as they saw it. The passion for old Roman architecture did indeed lead to an exaggeration of the actual. The background and wings of a picture are sometimes overloaded with classical temples and palaces, porticoes and triumphal arches, quays and bridges, which would be highly inconvenient for traffic. But the earlier Gothic and the later Romanesque are frequently depicted side by side as they actually existed. Bonfigli, as Mr. Heywood well points out, is invaluable in this respect in his fresco of the Siege of Perugia by Totila, and yet more in that of the funeral of S. Ercolano, showing the Churches of S. Ercolano, S. Domenico, and S. Pietro. In many cases we can learn the exact state in which many of the ancient monuments then were, the Colosseum, the Temple of Vesta, the Amphitheatre of Verona. In Carpaccio's picture of S. Ursula's visit to Rome we see the Castle of S. Angelo in all its glory, just as it was when the *condottiere* Cardinal Vitelleschi was trapped on its bridge and hurried into its dungeons. So it is with medieval architecture. We turn again to Carpaccio for the Piazza of S. Marco, for the bridges, the canals, the stumpy gondolas, the very chimney-pots, resembling flower-pots, which are still to be seen. Contemporary engraving contributes the Piazzetta with the two columns, and the Campanile without its steeple, just as a well-known engraving in Florence, of the last decade of the century, represents the unfinished Pitti Palace. There are pictorial plans of Rome, Naples, Genoa, Verona, Rimini, though the views of the chief Italian cities painted by Pintoricchio in the Belvedere have unfortunately perished. Many a picture preserves the tall towers of the nobles still unshortened, and the city walls and gates. Mr. Langton Douglas rightly dwells on Frà Angelico's exquisite care in adapting the details of the newest Renaissance style to the setting of his religious frescoes, especially those in the studio of Pope Nicholas V in the Vatican. Masolino and Masaccio must be thanked for the simple houses of Old Florence, with their small windows, projecting upper stories, and wide spaces of blind wall. The picture chronicle attributed to Finiguerra, which Sir Sidney Colvin has edited, is a treasure-house of mingled fantasy and reality. The editor points out the peculiar Florentine tiles, flat and curved alternately, the lion as weather-cock, the brackets on which to hang rods for birdcages or the family wash or Oriental carpets, and the great rings to hold torches. Such naturalistic details are at times incongruous, as when Adam, Eve and the Serpent have as their background a highly elaborate castle, which would exact from its inmates a lofty standard of dress. This was realised by the Magi, who in Gozzoli's picture are visiting the self-same castle, still in excellent repair. Adam, to judge by the square-headed battlements, was a Guelf, and so too Athens, according to Finiguerra, was Guelfic, probably as being a republic, while Nineveh, as the seat of monarchy, had battlements decisively swallow-tailed.

Interiors are as familiar as exteriors, bedrooms as sitting-rooms. If we would see a literary man at work in a really comfortable study we visit the S. Jerome of Ghirlandaio or Carpaccio. He has every object needed for the *ars scribendi*, down to paste and scissors, sand and markers. The hour-glass is there, but he has not watched it, and his little dog, with ears set back, is hinting that the time for his constitutional has long since come. Daniel does justice to the Elders and Susannah in his dining-room, where connoisseurs may envy the majolica jugs and dishes on the sideboard. S. Ursula's father was a king, but his bedroom was simple, with quite a modern French bed. Her own room was spacious and airy, with a carnation in the window and all arrangements for reading and devotion. With this may be compared the humble cottage room of Santa Fina, which has no furniture beyond bare necessities, a kitchen table and a plank bed. Both these saints remind us that tidiness is next to saintliness: there is not one object out of place, not even S. Ursula's slippers or her crown. A simple tent bedstead is represented in Piero della Francesca's beautiful Dream of Constantine, at Arezzo. In contrast to this Finiguerra places Sardanapalus in a luxurious bed-sitting-room, in which the elegant border of the bedspread is well worth copying. Two lady companions are busy with dress-making, presumably for their lord's own toilette, while a *bambino* rests in a cradle behind them. It is fair to add that, since this lecture was delivered, the character of Sardanapalus has been completely cleared from the traditional charge of feminism in a paper read to the Academy by Mr. Gadd.[1]

Contemporary fashions reach their height with Finiguerra's Queen of Sheba. She wears a two-horned head-dress and a long train held up by maids of honour, while she shakes both hands of an immaculately dressed Solomon. Helen of Troy runs the Queen very hard in fashion, especially on the day of her elopement with Paris. The train here also is long, while the back of the dress is cut low, and is of an exquisite fit. The sermons of S. Bernardino had clearly no permanent effect, though he had explained that only beasts wore tails, and that these feminine tails only accumulated dust in summer and mud in winter, causing bad language among ladies'-maids against their dirty mistresses. He preferred the simple, uniform skirt and shawl of the Roman woman, gentle or simple, which is, indeed, to be seen in fifteenth-century pictures, especially among ladies listening to sermons. The two-horned head-dress, as Sir Sidney Colvin has shown, has some importance in the chronology of art. It disappears, together with the long stiff train, about 1460, being replaced by the light, floating robes, with the head uncovered or slightly veiled, a fashion which gives such grace and ease of movement to the ladies of Botticelli and his fellows.

From birth to death the whole life of an Italian can be studied in contemporary art. For the birth Ghirlandaio in Santa Maria Novella gives pretty details of the baby, its mother and its nurses. Much earlier, however, Giotto showed the little nose being pinched into proper shape. For childhood Gozzoli may be studied at San Gimignano. The little Augustine is taken to school and caressed by the apparently genial master. But hard by is a naughty boy hoisted for the birch, a penalty which S. Augustine, according to his *Confessions*, often suffered. Others are working with their books and pens and slates and compasses. The same series affords one of the best examples of a lecture on Theology, from which dogs were not excluded, while a Law lecture may be seen

---

[1] [C. J. Gadd, "The Fall of Nineveh", *Proceedings of the British Academy*, vol. x.]

in an illustration in Frati's *Vita privata di Bologna*, and one on Classics delivered by Cristoforo Landino in an engraving in the British Museum. After college comes matrimony. Betrothal may be witnessed in pictures of the Virgin and Joseph. An actual marriage feast of 1427 occurs in an illumination which shows the groomsmen and bridesmaids walking arm-in-arm. Two illustrations from the story of Nostagio degli Onesti celebrate a wedding breakfast in which from the shields, the negro's head, and the *Palle*, the Pucci and Medici were concerned. It may be noticed here that gentlemen and ladies sat on opposite sides of the table. Shopping occupies a natural place; an Italian may be seen being measured for his shoes, visiting the drapers' booths for which Bologna was famous, buying silver plate at Florence; almost every trade, indeed, has its representation. Concerts are, of course, numerous, and every kind of musical instrument is familiar. Dancing, however, is not so common, and I know of no really good picture of games at ball, though reference may be made to figures in the background of Perugino's Delivery of the Keys to S. Peter. Pintoricchio in the Return of Ulysses shows the process of weaving and the humbler art of knitting.

Accidents often happened. A child is knocked over by a horse: a municipal employé is overcome by gases, and is with difficulty drawn from a well by two workmen and a pulley. This picture is, of course, named Joseph rescued from the Well. Hospital scenes are also provided by Piero della Francesca, and by the frescoes of Domenico di Bartolo and Vecchietta, showing life in the great hospital at Siena. Finiguerra has Aesculapius with a box of assorted pills, from which a brother practitioner or a patient makes a selection with a forceps. Apollo Medicus examines a medicine jar; the sick man watches him from his pillow, and the maid brings in a hot-water jug and basin. Even the result of a successful operation may be seen in an illumination by Mantegna, the victim's leg lying placidly by itself at the end of the room, while the surgeon wields a huge chopper. Cases did not always terminate favourably; death-bed scenes, humble and gentle, are found in abundance, with every detail of elaborate funeral

obsequies. Gozzoli, Ghirlandaio and Pintoricchio alone fur-
nish ample material for the death-bed and rites which follow.

People did not always die in their beds. In the background
of one of his most gorgeous scenes Pisanello depicts two poor
wretches hanging. At Florence the cheapest way to have your
portrait painted was to be hung, or, better still, to be condemned and run away, for then you were painted hanging
from one foot, which displayed the figure in a striking pose.
Castagno won his name of Andrew of the Gallow-birds (*degli
impiccati*) for effigies of the fallen Albizzi, while one of
Leonardo's earliest drawings represents a Pazzi conspirator
hanging by the leg. Botticelli himself was at the head of what
may be called the Hanging Committee.

Quattrocento art naturally teems with animal life. We know
the contemporary war-horses, race-horses and cart-horses,
with their trappings and harness, their curvetings, prancings
and ploddings. Pisanello could draw an admirable mule.
Cattle and donkeys, goats and sheep, are all familiar; among
the latter Piero di Cosimo has given immortality to a new
breed with tails touching the ground, which Lorenzo de'
Medici had recently imported into his model farm. The pigs
of S. Anthony, which were a constant trouble to every
medieval sanitary board, inevitably intrude. Pictorial rabbits,
if brought to life, would have been in sufficient numbers to
have stocked the New World. Dogs, of course, appear, of
every breed and shape, from mastiffs and greyhounds, through
spaniels and shaggy high-legged poodles, by what may by
courtesy be classed as Aberdeens and Pomeranians. They
have not all the patient virtue of S. Jerome's pet, still less the
active philanthropy of the little early sixteenth-century dog,
who in Ambrogio Borgognone's picture in the Brera trots
through the middle distance, holding in his mouth the daily
loaf, obtained from mysterious source, which saved the life
of S. Rocco, when cast out to die of plague from the gates of
Piacenza. Others, less amiable, fly at children, gnaw ladies'
limbs, fight with cats, and steal joints on the sly. Esau, a
careful master, kept his dogs muzzled, and gave them elaborate collars to facilitate identification. Mantegna noticed that a

couple of dogs in leash lie usually head to tail. Pintoricchio, a student of cat life, realised the irresistible temptation of a ball of wool.

Curiosity for strange creatures is typical of an age intensely interested in the East. Menageries of elephants, camels, dromedaries, bears, leopards and monkeys wind down the mountain roads, while above them all towers that miraculous beast, the giraffe, introduced to Florence under Lorenzo de' Medici. For this, Louis XI's acquisitive daughter, Anne of Beaujeu, begged in vain, but it could not be kept alive in spite of mountains of straw and generous fires. Among hagiological animals S. Jerome's lion is perhaps the most popular: it attended its master's funeral, but thenceforth vanished from artistic sight.

Favoured by subjects from sacred or classical history, the art of the century became an aviary and aquarium for birds and fishes known to Italy, and a haunt for real or imaginary reptiles; insects, attractive or revolting, fly or crawl across the picture. The butterflies among columbines and pinks in Pisanello's picture of an Este princess in the Louvre deserve a special mention. Few painters surpass or equal the birds and animals in the *intarsia* of Frà Giovanni in S. Maria in Organo at Verona. The subject is a large one, but reference may be made to an excellent account of it in Mr. W. N. Howe's *Animal Life in Italian Painting*.

I have dwelt solely upon the illustrative character of quattrocento art, and not upon its technique, upon its weakness, perhaps, from a purely aesthetic point of view, rather than on its strength. After the close of the century art was feeling its service to history narrowing, as she had sometimes wearied of her subjection to religion at its opening. She had become conscious of her knowledge and her skill; she craved to lead her own life, to escape from external control. Art for Art's sake became her manifesto. The historian, however, is thankful that its publication was so long delayed, that the life of a peculiarly attractive age had been represented as it appeared to sympathetic eyes, idealised or exaggerated perhaps, but not mythologised or classicised. If anatomy was being perfected, linear and aerial perspective formulated, chiaroscuro foreshadowed, so much the better; but these were not to the historian the essentials. He still goes to the quattrocento artists for the story which they tell, and for their way of telling it. And so, just for once, the historian feels at home in art. The art-critic may poke fun at our Gozzolis and Ghirlandaios, the "artist-journalists" of Italy, but we historians owe much gratitude to those who have left us volume upon volume of the Fifteenth-Century Illustrated Italian News.

VIII

AENEAS SILVIUS PICCOLOMINI, POPE PIUS II[1]

THE permanent popularity of certain figures in history is not always easy to explain. Relative importance is by no means the chief or only factor; the survival of the fittest is not the invariable rule. A tragic end will often make the fortune of heroine or hero, for this gives finish to the task of the biographer. But in the absence of striking incident the explanation may be found in perplexity of character. Character always lives, even when the circumstances which formed its environment are lifeless or dead-alive. Character, at all events, must be the secret of the abiding interest in Aeneas Silvius. It may be admitted that there is just a touch of tragedy in his death, but there was no notable episode in his career, and his pontificate had no marked effect upon the fortunes of the Papacy. Even within the fifteenth century his reign is of less political importance than those of Martin V, Eugenius IV, Sixtus IV and Alexander VI. Rome and the Vatican owe little or nothing of their store of treasures to him; in the encouragement given to art and letters Nicholas V stands head and shoulders higher. Nevertheless, Aeneas continues to exercise a fascination which seems always fresh, and biographers jostle round him. A new edition of his letters is in course of publication,[2] and Mr. Boulting's recent biography was only just in time to delay the appearance of another.[3] Mr. Boulting justly claims that his own book is the first self-subsistent life of his hero in English, but Dr. Creighton's treatment of Pius II is by far the most elaborate portion of

[1] [Reprinted from the *Church Quarterly Review*, January 1910.]

[2] [*Der Briefwechsel des Eneas Silvius Piccolomini*, ed. Rudolph Wolkan, vols. i, ii, iii. *Fontes Rerum Austriacarum. Diplomataria et Acta*, lxi, lxii, lxvii, lxviii (Vienna, 1909–18).]

[3] [W. Boulting, *Aeneas Silvius* (London, 1908); C. M. Ady, *Pius II* (London, 1913).]

his *History of the Papacy*, and it may be doubted if it is not as long as Mr. Boulting's separate work. Voigt's three substantial volumes, published between 1856 and 1863,[1] have never lost their authority, while Dr. Pastor is only less full than Dr. Creighton. The estimate formed by each writer differs from that of his fellows. At the one pole is the laboured indictment of Voigt, at the other the untempered panegyric of Mr. Boulting. The main interest, it will be found, is neither political nor ecclesiastical, but always personal. Aeneas Silvius was, indeed, in personality essentially human, a man who might have lived in any age, and in any age would have attained a certain measure of fame, though it has become increasingly difficult for the rays of a bright individuality to pierce the banks of cloudy commonplace which intercepts its sunshine.

Aeneas no doubt owes much of his posthumous fame to his literary gifts. He was, perhaps, the best man of letters and the best speaker that ever wore the triple crown. If only he had written in his own Italian language instead of in the Latin which custom demanded, he would rank among the chief of the world's letter and memoir writers. His literary versatility was marvellous. He wrote long hexameter poems, elegies, epitaphs and hymns, comedies and novelettes, treatises on education, grammar, rhetoric and horseflesh, polemical pamphlets and dialogues, geography and history—a history of Bohemia, of the Emperor Frederick III, of the Council of Bâle, even a history of Asia. But above all he is his own historian in his letters and commentaries, the latter of which are really diaries. Between them they extend throughout almost the whole of his career, and it is mainly these which explain his somewhat baffling character. For his character was a puzzle to his contemporaries, and its chemical ingredients have been disputed ever since.

So also is his success a puzzle. Others, it is true, with as little wealth and less gentility have climbed to St. Peter's chair, but they have usually pushed up through the ranks of

---

[1] [G. Voigt, *Enea Silvio de' Piccolomini und sein Zeitalter* (Berlin, 1856–63).]

one of the great Religious Orders, and by means of talents which normally secured promotion within these Orders, such as saintliness, deep learning, administrative ability. Aeneas was not a man of profound learning, not a theologian, not a canonist; least of all was he an administrator or financier. And he had no great Order to thrust him upwards. He was eminently individualist; he won his way by his personal qualities.

To which of these qualities did he owe success? To his utter lack of scruple, said some, to his opportunism, his skill in talking, his flair for the critical moment and for the right people. But we do not read his character thus. It may be urged that his force of character has been rated too high, and his morality too low. He had not really the genius to mould circumstances, nor even perhaps the stuff to fight them. Nor had he a creative intellect. What he possessed was a peculiarly impressionable nature, upon which circumstances could not fail to act. He might and did influence others by his powers of language, but he was in the first instance not the motive force but the receptive medium. The impulse came from stronger natures or stronger circumstances. Such men, if sufficiently great, are usually dubbed turncoats, apostates, hypocrites, opportunists. In fact this very impressionability is akin to opportunism. The latter is conscious, the former unconscious, and therefore far more effective if it be the inspiring power in one who has an unusual gift of expression.

For the development and utilisation of this gift of expression the times were unusually propitious. Aeneas was from early youth a secretary, and this was the golden age of secretaries. All the learned, all the eloquent men of Italy engaged in this profession. Their functions were extensive, for they were not merely scribes, but pamphleteers and orators. But the letter, the pamphlet and the speech were all vehicles of Rhetoric, that is of the Art of Persuasion. "Never except in ancient Athens", wrote Gregorovius, "did the Goddess of Persuasion exercise such power, never had Rhetoric enjoyed such high prestige." This was at once cause and result of the new diplomacy, and this, in turn, the outcome in great measure of the two first European Congresses, Constance and Bâle. Of this diplomacy Aeneas became the most persuasive interpreter. He was entirely conscious of the power of Rhetoric. He writes to an English friend, Adam de Moleyn:

Hold fast and enlarge the eloquence which you possess; think it most honourable to yourself to excel mankind in that, in which men themselves excel the rest of animate creation. A mighty thing is power of speech, and, to confess the truth, there is nothing that rules the world like eloquence. For whatever we do in politics, we do under the persuasion of language, and popular opinion cleaves to him who best knows how to persuade.[1]

This art of persuasion now seems almost lost. Our preachers and public speakers dilate, instruct, inveigh, but how seldom do they persuade! To sum up, we may conclude that the secret of Aeneas' success was Expression, the key to his character Impression. This, of course, does not exclude other qualities, such as self-seeking, intrigue, vanity, pleasantness. A great speaker is almost necessarily vain, because he must inevitably be self-conscious of the effect of his own words. So, too, pleasantness is associated with impressionability, which is akin to sympathy. But such qualities are not of the essence of Aeneas' character; they were the accidents, the inseparable accidents at the most.

It is by following the several phases of Aeneas' career that the qualities of Impression and Expression are best tested. He was the son of a Sienese gentleman so poor that he had to work like a labourer in his home at Corsignano. His eighteen children no doubt partly accounted for these straitened means. The boy was educated in the second-rate university of Siena. Intended for the law, he was carried away by the literary enthusiasm of the age, giving himself up heart and soul to the classical poets and orators, copying long extracts from books which he could not afford to buy. To the end he disliked law and lawyers, saying that they were usually dull men, and that they needed not talent but only

[1] [May 29, 1444. Wolkan, vol. i, Part I, Ep. 143.]

memory. Even now his industry was incomparable. Yet in spite of it he was popular, and won the life-long friendship of Mariano Sozzini, one of the highest, loosest and most cultured citizens of Siena—though a professor, and one of the best in Italy, and that of the hated Law school.

All of a sudden Aeneas fell under a different spell. S. Bernardino came to conduct a mission in his native city. The Franciscan's homely, direct eloquence and infectious piety almost swept Aeneas into a convent. His friends dissuaded him, and, as he afterwards thought, rightly, but his conscience was ill at ease, and he tramped all the way to Rome to consult the preacher as to whether he might righteously forgo his momentary impulse. This fact is of importance in estimating his character, for it is a proof that he had the potentiality for religion. This might never be energised, as Aristotle would say, but there it was through all his mundane, humanistic and even reprehensible early life. Of this one or two other illustrations may be given, though out of their chronological setting. When nearly wrecked off Scotland he made a vow that, if he were saved, he would walk barefoot to the Madonna's nearest shrine. This he did, trudging from Dunbar to Whitekirk in deep snow to the permanent injury of his feet. Some years later, in a letter to a friend, he urged the absolute necessity of fulfilling vows made in danger or sickness. And again we would quote in this connexion a very intimate letter, written in his comparatively unregenerate days:

He is a miserable man and without God's grace, who does not at some time or other turn back to his own heart and search himself; who does not amend his life, and ponder within himself on what the life which comes after this contains. I have sinned enough and more than enough. Now I know myself anew. Ah! may it not be too late![1]

After his preliminary studies at Siena, Aeneas had the delight of listening at Florence to two of the world's greatest scholars, Poggio Bracciolini and Filelfo. Now he became a

[1] [To Johann Vrunt, March 8, 1446. Wolkan, vol. ii, Ep. 6.]

poet and a Latinist, a receptive pupil rather than an original genius, a man of culture rather than of research. Both teachers bore their load of learning lightly. Greek to Filelfo and Latin to Poggio were as living languages, which they employed rather as men of the world than as grammarians. Aeneas was infected by their literary lightness, if he never absorbed their learning: in fact he never could learn Greek, though he used translations from it as part of his stock-in-trade.

On the return of Aeneas to Siena his chance came. The breach between Eugenius IV and the Council of Bâle had just begun to yawn. Cardinal Capranica, flying from the ill-tempered Pope to refuge with the Council, took the clever young Sienese with him as secretary. The youth had to find his bearings in the bewildering jumble of all the virtue and vice of Europe. By way of contrast he watched the entrance of the earnest, resolute Bohemian envoys with the sign of the chalice on their banner, and of the bright-eyed Emperor Sigismund, quick-tempered, open-handed and light of love. Fortunately Aeneas found decent service under one or other of the great ecclesiastics, papal and anti-papal, who visited the Council. Then he began the travels which meant so much to his impressionable nature, and which provided him with the material for his life-like exposition. In the suite of Cardinal Albergati, which included another future Pope, Tommaso Parentucelli (Nicholas V), he visited Milan in the days of Filippo Maria Visconti, saw Amedeo VIII of Savoy in his luxurious hermitage on Lake Geneva, and journeyed down the Rhine from Bâle to attend the Congress of Arras. Hence he was sent alone on a mission to the King of Scotland. Passing through Canterbury and Strood, where he heard the well-worn tale that the inhabitants were born with tails, he reached London, only to be deported. This entailed a terrible voyage from Sluys to Dunbar, whence he rode to the Court at Edinburgh. The stay in Scotland, the night of alarms when he had crossed the frontier, his journey through England in disguise and in the reputable company of a justice in eyre, all provided "copy" for his indefatigable pen.

After his return Aeneas spent seven years at Bâle, seven useless, wasted years, as he afterwards believed, for he learnt to condemn alike the life which he led and the opinions which he championed. Nevertheless it was at Bâle that his tongue and his pen found their true vocation, the art of persuasion. Aeneas was carried away by the reforming enthusiasm of the conciliar party among whom he now lived. This was another fresh impression upon his receptive mind. He explained in later years that he knew nothing of Eugenius IV or the Papal Curia: he believed all the exaggerated scandals that found currency at Bâle. His own talents had a fair field in the democratic atmosphere of the Council; he rose step by step to be its chief secretary, its most brilliant exponent, giving to it no new matter, but the finest expression of its dialectic, both on paper and in speech. The ill-feeling between Pope and Council became more and more acute, until the latter deposed the former, and elected as anti-Pope the hermit Duke of Savoy, Aeneas' former host. Here was schism in form. Lausanne, which Felix V made his Vatican, would become a second Avignon. This, however, was the Council's irremediable error. Moderate men were shocked at schism, and began to drift Romewards. The European States, France and Germany, while utilising the Conciliar programme, refused to recognise an anti-Pope. In Germany the Electors formed the so-called Neutral Union, which contained the germ of a National Church, Catholic in doctrine but rejecting dependence upon the Pope. It was a critical moment for the secretary of the Council.

Aeneas was not at first shaken; indeed the Pope of the future was now secretary to the anti-Pope. Yet his sensitive nature became conscious of the chill in the atmosphere. The Papacy of Lausanne was an anachronism, an absurdity. The world had no use for it; States that disliked the Pope at Rome were doing fairly well without a Pope at all. Aeneas in the course of his diplomatic missions was brought into contact with the German neutral party. Instead of persuading it by the power of his expression, he was himself impressed. It was a great occasion in Germany, for the young Emperor,

Frederick III, was going on his first ceremonial round. To him Aeneas, while on a mission to Frankfort, was introduced, and by him, for some totally unexplained reason, was crowned poet. The Emperor knew nothing about poetry and cared less. Had he given a diploma for the best-grown cabbage the compliment would have been appreciable, for on this subject Frederick was an expert. Nevertheless the title conferred some ornamental and practical privileges, and henceforth Aeneas signed himself *Poeta*. Soon afterwards he was offered a post in the Imperial Chancery, and left Bâle for ever.

At the Imperial Court Aeneas fell mainly under the influence of the all-powerful Chancellor, Caspar Schlick, a strong, coarse, capable personality. While the Italian interloper was snubbed and cold-shouldered by his German colleagues, Schlick showed him uniform kindness, making him almost one of the family and gradually using him as his right-hand man in the extraordinarily complicated diplomacy of Frederick III's reign. Before long Aeneas must discover that the Emperor's interests were not identical with those of the German neutral party, at the head of which stood the Electors. The Council of Bâle and the Electors had, in their several ways, a disintegrating, antimonarchical tendency. If the original aim of the neutrals had been the creation of a national German Church, the object of the princes now seemed to be the strengthening of their own particular secular authority by absorption of the ecclesiastical. The result would be a group of princely territorial churches, such as that which was achieved by the Reformation, and this was, of course, directly opposed to the interests of the monarchy. Thus the natural ally of the Empire could only be the spiritual monarchy of the Pope: the old rivals, Empire and Papacy, must lean against each other for support.

This new policy was enforced upon the papal side by two of the greatest spiritual influences of the day, the Cardinals Cesarini and Carvajal, both of whom Aeneas met at Vienna. He had in earlier days been deeply impressed by Cesarini, who had once warmly advocated the conciliar cause. Cesarini was a man of saintly life, of untainted honesty and great personal fascination: he shared, moreover, all the literary and humanistic interests of Aeneas. Carvajal had an exceptionally strong will, an unalterable attachment to the Papacy, and an unequalled knowledge of the judicial and political bearings of his cause. It is noticeable with a view to Aeneas' future life that these two men were now (1443–44) the apostles of the crusade against the Turk. Cesarini himself fell in 1444 in the terrible rout of Varna.

Steeped in these influences Aeneas visited Rome in 1445 on the Emperor's behalf. He had never seen the city since he had tramped thither as a boy to consult S. Bernardino. Now he was formally reconciled to the Pope, and henceforth became the vehicle of expression in the negotiations which led to the reconciliation of the Empire with Eugenius IV upon his death-bed, and under Nicholas V to the Concordat of Vienna. This regulated the relations of Germany to the Papacy down to the Reformation: it may be said either to have caused or to have delayed the Reformation. Persuaded himself, Aeneas had with persuasive eloquence worked on others. His good sense, his moderation, arising from his power of seeing many sides, had made him an efficient mediator. His tongue and pen worked together like a well-trained pair.

Shortly before his reconciliation Aeneas had received two small benefices in succession, the first in the Sarnthal, the second at Aspach in the diocese of Passau. It is not certain that he resided at either, though he gives a graphic description of the customs of his mountain parishioners in the one, and wrote his opening sermon for the other. He did not, in fact, take priest's orders until after his return from Rome nearly a year later. This was late in life, and only after many searchings of heart as to his ability to keep his vow. Such scruples were not common among men of his class, who looked to clerical preferment as a means of livelihood and advancement. Aeneas had not been a good young man, nor even a good middle-aged man. This much is known not only from the self-reproach of his later life, when an over-sensitive character might have exaggerated early lapses, but from his own absolutely contemporary letters. While in Scot-

P

land he was tempted by one of the fair and sensuous women whom he describes; at Bâle he made at least one serious slide from the path of virtue. This latter he defended in a letter to his father with an impudent cynicism which is very unpleasant reading. Other letters give evidence that he enjoyed without scruple the loose life of travel, Council and Court. When he was forty he wrote a novelette describing a love adventure of his patron, Schlick.[1] This is highly improper even for those days, and, what is worse, he confesses to writing it against his conscience. The only excuse which he could find in later life is that, though the story was bad, the moral was good. He complains that the public read the story and skipped the moral. It is fair to the public to add that the moral comes only on the last page.

Aeneas had without question the sensuous temperament with which an impressionable nature is often cursed, and his pleasant, winning manners made success the easier. On the other hand, his natural refinement saved him from the orgy of drink universal among his German associates. He speaks with disgust of the men of position who trained their sons from earliest youth to become champions in the art of drink, of the great nobleman who would visit the night nursery, and force wine down his children's reluctant throats as a test of their legitimacy—for there could be no true child who was not thirsty of nights. For his sobriety Aeneas claims no credit; he did not drink, he confesses, because drink was no temptation.

However bad Aeneas' previous life, there is no question that his ordination amended it. He had early dwelt upon the sanctity of vows: the very scruples which had delayed his orders forced him to respect them. Henceforth even the light and frivolous character of his confidential letters changes. In 1447 he became Bishop of Trieste, and on the disgrace of Schlick he retired for a time to his diocese. This, the only pastoral episode in his career, was a matter rather of compulsion than choice, and he soon resumed his wandering

---

[1] [*Eurialus et Lucretia*. In the form of a letter to Mariano Sozzini, July 3, 1444. Wolkan, vol. i, Part I, Ep. 152-3.]

diplomatic career. He engineered the Emperor's marriage with the beautiful and well-dowered Eleanor of Portugal, and then his coronation visit to Rome. During this journey he personally escorted the princess to the Emperor; the meeting took place in his own city of Siena, of which he now became Bishop. During this period he was perpetually on the move between Italy, Vienna and Bohemia, until in May 1455 he left Germany for ever. Increasing infirmity confined his activities to Central and Southern Italy. Calixtus III made him a Cardinal, and this was, perhaps, the happiest and most peaceful epoch in his life, for he devoted himself mainly to historical work and leisurely travel. On the old Spaniard's death in 1458 he reached the summit of all ambition: he was elected Pope.

At this time we must picture to ourselves a little man with back somewhat bent, and a scanty fringe of hair prematurely white, a pale face lit up by smiling eyes, which, however, could flash sudden fire if his hot temper were aroused. His health had been always weak: gout, he wrote, was quite an old companion; his feet were astrologers which infallibly foretold the coming of the equinox. One of his letters gives a schedule of the maladies from which he suffered within a year: pains in the head and then in the feet, weeks of acute agony in the waist—to say nothing of complaints more fitted for a medical journal. The worst of it is, he continues, that illnesses are so quick to come and so slow to go: they arrive by the pound and leave by the ounce. Yet he never shirked his work for illness: when Pope he never would refuse an audience from pain; the only sign, as he spoke, was a slight drawing of the mouth, or the pressure of his teeth upon the lower lip.

The Papacy of the fifteenth century was an institution not very spiritual, scarcely indeed ecclesiastical. It seemed to reflect in turn all types of Italian life, as on the slides of a magic-lantern. John XXIII had been a *condottiere*, and before that, perhaps, a pirate; Martin V a great Roman noble with a talent for political reconstruction; Eugenius IV was, indeed, a friar and a total abstainer, but his reign was spent in terrestrial quarrels; Nicholas V was a librarian, a book collector and a builder; Aeneas' immediate predecessor, Calixtus III, was, like a true Spaniard, absorbed in the Crusade, when he was not scheming principalities for his nephews, but his very short pontificate was mainly spent in bed. Aeneas himself had not owed his triumph to his spiritual but to his diplomatic qualities. It was the victory of style, of rhetoric, of the new diplomacy; the result of extraordinary experience in international complications. That his negotiations had turned largely on ecclesiastical questions was fortuitous; he himself complained of the obstacles which theology threw in the way of diplomats. It was not through the parish and the diocese that he had reached the Cardinalate and the Papacy, but through the *coulisses* of the Imperial Court.

What use would Aeneas make of his magnificent opportunities? The more natural alternatives were two: either he might follow in the steps of his former friend and near predecessor, Nicholas V, and make Rome the intellectual and artistic capital of the European world; or he might take up the process of Martin V and Eugenius IV, and convert the loosely knit and semi-independent Papal States into a centralised polity, a rival to the Italian secular powers. For this latter task his long career of diplomatic intrigue gave him a peculiar aptitude. But on these obvious alternatives he turned three-quarters of his back. He had, perhaps, outlived his early literary impressionability. He knew too well the moods, the morals, the manners of the literary lions. Their elation had been ecstatic when one of their own class had been given boundless powers of patronage, but elation damped off under disillusion. Pius II wrote his more important Bulls and Briefs himself: there was no need for a Valla or a Poggio; he needed his money for other purposes than for pompous panegyrics after Cicero, or for translations from the Greek. Upon the art of Rome he left little trace: his only important monuments must be sought in his little native village of Corsignano, re-christened after him Pienza. He intended his birthplace to be the country seat of Pope and Cardinals, and so here in a miniature square of about the size of a large college quadrangle may be seen the epitome of Italian architecture of that age, the cathedral, the Bishop's palace, the town hall with its loggia, the city well with its bucket, and by it the palace of the Piccolomini, still inhabited by noble members of the house.

For the Papal States Pius II did little more than for their capital. He neglected their fortresses and made no annexations. In Italian politics he did indeed play a considerable part, at once original and successful. Against all traditions of papal policy he supported through good report and evil the Aragonese claimant for Naples, the bastard Ferrante, against the brilliant Angevin, John of Calabria, son of René of Anjou. He believed that the Aragonese with no other ties would found a national dynasty, and close Italy to the quixotic enterprise of French adventurers. Yet for all this he cared comparatively little; his imagination was stirred by quite other aspects of the Papacy. Among all the reigns of the fifteenth century his alone has an antiquarian flavour. He seemed to be playing at the Popes of old, though he was sufficiently in earnest. Just as his curiosity was excited by every relic of the old world in and about Rome, so his whole nature was impressed by the old claims and glories of the Papacy. After all, visions of the Roman Empire might easily beset an imaginative Pope. "The Papacy", wrote Hobbes, "is none other than the ghost of the deceased Roman Empire, sitting crowned upon the grave thereof." For Pius the Papacy was no petty Italian State, but the world ruler.

Just as Aeneas' character had yielded to the seductive influences of Bâle and Vienna, so now it adapted itself to the environments of his new ideals. His life had become spotless. He was frankly ashamed of his early principles and actions, and was not ashamed of openly confessing it. He consoled himself with the example of St. Paul and St. Augustine. "Aeneam rejicite, Pium accipite" was his cry after his election. He did his best to reform the morals of the Curia, rebuking Cardinal Borgia for his unseemly dances, reproaching the whole Papal Court with its luxury and extravagance. Bred among the humanists, he rejected their advances, to their infinite disgust. Nourished on the democratic ideas of the Council, he became the strongest assertor of papal supremacy over all powers temporal or spiritual. Of this supremacy his Bull *Execrabilis*, condemning all who appeal from Pope to Council to the penalties of heresy and treason, is the most positive expression. Addressed virtually to the King of France, it was a *brutum fulmen*, an unexploded bomb in its own day; but ever since it has been treasured in the papal armoury as one of the most effective weapons, as the choicest and extremest utterance of ultramontane claims. The moderate and temporising negotiator, who had almost seemed to feel the weight of the Hussite arguments—so strongly did he put them—would not be content with nothing less than unconditional surrender of the elected King of Bohemia to Roman doctrine and Roman overlordship. As Bishop Aeneas had outspokenly recognised the bluntness of the papal weapons of offence; as Pope he was blind to the spiritual impotence of his office in a wholly material world. As Bishop he had written that all men would belong to any religion which their rulers recommended; as Pope he expected princes and subjects to follow him in the cause of the Cross against the Crescent, a cause which he had once proved to be a chimaera.

This cause of the Crusade towards the end became his supreme preoccupation; upon this he lavished all the resources of the Papacy and squandered his own health. The secular princes, from the Emperor downwards, were prodigal of promises, but of nothing else. The stately congresses produced tall talk in plenty, but neither arms nor men. Princes laughed in their respective sleeves at the quixotism of the senile Pope, or believed his Crusade to be a mendicant's imposture. Only Austria, Hungary and Venice seemed immediately threatened. Yet who can say that the Pope was wrong? Hungary was ultimately to be the playground of the Turk; Italy herself was saved only by an accident. The Turks were rapidly spreading along the opposite shores of the Adriatic from the Morea to Dalmatia. A few years after the Pope's death a large force actually landed at Otranto, and, but for Sultan Mohammed's death, they would have come to stay.

Their discipline, their mobility, their simple commissariat, which may be described as Liebig's Extract, gave them an incalculable advantage over European troops, either half-hearted mercenaries or untrained levies, with no discipline, and with such large appetites, both of man and horse, that the first tactical considerations must be those of drink and fodder.

As a forlorn hope, Pius himself took the Cross: he would shame the princes of Europe into following his lead. The actual Crusade upon which he set forth from Rome would be farcical, were it not pathetic. A river barge contained the handful of Cardinals and secretaries. The very first night Pius was so ill that he could not leave it. The drowning of a single rower totally upset the champion who was to lead the hosts of Christendom to death or glory. Leaving the waterway, the little party struggled across the Apennines under the scorching August sun, dropping now one and now another of the number from fever or white feather. Pius himself was carried in a litter, and from time to time the attendants drew its curtains that he might not see craven Crusaders trooping homeward from the coast.

At last he is at Ancona, and, like the remnants of Xenophon's ten thousand, he could cry: "The sea, the sea!"—that sea which meant to him, not the safety of retreat, but salvation to be won by conquest. All that was needed to carry him to the realisation of his later and nobler dreams was the stately Venetian fleet. For this he looked in vain from the Bishop's palace on the bold headland, which elbows out into the sea southwards of Ancona. Below it in the town was gathered a riff-raff of so-called Crusaders, the physical and moral scrapings of Italy, neurotic fanatics or broken adventurers, clamouring not for fight but food—men whom the Pope could not pay with ducats but only with indulgences, which indeed most of them sorely needed—men who sold their arms to buy their passage home. Meanwhile across the narrow Adriatic the greatest soldier-statesman of his age, Sultan Mohammed, stretched out his hand against the Christian republic of Ragusa, which made clamorous appeals to the Pope for aid. A septuagenarian Cardinal and two ill-found galleys were all the succour that the head of Christendom could offer.

As day followed day, fever fought against the will. At length Pius was carried to the window to see the Venetian fleet sail in, a truly majestic fleet, with the world's first admiral, the Doge himself, commanding, but a Doge so sceptical, so unromantic that he sent his doctor ashore to ascertain whether the Pope was really ill or only shamming. Pius proved his good faith by dying within the second day. The death-bed scene is entirely human in its higher affections, its unexaggerated penitence, its clinging to family ties, which Pius was not unjustly considered to hold too dear. The scene itself and the setting of the story prove that the Renaissance, even the use of the classical instead of the vernacular tongue, had not destroyed the simplicity of Italian life or language.

Dr. Creighton wrote that Pius was lucky in the moment of his death. Lucky is not a happy phrase for one who deliberately wrought himself to death in a grand but hopeless cause. Rather than his luck it was his atonement. For a saint it would have been a small sacrifice, for saints get used to sacrifice. But this was a man with few of the characteristics of a saint, one who had drunk deeply of the pleasures which one of the most pleasurable of all ages had to offer. The death scene at Ancona was not a lucky ending, but the fitting, the necessary consummation of an improving character. It is true enough that there was an element of accident in this improvement, that it was the result of circumstances working upon a susceptible, impressionable temperament. Yet even so there is comfort in the thought that merit is not only to be found in the strong formative characters, but even in our very susceptibilities and faculties for impression, if only the human wax is deep and pure enough to take the impress of the diviner seal.

If we turn from Aeneas' character to his career, it must be confessed that its brilliant course ended in darkness. He might have been an ideal Pope, peace-maker among Catholic nations, uniting Europe against the Turk, subordinating temporal to spiritual interests. The need was great, but the time was past. Men were more interested in nationality and national Churches than in the cosmopolitan universality of Christendom. What was yet more tragic—they never believed that Pius was in earnest. They could not understand the contradictions of an impressionable nature. Pius might shake himself free from the sins of his earlier life, but not from the scandal. Even his last journey was watched with incredulity; he was credited with sinister motives, or with the intention of starting merely to slip home again. His gift of persuasion had at last played him false: his power of expression had failed to convert others to the strongest impression of his life. And this is usually so with leaders, political or religious, who have not the true creative faculty, such as was possessed by Hildebrand or Calvin, by William the Conquerer or Solyman, by Bismarck or Cavour. Faith may remove mountains, but there comes a time when persuasion breaks its point against prejudice. Thus it was with Pius, with Savonarola, perhaps with the one great persuasive statesman of our own age and country. Rhetoric after all, even in its highest sense and most perfect form, is not the ruler.

The literary gift of Aeneas is precisely that which might be expected from his character; it is the photographic art of receiving and transmitting impressions, the power of seeing and making others see. His letters are, like those of all the humanists, often overladen with tags of classical learning, but his unusual experience of travel and his boundless curiosity make them of far higher interest than those of the great scholars upon which they were modelled. Aeneas seldom sees a place without describing its geographical situation, its history, the character of its people. He has an eye for any little salient detail. Thus when he visits the Hussite stronghold, Tabor, he notes the carving of the sacramental cup above the gate of entrance, just the object which would attract the traveller's eye, but which nine out of ten would omit to mention. His history of Europe is quite as much a treatise on geography and ethnology as a narrative of events, and this is true even when he is writing from hearsay evidence

only, as in the case of the Slavic-Teutonic borderlands north
and south of Bohemia. Scotland, on the other hand, which
also lay half within and half without the pale of civilisation,
he knew at first hand. Here he distinguishes between two
Scotlands, the cultivated and the wild, each with its distinct
language. But even the former was cold and poor and somewhat treeless. Towns had no walls, and houses no mortar;
the roofs were of turf, the door curtains of oxhide. The horses
were unshod and ungroomed. Beggars received lumps of
coal as alms instead of money. But there were compensations
for a materially minded young secretary. The women had
lovely fair complexions and were susceptible; kissing in Scotland counted for less than handshaking in Italy. The oysters
were larger than in England. Aeneas knew how to make himself acceptable to the Scots; nothing, he writes, pleased them
so much as abuse of the English.[1]

The two letters which respectively describe Bâle and
Vienna are good illustrations of Aeneas' descriptive skill, and
provide a telling contrast. Vienna was surrounded with ditch
and dike, wall and tower, whereas Bâle's defences could not
have withstood the sieges of Italian warfare; she was defended only by the unity of her people and their contentment
with their government. In both the houses were solidly built
of stone, and were full of fine furniture, but in the Austrian
capital Aeneas noticed rather the spacious stables and the
cellars, for subterranean Vienna was said to equal her super-
structure. At Bâle he dwells on the domestic refinement,
comparable to that of Florence, on the well-kept courts and
gardens, the fountains as numerous as those for which Viterbo
is still famous, on the comfortable heated halls, glazed and
panelled, where the family dined or worked or slept in the
company of numerous tame singing birds. Bâle was, indeed,
a picturesque town, as seen from the neighbouring hills, with
the steep roofs and the overhanging eaves, the sun glinting
on the painted windows of church or mansion, and on the
roofs the well-known storks' nests, which the inhabitants
never disturbed, either because they would not hurt a harm-

---

[1] [*Commentarii*, lib. i. Cf. also *Europa*, cap. xlvi.]

less bird, or because the legend went that storks, if robbed of their young, set fire to the robber's house. At Bâle the aristocrats danced solemnly in exclusive ballrooms to which no *bourgeois* was admitted, unless, indeed, he were peculiarly rich. The citizens in general danced or had athletic sports, or played primeval croquet in the grassy meadows outside the town, beneath elms and oaks trained from saplings to spread wide their boughs. Life in Vienna was one unceasing brawl, with its daily and nightly tale of victims. Students fought townsmen, and townsmen fought the gentry, or one trade union fought another. Private citizens thought it no shame to keep wine-shops to which they invited harlots and sots, supplying them with cooked food gratis to make them drink the more, and recouping themselves by short measure.

Neither at Bâle nor Vienna was the standard of morals or education high. In the Austrian capital conjugal fidelity was, according to Aeneas, a thing unknown, and the murder of inconvenient husbands was usual. Gluttony was the besetting sin of the lower classes, who spent a whole week's wage in gormandising and wine-bibbing on a feast-day. Some of the Bâlirs, too, spent most of their time in eating, but it was in the decent seclusion of their houses. These honest, simple citizens were also prone to wine and women, but then they saw no harm in this. Neither city cared for the humanities, for music or for rhetoric. If in Vienna they read Aristotle only in commentaries, at Bâle they had never heard tell of Cicero and the orators, and only learned Latin to go to Rome to beg for benefices. At Vienna there was, indeed, one professor, not quite unknown, who was said to have written not wholly useless books, but he had lectured for two-and-twenty years on the first chapter of Isaiah, and had not yet reached its end. It is not surprising that the undergraduates roamed the streets day and night, and were an unbearable nuisance to the citizens.

Justice was in both cities administered by unwritten law, but with what different results! In Vienna its elasticity gave immunity to the rich, and, moreover, the palaces of nobles and great ecclesiastics were beyond its pale. In Bâle justice was

absolutely pure: there was no escape for the powerful from
the breaking on the wheel, the drowning or burning, the
mutilation or slow starvation which their misdeeds might
merit. For here the elective magistracies, the Councils of
Twelve and Two-hundred, in each of which a third were
nobles, the Mayor and the President of the Criminal Court
found ready obedience, whereas the Austrian Prince's magistrates and police were totally inadequate to curb the lawless
populace. The Viennese churches were handsome and well
appointed, the clergy numerous and wealthy. In those of
Bâle Aeneas missed the monumental statues of the dead and
the religious pictures universal in Italy, but the stained glass
was beautiful, and the walls were enlivened by coats of arms.
High pews are not, as is often thought, a product of the Reformation. Ladies and their maids ensconced themselves in
pews the height of which was regulated by rank. When the
congregation stood, only the head of a great lady could be
seen, while a plebeian was visible from the waist upwards.
When sitting or kneeling they watched the progress of the
service through little windows in the panelling. To one institution alone in Vienna does Aeneas give unstinted praise—
to the House of Mercy, where fallen women sang hymns in
German. If they fell away they were drowned in the Danube,
but lapses were almost unknown, and the girls stood in
excellent repute. The easy-going life of comfortable Bâle
with its snug rooms and cosy pews was, to judge by Aeneas'
own experiences, not sufficiently strenuous to develop
penitence.

The above passages bear mainly on Aeneas' study of
national characteristics, but he also had, to an unusual extent
for that age, a perception for national scenery which is at
once geographical and aesthetic. Thus not only does he hold
an honoured place in the science of geography, but in the art
of word-painting. Among many instances of this art may be
cited his description of the banks of the Rhine from Mainz
to Cologne, the like of which for jocund beauty the whole
world cannot show; of Genoa rising from the quay of its
curving harbour up narrow footways bordered by lofty

marble palaces to the hill-top; of the deserted shores of Ostia or the wooded heights of Subiaco, peopled by anchorites; of the view over Southern Tuscany from Monte Amiata, favourite scene of his summer sojourning.

Versatile as he was, Aeneas could adapt his style to rapid narrative no less than to leisurely description, and the narrative is often spiced with humour. Examples of this are his accounts of a quarrel in the Council of Bâle, of his own election as Pope, and better still of the coronation of the anti-Pope Felix V, or, in a lighter vein, of the four-oared boat-race on the lake of Bolsena, or the races for horses, donkeys, men and boys at Pienza, in honour of the dedication of the new cathedral. But the passage which is deservedly most often quoted is that which portrays the excursions and alarms of a night on the Anglo-Scottish border. Aeneas had crossed the Tweed with his guide, and sat down to dinner in a cottage with the owner and the parish priest. The women from a neighbouring village flocked in, and stared at the stranger as Italians would at an Indian or Ethiopian. They catechised the priest as to what country he belonged to, what his intentions were, and whether he was a Christian. There was plenty of chicken and goose, but no bread or wine. Aeneas had thoughtfully brought a small supply of both, and this increased the curiosity, for the natives had never seen white bread or wine. The men, after touching the one and smelling the other, made him divide his stores among the women who were with child. After a long supper the priest, the men and the children took their leave, and trooped off to a distant tower for fear of a raid by the Scots at ebb of tide. All Aeneas' prayers could not induce them to take him with them, nor were they gallant enough to take the ladies, though these were good-looking girls and handsome young married women; they believed that the Scots would do them no harm, for they did not regard violation as any harm. So some hundred women sat round the fire throughout the night, chatting with the guide and cleaning hemp. Suddenly there was a barking of dogs and a cackling of geese. The women fled in all directions, and the guide took to his heels.

Aeneas thought it wiser to lie still in the straw and await events, for if he ran out he would be at the mercy of the first comer. The anxious moment was soon over, for the women and guide came back with the news that it was friends and not foes that had arrived.

This passage is expressive of the feeling for time and movement which is natural to an impressionable nature. It was written down in the Commentaries long after the event, but it is clear that the picture had never faded from the writer's mind. This gift is rare among the humanist writers of the early Renaissance; there is, indeed, a certain modernity about it, a proleptic echo of De Quincey.

It will have been realised from this sketch of the career and writings of Aeneas that he was never merely a man of letters. Both before and after his pontificate he led an adventurous or an active life. He has been called the Italian Special Correspondent in Germany, and this phrase happily expresses for his earlier period the conjunction of life and letters. Yet his memory has survived, not for what he did but for what he wrote, or rather, it should be said, for what he was. He still lives, and is likely to live, because he has given such vivid expression to his own impressionability, because he is the embodiment of the spirit of autobiography.

IX

THE MEDICI ARCHIVES[1]

RARELY, if ever, can documents concerning a single family
have come into the market which have such a range as
A.D. 1084 to 1771 and are of such importance as the Medici
archives which are to meet their fate at Christie's on February
4 and the three following days.[2] They form, needless to say,
a collection of consummate interest for all students of Italian
history. The name Medici first appears in the second document, dated December 5, 1240, which relates to the bank-
ruptcy of Guido Guerra, whom Dante has immortalised in
canto xvi of the *Inferno.* In this Ugo and Galgano de' Medici
appear among the creditors. The earliest Medici mentioned
in the catalogue as holding public office is Bonino, who as
Gonfalonier of Justice grants a pardon, which is signed by
Salvi Medici, notary public.[3] The Medici, however, had been
before this a powerful and troublesome family throughout
the stormy times which preceded and followed Dante's exile.

The first section of the documents is mainly concerned
with deeds of gift and sale, marriage contracts, wills, receipts,
powers of attorney, legal opinions, presentations to benefices,
papal briefs, patents of naturalisation and nobility. An illustration is given of one of two briefs by Leo X, written and
signed in the beautiful handwriting of Bembo.

From an historical and biographical point of view the chief
value of the collection consists in Lorenzo's letters, of which
166 are holograph, and which, together with other political
documents, form the second and third sections of the catalogue. Most of the letters were written to Pietro Alamanni,

---

[1] [Reprinted from the *English Historical Review*, January 1918.]
[2] *Catalogue of the Medici Archives, the Property of the Marquis Cosimo
de' Medici and the Marquis Averardo de' Medici* (1917).
[3] [Dated October 14, 1312.]

Florentine ambassador first at Milan and then at Rome, beginning with May 11, 1489, and ending with March 20, 1492, very shortly before Lorenzo's death. With these are many dispatches from the *Otto di Pratica*, a committee for affairs of state, and some from the official government, the Signoria. There is, however, a gap from October 1489, the close of Alamanni's embassy to Milan, until his arrival at Rome early in 1491. This correspondence was, as was customary until long afterwards, the property of the ambassador. The present owners are the descendants of Giovenco, second son of Averardo, who died in 1314, from whom Cosimo and his brother Lorenzo, ancestor of the grand-ducal line, were derived in the fourth degree of the elder line. Raffaello de' Medici (1543-1628) married Costanza Alamanni, who in all probability brought these documents to the junior branch of Medici. A few other letters of interest are also comprised in the second section, notably one from the good-natured Leonello d' Este to Lorenzo's grandfather Cosimo, begging him to have no reserve, but to "open his bag" as he would to a son, and several from Ludovico il Moro. Illustrations of the caligraphy of these notabilities are printed, as is one of a letter from Caterina Sforza. Charles VIII of France also figures among Lorenzo's correspondents.

Pietro Alamanni was Lorenzo's intimate friend. He was knighted by Ludovico il Moro before leaving his post at Milan, and was intended to act as ambassador at Naples. On reaching Rome, however, he was detained by Lorenzo's orders, and was here "coached" by Pier Filippo Pandolfini, who had represented Florence at the Vatican since Lanfredini's death. Alamanni was apparently modest as to his ability to cope with a group of clever and experienced cardinals belonging to different political factions. He wrote, however, that he had visited most of them with Pandolfini, and found them much like ordinary men: when young he had to please several ladies at the same time, and often with success, but Lorenzo knew that he had failed one St. Lucy's eve, and, with all his good will, this might happen with one of the cardinals. Lorenzo replied on January 15, 1491, that he knew that as a young man Alamanni had to keep two or three ladies amused together, and that the cardinals would give him no greater trouble: all that was needful was to be discreet, to say nothing that could displease anyone who confided in him, to try and gain with everybody and lose with no one. This was the ideal of diplomacy which Lorenzo impressed upon his envoys. These letters of Lorenzo have never apparently been utilised. Fabronius has printed several addressed to Alamanni's predecessor at Rome, Lanfredini, and B. Buser in *Lorenzo als Staatsmann* gives one addressed to Alamanni on May 17, 1491, but this does not exactly correspond with any analysed in the catalogue. As is often the case, the reader is tantalised by only getting one side of the correspondence, but, if Alamanni's books of Minutes for his letters should fall to the same purchaser, they would to some extent fill the gap.

Lorenzo's chief task was to prevent a renewal of the recent war between Innocent VIII and Ferrante of Naples. The King still held captive some of his barons, whom Innocent thought secured by the treaty of peace, and whose release he, as suzerain of Naples, peremptorily ordered. Ferrante also refused to pay the customary tribute, which had indeed been waived by Sixtus IV. The quarrel was accentuated by the revolt of Ascoli, the picturesque city on the Tronto, often a bone of contention between the Papacy and Naples; the citizens had added to this iniquity by raiding the little papal town of Offida. Ferrante marched troops up to his frontier under Virginio Orsini, a near relation of Lorenzo's wife, who had left Florentine service for the purpose. Thus was trailed a coat on which the passionate Pope was only too much inclined to tread. Lorenzo's plan was that the two neutral members of the long triple alliance between Milan, Florence and Naples should combine in effecting a reconciliation. He was sincerely anxious to protect the Pope, whose son Franceschetto Cibò had married his daughter. Innocent was not a comfortable client for a would-be mediator. Lanfredini had described him on October 21, 1489, as a perfect simpleton, whose passion was such that if Lorenzo alone gave him

Q

any encouragement, he would do violence to his own instincts, both in the matter of spending money, and in seeking adherents outside Italy.[1] Innocent threatened Ferrante with deprivation and interdict, and Virginio Orsini with excommunication, an *operazione diabolica*, as Lorenzo called it. He had thoughts of retiring to Avignon, which his mentor told him would do no good at all. On the other hand, Lorenzo's professed partner in the mediation was a most untrustworthy ally. Ludovico il Moro mistook complexity for cleverness: he was never content with one combination at a time. Lorenzo believed that he did not himself know what he wanted, that he would finally act as his mood dictated, and end of his own accord by giving himself away cheap. This is precisely what was to happen in later years. Ludovico's natural inclination would have been towards Ferrante, who had helped him to the government of Milan, and whose granddaughter had married the young duke, Ludovico's nephew and ward. The marriage, however, was not a success; several of Lorenzo's letters relate to a project of Ludovico for engineering a divorce between the young couple and marrying the wife himself. This, thought Lorenzo, might satisfy Ferrante; but the scheme came to nothing, and Ludovico married Beatrice d' Este, the prime cause of the rupture with Naples and of the troubles of Italy throughout coming centuries. Between the Pope's ill-humour towards himself and Ludovico's bad manners towards the Pope, Lorenzo confessed that he did not know where he stood.

Alamanni was, after all, right in his original nervousness as to dealing with cardinals. Never had faction run so high in the college as among the wealthy, high-born cardinals whom the old Pope, at once weak, obstinate and passionate, was quite unable to control. Lorenzo's letters constantly refer to *il Maleacense* as being the evil genius at Rome. This worthy is not identified in the catalogue; he was Federigo da San Severino, son of Innocent's late captain-general, Roberto, count of Caiazzo, who, when bishop-elect of Maillezaix (a suffragan see of Bordeaux), had been nominated

[1] Buser, *Die Beziehungen der Mediceer zu Frankreich, 1434–94*, p. 522.

cardinal with Giovanni de' Medici. Lorenzo was anxious to keep his son from contact with him, and it may be noted that long after his death the Cardinal Medici and the Cardinal San Severino respectively represented Pope Julius II and the schismatic council of Pisa in the battle of Ravenna. This Pope, as Cardinal Giuliano della Rovere, was also suspected by Lorenzo, but, as he was a rival of *il Maleacense*, Alamanni was instructed to be civil to him. Lorenzo's chief reliance was on the Genoese cardinal of Santa Anastasia, whose favour he thought cheaply bought by the reversion of a Florentine benefice of 200 ducats, the occupant of which, his own natural brother, was in excellent health at the time of writing.

It was clear that a conflict between Rome and Naples could not be localised; it could not even be confined to Italy. The northern, western and eastern powers were all on the lookout. The Pope was alarmed at the news that Matthias Corvinus had occupied Ancona and was intriguing with the lords of Camerino and Pesaro. As the King's second wife was the daughter of Ferrante it looked as if there were a combination between Hungary, Naples and the papal feudatories of Romagna and the March. Ludovico's action was also even peculiarly ambiguous. Matthias, however, convinced Innocent that his action was directed against Venice, who had robbed the Hungarian crown of the Dalmatian coast. Matthias had an interest in cajoling Innocent with a view to the transfer to himself of Prince Djem, whom he wished to utilise in his intended campaign against Bajazet. Lorenzo had hinted at an alliance between Florence, Venice and the Pope, if pressure upon the last became serious. He dissuaded Innocent from surrendering the custody of Djem, who had been entrusted to his care under special conditions by the King of France, the breach of which might cause grave offence.

The death of Matthias removed one danger to promote another. It is interesting to find that from this time Maximilian was feared in Italy. On January 27, 1492, Lorenzo advised Innocent to keep on good terms with him as he would probably be Emperor—"It seems to me that he may serve the Pope as a stick for all the dogs, for every man in Italy is afraid of him". On February 6 he adds that Venice in fear of Maximilian wants a general Italian league: the Pope should decline, for Maximilian thinks that Italy is hostile, and if the Pope joined the league he might be thought to share those feelings; there was time enough to join the league when Maximilian threatened Italy. On the other hand, Innocent was warned not to alienate Maximilian's enemies. Thus, when the news arrived of Charles VIII's intended marriage with Anne of Brittany, already married by proxy to Maximilian, the Pope was in a quandary. Lorenzo could only advise that, on Charles' request for a dispensation, Innocent should procrastinate by the usual resource of a committee. His penultimate letter before his death recommends the dispensation, mainly it would appear to stop some scandal about himself. The diplomatist who is often mentioned as well fitted to negotiate between Maximilian and Charles VIII is Raymond Perault, archdeacon of Aulnis in Saintonge, and afterwards one of Maximilian's chief counsellors. He is represented as being a good man and popular both in France and Germany. Yet another danger to Italy, as Lorenzo thought, was threatened by the intervention of Ferdinand and Isabella in the dispute between the Pope and Naples. Their purpose was ambiguous: either they might be backing their relation in more drastic action against the Pope, or, yet more perilous, they might be currying favour with the latter with a view to the replacement of the illegitimate line at Naples by the legitimate branch of Aragon. Lorenzo could never rest until their envoys had left Rome; Granada from henceforth occupied all their energies.

Rome and Naples finally made peace behind Lorenzo's back. He professed to be greatly pleased, but his letters prove that the neglect had nettled him. He advised Alamanni to keep clear of the negotiations for fear of alienating Charles VIII, who would not like them; he stated that the peace was unpopular throughout Italy, and expressed a somewhat scornful opinion on the likelihood of its permanence. In the later stage of negotiations Ludovico il Moro had almost dropped out of the picture. His marriage with Beatrice d' Este and the rivalry between her and her cousin the duchess had made him unacceptable to Ferrante as a mediator. Lorenzo, too, had a poor opinion of his diplomatic ability; Ludovico was, indeed, too subtle to be sound.

It may be confessed that these papers relate to the least eventful period of Lorenzo's career, because his fortunes and those of Florence were not directly involved in the dispute between the Pope and Naples, though, of course, in the delicate balance of power, and under the covetous eyes of three great ultramontane or ultramarine States, the slightest shock might bring ruin upon all Italy. The value of the letters consists mainly in their admirable illustration of Lorenzo's diplomatic methods, and even of his character, now that years and ill-health had tempered the more adventurous impulses of his youth. At this crisis he was all against adventure; his aim was compromise which should leave neither Pope nor King the stronger. Yet compromise must not be too rapid, or he would lose the strong position which his mediation gave. There was probably, too, a very human element of jealousy; he must be the universal *homme nécessaire*, must know everything, influence everybody, and decide everything. As he was not technically ruler of the State he frequently acted through independent agencies. Sometimes he employed a private envoy side by side with the official embassy, or the agents of the Medici bank, for instance the Sassetti and Spinelli of Lyons, to whom there are several references in these letters. In this case, however, he is acting through the regular ambassador. Yet the reader will see at once that Alamanni's correspondence with Lorenzo was far more intimate and important than was that with the Eight and the Signoria by whom he was formally accredited. The practical authority of the Signoria had for generations been shadowy, but the Eight were the committee for State affairs, which had formed an essential part of Lorenzo's constitutional experiments of 1480; they were selected for their experience, and not by the haphazard method which determined the personnel of the more dignified Signoria. Nevertheless, the Eight were left very much out in the cold, so much so that Lorenzo's secretary, Bibbiena, thought it prudent to warn Alamanni to write more often and more fully to the Eight, who had been heard to complain of the dryness of his dispatches; of course he need not let them into affairs which should remain secret between him and Lorenzo, but *verbum sap.* Not even much secretarial confidence is to be traced in Lorenzo's correspondence. All important letters are written in his own clear and careful hand, whether in cipher or not; he even copies himself the documents which he encloses, adding in one an imitation of Ferrante's elderly but florid autograph. His industry must have been portentous; in one letter he complains that he had been writing all day and was tired.

After full allowance for an element of vanity or self-interest the letters prove that Lorenzo had a genuine love for the peace of Italy and a horror of foreign intervention. Not only does he strive for peace between Rome and Naples, and the avoidance of all offence to Charles VIII and Maximilian, but he does his utmost to quench every spark which issues from the inflammable and explosive material in the little States which lie to east and south of Florence. Romagna had recently been disturbed by the murder of Girolamo Riario at Forlì and that of Galeotto Manfredi at Faenza. It was Lorenzo's task to support Riario's widow, Caterina Sforza, against the assassins, and to consolidate the government of Manfredi's heir. In several letters he urges the Pope to be on more friendly terms with Caterina, if only for the sake of papal security. He persuades Innocent to recognise the prevailing families of Baglioni and Vitelli in Perugia and Città di Castello, and so put an end to generations of faction. The exiles of one small State could always take refuge in another, and make it the basis of attack on the victorious government. Again and again Innocent is implored to encourage an alliance between Siena and Perugia and Urbino, and so put an end to the chronic restlessness. Through Lorenzo's agency much was really effected. If he finally had no part in the actual terms arranged between Innocent and Ferrante, it is certain that but for him Pope and King would long ago have been at war. It is the highest testimony to his pacific influence that the terrible Italian tragedy that was to follow was attributed to his untimely death.

The letters of Lorenzo, the Eight and the Signoria contain many references to Florentine affairs unconnected with foreign politics. Alamanni was instructed to obtain the Pope's permission for the settlement of Jews at Florence. The agreement with the moneylenders was renewed from time to time. On each renewal, urged the Eight, the city suffered, but a great city must have Jews: if usury were wrong, the Jews were the sinners, and the Church had no concern with their souls, while the Christian borrowers were punished by having to pay an exorbitant rate of interest; if men had no Jews from whom to borrow money, they were driven to cheat and steal in order to get it. It may be mentioned that three years before this petition Frà Bernardino of Feltre was expelled from Florence after preaching in favour of a State pawnbroking institution. Such sermons frequently led to attacks upon resident Jews. Alamanni also had to beg the Pope to allow the assessors of taxes to examine the real ownership of property purporting to belong to persons in holy orders. Families were in the habit of fraudulently transferring all their property to one clerical member in order to escape taxation, although the other members actually remained in possession. This caused a grievous loss to the revenue, especially at a time when men seemed less willing to make any sacrifice for the State than they ever were before. It appears also that young Florentines of position were disinclined to sacrifice their celibate freedom. Lorenzo and his secretary, Piero da Bibbiena, had done their best to persuade Alfonso Strozzi to marry Alamanni's daughter, but he had been evasive, though protesting that he would not marry against Lorenzo's orders. Many other Florentine gentlemen were also vainly trying to marry off their daughters, if that were any consolation to Alamanni. It is notorious that Lorenzo laid great stress on his command of the matrimonial market; it was his resource against dangerous family cliques.

Church scandals form the subject of a good many letters. The Eight kept protesting against the interdict laid on three Florentine churches at the instance of Arnolfo de' Bardi on account of certain payments due to him. The Priors of Assisi beg Lorenzo to implore the Pope no longer to neglect the disorderly life of the nuns of Santa Chiara, which dishonoured the house where the saint's body was preserved. The men of Pieve San Stefano complained that they had built a convent for the Franciscan friars, who were now living in a disorderly manner. The Florentine Signoria pressed the Pope to abolish the reservation of Florentine benefices for cardinals' nominees, and to keep them for Florentine clergy; the nominees were in many cases men of a vile and unworthy description, and God's service was gravely prejudiced. The general of the Camaldunenses petitioned the cardinal of Siena for leave to reform the convent of San Benedetto, which badly needed it. Lorenzo writes that there was an outcry in Florence against an attempt of the Strozzi to eject the incumbent of Pieve di Ripoli, a very old man and yet more poor than old; Lorenzo had been moved by the old man's tears, and, though the whole Strozzi family would be at him, begged the Pope to let him stay. The hunt for benefices was of course fast and furious throughout the Church, and Lorenzo certainly led the pack. It would be tedious to enumerate the endowments for his son Giovanni which he begged of the Pope through the agency of Alamanni. He would rather have ten benefices in Tuscany than thirty abroad, but the boy, not yet proclaimed cardinal, possessed them in the Milanese and the kingdom of Naples. Hints were made for the great abbey of Farfa, if the Orsini abbot were to die, and his family should quarrel over the succession. Alamanni was to watch for any benefice that fell vacant, for those in the Papal States were bestowed by the Pope before the news reached Florence, and so too the French ones by the King in France. Charles VIII himself made Lorenzo his broker, begging him to obtain a cardinalate for Pierre de Laval, Archbishop of Rheims, protesting against the bestowal of Tournai on the Cardinal of Santa Anastasia instead of on his faithful councillor, Louis Pot, and threatening, if the Pope did not treat him fairly, to have recourse to means which he would be sorry to use. Alamanni was empowered to offer the notorious Cardinal Balue a tip (*beveraggio*) if he would facilitate negotiations. Balue's death offered a splendid opportunity, for it was said that his benefices were to be divided at once; Lorenzo was, indeed, touting for the bishopric of Angers for Giovanni while the cardinal was on his sick-bed.

Innocent's very catholic taste for wine was a valuable asset for Lorenzo. No reasonable man would regard a present of a few dozens as a tip or bribe. Lorenzo wished to wheedle benefices, to shorten the three years during which Giovanni's cardinalate was not to be published, and to soften the Pope's heart towards Ascoli or the King of Naples. Couriers were consequently laden with all the bottles which they could carry of *Vernaccia*, which went as well with the ortolans which Innocent loved as with the eels so dear to Martin IV, or else with *Casentino vermiglio* or *brusco*, with the still excellent *Montepulciano*, or the *vino greco* which was sometimes hard to find in Florence or S. Gimignano. Alamanni, in a letter of April 19, 1491 (not here printed), wrote that the Pope asked for several bottles by letter post of wine that should be full flavoured, and not sweet but strong. Wine was supplemented by breadths of cloth, white, black or pink, and the choicest damask. The donor's greatest wish, he wrote, was to keep him merry and cheerful. Lorenzo was indeed the most obliging of men; at the request of the Venetian ambassador at Rome he makes and forwards a collection of the songs both sweet and serious of the Bohemian composer, Heinrich Isaak; at another time he gives much thought to a tomb for the great Francesco Sforza, but cannot think of a sufficiently worthy artist. In these years his health was failing fast. He had an idea in October 1491 of a visit to Rome to exercise his personal influence on the Pope, as formerly, at the great crisis of his life, on Ferrante of Naples. But his journeys now were from one sanatorium to another. In February 1492 his son Piero wrote to Alamanni that the gouty humours were spreading from the feet and hands all over his body, under the skin and in the joints and muscles; there was little fever, and Pier Leoni said there was no danger; he was strong and robust but very restless, and could not attend to any sort of business. Pier Leoni's diagnosis of the malady and analysis of the qualities of the several medicinal waters may still be read with interest by those of gouty temperament in Fabroni's *Vita Laurentii Medicis Magnifici*, ii, 391.[1] The doctor, by the way, had, the patient tells Alamanni, given him a fright, because it was rumoured that he had fled from Padua owing to threatened persecution for practising the black arts. In March Lorenzo was unable to talk over Milanese affairs with his close friend, Pier Filippo Pandolfini, who was on his way from Milan to Rome. A week later, on March 10, Giovanni made his formal entrance into Florence as cardinal, and thus the great wish of his father's later years was gratified. His last letter is dated March 20; on the night of April 8 he died.

The earlier part of the fourth section of the catalogue has not the same importance or continuous interest as those which precede it. The letters comprised in it are of a somewhat miscellaneous character, and their main value often consists in the autograph. But Francesco di Giuliano de' Medici held important offices in the State, and was in constant touch with his cousins of the elder line and their intimate associates. Thus we find a letter from Giovanni, afterwards Leo X, written when a boy of nine, and, as the illustration proves, far better than those of most modern boys of three times his age. There are many from his good-natured brother Giuliano, and one from his sister Lucrezia Salviati. Others are from the hand of Poliziano, Pietro Ardinghelli, Federigo and Filippo Strozzi, and the latter's wife, daughter of the luckless Piero de' Medici. Among the

[1] [For an analysis of Lorenzo's constitution from the medical standpoint cf. G. Pieraccini, *La stirpe de' Medici di Cafaggiolo*, vol. i (Florence, 1924).]

most interesting documents is an apologia written to Francesco di Giuliano's son Francesco by Lorenzino, the assassin. of Duke Alessandro; of this a full copy is given. Francesco's son and great-grandson, both named Raffaello, were constantly in high employment under the ducal and grand-ducal lines. Thus all members of this second house of Medici are well represented from 1541 to 1601. There are many letters of Cosimo I, one of his wife, Eleanor of Toledo, many from the notorious Bianca Cappello and her husband, Francesco I, and so forth down to Fernando I and his wife, Christine of Lorraine. In Fernando's correspondence there are frequent allusions to the rebellion of the audacious Alfonso Piccolomini, which might have proved serious owing to the connexion of his family with Siena, which had none too willingly accepted the personal rule of the Florentine despots. Raffaello's manuscript book with cipher key containing copies of his dispatches during his embassy at Ferrara in 1589 and 1590 must be a valuable source for the politics of a critical time. Another document contains the instructions given to him by Christine of Lorraine on his mission to the court of Nancy. Raffaello was to suggest to her father, Charles II of Lorraine, that her husband should effect a reconciliation between him and Henry IV: good Catholics, indeed, ought to have no dealings with Henry, but the Catholic League had done nothing for the Duke, and the war was only causing grievous suffering to Lorraine. In later pages are notes on letters from Cosimo II, Fernando II, Tilly, Richelieu, Louis XIII and Louis XIV, followed by a list of grand-ducal proclamations and of ordinances on trades and professions.

The catalogue concludes with documents which are necessarily briefly mentioned, but which will certainly prove to be of the highest value for economic history. They consist of ledgers, account-books and letter-books, mainly of the fifteenth and sixteenth centuries, and cover the whole ground of agricultural, manufacturing and commercial life. On one document is a precious note in the handwriting of Cosimo, *pater patriae*. Many give prices of wine, agricultural produce

and stock down or up to donkeys. There are payments of
taxes, purchases and sales of government stock, termed
Monte Comune, sales and leases of houses and shops in
Florence. The Art of Wool occupies the longest place; here
we have the prices of cloth and rate of wages throughout
long years, the imports of raw wool from Spain, the export
of cloths to Adrianople to be finished, the costs of transit
from Florence to Ancona and thence to the Levant, or from
Florence to Leghorn and forward to Lyons. Dealers and
agents are found among Turks and Jews at Constantinople,
Adrianople, Pera, Brusa and Gallipoli, which seems to have
been a centre for Syrian and Levantine trade. Other con-
signments pass to Ravenna, Ragusa, Rome, Messina and
Palermo. Closely connected with the woollen trade is the
Art of Dyeing, and for that especially important is the supply
of alum. In an earlier section Lorenzo solicits briefs from
the Pope to facilitate the recovery of alum purchased by
Henry VII. Alum leads us to soap, and soap is a usual
companion to spices and sugar. The Art of Silk and that of
the Jewellers find ample illustration; the luxuries extend to
velvets, belts, purses, knives and forks of silver and gold,
and all kinds of personal ornaments. Those who have ultimately to explore this mine of economic information are
greatly to be envied.

The catalogue itself with its excellent introduction by Mr.
Royall Tyler, its full genealogies and beautiful reproductions
of documents, is a book of high permanent value. It is
impossible not to feel deep regret at the prospect of the
breaking-up of this unique collection, even though portions
of it may be made more available for students of history than
in the past. It is sincerely to be hoped that at least the correspondence of the years 1489 to 1492 may escape disruption,
and in like manner the collection of economic documents.
The ideal would be the restoration of the whole to Florence,
and a permanent home in the Laurentian Library in prefer-
ence to the somewhat dingy Archivio, to which scientifically
they would belong.

[EDITOR'S NOTE.—The subsequent fate of the documents which form the subject of this essay has been as follows. The sale advertised to take place on February 4, 1918, was stopped by order of the Italian Government, and the most valuable items of the collection were scheduled as official papers, and thus the property of the State. When the much depleted archives were again offered for sale, some documents were acquired by the John Rylands Library of Manchester, while the account-books and other mercantile records, together with what was left of the diplomatic correspondence, were bought by Mr. Gordon Selfridge and presented to Harvard University for use in its School of Business Administration. A volume entitled *Florentine Merchants in the Age of the Medici* (Harvard University Press, 1932), edited by G. R. B. Richards, contains translations and analyses of some of the mercantile records, dealing especially with Florentine trade in the Levant.]

X

MACHIAVELLI AS POLITICAL THINKER [1]

THE name of Machiavelli is probably better known than that of any political thinker with the exception of Aristotle and Plato. Yet this notoriety was won by a little pamphlet which can be read in two hours, to which he himself only attributed a transitory importance, and which, according to Hume, contains nothing which everybody did not know already. Machiavelli wrote much else—a treatise on Livy, a long history of Florence, a novel, plays, diplomatic reports and private letters. Few besides hardened historians or inquisitive men of letters ever look at these. I should doubt if 5 per cent even of this enlightened audience have read through the *Discourses upon Livy*, upon which the writer expected his fame to rest. *The Prince*, and *The Prince* alone, has given him immortality. Since it was first printed, it has been the theme of volume upon volume in every European language; it is the subject of warm controversy to the present day. The literature, in fact, has become so vast that in an hour's space I can only flutter across the characteristics of the book, the origins of its composition, and the secret of its interest.

Machiavelli was born in 1468 and died in 1527. The year 1512 marks a conveniently sharp line between the two aspects of his career. From 1496 he had been the highly placed, hard-worked civil servant, Secretary to the Ten, the committee for military and state affairs. After the fall of the republican government inaugurated by Savonarola, and the return of the Medici to Florence, he was excluded from political life, and relegated to his little, very countrified estate at San Casciano. Here he had only too much leisure for his active tastes, and here he read and thought and wrote. Fortunately,

[1] [Read at University College, London, on March 4, 1920. Reprinted from *History*, July 1920.]

from time to time he enjoyed the stimulus of the most cultivated set in Florence, which met in the beautiful Rucellai
Gardens, and discussed the drafts from which his works
were later published. Late in life he was reconciled to the
Medici and commissioned to write his history of Florence,
leading up to the glorification of that House.

Sharp as the contrast is, the first period had an immediate
influence upon the second. The official had accumulated the
evidence upon which the philosopher's conclusions were
based. His experience for a public servant of no great family
had been extraordinarily wide. He had been sent, not indeed
as ambassador, but as observation officer, to France, to
Germany—that is, to Switzerland and the Tyrol—to Caesar
Borgia, to Julius II. He took a principal part in negotiating
the surrender of rebellious Pisa after the wearisome war of
fifteen years. Above all, he had shown some practical ability
in initiating and organising a native Florentine militia which
was to replace unreliable auxiliaries and corrupt *condottieri*.
The militia, by running away from Spanish regulars at the
storming of Prato, had really caused their founder's fall, but
the civilian was justly proud of his military achievement,
which was indeed the key to his future writings.

With most men study precedes experience; by Machiavelli
experience was applied to study. After his disgrace he could
devote his time to the ancient historians, whose works had
always excited his interest, *e.g.* during one of his missions
he wrote with urgency for a copy of Plutarch's *Lives*. Many
of you have read the letter which tells how, after a sordid and
squalid day, he puts off his dirty, muddy clothes, dons royal
robes and enters the courts of the great ancients, holds converse with them, and feeds on the food which alone is for
him, and for which he was born. In those four hours he
forgets his worries, he fears not poverty, has no dread of
death, is all absorbed in those classic authors.[1] Machiavelli
was too industrious to be content with reading, which is the
easiest form of indolence, or even with thinking, which by
itself is barren; he must needs be doing, and the only activity

[1] [To Francesco Vettori, December 10, 1513.]

possible was to write. He settled down to a commentary on the First Ten Books of Livy, because he saw in the Roman Republic the ideal State, well balanced as between the classes, possessing in the consulate an element of efficient monarchy, and above all so fully armed that it was able to compass the unity and peace of Italy. Italians were after all Romans; could they not revert to their original principles, could not a model republic be revived on the old Roman model? To this commentary he gave the title of *Discourses on the Decades of Titus Livy.*

What was Machiavelli's aim in writing the *Discourses*? Much the same as that of Aristotle in writing the *Politics*, though he took a different way of reaching it. Both strove to discover the ideal form of government; with both, the practical test was stability, for in Italy, as in Greece, the lack of stability had been the fatal flaw. Aristotle's method was the analysis of all existing forms, not did he despise that of ideal systems such as Plato's. Machiavelli was too pessimistic for the former process, and too practical or sceptical for the latter. Contemporary Italy was too corrupt to offer any gleam of light, with the exception of Venice, but her constitutional excellence was in his opinion outweighed by her vicious military system. He did, indeed, turn to France as presenting in her Parlement a model of justice, and once to England to praise her exercise of arms in time of peace. He had, however, this advantage over Aristotle, that there was a long historical past behind him. There is a universal tendency to look back upon the past as a golden age, or at least a superior age. Thus then Machiavelli, as Dante, being Italian, looked back to an age when Italy was really great, with this difference, that Dante idealised the Empire, and Machiavelli the Republic. Machiavelli was a republican by instinct and profession, and was not wholly disillusioned by the calamity of the Florentine Republic. His remedy was in politics, as in religion, in law and medicine, to revert to first principles. St. Dominic and St. Francis had for a time stayed the corruption of Christianity by restoring the ordinances of its founder. Machiavelli would do the same for the State by minute research into the history of the greatest republic that had as yet existed, that of Rome. Petrarch, he would have said, had made a fundamental error in drawing a hard-and-fast line between ancient and modern history. Roman history was not merely a collection of interesting incidents, useful only for rhetorical ornament; it was for those who read it with insight (*sensamente*) an infallible lesson for the present. In the State as founded by Romulus and continued by Numa he found good arms and good religion. These were the irreducible minima. Without good arms you could never have good laws, without religion good arms would only end in anarchy. On the foundations laid by the Monarchy the Republic built up the Roman State.

If Machiavelli was so deeply interested in the Roman Republic and its possible adaptability to existing Italian needs, why did he suddenly turn from it to compose *The Prince*, the very negation of a republican system and having no relation to pre-Imperial Rome? The immediate reason, perhaps, was that he was out of work and poor; his active mind longed for exercise, and his material instinct for the flesh-pots of Florence. The natural, the inevitable recourse was to a patron. There seemed no more chance for the republican government that had been overthrown; Machiavelli's late chief, Piero Soderini, had been led weeping from the Palazzo by four young aristocrats, and was now an exile at Ragusa. The Medici were firmly in the saddle at Florence, with the good-natured Giuliano as their representative, while his brother Leo X supported him with all the power of the Papacy. If Machiavelli had personal feelings of hostility, it was rather to the aristocrats who had betrayed the Republic than to the Medici who took advantage of the treason. After all, Machiavelli had not been one of the rulers of the State, but a mere employé. Why should he not be as useful to a new prince as the Kaiser's minister, Dr. Solf, to a new Republic? Guicciardini later adopted the same course, and his defence applies to Machiavelli.

This is the material, external side of the question, which makes *The Prince* a *livre de circonstance*, a personal bid for office. But there is more than this. Machiavelli had a gospel to preach, that of Italian liberty. He had seen with his own eyes his country disgraced and destroyed by French, Germans, Swiss and Spaniards. If Venice with all her power had been overthrown, what chance could there be for Florence, which without ruinous foreign aid could never even have recovered her own rebellious city of Pisa? Italy had sunk so low that to be freed she must be re-created. For creation Machiavelli always held that individual energy was essential; a State must be started on its course by a personality, a Romulus, a Moses, a Theseus, a Cyrus. He could not even conceive of the French institutions, which he admired as a model of constitutionalism, as being a growth; for him they were the conscious work of some unknown founder in the past. Here, then, comes in the individualism which is so prominent a feature in the Italian Renaissance. But also, as a clever and experienced bureaucrat, he had acquired the cult of efficiency. He must regretfully admit that democracy, as far as he knew it, was abandoned to the cult of inefficiency. In Italian city States republican constitutions had almost all given place to despotisms, because this was the sole refuge from the anarchy of faction. The Golden Ambrosian Republic of Milan, which had started with such bright hopes, had split into fragments the great Visconti State, the nearest approach to unity that Italy had known, and had ended in an orgy of mob rule and fallen a prey to an efficient soldier. The Savonarolist Republic of Machiavelli's own day had shared the fate of that of Milan, and yet she had in Savonarola her individual creator, her prophet, her Moses; but then he was inefficient, because he was unarmed. Even Venice, admittedly the best model of the mixed State for which Machiavelli had been searching in the *Discourses*, had failed in the supreme test of war.

At such a crisis could his patriotism be content with the arid and stale discussion of Aristotle's analysis of constitutions handed down from generation to generation and reaching him, not through the original, but through Polybius? Might he not exclaim with Pope: "For forms of government let

fools contest, whate'er is best administered is best"? The
times needed a creator who must be efficient, and, to be
efficient, must be armed. With such an one he had been
brought into close contact; during his mission to Caesar
Borgia he had won his favour, received his confidence; this
was the most exciting episode of his life. Caesar had actually
created a new considerable State, which might, thought
Machiavelli, have been a nucleus for a united Italy; he had
got rid of his mercenary captains, and rendered himself less
dependent on his French auxiliaries by the introduction of
national service, from which Machiavelli had copied his own
scheme. Caesar had, indeed, failed, but this, thought Machiavelli, was due to an accident, his own illness at the moment
of his father's death. He must then find a replica of Caesar,
of whom he writes, "I should not know what better precepts
to give to a new prince than the example of his actions". "I
shall never hesitate to quote Caesar Borgia and his actions."[1]
For his replica of Caesar, Machiavelli naturally turned to
the ruler of his own State. Italy could not be united by a
Florentine Republic; it might be by a despot working from
Florence as his base. The popular house of Medici, backed
by the power of the Papacy, stood surely a better chance than
the hated alien house of the Borgia Pope and his bastard.
When Giuliano died, Machiavelli transferred the dedication
to his nephew Lorenzo, who had more youth, more violence,
more ambition. Lorenzo took no notice of the disgraced civil
servant's brochure, and Machiavelli's sole reward for his
trouble was a reputation enviable or unenviable with posterity.

By my title I have begged the question whether Machiavelli is a political thinker, but I suppose that any man who
really thinks much upon politics, and does not merely think
that he thinks, may claim the designation. Can we place him
a stage higher and call him a political philosopher? This im-
plies originality, constructive power and method. Where then
is his originality? Why has he been called the founder of a
new epoch in political science, the first philosopher since
Aristotle and Plato? Why, again, has he been singled out as

<hr>

[1] [*Il Principe*, cap. vii.]   [2] [*Ibid.* cap. xiii.]

being pre-Baconian? Bacon himself has supplied a partial answer in what may be called a grace to be repeated before sitting down to a feast of Machiavelli's works: "Gratias agamus Machiavello et hujus modi scriptoribus qui aperte et indissimulanter proferunt quid homines facere soleant, non quid debeant".[1] In Bacon's opinion he discredited the utopia; he certainly caused a reaction against the formal panegyric, the formal diatribe, the literary stock-in-trade of the Renaissance, which devoted its talents to form rather than to thought. His conclusions were founded on facts, on personal observation and historical analysis. His method has been called inductive—historical is a better phrase, because in so huge a field as that of politics induction must be so incomplete as to be almost worthless. In his own words, "I have thought fit to follow the actual truth in my subject rather than an imaginary view of it. Many have imagined republics and principalities which have never been seen or known to exist in reality, for there is so much difference between how one lives and how one ought to live, that he who leaves what is actually done for what ought to be done is learning the means to his ruin rather than to his salvation, for a man, who under all circumstances wishes to make what is good his object, must necessarily come to ruin among so many who are not good."[2] Politics, that is, must be studied by and for themselves, they must not be confused by ethics or religion. Historical his method certainly is. From the lessons of Roman history he laboriously feels his way towards the formation of a model republic; for The Prince he selects his instances partly from the Roman Empire and the Macedonian monarchy and the tyrants of Sicily, partly from his own experience of Caesar Borgia. The third work of the trilogy, the Arte della guerra, is, as has been admirably shown by Mr. Burd, almost a cento of quotations from classical authors artistically woven into a treatise half military, half political.

At times, however, the uncomfortable question arises: Is his history always apposite, and, if not, what is the value of

---

[1] [De augmentis scientiarum, VII, cap. ii.]
[2] [Il Principe, cap. xv.]

the lesson to be learnt from it? Guicciardini's critical faculty
at once fastened upon a flaw. "How greatly do those deceive
themselves, who at every word quote the Romans. It would
be necessary to have a State under the same conditions as
was theirs, and then to govern on that model; but when the
respective characters are out of all proportion, the attempt
also is as much out of all proportion as it would be to set an
ass to run a horse race." [1] Machiavelli, in other words, does
not always argue *in pari materia*. If only he had left Rome
alone and put side by side with Caesar Borgia, as he very
occasionally does, the despots of Milan, Verona, Padua or
Rimini, *The Prince* would have been a precious handbook
of Italian medieval history, worthy of being set side by side
with Aristotle's *Politics*, the very grammar of Greek history.
Guicciardini's criticism might be carried further still; it might
be argued that Machiavelli's conclusions rest not always on
proofs but on authority, that a text of a Latin author counts
as much to him as a text of scripture to Dante and his
contemporaries.

Hence the extraordinary contrast between the sagacity
bred of experience in the Florentine Chancery, and ripened
by diplomatic opportunities at home and abroad, and the
plagiarist commonplace derived from solitary study of moral-
ising historians. The pedant and the politician were never so
curiously blended as in Machiavelli.

And yet, further still, is there not in Machiavelli's political
works an element of the utopia, an imaginary ideal State,
ideal not indeed for the governed but for the government?
"It is an unsafe thing", says Harrington, writing on Machiavelli, "to follow fancy in the fabric of a commonwealth."

I need not dwell on other faults of Machiavelli, on his
frequent contradictions, on his using the selfsame fact to
prove two opposite conclusions, on his somewhat shameless
selection of his evidence, of which I will give a single instance.
In pushing his military hobby to its extreme, he says that
every successful ruler must be a soldier, leaving out of sight
Gian Galeazzo Visconti, who was far nearer giving unity to

[1] [*Ricordi politici*, cx; *Opere inedite*, vol. i.]

Italy than Caesar Borgia or Francesco Sforza, or Charles V, the most successful king of France, who spent his time on his knees rather than in the saddle. These latter faults are natural, for Machiavelli was writing with a view, not to abstract philosophical truth but to practical politics, and what political writer does not pick his instances and doctor his statistics? But also this predisposition to formulate, according to his favourite phrase, "a rule which never or rarely fails" is a defect of his quality, of the piercing vision which looks through and behind facts to principles. He clutches at principles, and is too impatient to collect its proofs.

Machiavelli was always searching for method but never quite found it. His want of scholarship made him uncritical as to his sources and to the conclusions to be drawn from them. Method, after all, is the instrument of constructive power, and of this he had but little. The form of the *Discourses*, it is true, being a collection of notes on chapter by chapter of Livy, did not lend itself to construction, though he might derive therefrom some general principles of interest. *The Prince* is more compact, it has some sort of plan, but the scheme has little originality and no completeness; it is little more than a series of maxims for government by force or fraud derived from the existing or historical despotic state. As a work of philosophy, it cannot be compared with the *Defensor Pacis* of Marsilius, or even with the *De Monarchia* of Dante. It is not even an utopia, because this is a constructive work of the imagination, even as a political philosophy is that of the intellect. An utopia, such as that of More, or of Campanella or Butler's *Erewhon*, professes to picture the whole framework of a dreamland people. No one can claim this for *The Prince*, though it has been called an utopia not for the governed, but for the government. There is, however, in an utopia an element of prophecy, looking forward to a future better than the present or the past. Machiavelli was no prophet, unless a prayer for Italy's unity, when it was quite impossible, constitutes a prophecy. In this there was no originality, for poets had sung of it; rulers before his day, such as Gian Galeazzo, had thought it almost within their reach; and many, among them Machiavelli himself, feared in his own time that such was the deliberate aim of Venice.

Machiavelli's insight, acute as it might be, was confined to facts, to specific objects. He was too short-sighted for distances, he had no sense for atmosphere. Even while he wrote, there were great, if distant, events in the far East and West which would reduce to yet lower insignificance the petty States of Italy, which were all his world; there were movements of thought, which long before his death would shake all Europe, but all these were outside his focus and foreign to his feeling. *The Prince* gives no real evidence of constructive power, whether philosophical or imaginative. The realisation of his scheme would have been a mere mechanical extension of a faulty system from one territory to another until his buckram hero misgoverned the whole of Italy.

How is the more fundamental weakness in Machiavelli's philosophical structure to be explained? I think by his belief in the theory, common in his day, of an historical cycle; there is always a definite amount of evil and of good in the world, neither more nor less; a given nation never stands still, it is always ascending or descending, but cannot escape from the cycle, cannot in fact progress. Thus, it is often said that Machiavelli had no idea of progress, of evolution, which is the cardinal feature of most modern political science. Thus revival takes the place of reform, whether political or religious. As St. Dominic and St. Francis reverted to the practice of the early Benedictines, and the spiritual Franciscans to that of St. Francis, so the Italian politician must hark back to the system of his forefathers, the ancient Romans. Yet, even so, he is not quite logical, for he seems to think it impossible that this latter goal should ever be really reached. Italy, the corruption of the world, was obviously at the bottom of the wheel, and Machiavelli despairs of her ever reaching the top. This is what is called Machiavelli's pessimism, which is at once historical and ethical. He was a disappointed man, had seen little of the better side of human nature; his own moral standard was distinctly low. For him, men were by nature bad and not good; if ever they were good, it was because they were forced to be so; "of men, speaking generally, it may be said that they are ungrateful, fickle, deceitful, cowardly, greedy; so long as they are getting anything out of you, they offer you their blood, their goods, their lives, their children, when the need seems far distant, but when it is near at hand they turn against you".[1] The people being bad, the ruler cannot be good, for to be good would be his ruin; the ruler must be what his subjects make him, he must have no good faith, no mercy, no scruples, no half-measures; he must be beast as well as man, fox as well as lion, must pretend to be what he is not, and pretend not to be what he is. He may have personal virtues or vices, but he must select from each category those which will not prejudice his power. The people, bad as they are, for selfish reasons, would like their prince to have all the virtues. So he must appear peaceful, faithful, humane, honest and, above all, religious. The most successful ruler of his time was Ferdinand of Aragon, who used religion to justify all his enterprises, however cruel. The cant of Ferdinand, the force of Borgia, are the essential qualities for all rulers to acquire. It must be noted that this doctrine is preached by Machiavelli, not only in *The Prince*, which is a somewhat fancy sketch of a typical Italian despot, but in the *Discourses*, where the people are to have their full share in the government. Truly a melancholy picture, no wonder that it would be found in practice that no policy that could be adopted could be good; all that could be done was to choose the least bad— the last word in political pessimism.

If Machiavelli's philosophical method was defective, if the subject of the *Discourses* was an ideal Italian republic, which never was and never could in those days have been founded, and that of *The Prince* a despotism which has revolted future generations, and that of the *Art of War* a civilian's military text-book which decried the use of gunpowder, why do we persist in paying so much attention to his works? Partly, no doubt, for the perfection of his style. Partly, also, for his

---

[1] [*Il Principe*, cap. xvii.]

patriotic cry for a free and united Italy, to which we shall return. But apart from style and patriotism, from a purely politico-philosophic point of view, the study of the *Discourses* and *The Prince* is well worth while, for they touch on the relation of the individual to the State, which still perplexes us, and must always do so. Here it is that the study of antiquity by so penetrating and so modern a thinker has proved a real contribution to political thought. Machiavelli learnt from both Greece and Rome that the State must be supreme, but he had more affinity with Rome than Greece. For the individualist development of the Italian Renaissance the Greek State was perhaps too all-absorbing; it dominates too many sides of the individual's activities. Many of our own problems Machiavelli scarcely touches. He never treats of education (though he may presuppose a training in the ἦθος of the State). On economics, which fill the largest place in a modern work, he merely advises the prince not to tax too heavily, and not to confiscate his subjects' land; he quotes with approval the voluntary taxation on Auberon Herbert's lines, which he found in Switzerland. On the relation of the sexes, he has no word beyond the suggestion that the best way to win a woman's affection is to beat her. Yet his successor, Campanella, reverts, in his *City of the Sun*, to the extremist views of Platonic sexual-communism and to equality in the service and the privileges of the State. In only a few sentences does he refer to the ruler's duty to protect and further agriculture and commerce by appropriate bonuses, and to encourage by his presence popular gatherings for feasts and spectacles, and yet these were prominent features in the policy of most Italian States whether monarchical or republican.

Machiavelli had more affinity with Rome than with Greece; he prefers the intensive but more limited range of the Roman State, which may be summed up in one word— Discipline. That was what Italy and, above all, Florence needed. Livy taught Machiavelli that the power of Rome rested on religion and on arms, *i.e.* on spiritual and physical discipline. In the fourteenth century, the religious question had taken the form of the relation of the civil power to the Papacy. This had been almost the whole purport of Dante's treatise, and the most interesting topic in that of Marsilius; the contest raged for centuries through every State in Europe. Machiavelli's peculiarity is that he adopts almost in its entirety the pre-Christian governmental point of view, though, except in one respect, he has no quarrel with Christianity. The passage in question suggests that Christianity weakened the warlike, virile character of the citizen by unduly exalting meekness and humility.[1] To the text "the meek shall inherit the earth" he would reply, "the meek might inherit, but the warlike might say: 'This is the heir, come let us kill him' ". Even this criticism he watered down by adding that it was probably not a correct representation of the Founder's teaching. Machiavelli had, indeed, no use for an unarmed prophet such as Savonarola, who, in spite of saintliness and his early popularity, fell because he was at the mercy of a riot. As against this, the simple people of Switzerland and the Tyrol were at once the most Christian and the most warlike. Machiavelli's quarrel with the Papacy was not that it was Christian, but anti-Christian, anti-religious, that thanks to it the three Latin nations had become the corruptest of the world, that religion flourished in inverse proportion to its nearness to the Papacy, that, if this were transplanted across the Alps, the German nations would soon become as corrupt as the Latin. For Machiavelli as for Dante, the chief cause of this corruption was the temporal power of the Papacy, and this he felt the more strongly because it thwarted his ideal of a united Italy. Machiavelli had, indeed, like Dante, been singularly unlucky in his Popes, Sixtus IV, Alexander VI, Innocent VIII, Julius II, a far from reputable *partie carrée* (the few months of Pius III may be omitted).

Machiavelli has often been misrepresented as holding that religion was merely an instrument of government. An instrument it might be, but it was much more. It was part of human nature, and no ruler could neglect it—nay more, it was the very base of a well-ordered State; there was no better

---

[1] [*Discorsi*, lib. ii, cap. ii.]

proof of the decadence of a nation than the contempt for
divine worship. The Roman republic owed her two centuries of glory even more to Numa than to Romulus, for
religion is essential to the maintenance of *una civiltà*. The
Samnites in adversity found in the revival of religion the
only hope of regaining their lost manhood. Thus, he warns
the new prince to respect and even encourage the ceremonies
and superstitions of his subjects even if he does not believe
in them. If the prince had no religion, he must, at least,
pretend to have it; Ferdinand of Aragon owed most of his
success to making religion the cloak of his most striking
enterprises. The unity and character of a State depended on
religion. If religion had been maintained in the Christian
States, they would be far more happy and united than they
were. Where there is religion, arms can be introduced; where
there are arms and no religion, the latter can with difficulty
be revived. Machiavelli was probably an agnostic, but he
cannot be fairly called an atheist, and he deserves credit for
a wide tolerance. William the Silent has often been credited
with the invention of religious tolerance; he had only to read
chapters 11 and 12 of the *Discourses* to find it. Were Machiavelli alive now to discuss the place of religion in education,
he would with certainty be undenominationalist, but not
secularist.

However much Machiavelli respected religion, his personal
interest was in arms. Good order required good laws, and
good laws could only be enforced by good arms. Thus, the
Roman military system became the foundation of all his
political thought. Both the *Discourses* and *The Prince* work
up to this and it receives its completion in the *Art of War*.
He had seen the Roman system practically adopted by the
Swiss, so thoroughly, indeed, that at one moment he had a
panic fear that they would conquer all Italy. But to have good
arms the State must be supreme; the individual must sacrifice his liberty, and, if necessary, his life to the State. The
system advised was so rigorous that no modern nation
adopted it until Prussia set the fashion. Yet, Machiavelli
was not militarist in the Prussian sense. Soldiers and officers

were to remain citizens; a campaign ended, both returned to their normal civilian occupations; a military caste he would have regarded as an evil as great as the *condottiere* system. But the chief duty of the ruler must be the training and upkeep of the national army. For this purpose, a prince doubtless had advantages over a republic; the wholly imaginary Castracane and the not wholly real Caesar Borgia were made his models. But this did not entail irresponsible autocracy, for the whole people could not be armed, unless the whole people consented. And a popular army must consist mainly of infantry, and thus infantry comes to be the backbone of a national force.

This popular service leads to another side of Machiavelli's principles, which has a very modern bearing, that is the share of all classes in the service and in the government of the State. His instincts are radical, he believes in the people rather than in the upper classes; from the governmental standpoint, rule based upon the people is more durable; the people is more loyal, more easily satisfied; it wants, not to oppress, but merely not to be oppressed; ignorant as it may be of general principles, it has a sound instinct for particulars. Against the upper class Machiavelli seems to have a personal prejudice, yet he would not exclude it from the construction of the State. Even the despot of Caesar Borgia's type cannot dispense with either people or nobles; he must rely upon the people, but must also satisfy those humours which, being unsatisfied, lead to trouble. It must be remembered that the people, in Machiavelli's sense, would include the middle class, a large and intelligent body in Florence. Government, then, must not rest on Junkerism, on *bourgeoisie*, or on labour; it must be compacted of all classes. All must be enlisted in the service of the State; the State must be framed for the benefit of all classes, but it must control all classes. If such a State were to expand, and Machiavelli meant it to expand to the limits of all Italy, the provinces annexed must be made, not subjects, as was the usual Florentine practice, but companions, as in ancient Rome; the Italian State would be in a sense a federation of provinces, resembling that of the Swiss cantons. Here at last in the *Discourses* rather than in *The Prince* there is evidence of constructive thought. Outside the limits imposed by the State free play was left for individual tastes and energies, but within them the State was all in all and over all—*Deutschland über alles* in the true sense of that much-abused phrase.

These subjects of modern interest are illustrated in the *Discourses* rather than in *The Prince*, and yet it is on the latter alone that Machiavelli's fame has rested. How is the extraordinary vogue of this little pamphlet to be explained? In great measure by the date, not of its composition, but of its publication (1531). The second expulsion of the Medici, the revival of fierce republicanism with the martyred Savonarola as its prophet and the Holy Ghost as its patron, the gallant defence of Florence and its tragic fall, produced a violent reaction against Machiavelli as being in *The Prince* the parasite, in the *History of Florence* the panegyrist of the Medici. European interest was aroused. *The Prince* became the text-book for would-be absolutists, the target for lovers of liberty. The question was one not only of politics, but of ethics. No one had ever stated the cause of the Is against the Ought To Be so trenchantly as Machiavelli. This had been to his contemporaries an academic commonplace, but to the stirred consciences of the Reformation and the Catholic Revival it was a vital question of morals. Jesuits and official Papalists denounced it as subversive of religion and papal authority, Protestants as dangerous to morals and to liberty. The indifferents, the realists, the new men of science, rallied to Machiavelli's defence. Do the same principles apply to State and to individual practice? Is there a national as there is a personal conscience? The controversy was afoot, and every newspaper editor knows how much easier it is to start a controversy than to stop it.

The interest in Machiavelli's call for the liberation of Italy was more intermittent, but it naturally rose to fever-heat with the *Risorgimento* in the middle of the last century. Dante, who had summoned a German Emperor to give peace to Italy, fell out of favour, and Machiavelli, who had called upon Italians to expel the foreigner by force of arms, became the popular literary hero. And yet of the two greatest figures of the *Risorgimento* Mazzini condemned him as causing the moral ruin of Italy, and Cavour preferred Guicciardini as the better guide for the practical statesman.

This call, however, contained in the last chapter of *The Prince*, and somewhat loosely attached to the structure of the pamphlet, is in chief measure the true cause of the writer's fame, and that for the beauty of its words. It is probably the finest patriotic cry that ever issued from any language. It gave value to the little book, which was aided by its very shortness and its very easiness. And here we have reached Machiavelli's chief claim to immortality. He had an incomparable style, the least ornate, the least redundant, the most simple and direct, the clearest and most forcible of all Italians of his day, or perhaps of any day. It is at least remarkable that his two works which are at all widely read, *The Prince* and the *History of Florence*, are those which best lend themselves to the display of style. Of these *The Prince* is the finer as being the younger, the less laboured and conscious. His style is so perfect because it is so genuine, because it comes hot from the furnace of his feelings or his thoughts. Had he been a characteristic Renaissance humanist, he would have cast about for added ornament; the product would have cooled and lost its savour. Most of us find that we cannot write as vividly as we think; there is a gap between the thought and its expression. With Machiavelli it was not so. Whatever his contradictions, he felt so keenly on the subject which he was treating that thought and expression were almost simultaneous.

A recent writer, Alfredo Oriani, has called him the painter of politics, his gift being that of the brush rather than of the brain. His art is pictorial rather than philosophical; *The Prince* is a flash-light representation of the policy of an Italian State as Machiavelli saw it. Others have called him the reviver or creator of political thought. Oriani, who sets no value on his philosophy, proclaims him, more truthfully to my mind, the creator of modern Italian prose, and that is glory enough for any man.

XI

AN ITALIAN ADVENTURER [1]

(AN EPISODE IN THE WAR OF THE LEAGUE OF CAMBRAI.)

A MAN can so easily be pleasant if he has no principles. Leonardo Trissino was a member of that community of agreeable scamps who are popular with everyone except their near relations. He married young, his wife being his cousin Tommasina Trento. The Trissini and the Trenti were two of the leading families of Vicenza, enjoying their full share of the municipal honours which the Venetians, most liberal in the matter of local government, left to the discretion of their mainland towns. Leonardo was married in 1493, and before long he was fast in the grip of the Jews. His father-in-law, as usual, bore the brunt; he engaged to satisfy Leonardo's creditors, taking over the administration of his estate. Before long he had also to find a home, and make future provision for his daughter and grandchildren.

Agreeable as Leonardo was, he one night killed a man. The victim was a knight, a doctor of law, and a public official; and Leonardo Trissino was forced to fly the country. Several of the exile's letters still exist. They are always appeals for money, which, curiously enough, he always seemed to get. Tommasina is never mentioned, but the money must be sent in desperate haste; it is almost unnecessary to add that the writer had been extremely ill, but was now a little better.

Leonardo's letters were usually posted from the Brenner

[1] The writer is under great obligations to an article in the *Nuovo Archivio Veneto*, ii, 1, by the Abbate Domenico Bortolan. From this he has derived many details of Trissino's career not given by Da Porto and Sanuto. [Reprinted from *Macmillan's Magazine*, July 1896. Bortolan's article, "Leonardo Trissino celebre avventuriero", is in *Nuovo Archivio Veneto*, vol. iii (1892); an article in vol. ii (1891) by P. Zanetti, on "L' assedia di Padova del 1509", has also been utilised by the author.]

Pass. An exile from Vicenza would naturally make for Trent and thence for Innsbruck. The Emperor Maximilian had, for political and pecuniary reasons, married a Milanese wife, Bianca Maria Sforza, whose household was controlled by one of the Emperor's chief favourites, the Prince of Lichtenstein. When Maximilian came, as was his custom, to hunt chamois in the Tyrol, Prince Lichtenstein came with him, and brought in his train the Italian refugee who was, like many unsatisfactory characters, an admirable sportsman. Trissino not only kept up with the Emperor in his venturous scrambles, but sometimes beat him. Maximilian was too true a sportsman and too great a gentleman to be jealous; he dubbed his comrade a Golden Knight.

It is still a tragedy to have to leave Vicenza, even though no wife be deserted, though the only creditor be the landlord of the comfortable hotel, and though all that has been killed be time. The city is set upon the plain, but the Bacchiglione which sweeps round it has still the swing of a mountain torrent, and the grove of plane trees without the gate gives a sense of cool and comfort unusual to Italian towns. Northwards stretches the fruitful plain, broken by ridges which are the outposts of the Alps; Catherine Cornaro's classic home of Asolo still stands upon its wooded height; the walls and towers of Marostica, still intact, lie like an outspread fan upon the mountain slope; the ramparts of Bassano bar the narrow outlet of the Val Sugana pass, which leads into the very mysteries of the Alps; the northern horizon is a broken hazy line of rock and snow. But Vicenza, strange to say, has a mountain of its own. Immediately outside its gates to the south rises the steep ridge of Monte Berico, an unexpected and eccentric outcrop from the plain. Hereon are the summer houses and the gardens of the Vicentine gentry. Beyond them wood and copse, with violets, Christmas roses, snowdrops and yellow wood anemones, tempt the walker for miles along the promontory which breaks the level sea of Lombard plain, whose ripples are the young waving wheat and its billows the lines of mulberry and elm.

Vicenza is a conservative town; still the centre of a rich

agricultural district, it has never suffered the social and archi-
tectural distortions of active manufacture. The great families
of the fifteenth century, the Da Porto, the Trissini, the
Thieni, the Trenti, are the leading gentry still; they live in
their old palaces; they occupy the same seats in their respective parish churches beneath the memorial slabs of ancestors
some centuries apart. On the plain their great villas, half
farm, half country-house, stand back from the old highroads
among their ricks and vineyards and the cottages of their
hereditary tenantry. Life in the rural districts between the
Alps and the Po changes only with the cycle of the seasons.
The deliberate oxen with their creaking carts, the toy ladder
of the vinedresser, and the Vergilian plough, the three-
cornered spade and the clumsy pruning-hook are as they
were two thousand years ago.

Vicenza is beautiful to-day, but at the moment when
Leonardo fled it was at the zenith of its glory, for it never
quite recovered the storm and stress of the succeeding years.
It is true that since then Palladio encased many a noble's
house with columned fronts, at once pedantic and poetic,
hybrids of severe knowledge and exuberant imagination. In
the palaces of Trissino's friends the round-headed Romanesque windows relieved by little diamonds and cubes of projecting brick, remnants of which a sharp eye may sometimes
even now detect, had given place to a frontage of Venetian
Gothic. But the peculiar glory of the Vicentine palace was and
is its Gothic balcony, hung on gala days with Oriental carpets
on which the ladies leaned to watch the horsemen pass. In
the broad court behind the house the fountain plashed and
the hounds lay slumbering in the sun. In the shade of the
wide balcony above, or in the gardens on the hill, the young
Vicentine gentry read their poems to each other or discussed
the philosophy of love. Among the cynosures of this cultivated group was the main authority for our scapegrace hero's
story, the young Luigi da Porto, poet, letter-writer and
novelist, the author of the piteous tale of Romeo and Juliet.[1]
As yet, however, he was still fresh from his training in the

[Cf. *Lettere storiche*. Ep. 21-5 are especially concerned with Trissino.]

court of Urbino, the nursery of high culture, graceful soldiery and fine manners. Another ornament was Leonardo's
cousin, Gian Giorgio Trissino. He too had his failings in
domestic life, but his spirit of adventure found vent in literary novelties; as a writer of Platonic dialogues, and of the first
real Italian tragedy, *Sofonisba*, he found wealth and fame
far beyond the limits of his native town.

Under Venetian rule Vicenza had enjoyed peace for more
than a hundred years, and this through the troubled fifteenth
century when other Italian States, when France and England,
Spain and Germany were racked by perpetual war. It is hard
to realise to the full the bearings of such unbroken rest.
What great Continental city can even now boast that it has
seen no hostile army since 1790? But some little foretaste of
trouble, thanks to Trissino, Vicenza had in 1508, the year
which preceded that of wrath. The Venetian armies were in
the mountains on the frontiers of the distant Friuli, beating
back the Emperor's troops from Cadore, the home of the
young Titian. Of a sudden the news reached Vicenza that
some seven thousand German foot, with three hundred
horse, had on a dark rainy night scaled the mountains to the
south of the Val Sugana, and were on the march over the
wild table-land of the Seven Communes. This district was
inhabited by a German colony which some two centuries
before had pressed downwards from the Alps, and then,
when the tide of Teutonism ebbed, had been left stranded
as on an Italian Ararat. To the present day it speaks an old
German dialect and leads an old German life. If these Imperialists crossed the table-land, nothing could save Vicenza.
Many families fled the town, and in the Seven Communes
the villagers, with their priest and cross and sacrament at
their head, went out to propitiate or conjure the unwelcome
apparition. The invaders retreated as suddenly as they had
come; the country was probably too inhospitable for their
maintenance, for, as a Venetian envoy at the Court of Charles
V once wrote, in a German army the horses eat and the men
drink so much that they are slow to move and difficult to
keep. Then came the news that the leaders of the band were

four Venetian exiles, and that one of them was Leonardo Trissino.

In the following year the League of Cambrai had banded Europe against the Republic of Saint Mark, and all her mainland territory was in a turmoil. Her chosen leader, Bartolommeo d' Alviano, visited Vicenza and examined the defensive possibilities of the town. He began to draw a ring of trenches round the city; suburbs were destroyed, gardens wasted, mulberry trees cut down. Worst of all he must needs enclose a part of Monte Berico within his lines, and the luxurious villas and gardens of the gentry must be sacrificed. The peasants, instead of gathering their spring crops and tending their vines, were impressed for work upon the trenches; others were driven from their homes and lost their all. There was loud lamentation; the nobles sullenly complained that the sacrifice was vain, that should the Venetians be beaten in the field the works would not be ready for defence, and that if they held their ground they would not be needed. But Alviano, a rough swaggering soldier, would take no denial; a Roman Orsini by adoption, he took upon him the overbearing manners of the house which to the gentler Florentines had long been a byword. As war came nearer, Cremonese gentlemen passed eastwards under Venetian escort, that their disaffection might be damped by the air of the lagoons until the storm was over. Then through Vicenza, westwards towards the Adda, poured Alviano's levies, clad in his colours, in tight parti-coloured stockings and jerkins of red and white. Mere militia were most of these, men who had never known war, and were torn weeping from their homes. They would make little fight, said the professional cavalry officers and young nobles like Da Porto; yet when they were called milch-cows by the regulars they proved quarrelsome. A month more and Alviano was a prisoner in the great rout of Vailà. The lion of Saint Mark himself could not have fought more fiercely than the too venturous general. The milch-cows had gone straight at the French, a feat unparalleled for Italian infantry of that age. They had beaten back the foot and charged the guns, only to be mown down line behind line by the unrivalled

French artillery. Bayard, with his rear-guard wading to the waist through the flooded meadows, had completed the discomfiture. But never, said the experienced Captain Lattanzio of Bergamo, had he seen infantry fight like these raw recruits.

Nothing could now stay the French advance which swept forward to the Mincio. Here at length it paused, content with hanging the defenders of Peschiera from their ramparts for daring to resist a King of France. The King had conquered his allotted share; the land from the Mincio to the lagoons was Maximilian's portion. Verona, Vicenza and Padua shut their gates against the retreating troops. In the panic, the Venetian governors, the Captain and the Judge, lost their customary influence. The local gentry once more, after a hundred years, reassumed the lead. Popular as Venetian rule was with peasants and artisans, the nobles were seldom quite content. They resented their inferiority to the Republic's Rectors who came to rule them; they found little employment in the Republic's service; their faction-fights were quelled, and any injustice towards the poor rigorously repressed. Now too they were tempted by the prospect of imperial titles, while a foreign Emperor would ride with a looser rein "the restive Italian steed" of Dante's verse.

Strangely enough there was no Emperor to take the magnificent territory left at his disposal. Maximilian was hunting in the Tyrol; he was no longer young, but for him a pair of cities was never worth a chamois. In their perplexity the Vicentine nobles bethought them of their townsman, Leonardo Trissino. His own and his wife's relations begged him to offer to the Emperor the city which would give itself to the first comer; they implored him to return, promising money and all that he could need. Trissino went joyously to Prince Lichtenstein; with an imperial commission he would win the whole Trevisan March, nor cost the Emperor a ducat or a man. The Prince dispatched him on his venture, promising to send the commission after him: he thought to himself that no German officer could go without a considerable force, and he had not the money to raise a soldier; should

Trissino prosper, well and good; if he should fail, there was no great loss, and his master was not committed.

Trissino crossed the Brenner to Trent, and there he found six Stradiots, light horsemen from Albania, deserters probably from the Venetian army. With these as a nucleus he gathered some ten horsemen and sixty foot and went on his way to Roveredo. Meanwhile his extemporised force began to dwindle, and he soon found himself at the head of some five-and-twenty ragamuffins, "bandits, charcoal-burners and vagabonds, all black and greasy, dirty and tattered". Of brave words and men in buckram, however, Trissino had abundance. He wrote to the town of Schio, which had imperial sympathies, ordering quarters for five thousand foot and four hundred horse; he had already demanded the submission of Vicenza; if she would not open her gates to Caesar, he would spare neither life, property nor sex.

The Venetian governors were still in Vicenza, but they had sent off their artillery and ammunition, their books and military chest to Padua. They vainly protested against the proposal of the local Committee of Government to surrender to Trissino. Sensible as all Venetians were they recognised defeat; they abandoned the insignia of office, closed the governmental palace, and refused to administer justice. A deputation of nobles and lawyers, clothed in silk, with gold chains round their necks, rode out to Malo to beg the exile to re-enter his native town. They persuaded him without much ado to abstain from quartering upon the city his numerous phantom force. Trissino was by this time in condition to meet his fashionable friends, for his ill-used father-in-law had made him a present of £10, and sent him twenty yards of velvet with five yards of gold braid. Thus on June 5, 1509, Trissino returned in splendour after fifteen years of exile, escorted by some eighty horsemen to the sound of drums and trumpets and clanging bells. The Committee of Government gave him the keys; its spokesman made an elegant address, to which he paid no attention and attempted no reply. Leonardo had in fact almost forgotten his native tongue; but he pleased everyone by his modesty, and was equally agreeable to all comers. The self-appointed Governor dismounted at the Captain's palace, where a magnificent dinner awaited him. Hence the town-crier received the order that no townsman should bear arms, and that fathers should be responsible for the transgressions of their sons and masters for those of their servants; "A most unheard of notice," wrote the Venetian chronicler of these events, "learned by him from the barbarous Germans beyond the mountains, who are always studying how to be more cruel". The order was doubtless needed, for the departure of the Venetian governors, who had slipped from their houses in plain clothes and ridden off for Padua, was the signal for disturbance. Some of the citizens had marched round the town in arms, crying *Empire, Empire!* But these were met by the men of the poorer suburb of Saint Piero headed by one who carried a banner with a cock thereon, and these artisans with shouts of *Saint Mark, Saint Mark!* set upon the aristocrats and slew a doctor of laws and others. Nevertheless the classes beat the masses back and hoisted the banner of the Empire. Then in the great oblong piazza night was made merry. From the Captain's palace and the Court of Justice torches flared and huge candles flickered; a barrel of powder was bought to pass for fireworks; a blazing bonfire on the pavement threw up its sparks as though to top the giddy height of the ruddy bell-tower. Italian men are easily made boys; and in nights so short it is waste of time to think of the long to-morrow.

At the head of the chief square in every Venetian town stands a column, and on it the winged lion with its paw upon the open gospel; it is the symbol of Venetian sovereignty. This lion was by Trissino's orders dashed into atoms on the pavement, and replaced by a trumpery gilded eagle. The item of payment to the destructive mason may still be read. To the artistic Da Porto this was a Vandal's act; he cared not for the shame done to Venice, but for the ruin of a masterpiece of beauty, such as the most famous sculptor of the ancient world might well have carved. The lesser people loved their late masters and their lion. They gathered together the broken limbs and hid them till better times. The

less comely parts, however, were seized by some nobles of
Cremona who had escaped from Venice and were passing
homewards through Vicenza. As they rode through Monte-
bello, a large village towards Verona, they jested indecently
at the poor fragments of the lion, whereon the villagers fell on
them in fury, wounding many and killing some. This was
perhaps the first symptom of reaction in favour of Saint Mark,
for before long every strong village was a hornets' nest to
German and French invaders. The peasants would cut off
the convoys, break the bridges, delay the siege-trains. Day
after day they watched the Marquis of Mantua, a fierce enemy
of their lords, until at length they pounced upon him sleeping, and seized him in his shirt. The secret of this was the
Republic's even-handed justice, elsewhere in Italy unknown.
"One thing", wrote Bayard's biographer, no friendly witness,
"must needs be noted, that never on this earth were lords so
well loved by their subjects as the Venetians have always been,
and this alone for the great justice wherewith they rule them."
One hundred and fifty years later Harrington bore witness
to Bayard. Since then English and French ignoramuses and
idealists have conspired to blacken the aristocracy, which
knew and did its duty to the only grateful poor.

Trissino, meanwhile, had been invited to take Padua in his
master's name. To make his entry more effective he hired a
hundred barefoot German *Landsknechte* for the day, and
pressed into his procession all the nobles of Vicenza. Da
Porto, opportunist beyond his years, unwilling to commit
himself so far, pleaded a bad arm, but Trissino would take
no excuse. The Paduans who rode out to meet their new
ruler returned almost mad with joy: he was the most generous
of mankind; he would give to the citizens every imaginable
privilege, and would divide among the nobles the wide estates
of the Venetian gentry; the Emperor would confirm his every
act. No wonder that the guns thundered and the fifes played,
and the ladies waved a welcome from their balconies as the
dandy Governor rode by. Then it was that the lion over the
doorway of the Captain's palace was blown into the air by
bombards thrust into its belly, while the Buzzacarini dragged

from their store-room an imperial banner hidden for a hundred years. As its mouldering folds first flapped in the unwonted wind, the Captain alighted at his palace, where he found board and lodging to befit a king.

A king in truth Trissino was. For fear of offence none dared to ask for his commission. From the furthest corners of the Friuli came great noblemen to crave imperial confirmation of their fiefs, or soldiers to beg the command of imaginary squadrons. Trissino himself would laugh with Da Porto at the eagerness with which all who had any job to perpetrate would turn to him, as though he was the Emperor in person. The Venetian troops were ordered off the territory of the Magnificent Paduan Republic. Paduan nobles were commissioned to replace Venetians in the fortresses and dependent townships. All the irksome duties upon comestibles were abolished, and never was living so cheap in Padua; wine there was in such plenty that it cost nothing; a halfpenny would buy seven eggs or a pound of meat. The order was issued that everyone, under a penalty of fifty ducats, should sweep the front of his own house; and everyone obediently swept. But after all the main function was to command the troops, and of troops there were none. Trissino, imitating the methods of Alviano, attempted to enrol militia. He ordered all the peasants of the territory between eighteen and forty-five years of age to muster in Padua for drill. Some five hundred obeyed the summons, and on the summer days Trissino could be seen in the piazza eating cherries while he drilled his troops. He undoubtedly dressed his part. A dandy by nature, he could now satisfy his vanity at his country's expense. Very effective he looked in his white velvet tunic frogged with gold, his little gold cap stuck on one ear, his beard worn in the German fashion, and always a bunch of flowers. When he was tired of drill he dismissed his peasant soldiers, each with a coin to buy their lunch; for dinner he told them they should have half a ducat or more, and yet they grumbled. Peasants are rarely content when overfed and overpaid.

Meanwhile outside Padua matters went none too well.

Trissino had no administrative genius. The roads were at the mercy of disbanded soldiers and loyal peasants; the Paduan merchants could not travel. Bassano, indeed, and Asolo tendered their submission. Treviso, the third great city, which should complete the conquests promised by Trissino, sent a deputation to offer him the keys. But he was too timid or too slow; he feared the Venetian forces encamped at Mestre, and his delay gave time to the popular party to memorialise its Venetian masters. When Trissino's trumpeter arrived he was well-nigh killed. A popular tumult, headed by a furrier, overawed the gentry. The Venetians took heart and threw in troops; the suspected nobles were carried off to Venice. Nor was this the only check. Another luckless trumpeter was sent to summon Cividale; but out came Paolo Contarini the *proveditor* and one hundred Stradiot horse, and gave the trumpeter such a fright that never would he go near the town again.

In decrying the Italian soldiery of this age modern writers too blindly follow Machiavelli, whose purpose it was not to write history, but to prove theories. For him every hired captain was a coward, a sluggard and a traitor. Yet many soldiers of fortune and men of birth, from all parts of Italy, stood firm by Venice in her darkest hour, reorganising her beaten and disordered troops, until they once more met the barbarians on no unequal terms. Such officers were Mariano dei Conti from the Roman Campagna, and Count Pietro Martinengo of the richest house in Brescia, courteous gentlemen and well-knit athletes. These two, indeed, fell in the first battle near the Adda, side by side, for they had sworn to stand together though their men had fled. But Lattanzio of Bergamo and Zitolo of Perugia fell one after the other at their guns when the Venetians, after the tide had turned, strove to hurl the Franco-Spanish-German forces from Verona. Dionisio da Naldo throughout the war kept training the fine infantry which took their name from his little Romagnol village of Brisighella. From Tuscan Prato came the Knight of Saint John, Frà Leonardo, who from hatred to the French offered his services to Venice in any capacity which she might choose. He was no hireling, for he gave his whole fortune, five thousand ducats, to the Republic that she might use it in her need. He too fell late in the war at the head of his light horse, and the French grieved because they had not taken him alive to murder him. Another Tuscan was the one-eyed Baldassare Scipione of Siena, who fought through the war from end to end, from the western frontier of the Adda to the easternmost corner of Friuli; who was taken fighting at the Adda, and again at the terrible storm of Brescia; and who performed the last exploit of the war by saving from the scoundrelly Swiss allies the artillery which they had sought to steal. Baldassare was the fastidious Da Porto's ideal of a soldier, a fierce but scientific fighter, combining a high character with literary culture. The one chivalrous champion of Caesar Borgia, he had posted in all the chief squares of Europe a challenge to any Spaniard who should deny that their Catholic Majesties had not disgraced their honour and their crown by their treachery towards his fallen chief.

Upon one of these men of ancient virtue, one otherwise unknown to fame, the clever adventurer Trissino chanced to stumble. He sent a herald to the Venetian camp to order Bernardino Fortebraccio, the leader of a thousand horse, to come and tender his submission to the Emperor, otherwise he would confiscate his patrimony at Lonigo, and arrest his wife and children who were at Padua. The old soldier's reply is an answer not only to Trissino but to the Florentine slanderer of Italian soldiery: "I have no wish to desert my duty to the Signory. For sixty years past I have been her servant and have eaten her bread, and if I had a hundred sons I would give them all for her, and would take no heed."[1] When, too, Trissino sent a governor with a hundred foot to the walled township of Mirano, Alvise Dardani held the fort with a handful of peasants from the neighbouring villages and the official slunk back to Padua.

In winning Padua Trissino virtually lost Vicenza. This was natural, for in Italy municipal patriotism was so strong that every city hated its nearest neighbour. The Committee

---

[1] [Bortolan, *op. cit.*, from an anonymous Venetian MS. chronicle.]

of Government could keep no order. As soon as the imperial eagles were hoisted, exiled malefactors flocked into the town and lorded it over the citizens. They set fire to the palace and the town-hall, and burned the books wherein the sentences against criminals were registered. The new government of Padua was protectionist and forbade the people of Vicenza to sell their produce in the Paduan market. This infuriated the lower classes, already devoted to Saint Mark. When a Venetian trumpeter under safe conduct rode up to the walls, the men of the suburb of San Piero with cries of *Marco, Marco!* escorted him to the public square, thinking that he had come to take the lordship of their town for Venice. Each country makes its little revolutions differently. Englishmen rechristen their Local Board; Frenchmen change the terminology of their streets; Italians would throw something, or somebody, into a river or on the pavement. Thus when Charles VIII had entered Pisa, the people threw the Florentine lion from the bridge into the Arno; and when a few years later the Emperor appeared, they served the statue of the French King as they had served the lion. So too at Vicenza the mob threw the gilded eagle from his column, and finding in the cathedral some banners of the late Bishop with the emblem of Saint Mark, they hoisted them in the eagle's place. The upper classes barricaded themselves in their houses, but the people sacked the Captain's palace which was sumptuously draped to greet the arrival of the Imperial Commissioner. Even Trissino had now lost his spell. He wrote to the commune demanding suitable apartments and sufficient funds for the entertainment of himself and his court. He was answered that the city could not undertake the burden; and when he appealed to the Benedictine monks he received a similar refusal. Nevertheless he came by torchlight with fifes and drums and a company of Germans; he wore a wreath of ivy, and his little cap set jauntily on one ear covered but the one half of his head and seemed like to fall. His sojourn was for one night only, for he was forced to lodge at his own house and at his own expense. This visit made matters worse, for he persuaded four hundred Vicentine soldiers to follow him to Padua, and on their arrival they found the gates shut in their faces. Paduans were too proud to be dependent on Vicentines. In return the soldiers ravaged the surrounding fields, and two were caught and hanged at eventide with their faces veiled. Such lynch-law did not improve the feeling between the neighbour towns.

The Venetians naturally tried to bribe Trissino. Andrea Gritti promised that, if he would restore Padua, a complete amnesty should be granted and Vicenza allowed to choose her own master; Trissino should be first Baron of Saint Mark; he should receive a grant of a fine palace in Venice and £50 a month for the expenses of his table. In addition to this were offered to him the two strong towns of Cittadella and Castelfranco, which face each other, the one with its circle, the other with its square of walls and towers. Of these Trissino should be Count with free sovereignty, while a hundred cuirassiers, two hundred light horse, and five hundred foot were placed under his command. Trissino was an adventurer, but not a common blackguard. He played the grand game, and refused the bribe. His mother city of Vicenza, he replied, would receive the widest privileges from the Emperor; for himself he looked for nothing. The Republic did not despair of at least conciliating their influential foe. Many Venetian nobles had for some time past withdrawn their capital from trade and invested it in real estate upon the mainland. They had thought that in abandoning their sovereignty they would still retain their private property; but they found themselves mistaken. Trissino scheduled their estates, and it was reported that half would be applied to the benefit of the Paduan municipal pawnbroking office, and the other moiety to the advantage of the town. Meanwhile the crops were ripe, and their proprietors were chafing to gather them. The Venetians strove to induce Trissino to respect the rights of private property. Hearing that he had sent to Mestre to buy a race-horse, the Government presented one, a strange gift from the city of canals. More than this, the Secretary who conducted negotiations was empowered to offer £1000. It is not known that Trissino took the bribe; but he courteously allowed the Venetian gentry to harvest their crops for the current year.

Encouraged by this concession, the Republic sent Francesco Cappello to renew its former offers. Trissino cherished a warm regard for the old man who, when ambassador in Germany, had befriended him in exile; and he had excepted his property from the schedule of confiscation. Cappello, under pretext of an embassy to the Emperor, took his chaplain, his secretary and his barber, and made Padua the first stage of his fictitious journey. For further security he disguised himself in a Hungarian dress. But as he entered the gate, some soldiers who had served under him at Trieste recognised the magnificent old man, and reverently saluted him. A little further a woman, looking him hard in the face, cried, "Hurrah for Saint Mark!" A secret interview with Trissino was contrived, but the Paduan nobles, very jealous of these negotiations, got wind of Cappello's presence. Trissino, moreover, was no longer the sole master, for on the same evening as his friend three Imperial Commissioners arrived at Padua. Cappello slipped safely down the Brenta as far as Strà, but here he was arrested by fifty horsemen. It nearly went hard with the old diplomatist. In spite of his commission to the Emperor, in spite of his indignant protests on the violation of the law of nations, the provisional Government of sixteen members debated a motion for his immediate execution. The turn of a single vote would have cost his life.

The great coalition against Venice was now showing signs of loosening. The King of France retired from the Mincio to make his triumphal entry into Milan. Ferdinand of Aragon and the Pope had taken, almost without resistance, all that they desired. The Emperor was timidly clinging to the southern fringes of the Alps, concentrating his forces at Bassano and the neighbouring walled townlets; his unpaid troops were demoralised by plunder. The Venetians plucked up courage; the nobles had now realised that in abandoning the territory of their State, they were losing their means of livelihood. In the Senate it was debated whether the Levant or

Italy, the sea or land, offered the fairest field for Venetian enterprise; the issue was a resolution, carried by one vote only, to retake Padua. The town was weakly held. Trissino and the imperial officials had but some three hundred Germans, a few Italian lances, and the volunteer companies of Paduan nobles; the populace was eager to welcome Venetian rule. Padua was so near Venice that the fortifications had been allowed to crumble, and Trissino, bent on remitting instead of raising taxes, had never looked to their repair.

On the night of July 16 all Venice was astir. Andrea Gritti, the soul of the enterprise, had marched the regulars up to the eastern gate of Padua. Every available boat from every township on the lagoons, from Murano and Malamocco, from Torcello to distant Chioggia, had been ordered to the channels of the Brenta. Thither passed the crews and the workmen from the Arsenal; the nobles came in their barges, the citizens in their gondolas and pinnaces. Some twenty thousand men in a flotilla of four thousand boats were gathered on the Brenta. From the villages on the banks poured forth the peasants, full of fight against the plundering Germans and the Paduan rebels. Yet with all this stir the secret was strangely kept, and on that July night all Padua was sleeping. At dawn of day on the 17th, the anniversary of the day on which a little more than a century ago Padua had first fallen, three waggons with loads of wheat summoned the guard to open the Codalunga gate, where now there stands the monument of the Venetian victory. The last waggoner stopped upon the bridge, and then the Venetian horsemen dashed in from their ambush and held the gate. The Greek light horse, the Uhlans of their day, galloped forward to explore the streets; the gentry were in their beds, the people made common cause with the invaders, and the main Venetian force pushed its way into the town. Trissino was the first to mount, but he and his two hundred followers were thrust back to the marketplace. They barricaded themselves in the Captain's palace; but the doors were dashed in, the lion banner once more floated from the balcony, while the great bell clanged out the Venetian triumph. Trissino, however, was not yet caught.

From the palace he broke through the wall into the stronger castle; and here he and his comrades were safe for at least a night.

Meanwhile through the gates and over the walls of Padua poured soldiers, villagers and farmers, pillaging the houses of the nobles and the Jewish money-changers. Then towards midday arrived the great flotilla, detained for some hours by fifty brave Germans who had defended the half-way fort of Strà. Nobles, fishermen and boatmen joined indiscriminately in pillage; in vain Gritti risked his life, rushing among the plunderers sword in hand, until at nightfall he got the mastery, and hanged the plunderers forthwith. Next morning the Venetian mortars were dragged to the piazza and opened fire upon the castle. Seven shots sufficed to effect a breach. Then Trissino called for a parley at the postern. He bargained for his own life and that of the imperial treasurer, surrendering his other comrades at discretion. He took the gold chain from his neck and gave it to a Venetian officer; but Gritti, always the most generous of victors, returned it, saying, "You shall wear this with honour". Yet Trissino did not escape from Padua without humiliation. As he passed through the streets to the river-gate, a poor old woman struck him with all her might and cursed him like a Fury. All Venice was waiting to see the captives come; but their arrival was purposely delayed till night, and only the nobles were abroad when they were landed in front of the Doge's palace. Lorenzo Loredano to the other prisoners gave a courteous greeting; but to Trissino he vouchsafed no word, although the adventurer was still finely dressed with his golden cap, his massive chain, and his white velvet tunic frogged with gold.

The prisoners, ten in all, Germans and Italians, were kindly used. The Ten examined Trissino, and finding him suffering from a wound, gave him a better prison. Maximilian did not forget his brother sportsman. Personally, and through Prince Henry of Brunswick, he complained of the treatment of the captives, and threatened reprisals. The Doge replied that the Emperor was misinformed, that the prisoners, including

Trissino, were kindly treated and were only prevented from escaping. Towards the close of the year Trissino and others were taken from the prison and lodged in the Captain's house, where they could freely hold intercourse with their fellows. In February 1510 the four chief Germans abused their privilege, and while the guards were guzzling, broke through a walled-up doorway and escaped. Trissino paid the penalty, for he was led back to the strong prison, and here just one year later he died of a broken heart.

Thus ended a remarkable adventurer, with his high ambitions, his winning manners, his love for velvet and gold braid and flowers. He had played for a high stake; that he lost was not all a fault of his. Without a ducat or a trooper he had kept his word, and won for the Emperor a priceless territory. Had Maximilian followed his friend in the field as keenly as he followed him in the chase, the quarry might never have been let slip. Yet Maximilian was a man of sentiment and was not forgetful. When in the half light of a wet November morning the lion of Saint Mark sprang upon Vicenza, the house of Trissino fled from its claws, and for love of its scapegrace member found shelter with the Emperor. And when after seven years of fight the war grew weary, Gian Giorgio Trissino was chosen to negotiate the peace; for Maximilian was known to cherish the name of his agile comrade in the breezy Tyrol mountains, who in his cause had pined to death behind the prison bars above the sluggish waters of the canal.

XII

THE SPANISH COLLEGE IN THE UNIVERSITY
OF BOLOGNA[1]

DAILY the indefatigable omnibus of the Hotel Brun at Bologna disgorges its tale of tourists into the noisy paved courtyard. The first thought with all is, very properly, the hour of dinner: the second with most is, very improperly, the hour of the earliest express on the morrow. Of those who remain to explore Bologna, few are aware that within a short walk of their hotel is to be found an institution absolutely unique outside the Universities of Oxford and Cambridge. Between the Via Belfiore and the two streets which converge into the Via Saragozza lies a triangular island enclosed by walls. Herein lies the Spanish College, the sole survivor of the numerous colleges which once graced, or as educational reformers would believe, disgraced the Universities of Italy, France, Germany and Spain. "This is", says Denifle, "weakly though it be, a survival of the Middle Ages, the solitary example on the Continent." The Spanish College is no seminary for the education of pupils in a particular faculty, nor is it an aggregation of lecture-rooms. It is a corporation consisting of a Rector, and of, what would be called in England, Bachelor Fellows: it holds real property, and its principle is still the idea of a common home for students of a common nationality, which was the basis of most of the colleges of the Middle Ages. Its members matriculate in the

[1] This article is mainly based upon the notes and documents published, in 1880 at Madrid, by Don Pedro Borraj-o y Herrera and Don Hermenegildo Giner de los Rios; partly on two visits made by the writer. The account of the College given by Sepulveda is invaluable but scanty. Illustrative matter has been gleaned from Don Vicente de la Fuente, *Historia de las Universidades en España* (Madrid, 1885), and from Denifle, *Die Universitaten des Mittelalters* (Berlin, 1885). [Reprinted from *Macmillan's Magazine*, March 1888.]

University, and take their degrees in the ordinary course. But the visitor will not find a large number of undergraduates residing within its walls, though excluded from the corporation. This is a peculiar and comparatively modern accretion of the English College. The Spanish College is in a manner the All Souls of Bologna, whilst the status of its Fellows has some resemblance to the now obsolete Taberdars of Queen's at Oxford. The building itself is a small English College translated into Italian. By the gateway is the porter's lodge, opposite it is the chapel, adjoining the latter, upon the first floor, the Rector's lodgings. The quadrangle contains a well, a more practical form of the Mercury of Christ Church; and on each of its two lateral sides are the Fellows' rooms, on the ground and on the first floor, but, being in Italy, they are naturally protected by a loggia, or open corridor. Opposite the chapel and over the entrance are the dining-hall, the library and the common rooms. In addition to this there is a fine hall of reception in which hang the few portraits that have been spared to the College, while it possesses a luxury to which even All Souls has not yet attained—an excellent billiard-room.

But to the visitor from an English University perhaps the most interesting feature of all consists in the Fellows' rooms. They are an almost exact reproduction on a small scale of those which house our own undergraduates. The sitting-room and the bedroom communicate, and both are inexpensively but comfortably furnished. There is the same modest supply of books, the same erratic taste in pictures: we find an occasional piano or other instrument of torture: we become acquainted with the features of the owner's nearest or prettiest relations: the pair of foils replaces the cricket-bat and the racquet. May it be added that the bedroom is infinitely cleaner?

Sepulveda, himself a member of the College, has left a vivid picture of its appearance early in the sixteenth century. The library then adjoined the chapel: the hall had enjoyed a pleasant view of the Apennines, but was too far from the kitchen, and another room had recently been used. He describes the tennis-court and the shady garden with its canopy of vines, and dwells with enthusiasm on its well-drained cellar. The quadrangle was then adorned with trees and shrubs: "In the middle of the College lies a court planted here and there with trees, with laurel, box and jessamine, as people call the plant". The ornamental parts of the College, the façade, the gallery, the portico and the chapel, have been remodelled or rebuilt; but the little vaulted rooms are probably much the same as when they were first inhabited, nor has time destroyed the picturesqueness of the garden.

The origin of the Spanish College dates from the golden age of collegiate life, and few save royal foundations can boast a more distinguished parent than Cardinal Albornoz. He was employed by the Papal Court of Avignon in the apparently hopeless task of recovering its territorial possessions. He was a soldier, a statesman, and an administrator of the first order, and he carried his commission through. Bologna became naturally the centre of his operations. The town owed to him its canal, and in return, he determined that its University should benefit his countrymen. In his will, made at Ancona in 1364, he appointed the future College his residuary legatee; but even before his death he provided his relation, Alvarez de Albornoz, and his chamberlain with sufficient funds for the purchase of land and the building of the College, which was completed in 1367. Shortly before the founder's death, Albornoz himself drew up the statutes, which most unfortunately no longer exist, and Alvarez de Albornoz resigned his office into the hands of Alvaro de Martinez, the first Rector elected according to statute, by the members of the College. Under the founder's will the site of the College was to be within convenient distance to the schools: it was to contain a chapel, a courtyard, lodgings and a garden, and the endowment was sufficient to support a Rector, twenty-four students who were to reside for eight years, and two chaplains. Albornoz himself called his foundation La Casa Española, but its official title became Collegium majus Sancti Clementis Hispanorum.

Solitary survival as the Spanish College now is, at the time of its birth it had many sisters. The fourteenth century was pre-eminently the age of collegiate foundations, though not a few may date from the thirteenth. In the Cardinal's own University of Toulouse three colleges had been founded between 1337 and 1360, two more in 1363, another in 1364, while three immediately followed the foundation of the Spanish College. He was thus thoroughly acquainted with the collegiate system. In Bologna itself it had long existed. Its first college, intended for scholars of Avignon, had been founded in February 1257, the same month and year to which the Sorbonne owed its origin, though the character of the latter was different. Since then a college for natives of Brescia was built in 1326, and another for students of Reggio in 1362–63. At Paris a very large number of colleges was founded in the course of the century, almost all of a national or provincial character. At Oxford the foundation of Queen's precedes, that of New College shortly follows, the Spanish College. At Cambridge, Pembroke, Gonville, Trinity Hall, Corpus and Clare are all within twenty years of it. The same may be said of the earliest colleges of Padua, Perugia, Montpellier, Avignon, Cahors. The great Collegium Carolinum of Prague dates from 1366, and the first colleges at Heidelberg and Vienna fall within the century. Colleges have been more tenacious of life in Spain than in any other Continental country, but no greater mistake can be made than to suppose that the Cardinal brought his system from his native country. The earliest college, that of Lerida, can hardly have existed: the second, the famous Collegio mayor de San Bartolom of Salamanca, was founded consciously on the lines of the Spanish College of Bologna in 1401. It served also as a model, at the request of the people of Siena, for a college which, in 1408, Gregory the Twelfth formed out of the Casa della Misericordia. Foundations at Valladolid and Alcalá, at Seville and Salamanca, owe their origin, their privileges or their statutes to their compatriot at Bologna. It is noticeable also that a second college for Spaniards was founded at Bologna, funds connected with which apparently existed until quite recently.

The Casa Española prospered, if it did not grow. Favours were showered upon it from all quarters. Charles V placed its doctors on an equal footing with those of Salamanca and Valladolid. Philip II recognised the degrees taken by its members as equivalent to those taken in the national Universities, a privilege rarely conferred on foreigners. Its servants wore the royal livery. The Popes were even more practical in their patronage. They exempted the College from taxation, civil or ecclesiastical, and gave it the right of annual presentation to one of the Spanish prebends reserved to the Papacy. The Rector had the grant of jurisdiction, civil, criminal and ecclesiastical, over all members and servants of the College. Equally liberal was the Senate of Bologna, which exempted the College from contributions to the town, and excluded the building from the town-numbering, as being Spanish territory. In the eighteenth century it regarded the College as a Casa Nobile, with the result that the municipal authorities had to be invited to the Founder's Days.

The natural result of the prosperity of the College was that it early came into collision with the University. There were grave questions of precedence which had to be referred to the government of the town. The most important was settled by the governor, the Bishop of Concordia, in 1436, who decided that the Rector should rank second to the Rector of the University. But to modern readers there was a far more interesting cause of jealousy between the College and the University. Within the College lectures were given in all the branches of study to which the members devoted themselves; and so excellent was the teaching provided by these lectures that the professors of the University found their own classes dwindling. No doubt the Bolognese professors, like their modern compeers, were righteously indignant that the college tutor should demean himself so far as to lecture with a view to "the schools". At all events they preferred their complaints on the subject to the Senate of Bologna. The latter acted in a spirit of compromise quite foreign to a modern Government University Commission. It ordered the discontinuance of the obnoxious lectures, but directed that four professorial Chairs should be given to members of the College. The modern tutor might well be content with such a compromise.

A lighter form of skirmishing was carried on between the students and the Jews, if that may be called a skirmish where the fighting is all on one side. It appears the students had acquired the habit of snowballing the Jews, who finally compounded by a handsome gratuity. The subsequent expulsion of the latter by the town was obviously a dead loss to the College; but in compensation, on the first day of snow, several snowballs were presented upon a silver waiter to the municipal authorities, who thereon paid the scot originally exacted from the Jews. A similar ceremony took place at the presentation of the Rector to the Legate, the Archbishop and the Gonfalonier, but as the Rector was elected at the beginning of May, it is difficult to see, even in Bologna, whence the snow can have been procured. Whatever truth the story may contain, the fact remains that the presentation was called "The Gift of Snow".

The life of the College for the first century and a half of its existence was apparently solely connected with the affairs of the University. The only exception may be said to have been the shelter which it afforded to the first printers in Bologna, who were driven within its walls by an outbreak of the copyists who saw their occupation gone. The first book said to have been printed within the College, a manual on Law, by Pedro, Bishop of Brescia, is still one of the treasures of the library.

The establishment of the Spanish power in Italy necessarily gave the College a political complexion which was not favourable to its best interests. The tendency to interfere in Italian politics very early showed itself. In 1511 the students joined the Spanish troops allied to Julius II in the attack upon Mirandola, and lost two killed and one prisoner. The French troops who restored the Bentivoglio dynasty lodged in the College, and, as usual, looted it. The Spanish War of Succession was the cause of a fresh series of troubles. In 1703 the Duke of Castiglione was sheltered in the College during his negotiations with the Prince of Mirandola for the admission of French troops into his garrisons. The students seem warmly to have espoused the cause of Philip V; but in 1708 General Daun removed the Bourbon arms, and temporarily shut up the College, which he forced in 1709 to recognise Charles, though it does not appear to have resumed work till 1715. Equally serious were the events of the wars which followed. In 1735 the Duke of Montemar took up his quarters in the College, which became a voluntary arsenal for munitions of war. In 1743 the Fellows gave up their rooms to wounded officers from the field of Campo Santo, and when the Austrians compelled the retreat of the Spanish troops on Naples, more than one hundred of these poor fellows were left in the town. These had recourse to the Rector for means of escape: he collected barges which were professedly to be freighted with grain from the College estates, and shipped the officers down to Comacchio.

That the College survived the French Revolution is perhaps the surest test of its vitality. After the establishment of the Cisalpine Republic it was deprived of many of its privileges, and probably only saved from extinction by the exertion of Talleyrand. It dragged out a precarious existence until 1812, when by Napoleon's orders the agricultural property was confiscated under pretence of debts due from the Spanish Government. The furniture and the portraits of old members were sold. The latter must have been more interesting than artistically meritorious, for they were knocked down at an all-round price of two francs the dozen. At this period paintings by Rafael disappeared from the College, and the great fresco representing the coronation of Charles V by Pope Clement was irretrievably ruined. The College was put up to auction, and, finding no purchaser, was converted into a workhouse. The library was fortunately saved by Mezzofanti, who secured it for the town, by which it was afterwards restored. On the return of peace the re-establishment of the College was made the subject of negotiations between the Papal, Austrian and Spanish Governments. The original estates were irrecoverable, but the College was endowed, with lands of a corresponding value, situated chiefly in the March of Ancona.

The ship had weathered the storm, but very nearly foundered in the calm which succeeded. In 1853 a royal ordinance deprived the College of its most cherished privilege, that the degrees taken at Bologna should rank as those taken in the national Universities. On the death of the Rector in 1855 the Dean, Don J. Maria Irazoqui, received, instead of a notification of the appointment of a successor, an order to deliver over to one Marliani the whole of the College property within the space of twenty-four hours. The Dean foresaw that the transference of the property to a Government Commission was but a stepping-stone to the suppression of the College. There was apparently a project for transferring the revenues to the support of a Seminary at Rome. Such action on the part of the Spanish Government of those days would correspond to a scheme on the part of an English Government for transferring collegiate revenues to the support of technical education in the large towns. Practical utility would be urged in both cases. A somewhat later, but still more imbecile, idea was the conversion of the College into a School of Art for Spanish painters. Re-painting rather than painting would certainly have been the natural result of study in the Pinacoteca of Bologna. The Dean, however, stood up manfully for the sacredness of the founder's wishes, and for the cause of liberal education. The privileges and the prestige of five centuries could not be transferred to the growth of a day. "The result", he writes, "would be the extinction of a foundation which has produced men of such renown, with the object of creating another whose members would study with a view to successful competition for ecclesiastical prizes rather than to eminence in research."

The gallant Dean was no mere obstructive: he was prepared with a new scheme better adapted to the exigencies of the day, and he won his cause, receiving for reward his appointment as Rector. The last great danger which the College had to undergo was due to the establishment of the new kingdom of Italy. In 1861 the government decreed the sequestration of the College: its seals were put upon the doors of the Bursary, and the Rector was forbidden to interfere in the administration of the revenues. Here again Irazoqui was successful by means of timely appeal to the Spanish Government. Nor was he forgetful of the interests of his colleagues. He made in 1875 an application for the increase of the Fellows' stipend. He represented that the sum of four hundred reals (about four pounds of our money) allowed under the statutes of 1365 were quite inadequate to meet modern necessities, and petitioned for its increase to three thousand reals (about thirty-two pounds). The stipends were raised, but not to this amount. It is doubtful if the revenues could have supported the charge, for the net income in 1873 amounted to not more than thirty-five thousand one hundred and nineteen lire (about fourteen hundred and five pounds).

This slight historical sketch will show that the Spanish College had a reason for its existence which was the cause of its vitality. Notwithstanding the great power of the University of Bologna the College was not outgrown by, nor absorbed in, the University system, as has been usually the case on the Continent. The shocks which it has suffered have been purely the result of external political circumstances, arising mainly from the position held by the Spanish crown in Italy, which rather endangered than guaranteed its existence. The sole exception perhaps was the threatened Government Commission of 1855, which was the more dangerous because it was a self-conscious mania for reform, and a pedantic governmental fussiness which ten years previously had closed the career of the whole collegiate system in the mother country.

If, however, what may be called the external history of the College has its interest, its internal life as illustrated by its statutes gives a far more vivid idea of collegiate life in Italian or Spanish Universities. Every member of a University is of course aware that statutes may survive long after they have ceased to be operative; yet it may safely be averred that in all cases there has been a time when they had a practical meaning.

The earliest statutes were modified by several of the Popes of the Renaissance: some of those made in 1536 are still preserved, though the complete scheme from which the following details have been extracted belongs to 1648, and was the work of the Protector, the Cardinal de la Cueva. In it, however, are imbedded a great portion of the earlier statutes, subject to modifications intended to meet the change of circumstances. The editor of Sepulveda's works states that the statutes framed by him in 1536 still for the most part ruled the College at the date of publication in 1780. Moreover, those of 1648 closely resemble many collegiate statutes of the fifteenth century. The College now consisted of the Rector, thirty-one members and four chaplains. The Rector must be in orders, at least twenty-five years old, and a member of at least two years' standing. He was elected on May 1, held office for one year and was not re-eligible. The method of election was that peculiar mixture of voting and lot well known in the Italian municipalities. The names of all members of over six months' standing were enclosed in balls of wax and thrown into a basin of water. One of the chaplains, with his eyes carefully shut, drew ten names, and out of these ten another chaplain then drew three. The members thus drawn were the electors. They were themselves ineligible, were allowed to hold no communication with the other members, nor to eat and drink until they had completed the election. If they agreed upon a candidate no more formalities were necessary; but if they could not decide between two or three candidates the basin was brought into play again, and the Rector drawn by lot. Notwithstanding the obvious element of chance, the election was perhaps not more liable to accident than that of Heads of Colleges at the present day. A chaplain with his eyes shut will occasionally make as good a choice as a Fellow with his eyes open.

The Rector once elected was a person of great importance during his year of office. Not only was he the second personage in the University, but he might be elected to the Rectorship of the University, in which case, however, the College economically withdrew his Fellowship and salary, giving him only an allowance of wine. He exercised a general supervision over the discipline and the estates of the College, and twice a year he was required by statute to inspect the Fellows' rooms. Young and inexperienced, however, as he must often have been, it was necessary to prevent negligence or favouritism by as severe and detailed a scale of penalties as that applied to the other members of the College. He exercised jurisdiction—civil, criminal and ecclesiastical—over all persons connected with the College; but his action was checked by the direct intervention of the Cardinal Protector, and by the yearly visitation of the Archbishop of Bologna and the Abbot of St. Michele del Monte. His year of office did not count among the eight years of the tenure of his Fellowship, and he received a salary of one hundred and fifty pounds Bolognese (a little more than six pounds of our own money). Of this, however, one-third was only paid on his vacating office in the event of good behaviour, while two-thirds had to be spent in dress "for the credit of the College". A survival of a similar idea may possibly be seen in the tall hat and black coat which the most light-hearted of laymen think it proper to adopt in England on election to the Headship of a House. The Rector held College meetings from time to time, but ordinary business was transacted with the aid of a committee of four, who were annually elected by lot. An unpleasant part of his duties was the obligation to remain in Bologna in the case of plague. In this event two companions were chosen by lot, unless indeed two members volunteered. The same practice prevailed in Spain. Pedro Torres in his diary relating to Salamanca writes: "On July 6, 1507, the members of the College drew lots for the plague".

Of the thirty-one members, ten were to be students in Theology and twenty-one in Law, Medicine being now excluded. They must have studied at least four years in a Spanish University, and have taken or qualified for the degree of Bachelor. If Canonists they must have studied both Canon and Civil Law, and if Theologians, Philosophy, Theology and Grammar. No encouragement was given to those nervous, uncomfortable students who are always changing their minds and their schools. A member once elected must adhere to his faculty, though he might study other subjects in addition. The right of presentation lay with the Bishop and Chapter of the dioceses with which the Founder had been connected, while three presentations were reserved for Founder's kin. If there were not qualified members, or if the Bishops failed to present and the College therefore declined in numbers, it was empowered to nominate from other dioceses.

All candidates must be at least twenty-one years of age, and must be of legitimate birth and Christians born and bred (*Christianos viejos*): there was to be no taint of Jewish or Moorish blood. This qualification existed in Sepulveda's time, but it probably dated from the fanatical period of Ferdinand and Isabella. At Siguenza, the "new Christians" were expelled in 1497. The riches of the father did not disqualify, but a limitation was placed on the private income of the candidate. Members of Religious Orders were not admitted as candidates, nor those suffering from infectious diseases or other inconvenient complaints. Nor might a candidate be married, nor have been a servant at another College, nor must he have a father, brother, uncle or nephew in the College.

The candidate was expected to reside in Bologna for thirty days, was then subjected to an examination *in viva voce*, and finally to the ballot. It appears doubtful if the College often or ever reached the full numbers of the Foundation, and this perhaps is not surprising. Thirty days' previous acquaintance, an examination *in viva voce*, and the use of the ballot, might keep down the number of Fellows in many a college—to say nothing of the previous qualification of *Christiano viejo*.

Once admitted, the young Fellow fared well. The complaints which Londoners make as to the sleeping accommodation of an Oxford College would have been hypercritical. The beds of the Spanish College were required to have the normal number of legs, two woollen mattresses, one of straw or feathers, a pillow equally well stuffed, two blankets and four sheets. The sheets were to be washed at least once a month under penalty of a fine of five soldi (twopence halfpenny). Besides this, the furniture consisted of a chest with lock and key, a copy of the statutes, presses for clothes and books, a reading-desk and other tables necessary for study.

The diet may be regarded as monotonous. It consisted of soup, the quality of which was to be regulated by the Rector, two pounds of veal, which on fast-days was to be replaced by fish and eggs, and dessert to the value of five soldi. There were only two meals a day. If a student for devotional reasons wished to fast he was allowed the full commons for the day at breakfast. On feast-days an addition was made to the fare of half a fowl or pigeon, or a capon from the College estates. No private delicacies were allowed to be brought into hall, nor was eating or drinking permitted in private rooms except when strangers were invited to dine by the members with the Rector's permission.

Strict regulations were made as to behaviour and dress when the members of the College left its walls. During the hours of lecture they must only use the streets leading direct to the schools. No member was allowed to go out without a companion; but a senior might always call upon a junior to accompany him on his walk, and a severe penalty was attached to refusal on the part of the unfortunate junior. The dress consisted of a black gown reaching to the heels, with sleeves and a wide collar, and a *beca* of purple cloth. The latter was a kind of hood, which, however, fell over the shoulder and chest. In Spain its various colours distinguished one college from another. The Spanish students at Bologna also wore the woollen scapular, which the Italians had discarded "as an uncomfortable and useless encumbrance". The modern undergraduate who abhors the use of academicals would endorse Sepulveda's criticism on the conservatism of the College Dons. "This, if I may say what I think, is a nuisance with which we might well dispense, as being both inconvenient and undignified. We should indeed have done so long ago, but for the obstinate opposition of certain conservative bores." Boots and stockings must be black, and the head-dress was to be a decent sombrero adorned only with a twisted cord. Inside the walls the black gown of the College was to be worn, and no light suits were allowed in chapel.

Two gowns of black cloth and two purple hoods were given by the College to each Fellow in the course of his eight years' residence. The Rector only was allowed to array himself on public occasions in expensive silk or cloth cassock and gown, and, contrary to present etiquette at Oxford, pictures represent him as wearing elaborate gloves. In Spain at Alcalá the presentation of gloves formed a part of the ceremony on taking the Doctor's degree, a custom which has descended to the modern University of Madrid. Statutes upon dress are notoriously the hardest to observe; and as at Oxford the black or subfusc raiment is not invariably worn, and as undergraduates may be seen in the streets without cap or gown, so at Bologna, at a somewhat later date than these statutes, we are told that the students of the Spanish College were in the habit of dressing *à la Francesca*. At the present day apparently it is only the Rector who even possesses a gown, and the dress of the students is unexceptionally modern, and eminently non-academic. If the stranger is anxious as to the costumes of the old Spanish University, he will most easily find these at Coimbra. Great attention was naturally paid to the religious needs of the College. The chaplains were not members of the Corporation, and they had no right of attendance at College meetings; but they lived in common with the Fellows, and like them had their commons and their allowance of oil and candles for midnight study. They were permitted to study Theology or Canon Law, but were not allowed to hold any office which might clash with these duties. If they took their degrees the College allowed them four pounds Bolognese (about three shillings and fourpence) for purposes of entertainment. Chapel was compulsory twice a day, but attendance was rewarded by four pounds (Bolognese) a year, while absence was punished by deprivation of battels. On feast-days, if a member was late for mass he lost his wine for breakfast, and if he was not in before the gospel he sacrificed his portion of fowl. Under pain of expulsion the members were obliged to confess at Christmas, Easter and the Assumption of the Virgin, and the Rector also on All Saints' Day.

Study was not necessarily very severe. Each student must devote one or two hours a day to his faculty either in his own room or in the library. It was the business of the Visitor to ascertain that each student gave satisfactory proof of his year's work. Every Saturday evening there was a debate, in which each member in order of seniority had to maintain three conclusions on subjects connected with his faculty. These were posted on the hall-door the previous evening. The argument was opened by the youngest member, and the Rector had the duty of directing the debate and of summing up. A strong feeling of *esprit de corps* existed in the College, and every precaution was taken that it should not be disgraced by the idleness or stupidity of its members. No Fellow might read his exercise for his degree in public until it had been previously heard in College and received a majority of votes. A member might read a paper in the chapel, which was open to the public, but only after it had received the sanction of his companions. So, too, with due licence from the College, he might give lectures within or without its walls. If any Fellow sought a post or a Chair in the University, all members of the College were bound to help him.

The Fellows probably worked hard, for there was little else to do. Brutal athleticism was conspicuous by its absence. The occasional mention of stables is not sufficient warrant for the existence of hunting, or possibly even of riding men. They were probably intended for the cart-horses or oxen from the estates, and for the bailiff's mules. But, as a great treat, a game of ball might be played on feast-days after dinner, but only with moderation and for a limited time. For this purpose there was a court behind the chapel, and the game was probably that of *pallone*, a kind of tennis which is still played by professionals at Bologna. Cards and dice were absolutely prohibited, except between Christmas and Easter, when they might be played under Rectorial supervision and in the Rectorial reception-room. But strangers were strictly excluded from all these unseemly pastimes. Nor was music regarded with any great favour, though a Fellow was allowed to sing or play in his rooms if he could do so without disturbing his colleagues or the neighbours. Strict rules were made against masquerading and dancing: the dances prohibited must have been of what is popularly known as a Spurgeonic character. The general discipline was strict. Blasphemy, bad language, fighting or quarrelling were severely punished. Theft was treated with comparative leniency. No ladies were admitted, even under pretence of attending service, or visiting the chapel. The Rector, however, might give leave for the admission of a mother or sister, or any female relation to whom no suspicion could possibly attach. After lock-up, the gate could only be opened by express permission of the Rector. But young men are alike at all times, and it was found necessary to inflict severe penalties on those who climbed over walls, or got out and in by windows. The walls of the College were high, and the benighted Spaniard had not the advantages offered by the top of a hansom cab; but doubtless even in those days a convenient policeman was willing to give "a leg up" for a consideration. The substantial Spanish or Italian *reja* must, however, have been much less easily removable than the English window-bar.

The scale of punishments was very precise. For ordinary breaches of discipline the sound principle was adopted that the heart is most easily touched through the stomach, and the deprivation of part or all of the day's commons was the usual form of punishment, even for the chaplains. But pecuniary fines were also frequently imposed; and for severer offences members might be locked up in their rooms or even in prison, rusticated for a period, or expelled.

The regulations respecting the property of the College were admirable. Within ten months of admission every member must make himself acquainted with its property within the walls of Bologna, and within two years he must visit all the agricultural estates. But no Fellow was allowed to pay such visits unless accompanied by the proper authorities. Unauthorised junior Fellows of an English College have been known to create a panic among the tenants by making amateur proposals for a peasant tenantry. The danger at Bologna was of a more practical character. The authorities feared that the needy Fellow might take a holiday at the expense of the College. Twice a year the Rector and the councillors went on progress round the estates, and six times a year the whole College had a picnic, for which double commons were allowed. The Rector had, as has been seen, the general supervision of the estates, but the Bursar (*Economo*) was a great personage. The members had formerly managed the estates, but their competence had not been remarkable, and under the statutes of 1648, the Cardinal Protector nominated a Spanish or Italian Bursar, not a member of the College, but a man with a practical knowledge of agriculture and agricultural contracts. He held office for three years, but might be reappointed. He had the letting of the farms by public auction. He collected the rents, which might be paid in money if it were considered advantageous, provided that sufficient wine and grain were reserved for the use of the College. He was personally present on the estates at sowing-time and at harvest. He saw that the land was properly manured, and that the conditions of the leases were kept with regard to rotation of crops and cutting of timber. The supervision of repairs was also one of his functions, though he was limited in the amount which he could spend without the leave of a College meeting. He was also domestic Bursar. He must see that the meat bought was of good quality and weight, and he must buy at advantage and with ready money. All salaries were paid by him, and he was obliged to keep an inventory of furniture, and proper books of account, which were annually presented to the Cardinal Protector; moreover he was audited every three months by the Rector. A book containing a list of the estates and their rents was kept in the library, so that all the members might have an opportunity of inspecting it. The debtors of the College paid money not to the Bursar, but to the Monte di Pietà, or other safe depository. On this the Bursar drew by means of a cheque signed by the Rector; but if the amount exceeded two hundred pounds (Bolognese), the councillors must also sign. No alienation of the College estates or of its books was permitted, though the outlying properties might be exchanged with the consent of the Car-

U

dinal Protector. More prudent than recent University Commissions the statutes provided not only for growth of income but for its possible diminution. Extra table-allowances were first to be sacrificed, and then the stipends of the Rector, Officers and Fellows of the College were to be diminished. In case of increase of value the unearned increment was to be invested in land, and half the proceeds to be given to poor "unattached" Spanish students in Bologna.

All important transactions concerning the estates had to be signed by each member of the College, as being a co-proprietor. The seal and valuable documents were kept in a chest in the chapel, of which the Rector and each of the councillors had a key; but the chest could only be opened by the five keys at once. All documents were to be copied, and negligence with regard to them was visited by severe penalties.

Equal precautions were taken with regard to the library. The catalogue was to be carefully kept. No book was to be taken out under pain of excommunication, and if a book were thus lost its value was to be replaced, and meanwhile the loser forfeited his commons and his salary, and was expelled if he failed to indemnify the College. Readers were directed to handle books carefully, not to leave them lying open, and the last man in the library was to shut the door under penalty of a fine. It is obvious on which side the Cardinal de la Cueva's vote would have been counted in the debate on lending books from the Bodleian Library.

The rest of the establishment consisted of a bailiff, to assist the Rector and Bursar in the management of the estate, a skilful cook and under-cook, a maniple, four servants and a porter. The maniple was responsible for the marketing; the porter might be an old man, and his chief function was to keep out of the College the boys who used to pester the students on their return home. Of the servants, one waited on the Rector, two on the Fellows, while the fourth cleaned the stairs and public rooms. Attached to the College were a doctor, a surgeon, a notary and an advocate who were usually paid in kind by grain and grapes. A barber and a washerwoman also attended weekly.

Such were the statutes which in the main governed the Foundation until the new scheme of 1876 came into force. In 1757–58, however, an important change was made in the position of the Rector, who, in consequence of an unseemly dispute on the election, was henceforth nominated by the Crown from among past or present members of the College, while the office became more or less a permanent appointment.

Under the scheme of 1876, the College was to consist of a Rector, two Chaplains, eight Fellows, a *Contador* and an *Economo* (senior and junior Bursar). The Rector is appointed by the Crown. He must have resided at least three years in the College, must be over twenty-eight years of age, and under forty-five. Married Heads of Houses are not regarded with favour. For the Rectorship, a bachelor or widower without children is preferred: at all events, if the Rector is married, his family is not allowed to live in the College. As of old, he has the general superintendence of the property and of discipline. It is interesting to find that the penalties contemplated by the new statutes consist usually of "gating".

The Fellows must be of legitimate birth, between eighteen and twenty-four years of age, and they must have taken the degree of Bachelor. They receive free board, lodging, service and medical attendance and an income of five hundred lire (twenty pounds sterling), while the College now defrays the expenses of matriculation. The new statutes still regard them as heirs of the Founder. They take formal possession of the property of the College in the presence of a notary, and their signatures are required in any important transactions connected with it. There are few detailed clauses as to study and discipline. A thesis has to be written once a year, which should be forwarded to the Secretary of State. Of the eight Fellows, the Archbishop of Toledo was to nominate two, who were to devote themselves to Theology or Canon Law. Two students of Jurisprudence were to be appointed by the Rector of the Central University of Spain: two nominations fell to the Secretary of State, one to the Rector of the Spanish College and one to the family of the Founder. Members appointed by the Secretary of State are expected to study diplomacy, while one at least of the remaining two should devote himself to scientific agriculture. A ninth place was open to any candidate of the Founder's family who was otherwise qualified. The statutable numbers, however, have never been kept up. In 1797 there were ten Fellows. In 1874 there were four, exclusive of the Rector. At the time of my visit there were apparently five, and of the two with whom I had the pleasure of making acquaintance, one was studying for the diplomatic career, the other was working at Natural Science. Their opinion was that their own country offered an equally good education in Law, but that the Natural Science school of Bologna was far superior. Regulations appear to have been relaxed ever since the last statutes, under which there was a resident chaplain who said mass daily, though attendance at chapel was only compulsory on feast-days. The resident chaplain and the daily service have disappeared. The stern old regulations as to the admission of ladies have become a dead letter. It is doubtful indeed whether the authorities have risen to the pitch of liberality attained elsewhere, and that the fair artistes of the Bologna theatres are permitted to grace by their presence the services on Sunday evening; but at all events English ladies are allowed to enter under pretence of visiting the chapel, even without the special licence of the Rector. It is possible that they may be classed among "those female relatives, to whom no suspicion can possibly attach".

Notwithstanding such modifications, no institution perhaps of such an age has in the main followed so closely in the lines laid by its Founder. Any divergence has been rather in the direction of quantity than of quality. The Spanish College has retained to a remarkable degree its national exclusiveness, survivals of which still linger in the form of provincialism in the English universities, sometimes accounting for the traditional enmities of certain colleges, the origin of which has been long forgotten. It shares, too, with the English colleges the very great merit of providing a common society for men whose studies lie in opposite directions; whereas, on the Continent, most of the modern so-called colleges, the clubs and the seminaries are based on the narrow principle that birds of a faculty should flock together. Small as the Spanish College is, and narrow as is its sphere of action, it is yet a living protest against the principle which is almost universal upon the Continent, and which is rapidly infecting England, that education consists solely in the acquisition of knowledge. For this, and for other reasons, let us hope that it may live long.

[EDITOR'S NOTE.—The Collegio di Spagna has survived the Spanish revolution and continues to flourish on the lines here described. In 1932 there were nine members in residence; law, medicine and diplomacy were among the professions for which they were studying. Modernisation has introduced running water into the bedrooms, but it has left unspoiled the charm and dignity of this island of Spain in Bologna.]

XIII

A POLITICAL SURVIVAL [1]

THE REPUBLIC OF SAN MARINO

A SURVIVAL is usually interesting, but rarely exhilarating. It is wrapped in an atmosphere of spiritual depression. The Conservative would wish it away, as a mockery of the good old times. It inspires him with an active, painful feeling of regret. It is the old yellow love-letter, when life has outgrown love. The past had better die than linger. To the Radical at once sour and sanguine, sceptically contemptuous of the past, servilely superstitious as to the future, the survival is a grievance. Its subdued and faded tones are an eyesore, which his rose-coloured spectacles will not quite correct. It is a constant source of conscious annoyance. It has no right to be there—the past had better be killed than die.

The Republic of San Marino is a survival unique in the political world of Europe, and yet it has escaped the common lot. It is praised by Conservatives and Radicals alike. It is in fact a survival with two sides. On the face of its coins are seen its three medieval castles, on the obverse is read the magic word *Republica*, magic indeed, for this amulet has saved its life over and over again. Thus it is that intelligent Americans, in whose eyes republics are always right, will fondle San Marino as a little long-lost sister, older it is true by far, but fallen into Rip Van Winkle's slumber on an Italian mountain-side. They will complacently gaze upon it as upon a miniature photograph of their own Columbia, with its superfluous exuberance shaded down. Those who have half read and half forgotten the *Politics* of Aristotle seem to remember that he asserted republicanism to be the most stable form of government; for there are some to whom

---

[1] [Reprinted from *Macmillan's Magazine*, January 1891.]

294

republic and democracy are but synonyms. Yet deeper perhaps is the love of those who, standing now on the great level plain of Modern Europe, yet turn their eyes back to the devious mountain-tracks of medieval Italian life. To them the crags of San Marino are as to the scholar is the Pompeii of the plain—more indeed, for San Marino is a Pompeii undestroyed. Older also, for though we have called it medieval San Marino is in essentials prehistoric—a rural commune or group of rural communes such as existed in the Umbrian hills before Rome was known or Florence thought of, when Naples was a barren shore and Venice but a bank of mud. How then has San Marino not only maintained its communal existence but struggled into political sovereignty? The answer to the first half of the question is the easier. In the absence of ethnological deluge—and these usually leave the Ararats unswept—it is the nature of rural organisations to survive. It is only towns that change. In the chronicle of the country there are no births and deaths. It is past all the weight of the Bishop of Oxford and Professor Freeman to smother or drown the crone of the pre-Saxon village. The old witch will not sink, nor will she strangle. He who on a winter's day is plied with mead in an upland Dorset farm blesses the continuity of rural life, and realises that it must have been as old as its weather. But sovereignty is quite another thing. Rural communities bow readily to sovereignty; partly because they are not easily defensible—partly because they barely realise its meaning. Sovereignty in its essence is identical with taxation. The rural commune does not feel the weight of taxation so heavily. It is the rich *bourgeois*, not the poor agriculturist, who kicks against the prick of taxation.

The sovereign independence of San Marino is due to a series of happy accidents which were crystallised into a sentiment. The origin of the State is ascribed to a Dalmatian saint who fled from the early persecutions at Rome and dwelt in a hermitage on Mount Titanus. But it is impossible to believe that there was no earlier population. The mountain is a detached block standing free of the Apennines

—a short twelve miles from the sea-coast, easily defensible and commanding a fertile undulating district. The hill villages must have existed before the towns of the coast. As old as Illyrian pirates were the highland townships of Verucchio, San Leo, Urbino, Osimo, Loretto and, above all, San Marino. Yet, but for the saint and his noble benefactress Felicitá, San Marino would have shared the fate of other highland communes. This lady was a Countess Matilda on a small scale. She gave to the young congregation the proprietorship of the mountain, and the lower table-land was acquired by subsequent purchase and by the generosity of Pope Aeneas Silvius. But Felicitá could not give sovereignty —she could give no more than she possessed. The sovereignty had rested with the Roman Republic—the Empire— the Goths—the Greeks—the Germans. The Papacy itself had as much claim to San Marino as to anything which it possessed. It was included at all events in the donation of Pepin. In the pontificate of John XXII the Bishop of Feltro, who claimed the ownership of the town, proposed to sell it, partly because he needed money to restore his church, partly because the Sammarinesi were rebellious subjects — "not recognising superiors here on earth, and perchance not believing upon a superior in heaven".

Yet the Papacy appears in the thirteenth century to have accepted a judicial decision as to the sovereign independence of the Republic, and Pius II considerably increased its territory in 1463 at the expense of Sigismund Malatesta. The sovereignty of San Marino is therefore almost as complete a puzzle as that of the mysterious Royaume d'Yvetot. Neither can be explained by the ancient alod and the later fief. In after times it is strange also that the theoretical sovereignty of the Republic escaped the practical encroachments of more powerful neighbours. The Malatestas, originally lords of the neighbouring upland fortress of Verucchio, would willingly have made the whole ridge the backbone of their State of Rimini. But this very fact secured for the Sammarinesi the constant friendship of the lords of Urbino, whose magnificent fortress of San Leo is only a few miles beyond the little river

Marino which forms the western boundary of the State. Neither power could allow the other to appropriate so invaluable a strategic position. Florence by conquest or a system of commendation absorbed many of the communes of the Apennines, but her influence did not extend so far over the hills, unless indeed in the case of important outlets such as Forli which commanded a main highway from the Adriatic. The action of Visconti and Sforza was too intermittent in this part of Romagna to be a source of serious danger. But when Caesar Borgia had mastered all surrounding towns and was consolidating his principality upon the Adriatic, the Sammarinesi expected invasion from hour to hour. They appealed in vain to Venice for protection. Caesar Borgia had little sentiment either religious or republican, and Europe now would be a State the less but for the fateful supper in the gardens of Hadrian of Corneto. The Venetians who succeeded Caesar at Rimini cared little for the conquest of mountain towns; they were content if they could appropriate by degrees the seaports of Italy. Far more dangerous was the re-establishment of the Papacy under Julius II in her old nominal dominions. The Saint was likely to be but a poor protector against the Pope. Paul III would fain have given San Marino to his notorious nephew Pier Luigi Farnese. It was at this time also that the adventurous Florentine exile Piero Strozzi actually sent troops which were to converge from Bologna and from Rimini on Mount Titano. But night attacks are usually failures. The invading forces apparently walked round and round the frontiers in a snowstorm and retired discomfited at daybreak without a blow on either side.

From this time downwards the Fourth of June has been at San Marino, as at Eton, a high holiday. The Popes of the seventeenth century behaved with scrupulous moderation towards their tiny neighbour, and entered into formal treaties of alliance. But this dignified calm was followed by the wildest storm that the Republic has undergone. Alberoni became legate of the March. He was always characterised by a mania for unexpected annexation. Not discouraged by his

failure to conquer Sardinia and Sicily for Spain, he would
at least annex San Marino to the States of the Church. He
was indeed the Sir Theophilus Shepstone of the miniature
Republic. A memorial was drawn up by malcontents petition-
ing for annexation, and presented to the Pope. The Government, it was urged, was objectionably oligarchical, the
finances were in a desperate condition, the State-chest was
as empty as was found to be that of Pretoria with its humble
cash in hand of five shillings and fourpence. On the night
of October 17, 1739, Alberoni occupied the town and castle.
On the 18th he proclaimed the sovereignty of the Pope and
ordered all officials to swear alliance in the Collegiate Church.
It was then that the veteran general Alfonso Giangi cried in
thunderous tones, "On the first of October I swore allegiance
to the lawful Prince of the Republic of San Marino. That
oath I now confirm and thus I swear." The result was a
national rising. Alberoni is reported to have used the worst
of language and to have ignominiously run away. The loss
of the Republicans was as little as that of the Boers on
Majuba Hill, but Alberoni conducted his retreat with far
greater skill than the British officers. His sole loss was his
temper and his slipper. The latter is still shown in the Museum
of the Republic—no measures appear to have been taken for
its restoration in the subsequent treaty. The Government
naturally disavowed its agent. It had been falsely informed
of the condition of popular feeling. He was a prancing pro-
consul who had exceeded his orders. Such is the authorised
patriotic version of the incident. Alberoni's own recital,
which may be found in manuscript in the Ambrosian Library
at Milan, leaves an impression that there may have been
some justification for interference. The governing aristocracy
had, it is stated, between 1690 and 1700, become a mis-
governing oligarchy. The Council of sixty had been reduced
to twenty-three, of whom five or six were absentee nobles of
other cities, and even this reduced Council was manipulated
by an inner ring. Against these magnates no debt could be
enforced; they tampered with the laws respecting the supply
of bread and meat, and were corrupt in the administration

of State contracts. They systematically neglected the legal audit of accounts, one of them having refused to produce a statement for a space of twenty years. The taxes fell exclusively on the country folk and on those townspeople who did not truckle to the dominant clique. The territory had become a sanctuary for forgers, assassins and bandits from the Papal States. Some fifty or sixty malefactors were sheltered by the protection of the Republican Government. With reference to this charge it is noticeable that a similar grievance not so many years ago produced some tension in the relations of the Republic and the Italian Government. In another document Alberoni describes the actual process of annexation. This, he urges, was due to the initiative of the inhabitants themselves, who appealed to the Pope to deliver them from misgovernment. Of violence there was no thought. He set out from Rimini in a *calèche*, accompanied only by his chaplain. At Serravalle and the Borgo he was welcomed by deputations and the ringing of bells. No resistance was made to his entry into the city. The people of Fiorentino came to offer homage. Hearing that the malcontents were meditating a disturbance, he sent to Verucchio for a few soldiers, but these were replaced next morning by fifty men from Rimini. Meanwhile, until the arrival of the soldiers, the people of Fiorentino volunteered to guard his house. On Sunday morning the secretary brought the keys of the Rocca, but Alberoni refused to accept them except at the captain's hands, by whom they were subsequently delivered. During the next few days deputations came from the other villages, and the Cardinal undertook the reorganisation of the State, and for this purpose associated with himself the existing magistracy, especially Onofrio, afterwards one of the leaders of the opposition. He again raised the number of the Council to sixty and divided it into three classes. On Sunday, October 25, after celebration of mass by the Bishop of Montefeltro, the Councillors approached the Cardinal's throne to render homage and to take the oath. In the course of this function, much to his surprise, seven protests were raised, beginning with Alfonso Giangi, but the others continued to take the oath, the deputies from the country being peculiarly zealous. Alberoni then made a speech against the tyrants from whom his audience had suffered, and after this the people began to plunder the houses of the malcontents and were with diffi-culty restrained. In the evening the Secretary Martelli sent to pray for pardon, and his example was followed by others. The government of the new acquisition was entrusted to the Governor of San Arcangelo, upon which the soldiers and police, with the exception of six men, left the town. Albe-roni's recital does not unfortunately include the circum-stances of his own exit, but he states his intention of leaving on October 29. In the same collection of documents is a letter from one of the nationalist party, which also stops short of the catastrophe. He attributes Alberoni's unresisted entry to money spread broadcast among mendicants and dis-reputable rascals, and lays stress upon the terror exercised by the police and soldiers, especially those from the tradi-tionally hostile town of Verucchio. He admits, however, that the rebellious inhabitants of Fiorentino supported the Car-dinal, and that at first those of Serravalle were seduced by the representations of their parish priest. A short letter also exists in the Bodleian from one of the seven protesters. His house was plundered ten or twelve times after the celebrated mass, not by the people but by the soldiers. He lost the humblest articles of bedroom furniture, his clocks, his ink-stand, his sand-sprinkler. Just as his house was about to be burnt, he heard that on application he would be pardoned; upon which he and his associates called upon Alberoni to express regret. A pardon was granted and the property restored—or rather the vestiges that still remained of it.

No doubt *ex parte* statements were made on either side, but it appears not improbable that the inevitable tendency to oligarchy had manifested itself to some degree, and that the interests of the country districts had been subordinated to those of the greater families of the town. There is little doubt that the danger had a bracing effect upon the con-stitution, which might otherwise have fallen to decay. At all events the incident made the fortune of San Marino in history. All Europe, in the much decried eighteenth century, applauded the gallant little State, and the Papacy, it must be confessed, behaved with much generosity. It made another formal treaty and the merry Republicans established another whole holiday.

French republicanism was shot out suddenly like a load of bricks upon Italy. The republican general, Napoleon, after his victory at Arcola, was astonished to discover a republic so like—or unlike—his own. "Citizens," his agent Monge said, "the constitution of the States, your neighbours, may possibly undergo some modification. If any portion of your frontiers should be absolutely essential to you I am ordered by the Commander-in-Chief to beg you to let him know." The Government with consummate prudence replied with all the inflation of modern republican style, but begged to be allowed to remain in *piccolezza libertà*. Napoleon in his imperial days did the little State a yet kinder and more thoughtful turn. In the readjustment of Italy it would have been included in the new Italian kingdom. Marescalchi, the Foreign Minister of the new kingdom, consulted the Emperor upon the subject. "Upon my word," replied Napoleon, "we really must keep it as a republican specimen." Curiously enough, the existence of the Republic does not appear to have strained the relations of Castlereagh and Canning. Garibaldi was the next to ruffle the serenity of the mountain State. His republicanism was apt to be a little inconsiderate. Driven from Rome by Oudinot he suddenly appeared at San Marino at 2 P.M. on May 31, 1849. On the following day he posted a notice on the Collegiate Church. "Soldiers! We have reached the land of refuge. Our behaviour towards our generous hosts should be without reproach. This land will assure to us the respect which evil fortune merits. From this this moment I release my companions in arms from all engagements. They are free to return to private life, but I must remind them that it is better to die than to live the slave of the foreigner. Garibaldi." The hero himself did neither. He ran away in the night with his bravest comrades, took fishing-smacks and made for Venice. His less brave comrades and his generous hosts were left in considerable embarrassment. The Austrian troops at Rimini had threatened to invade the Republic if the fugitives were not surrendered. A very reasonable compromise was arrived at. Garibaldi should receive a passport for America; his companions should leave their arms with the authorities of the Republic and have full liberty to return to their homes without molestation. The result of Garibaldi's breach of the convention was that his less courageous comrades were imprisoned upon their arrival at Rimini. All good liberals howled at monarchical perfidy, forgetting some curious incidents which followed the Convention of Saratoga. Since that day San Marino has been the happy State that has had no history. The floodtide of Italian unity levelled all else, but left it high and dry. It is still a Sovereign State. Like Turkey it receives tribute from other Sovereign States. England pays Turkey tribute for Cyprus; Italy, as will be seen, pays San Marino tribute for tobacco.

It has been said that San Marino is a survival at once unique and not depressing. Neither point has as yet been proved. Several cantons of Switzerland have a constitution perhaps as old, but the growth of federalism has deprived them of their sovereign character, though not of their constitutional interest. A fairer parallel is Andorre, but its connexion with the Bishop of Urgel and its relations to France and Spain both account for and trench upon its sovereign existence. The survival of the Principality of Monaco is almost equally curious; but this is of later origin, and differs geographically rather than constitutionally from many a small German principality—or at all events until recent times finds its parallel in such pigmy principalities as Massa and Piombino. Moreover Monaco, if not Andorre, owes its continued existence perhaps not merely to chance, but to games of chance. More truly than Switzerland may it be called the playground of Europe. It is to the credit of the Republic of San Marino that she deliberately refused the bait. Alone perhaps among nations she resisted the advances of that attractive but mysterious tempter, a speculative syndicate. This was the answer of the Government to a report that a gambling concession had been granted. "It is not material prosperity that maintains the good renown of Free States, but rather the high virtues of Republicans at once proud and simple, the self-denial which in poverty is capable of rejecting riches, the courage which does not fear to stand in the face of danger, the greatness of heart which can contemptuously refuse all that might corrupt the people and injure the public welfare."

But this, the captious reader will urge, tends to prove rather the virtuous than the exhilarating character of the Republic. Then let him go to Rimini. Let him prepare himself by vigils, or rather by a sunny morning in the Tempio di Malatesta, the most exquisitely wealthy memorial of the Pagan Renaissance. Let him spend an evening hour on the old wooden pier, and follow with his eyes the red and yellow sails tacking as if not to catch the wind but the last rays of the setting sun. Let him watch the barelegged boys upon the outmost piles fishing with all the patience, not with more than all the success—but with far more than all the beauty—of the fishers of the Thames. Material deficiencies will not dispel his spiritual elation. His dinner will be above reproach; he will eat asparagus early, and he may eat it often. He will remember that Rimini was not merely a station on, but the terminus of a great Roman road. It keeps its Roman bridge, it keeps its Roman gateway, and there are those who keep horses still worthy of the Roman name. An early start, a pretty drive of a few miles, and the traveller rattles over a bridge which spans the Marignano, and he is out of Italy. He may imagine that he at once sees signs of a more prosperous and less heavily taxed community; he may recall Arthur Young's notable discourse on the effects of government as he passes the pillars that divide Spain from France. Certainly the Sammarinese is less niggardly in his treatment of trees. Hitherto nothing has been seen but elms and poplars, most Peruginesque in feathery lightness, for every branch that could be reached has been pared away. On republican soil there are well-grown trees, oaks even which would not disgrace a Hampshire homestead. At all events the three-peaked cap of Liberty is garlanded with flowers. The hill country begins at the township of Serravalle and the slow ascent hence to the Borgo is beguiled by patches of scarlet anemone, tulips, jonquils and narcissus, while to the rock itself cling primroses—in Italy a mountain plant—violets, hepaticas and purple corydal. The Borgo lies on a small plateau beneath the steep long ridge with its three crags crowned with castles. This is the business centre of the State; here is held the market, here is the inn, and here the horses are put up. Imbeciles and decrepits may be dragged by oxen hence to the town itself, though the ascent is not so tiring as Highgate Hill or Fitzjohn's Avenue.

The Sammarinesi farmers seen in the market-place are a good sample of strongly built, well-fed Romagnols. Sales are conducted with much animation. Two sturdy proprietors stand back to back; they turn only to give vent to words which sound like imprecations, while their gesticulations suggest an immediate appeal to fists or knives. A third party stands between the two; he caresses the one, he remonstrates with the other; his hands are raised to heaven; his voice is piteously plaintive. He pulls one by the shoulder, the other by an elbow, and finally by an apparently acrobatic feat he unites their hands. This is no blood-feud forgiven, but a harmless heifer sold.

The city itself is a tidy well-built mountain town of some four thousand inhabitants. It has its palaces wherein dwell the aristocracy of the Republic, its classical Collegiate Church which serves as its Cathedral, its arch-priest being the chief ecclesiastical authority of the Republic. The old arcaded palace of the Sovereign Council has recently been encased in a larger if not so interesting a structure. High above the town stands the Capitol, the Rocca. This is the point of culminating interest in the State. Hence on high holidays floats the blue and white banner of the Republic, and here are the curious clock and splendid old bell which summon to Popular Assembly or to Council. Few views have more varied historic interest than that from the tower-top. It

commands the territory of the whole Republic, corresponding almost exactly to the detached block of Mount Titano.
The dullest traveller must feel a thrill as he stands in such a
spot. He is on the acropolis of the solitary aristocracy or
polity that has survived in Europe, a state that, technicalities
apart, has remained unchanged for over fourteen centuries.
Beneath him is Ariminum (Rimini), for long the limit of
Rome's Republic. Beyond it is the Rubicon, the beginning
of the Empire. Around the mountain's base had surged
succeeding waves of Goths and Greeks, the hosts of Alaric
and Theodoric, of Belisarius and Narses. This rocky sunny
land is the forcing-house of Renaissance culture. From
Verucchio to Rimini we trace the Malatestas from their
cradle to their grave, saints and sinners, men of blood and
men of letters. Hard by is the land of the Dukes of Urbino,
Montefeltro and della Rovere. Francesco, their greatest,
saved probably the existence of the Republic. Readers of
John Inglesant will recognise in the Duke of Umbria the last
of these two illustrious lines. Caesar Borgia had drawn a ring
fence around the mountain. San Leo was the scene of his
most successful treachery, taken with its own cannon lent
by a too confiding friend. Here too an earlier and greater
Spaniard, Cardinal Albornoz, had re-established the claims
of the Babylonish Papacy. The skirt of Pesaro is the hem
of the garment of Caterina Sforza, wife for her third venture
of Giovanni delle Bande Nere, ancestress of Grand Dukes of
Tuscany, to whom France and Spain owe queens, and Brazil
an empress.[1]

Interesting, however, as are the personal and political
associations of the stretch of country around the mountain's
base, yet to some the constitutional interest of the town itself
will be more unique in kind. San Marino is a sanctuary for
old Italian municipal forms and usages, driven from shelter
to shelter before the march of national centralisation. The
existing constitution is a living lesson on medieval history.
Fortunately, also, it not only exists in practice but in print,

---

[1] [Giovanni delle Bande Nere was the son of Caterina Sforza, the
offspring of her marriage with Giovanni di Pier Francesco de' Medici.]

for the Statutes of the Republic were published at Forli in
1854, and in their more essential constitutional features there
has been little change. Theoretically, sovereignty in the last
resort belongs to the people, and of old this was practically
exercised by the Arengo, which thus has some correspondence
in meaning and functions to the Florentine Parlamento. The
Sammarinesi, however, were wiser than the Florentines.
When the increase of population and territory rendered a
gathering of the whole people an incompetent engine of
legislation, the Arengo was not allowed to remain as a
mischievous survival with ill-defined authority at the mercy
of the governmental wire-pullers. The prerogatives which
were reserved to the Arengo were small but definite. By the
clang of the great bell and the voice of the crier each household is summoned, under penalty of a fine, to send one
member to the General Assembly when it shall seem good
to the Captains to convoke it. Here by statute the election of
officials is proclaimed, a statement of receipts and expendi-
ture is published, as also regulations respecting roads and
watercourses, woodlands, watch and ward. Had the communal property been more considerable, the General Assembly might have retained more power. But whereas many
of the Apennine communes in the sixteenth and seventeenth
centuries wrested, or more probably recovered, from the
local lordlings the manorial or common lands, in San
Marino the enclosure of the common field appears to have
been singularly early, and in this respect the Republic is
exceptionally modern, or, as the advocates of land nationalisa-
tion would urge, exceptionally retrograde. Possibly the most
important right that still remained to the Arengo was that
of petition and of the presentation of grievance. But supply
was rendered independent of petition. It was after the
accession of territory granted by Pius II in 1463 that the
constitution of the State was fundamentally altered—a change
much more sweeping than the closing of the Council at
Venice. The people now delegated its sovereignty to the
Council, which was raised to sixty members, of whom forty
represented the town and twenty the country districts. As

in most Italian Councils numerically named, and as in all statistics, the figures did not represent the facts, but were conveniently elastic.

In 1600 an order of Patricians was established, to which was given one-third of the representation, and the Council now consists of twenty *nobili*, twenty *artisti*, artisans and shopkeepers, and twenty *contadini*, agriculturists. The harmony of the Republic is undisturbed by general elections, for the Council is recruited by co-optation. The members must be at least twenty-five years of age, and sit for life unless disqualified by crime or clerical orders. As of old at Venice, precautions are taken that family rings should not dominate the State, for but one member from each family may be chosen, and if personal interests are discussed in Council the statutes provide that relations to the third degree shall leave the hall. Some of the regulations for the conduct of business are noteworthy. The Assembly begins with prayer. The Arengatores are chosen by lot, who deliver their speech and give their vote first. The wearisome initiative of the professional bore is thus avoided, and the sensible but tentative and retiring member is forced to make up his mind and to extemporise his speech. No member is permitted to speak twice without special leave, and those who interrupt are fined. With such a rule the House of Commons could pay its clerks and subsidise its kitchen.

Members of Council, as those of the House of Commons in good old days, had their privileges. They could not be imprisoned for small debts. There may possibly be as in England an agitation for payment of members. The main object of the select candidate of the future will be to pay his debts, which after all is more conducive to the happiness of the greater number than the avoidance of their payment.

The composition of the Council is naturally a matter of supreme importance, for the State may be saddled with an incompetent legislator for the term of his natural life, it being a matter of common experience that the most incompetent legislators are neither criminally nor clerically inclined. Thus whereas in the election of executive officers for short terms from among the ranks of the Council lot is a constant element, in this the responsibility is fixed upon those who nominate the candidate. This is quite in accordance with the Aristotelian doctrine that the less important offices only should be filled by lot. Each of the Captains may nominate two persons, whose names are read aloud by the Chancellor. Each member of the Council may then make one nomination, after which the names are put to the vote. Relations to the third degree are not allowed to vote for their kindred.

A Council of Twelve likewise exists which may be mentioned for the sake of correcting the false impression that it is in any sense a Second Chamber or an Upper House. Its functions are mainly judicial or magisterial. It is interesting chiefly from the mixed methods of vote and lot so familiar to those acquainted with the Venetian Constitution. The statutes provide that sixteen members of the Grand Council be drawn by lot, eight from the town and eight from the country. From each of these bodies four are then chosen by ballot. The members hold office for a year, but in order that, in University phraseology, "the standard of the School may be preserved", four members of the previous year are added, a practice which was also prevalent in the Judicial Committees, the *Quarantie* of Venice.

At the head of the Executive stand the two Captains Regent. To them the statutes assign the sovereign authority and the power of the sword. They may not enter foreign service, nor leave the territory of the Republic for more than a fortnight, under penalty of a heavy fine and eternal infamy. They draw a small salary, and during their six months of office are free from all State burdens. The elections take place at the end of March and September. Twelve names are drawn by lot. Each of the persons so drawn secretly nominates a candidate to a committee consisting of the existing Captains, the Chancellor and two of the twelve preceding Captains. Of the number so nominated six are selected by vote, and their names are placed on slips in three pairs. These slips are tightly rolled and inserted into the middle of oval beads of ivory or wax. One pair is then drawn by a

young boy before the altar of San Marino, after celebration
of the mass, the other two slips are then destroyed. The
candidates must be resident natives, qualified by age and
character. For so small a state as San Marino the *divieto*, or
temporary disqualification, is somewhat wide. None of those
whose names were drawn as nominators may be elected, nor
one who has been Captain for the previous twelve years, and
no nominator is permitted to propose a relation. The Captains
enter office on May 1 and October 1, and these are gala
days in the Republican calendar. The new Captains and the
old meet in the Palazzo Communale and proceed in state
accompanied by a guard of honour to the church. Here mass
is celebrated, the existing Captains sitting upon their thrones
in the chancel, the selected candidates immediately below
them in the aisle. Then in the great hall an *egregius ludi
literaris*, or the State schoolmaster, or one of his best pupils,
makes a Latin oration dwelling upon the greatness of the
office and the responsibilities which it entails. This concluded, the new Consuls take the oath and receive from their
predecessors the standard, keys and seal of the Republic.

During the time of office the executive and judicial functions are very onerous, and it was foreseen that the men most
capable of governing would be the most disposed to avoid
the burden. But political abstention is in San Marino, as
in well-ordered republics of old, a crime. A refusal to be
elected is by statute followed by deprivation of citizenship,
eternal infamy and a heavy fine. Against this there is no
appeal, and a penalty is even inflicted on any who should
plead in the recusant's behalf. At the close of office the
Captains, as all other officials, undergo the scrutiny to which
Aristotle attributes so much importance. Two names for this
purpose are drawn by a boy from the roll of all the Council,
and the two persons thus drawn publicly nominate two
others to serve as Syndics. These are compelled to deliver
judgement within a very short period, so that the Captains'
anxiety as to the result of the scrutiny is not of long duration.
The only other executive officer whom it is necessary to
mention is the General. To him is entrusted the security of

the Republic, the command of the troops, and the appointment of their officers. The standing army consists of a select
guard of honour for state occasions, but the liability to
service appears to be universal, though the statutes provide
that the General may call out one member from each small
family and two from the larger, exemption being given to
doctors, scholars and officials. The office of General has no
regular duration, and owing to its more permanent character
it appears to have acquired a political importance that was
not contemplated in the statutes, so that it may almost be
described as a permanent Secretaryship of State. It is however, temporarily delegated, if the General be elected
Captain, in order that the highest officer of the Republic
may not also wield its military power.

The administration of justice retains some very characteristic features of medieval Italian life. It was believed throughout a large portion of Northern and Central Italy that impartiality could only be secured by the appointment of a
foreigner to the highest judicial office. In San Marino the
chief judicial adviser of the State, the *Commissario della legge*,
is still a foreigner, and so also are the six or eight handsomely
dressed policemen. The penal code fills a large portion of
the Statute Book and is well worth perusal, though it has
been radically modified in accordance with the humanistic
principles or prejudices of modern times. Capital punishment has been abolished. There is no Judenhetze. Of old
the San Marino noble who hoped to rise to political eminence
on the ducats of a Jewish heiress, lost possibly his heart but
certainly his head, and that of his wife to boot. He would
to-day but lose consideration. That, however, in San Marino
counts for much, perhaps for more.

Two of the three castles which crown the peaks of Mount
Titanus are unoccupied, but the Capitol serves as the State
prison. On the occasion of a recent visit it was unusually full.
Not only had a *poveretto* been confined for several months
for being too ready with his knife, but a party of four, including a woman, were lodged in gaol on a charge of murder,
the only such incident for seven years. They were found in

a tavern with the body of the murdered man, and none would give evidence against the other. Little sympathy was expressed for the victim, one of the least reputable members of the community, and indeed knife play seemed to be regarded, as in certain other quarters, as a gentlemanly vice, and to minister to the creature comforts of the offenders while in gaol was clearly not abhorrent to popular opinion. The commoner offences are characteristic of a hot-blooded people as all Romagnols are, and of a well-to-do population as all Romagnols are not. Offences against women are tolerably frequent, robbery very rare because the people are prosperous. Drunkenness is common, especially on market-days, for wine is cheap and farmers rich. "Of course," said the writer's guide, "they drink, for wine costs little." It is in all probability the poverty and over-taxation of South European nations that keep them sober rather than their nature or religion. A French traveller of the last century noticed that the Catalonians who worked and made money always drank, the Spaniards were idle, poor and sober. Drunkenness, he added, was the outward and visible sign of industry.

Citizenship of the Republic is most jealously guarded and with reason. Who would not wish to become a native of a territory singularly healthy, and enjoy an almost complete immunity from rates and taxes? A few market dues there may be, and the landed proprietors are required to send their quota of stone to repair the roads, but of taxes there are none. Formerly a salt-monopoly, that well-fought bone of contention on the neighbouring Adriatic shores, appears to have been a principal source of revenue. The expenses of government are now mainly supported by a sum paid by the Italian Government in compensation for the prohibition of tobacco-growing by State authority. Such a revenue is due rather to a happy accident than to economic skill; but it is fair to bear in mind that even before this arrangement State burdens were extremely slight. Official salaries are small and much work is practically unpaid; where the *honos* is, there falls the *onus*. To serve the Republic is sufficient guerdon.

In such a State can there be any political discontent? Are there those who think that a co-optative Council is an anachronism and that the form of the Republic is an oligarchy? The writer, being one disposed to cling to a bright past rather than to leap into the dark future, was startled to see the writing on the wall, *Viva il suffragio universale!* He has since been assured on the highest possible authority that this was the handiwork of some eccentric individual, or of some scatter-brained youth craving for novelty, and that such ridiculous manifestations are by the sane majority of the citizens noticed only with a pitying smile. Ridiculous indeed would be the application of the nostrums of modern democracy to this ancient State. It would be to mistake the whole basis of old Italian citizenship. At San Marino, as at Florence, citizenship consists not in the right to elect but in the right to be elected, and from this no class is excluded. It is true that vacancies in the Council occur but rarely, but each family may live in hope. Moreover, the State imitates the Venetian model in very large numbers of governmental officers. These not only give to many households a stake in the government, but they provide a gradual training for the higher posts. The statutes indeed present, except in respect of land, an almost perfect picture of State Socialism; the butchers and bakers have wellnigh the place of governmental functionaries, and the schoolmaster is appointed year by year. The State doctor inspects the chemists' shops and is bound on curiously satisfactory evidence of illness to visit the sick. Goats are prohibited from working their sweet but wayward will; indeed, as in many Apennine communes, they are forbidden entrance to the State.

Such is the character of the miniature Republic which Machiavelli might well have classed with Sparta, Rome and Venice among the most durable of States, and which all but satisfies the criteria of the Aristotelian aristocracy, a government founded not on birth, nor wealth, nor numbers, but on merit. Survival though it be, it is not without its lessons for the statecraft of the future. It is the final term in the development of local government. There may yet be those who hesitate to believe that all history consists in progress, who still furtively cherish the doctrine of recurring cycles, who believe with Machiavelli that in politics as in religion it is needful from time to time to revert to simpler and purer forms. To such the older masterpieces may still serve as models and not as curiosities. When all the larger political carnivora shall meet and rend each other in the great national bear-garden, when central administration shall have become yet more impossible, then there will be space and air for local government and worthy functions for local aristocracy. There may even now be citizens of large States taxed beyond endurance for fancies not their own, who cry with the Sammarinese noble when robbed of his household goods by the representative of centralisation and consolidation, *Magnus est Sanctus Marinus.*

XIV

A GRAND TOUR IN THE SIXTEENTH CENTURY [1]

IT was pleasant to travel with a cardinal of royal blood in the early sixteenth century. The Cardinal of Aragon, moreover, grandson of King Ferrante of Naples, though pious and clean-living, was not uncomfortably ecclesiastical or ascetic. He and his ten gentlemen all wore alike secular costumes of rose silk striped with black velvet. The cavalcade numbered thirty-five mounts, increased to over forty-five by grooms and musicians annexed in France. One mule carried the plate and crockery, another his eminence's bed, neatly packed in two bundles, while an advance-guard of two cooks saved the refined Italians from many a barbarism in the parts of Germany. Luigi d' Aragona suffered from gout, as might have been expected, but he was no mere sybarite. Peter Martyr of Anghiera found in him his most stimulating patron, and he had a cultivated curiosity for works of art, antiquities, musical instruments and scientific inventions. Thus his chaplain, Antonio de Beatis, might congratulate himself upon visiting ultramontane countries in such sympathetic company. Posterity may also congratulate the Cardinal upon his chaplain, for a grand tour in early days has rarely had a livelier diarist than Antonio.

The editor, Dr. Pastor, rightly brings into line the journals of two companions of the great Bohemian baron, Rozmital (1465–67), and that of the Castilian knight, Pero Tafur (1435–39); for they covered much the same ground, and are therefore useful for comparison.[2] In some respects, however,

---

[1] [Reprinted from the *Quarterly Review*, July 1908. Based on the diary of Antonio de Beatis (1517–18), written in Italian, and edited by Dr. Ludwig Pastor under the title *Die Reise des Kardinals Luigi d'Aragona, beschrieben von Antonio de Beatis* (Freiburg-in-Bresgau, 1905).]

[2] Leo von Rozmital, *Reise durch die Abendlände in den Jahren 1465–1467*, ed. J. A. Schmeller (Stuttgart, 1844); *Andancas é Viajes de Pero Tafur* (Coleccion de Libros Españoles raros ò curiosos, vol. viii, Madrid, 1874).

the closest parallel is the exactly contemporary description of Charles V's journey to Spain by Laurent Vital, whom Antonio must actually have seen at Middelburg.[1] Our diarist disclaims any profound knowledge of Latin, nor could he make profession of literary Tuscan. Being thus reduced to his native Apulian idiom, he writes as naturally as would a sensible tourist of to-day, while his art of seeing and making see selects just those salient features of a city or a nation which interest alike the historian and the traveller.

The Cardinal started from Ferrara in May 1517 and returned thither in the following January. His route lay over the Brenner to Innsbruck, and thence by Augsburg, Ulm and Nuremberg to Constance. The Rhine conveyed him to Cologne; and the Netherlands were reached by way of Aix and Maastricht. After some five weeks in Low-Country cities the party made for Calais, Boulogne and Rouen. A visit to Paris was followed by a journey to Caen and Mont Saint-Michel, whence the way led through Rennes, Nantes and Angers to Tours, Amboise and Blois. Lyons having been reached by Bourges, a wide sweep was made through Savoy and Dauphiné to see Chambéry, the Grande Chartreuse and Grenoble. From Valence the Rhone was followed to Avignon and Arles. Marseilles was quitted for a pilgrimage to Sainte-Baume; and, finally, a rough ride along the Riviera brought the travellers to Genoa, and thence to Milan, at that time, to Antonio's dire disgust, in French occupation.

Antonio was peculiarly fortunate in the personages whom he met during these nine months. At Innsbruck were the two young queens, as he calls them—Anna, the fiancée of Ferdinand, and his sister Mary, who became Queen of Hungary. The former was a girl of fourteen or fifteen, full of life and gaiety, with sparkling eyes, and a complexion which seemed all "milk and blood". Mary, younger by four years, was dark and not, to Antonio's taste, pretty. In Augsburg the Cardinal consorted with the wealthiest German financier,

---

[1] [*Relation du premier voyage de Charles Quint en Espagne* (Collection des Voyages des Souverains des Pays-Bas, vol. iii, ed. Gachard et Piot, 1881).]

Jakob Fugger; and at Mainz he caught a glimpse of the wildest German freebooter, Franz Sickingen. The Emperor Maximilian was unfortunately just missed, and thus we lose a companion picture to Luigi da Porto's lifelike sketch of eight years earlier. The reason was the necessity of hurrying on to catch the young King of Spain, who was on the point of sailing for his new dominions.

Charles was found at Middelburg. Antonio saw him first at mass and heard the chanting of the royal choir, the best church music then in Europe. Afterwards a papal nuncio presented a brief conferring the cardinalate on the boy bishop of Cambrai, whose speedy translation to the primacy of Toledo was a primary cause of Castilian revolt. Among the bystanders were Pescara, future victor of Pavia; John of Brandenburg, who was to console Ferdinand's widow, Germaine de Foix; and the fascinating Count Palatine Frederick, whose incipient love affair with the King's sister Eleanor had been roughly smothered the year before. At a formal audience Antonio saw the Court at closer quarters. His judgement of Charles is unusually favourable for those early days, when he was commonly reckoned a negligible quantity. The face was long and thin, and, unless he thought about it, the lower jaw dropped and the mouth fell open. Yet the expression was attractive and extremely dignified; and these are the precise characteristics on which Charles' visitors dilated in later years. The lank, straight legs were "incomparably beautiful"; and the Cardinal, an expert in horsemanship, pronounced Charles to have an admirable seat, befitting one who, as was later said, would have been the best light horseman in the Spanish army had he not been Emperor. Charles was punctual in his religious duties, attending daily one plain and one choral mass. He dined alone and in public, but not sumptuously, and, remaining at table, gave gracious audience to all comers, while the Catalan Bishop of Badajoz, interpreting in all languages, explained that the King could not as yet reply. The Cardinal talked long in Spanish with Margaret of Burgundy, whom Antonio thought not ugly, but of a truly imperial presence, lightened by that charming smile to which her portraits bear invariable witness. Like other men of taste, he found the King's sister Eleanor most bewitching.

A month later Antonio saw the French Court at Rouen. Francis I's amorous trespassings were already notorious, but he paid creditable outward respect to his young wife Claude, who was small, ugly and lame in both legs. Far handsomer was the King's mother, who was tall, plump, rosy and lively. She seemed to be about forty, so she might be regarded as "excellent stuff for more than another ten years". She was always with the King and Queen, and was absolute ruler of the State. Francis was of fair height and good appearance, in spite of his big nose; but the Cardinal thought his legs too slight for so large a body. He was active and very genial, delighting especially in stag-hunting. On the Feast of Assumption he confessed and communicated before touching for king's evil, which was believed to dry gradually after the king's touch and the sign of the cross. The Cardinal rode with him to a game of tennis, and then took part in a dance, but was prevented from hunting by an attack of gout in both feet, which tied him to Rouen for ten days. Such were the drawbacks of royal hospitality.

Other notabilities met in France were Lautrec, the ill-fated Duke of Bourbon, and Maximilian Sforza, the recently dispossessed Duke of Milan, now a satellite of the French Court. Antonio despised this prince, and contrasts him with his brother Francesco, whom he had met in Tyrol, and who was literary, strenuous and very sensible. More interesting than all was Leonardo da Vinci, who was visited at Amboise shortly before his death. The septuagenarian artist showed the Cardinal's party three of his pictures—a St. John the Baptist and a Virgin with Saint Anne, both now in the Louvre, and a Florentine lady, who cannot with certainty be identified, painted life-size for the late Giuliano de Medici.

It is true (says Antonio) that, owing to a certain paralysis having affected his right hand, no more good work can be expected of him. He has, however, trained a Milanese pupil (presumably Francesco Melzi), who works very well. And, though Messer

Leonardo cannot colour with the softness of old, yet he serves to make sketches and to teach others. This gentleman has written on anatomy in rich detail, and with pictorial illustration of limbs, muscles, nerves, veins, joints, intestines, and all that can be discovered in the bodies of men as well as women, such as none other has yet approached. This we saw with our own eyes; and he told us, indeed, that he had dissected more than thirty bodies, male and female, of all ages. He has also written on the nature of water, on various engines, and other things, an infinity of volumes, all in the vernacular, which, if ever published, will be full of profit and of pleasure.

A little later Antonio saw Leonardo's "Last Supper" in Milan, already, after the lapse of only twenty years, showing signs of damage "from the dampness of the walls, or some neglect or other". This is by many years the earliest definite notice of deterioration. It is not mentioned by the Frenchman, Pasquier le Moine, who, some two years earlier, had admired the realism of the detail: "To see the bread you would say that it was natural and not artificial; the wine, the glasses, the dishes, the table-cloth, and the viands are in like case, and so too the figures".[1] Antonio confirms the story that these figures were painted from the life after notable Milanese personages of the period.

Other well-known masterpieces Antonio saw actually in the making. Maximilian's monument in Innsbruck Cathedral was not completed before 1580; but the gigantic ancestors who stand on guard along the nave were already being cast in the Mühlau foundry. Eleven of the intended twenty-eight statues were finished, while some of the 128 small figures of saints, which were being made in Innsbruck itself, were also seen. This fixes the date of the twenty-three statues now shelved in the Silberkapelle, and proves that they were part of Maximilian's original design. In Brussels, too, the factory was visited where sixteen pieces of tapestry were being woven for the Sistine Chapel, at a cost to Leo X of two thousand golden ducats each.

The catholicity of Antonio's taste in art is remarkable. On

---

[1] [*La Conquête du Duché de Milan*, MS. Bibliothèque Nationale.]

visiting Ghent he thought the great Van Eyck the most
beautiful work in Christendom, for modelling, colouring and
the chiaroscuro—if it may so be called—of the Adam and
Eve, then at the extreme right and left of the picture, but
now long since removed. He could naturally appreciate
French Renaissance architecture, as at Gaillon or Le Verger,
because, though the fusion of French and Italian art was
chemical rather than mechanical, the Italian element was
always present. But he could equally admire German and
French Gothic, distinct from each other and from the Italian
Gothic, even of Apulia. It is not, however, always easy to
follow the humours of his taste; they may have varied with
his master's gout, which Antonio perhaps shared, for he in-
veighs against the cobbled streets of Avignon as being bad
to ride and worse to walk, and very ruination to the feet. He
extols the richly carved façade of Rouen Cathedral and its
two fine towers, one still unfinished, but at Saint-Ouen he
mentions only the treasury. Bourges he thought most beautiful, though it was not cruciform like most modern churches;
but Angers he condemns as ugly, for it resembled a long,
narrow chapel without aisles. Nantes and Bayeux both
appealed to him, while the church of St. Stephen at Caen,
which had been recently restored, he thought the best-planned
building which he had seen in France. Notre-Dame at Paris
had no charm for him, in spite of its size and situation. In
Germany he praises Speyer and Ulm, and is especially delighted with the masonry of Strassburg Cathedral tower, the
stones being all riveted without a grain of mortar. Nothing
could be less like Strassburg than the round Romanesque
cathedral of Aachen, yet this is highly commended as small
but exquisite. Among Netherlandish churches Antwerp and
Malines are singled out; and, although municipal architecture
is seldom mentioned, the town hall of Louvain is praised
for the delicately carved foliation of its façade.

While at Bourges, Antonio draws a striking distinction between Italian and ultramontane monumental art. Neither in
Germany nor France had he seen the superb and elaborate
tombs of Italy with canopies rising high against the church

walls. The monuments, on the contrary, were flat, resting on
the ground, with the figures either in high or low relief. Yet
he had seen many fine French tombs subject to Italian influences. He fully describes, for instance, that of the Duke
and Duchess of Brittany at Nantes, the figures in alabaster
resting on a black marble base, which, he says, for a modern
work was truly fine. At Saint-Denis the figure of Charles
VIII, unlike those of his predecessors, which were in half-
relief, was on its knees; while the magnificent monument of
Cardinal Amboise at Rouen might certainly be thought to
answer to Antonio's ideals. He had, however, probably in
his mind's eye the glorious Gothic sepulchres of Naples,
rising tier upon tier to the equestrian statue at the apex.
After all, for him no foreign cathedral could compare with
the triumph of Italian art, the Certosa of Pavia, the most
beautiful, lustrous and fascinating church that he had beheld
in all his travels. And, as for tombs, here was Gian Galeazzo
Visconti to the life, with his little beard of a very few
long, crimped hairs in the most fantastic fashion that nature
could have produced. In Pavia itself was Saint Augustine's
sepulchre, with an infinity of figures so exquisitely carved in
alabaster that no modern master could approach it. Experts
held it to be among the finest things in Italy; of foreign lands
there was no need to speak, for what could not be found in
Italy it were vain to seek elsewhere.

If the Certosa were Europe's most splendid church, Antonio was convinced, on reaching Milan, that Ludovico il
Moro's castle was its most sumptuous residence. Yet every
other country had its own show-places, in the description of
which the diarist is of first-rate importance. In Augsburg
Jakob Fugger himself played cicerone to the splendours of
his palace, the street front frescoed with bright colours and
gold, the walls inlaid with marble, the copper roof, the rooms
furnished some in German, some in Italian fashion. He
showed also the Fugger chapel in the Carmelite church, with
its own organ, mosaic pavement, and brilliant paintings; the
altar was enriched by figures after the antique, the oak choir-
stalls with prophets and sibyls in marvellous relief. The

financier took care to state that this chapel had cost 23,000 florins. But this he could well afford, as he could handle 300,000 in cash without touching his invested capital. He boasted that he had financed the nomination to every see in Germany, and some of them twice or thrice. Some 10,000 workmen were employed in his Hungarian and Austrian mines; and he was making handsome profits, though the rents were greatly raised.

At the ducal palace at Brussels Antonio was chiefly taken by the deer park, the maze and the tennis-court, "in which they play with racquets (*ricchecte*), and extremely well". The Nassau palace was reputed the masterpiece of the German type. Upon the huge central court opened halls and rooms panelled in oak with a wavy grain, like satin. Among the pictures were those of Hercules and Dejanira, fine figures entirely naked, and a "Judgement of Paris" with the goddesses exquisitely painted. There, too, were fantastic panels with landscape, seascape and skyscape, shell-fish and cranes, men and women black and white, birds and animals of every sort, all so natural and quaint that nobody, without seeing them, could possibly conceive them. Much cooking was needed in this hospitable household; and therefore in mid-kitchen was a wall with a fireplace on either side, and both could be used at once. Also there was much drinking; and therefore a mammoth bed of twenty-six palms' length by thirty-four was kept always ready with its full complement of pillows, sheets and counterpanes, for the count liked to see his guests drink; and, when they were too full to stand upon their feet, he had them thrown upon this bed.

The most delightful features of the palace of Blois were the library and the gardens. One Pacello, whom Charles VIII brought back from Naples, had planned the latter, and now, as head gardener, received high wages in the form of benefices. Here were grown all fruits of the Terra di Lavoro, small figs which, however, rarely ripened, oranges and lemons planted in tubs, and removed in winter to a covered orangery. The vegetables and salads, the endives and crinkled cabbages, were as fine as could be bought in Rome. The garden

Y

was entered by a corridor, which was ornamented with the head and forequarters of stags, made of wood but with real horns, and with wooden figures of Louis XII's favourite hounds and hawks. The galleries which encircled the garden served as a riding-school, and the Cardinal highly appreciated the stud, especially a dozen small Sardinian horses, a present from the King of Spain. These had beautiful mouths and were marvellously versatile, ambling like jennets, curveting like chargers, or padding along soft and sure as Highland ponies.

Of all foreign palaces the most notable was Gaillon, built in the heyday of the early French Renaissance, and costing Cardinal Amboise the enormous sum of 700,000 francs. He bequeathed it to his see, but it lay heavy on his conscience, and he is said to have cried upon his deathbed, "Would to God that the money spent on Gaillon had been given to the poor". The façade and the fountain may still be seen in Paris, but otherwise Gaillon has almost perished, and Antonio's description is the more precious.[1] The park of Gaillon was six miles round, protected by lofty walls. The square garden was cut by paths into yet smaller squares, each enclosed by wooden lattice-work painted green. There were a few trees, but it was planted mainly with box, rosemary and flowers. The shrubs were clipped into the form of horsemen, ships, animals and birds, while the flower-beds portrayed the royal arms and certain ancient letters. On one side, covered by fine wire-netting, was an aviary with stream and fountain, trees and shrubs, all for the pleasure of the birds. In the centre was an elaborately carved fountain, with a Cupid on its summit spouting water, and above it an octagonal pavilion of oak, enriched with blue and gold, each facet having its own half cupola. There was, too, a garden chamber for summer slumber, with windows of exquisite glass in its eight sides. An open colonnade led to a grass lawn from which a drawbridge gave entrance to the great court, with its fountains plashing high above huge marble monoliths and all its

---

[1] The *Memoirs of the Duc de Luynes* contain a full account of Gaillon in the eighteenth century, vol. vii, pp. 34-40.

doors and windows decorated with heads in classical style. In the balconies, which overlooked the park, were statues of Charles VIII, Louis XII, Anne of Brittany, the Cardinal himself and many courtiers, while the chapel contained statues of all the house of Amboise. The richly furnished rooms, upholstered in velvet, damask and brocade, the painted windows which cost 12,000 crowns, all contributed to make Gaillon the stateliest palace that Antonio had yet seen. Yet there was a fly in the Italian's amber. The fine library, as that of Blois, contained books with King Ferrante's arms, sold, in her necessity, by the unhappy Queen Isabella, while side by side were others looted from Ludovico il Moro, painful reminders of barbarian victories.

A taste for scenery is always worth watching in old travels. No modern tourist forgets his first sight of the lakes by the St. Gothard Hospice and the parting streams of Reuss and Adda. Similarly Antonio, though, like his contemporaries, he does not dilate upon Alpine beauties, was impressed by the two lakelets at the top of the Brenner pass and by the tiny streams of Sill and Eisack running respectively north and south from the watershed. All travellers have felt bound to notice the falls of Schaffhausen; but ordinarily the scenes which pleased Antonio were more humane. He could imagine, *salva honestate*, no more pleasurable sight than the meadow outside Nuremberg, with its close-clipped turf and the five rows of limes, unknown to Italy, with their pale, sweet-scented flowers. The soft beauty of Lake Constance touched him; but, above all, the reach of the Rhine from Mainz to Cologne, the banks covered with vines, the thickly planted towns and villages, and on the hills the knights' ancestral castles. As Tafur before him, he thought this the most beautiful river scene within his knowledge. At Breda the storks' nests on the thirteen trees around the church, all full of young, and the parent birds quite tame, were a lovely thing to see. On the house-tops too were nests of the aforesaid storks, who flew away each year to return to the self-same spot; nor did any citizen do them hurt. To all Italian travellers, Dante perhaps included, the tide of the North Sea was wonderful. "We rode", Antonio writes, "half a mile out at sea along the sand, it being ebb-tide at the turn, which does truly seem a marvellous thing."

Few more graphic accounts have been given of Mont Saint-Michel, the rounded mountain of natural rock planted on the sand, or, at full moon, in two leagues of water, and thence diminishing into the form of a pyramid or a diamond, with houses packed from base to summit, like the overlapping tiles of a cupola, and, rising above all, St. Michael's Church, with its tower so high that the view extended, so natives said, from England to the Pyrenees. "And indeed", adds Antonio cautiously, "it is so high and conveniently placed that, granted the visual power, this might easily be believed." The church itself was then not large, but the present choir was being built, which would be no small addition.

We are accustomed to picturesque description of the junction of the Rhone and Saône, yet very graceful is Antonio's metaphor of the swifter stream cleaving the more sluggish as a fine swimmer or a dolphin parts the waters of the sea; and, again, his skilful touch in comparing the ill-omened lighthouse fortress of Louis XII at Genoa to a falcon above its prey. The whole journey along the Riviera affords examples of the quick eye and terse expression. Antonio sees precisely what the modern traveller would now wish to have seen. He anticipated Lord Brougham's admiration for Cannes, a hamlet of a few houses, but offering lovely views and a charming climate. Very pleasant were the islands off the shore, on the larger of which was a monastery strongly fortified against Moors and pirates, already a scourge of the Riviera. He was, indeed, in a mood for appreciation, for the Bishop of Grasse royally entertained the party with fish as big as it was good. At Fréjus he admired the Roman aqueducts and theatre, not yet much injured; at Antibes the amphitheatre, the road paved with large white flagstones, and the arch with the (to him) illegible inscription, all ascribed to Hercules, who, said the Romans, visited those parts.

From Nice to Genoa there was not a palm's breadth of good road, nor anything but steep mountains and precipitous rocks. Yet he did not fail to admire Eza, a mere group of houses perched upon bare rock high above the sea, and, on the descent, the contrast of the olives and the carob trees, growing in infinite quantities almost to the mountain's base, and still so striking a feature in the landscape. At Bordighera the traveller revelled in the plains covered with olives, figs and vines. Then came San Remo, half upon the mountain-side and half upon the sea, with the thickest, biggest and most fruit-laden orange and lemon trees that he had ever seen. There also was such a quantity of palms that the town pro-vided France, Germany, Florence and Rome, for not yet had the Bordighera sailor's cry of "water on the ropes" secured for his native town the monopoly of palms for the use of St. Peter's. The palms, indeed, were scarcely pretty, for, then as now, they were tied up tight to keep them fresh; nor was their fruit of value.

From Savona to Genoa the riders had to keep their eyes upon the road, or rather the tortuous path, which it was the most dangerous thing in the world to ride, for precipices yawned beneath it. Yet the abundance of grain and the soft-ness of the air made it all a paradise; and Antonio could note the characteristic walled terraces whereon the vines were planted, so that torrential rains might not wash earth and vines into the sea. Tafur, who saw these shores from the sea, also thought them the most beautiful thing on earth, so thickly were they studded with houses that from Savona to Genoa it seemed one long city.

Antonio's quickness of eye is the secret of his fondness for bringing together distant objects and places in comparisons which resemble the travel-sketches of E. A. Freeman. The plain of Augsburg recalled that of Apulia, the paving of Malines that of the Campo di Fiori. Antwerp is compared in size to Bologna; Ghent has a circuit three times as large as Naples. The castle of Tarascon not unnaturally reminded him of the Neapolitan stronghold of the Angevins, the Castel Nuovo. Marforio is utilised to measure the size of the Saint Christopher in Notre-Dame. The tower of Strassburg Cathedral was higher than the Torre del Asinello at Bologna,

the cupola at Florence, the campanile at Venice, or indeed
any other tower in Italy, but he had never, perhaps, seen the
highest, the Torrazzo of Cremona.

Frontiers always interested Antonio. After describing the
defences of the Chiusa, the Venetian boundary, shrunken
since 1516, he shows that Germany, ethnologically, only
began at St. Oliver, five miles north of Trent, whereas the
line has now been pushed ten miles backwards to Salurn.
Maastricht bridge, which became so important in the coming
wars, divided the town, of which the Counts of Flanders were
suzerains, from the temporal lordship of the Bishop of Liège.
Of the bridge of Avignon, the Pope only owned forty of the
461 feet. Along these forty feet a Jew could safely walk; but,
if he overstepped them, he could be killed at sight. On
crossing the Var, Antonio heads his page with *Bella Italia*,
but he confesses that the nationality of Nice is dubious, its
derivation being *ni za ni là*—neither here nor there—while its
very eagle has one leg lifted in an attitude of suspense.

Like a modern tourist, the diarist noted that the lords of
Monaco acknowledged no sovereign upon earth. He describes
their masked batteries of bronze guns, their navy of one
heavily armed *fusta*, which levied a duty of 2 per cent on all
small vessels passing eastward, their army of 186 effectives,
now reduced to 126, the solitary instance of a retrenchment
of bloated armaments. Hard by, the Genoese Bank of St.
George owned Bordighera. Antonio calls this a huge pawnbroking establishment; but really it was a combination of
joint-stock bank and colonial company.

At the conclusion of each section of his journey Antonio
draws up a summary of national characteristics; and these
are of real value for social history. He treats Cologne as the
entrance to the Netherlands, and hence pauses here to render
his account of Upper Germany. On reaching Picardy he
describes the Low Countries, while the crossing of the Var is
followed by his impressions of France. The picture of Germany is the portrayal of substantial well-being; and indeed
this diary is printed as a supplement to Janssen's *History of
the German People*, to confirm his favourable view of German

society previous to the Reformation. Protestant writers have
doubtless too readily accepted the grievances of the insurgent
peasants in 1525 as photographic pictures rather than political pamphlets. On the other hand, the diarist's route lay
through prosperous districts of southern and western Germany; he only saw peasant life from his waggon, while the
wealthy cities gave the Cardinal's party of their best.

Facilities for transport in Germany and the Netherlands
were greater than in Italy, for the roomy four-wheeled waggons had four times the capacity of the Lombard carts. A
voyage down the Rhine in the large boats with their high deck
coverings, pictured in the contemporary engravings, must
have been one long picnic. Inns were excellent; and, even
where there were no vineyards, good red and white wines,
flavoured with rosemary, sage and elder, were always found,
though in the Netherlands they were dearer. This was here
an advance in civilisation, for Tafur describes wine as often
scarce; and once he would have been a total, if involuntary,
abstainer had not an abbess with an ample cellar invited him
to dinner. Beer was universal, but best in the Netherlands,
where it was brewed in infinite quantities. Water was put
aside by Tafur as painfully bad, while Antonio discards it as
soft and brackish. Long afterwards Montesquieu puzzled the
natives of Upper Germany by asking for a drink of water.

Meat was plentiful throughout Germany, and veal ab-
surdly cheap, for a calf could be bought for about ten shillings
at modern value. Both Antonio and Tafur relished the Rhine
salmon. Fresh fish were unfailing, for every host kept live
fish in a tank with water running through it. Near the water-
gate at Constance was a sphere set in the wall, whereon,
under each month, were painted the seasonable fish—a convenient guide for housekeepers. In Flanders fresh-water fish
were replaced by the salted kinds, not to speak of whelks and
oysters, small but abundant. Cabbages in Holland were so
huge that a man could scarce carry more than one; they were
salted for use in winter when snow covered the gardens.
Germans only appreciated cheese when rotten; and no Italian
could touch the highly esteemed but strongly odoriferous

green cheese flavoured with vegetable juices. One cheese in the Netherlands was, however, eatable; it resembled *raveggiolo*, goat's milk cheese. The tourists only tried the native dishes twice, just to taste them, for Germans had a bad habit of cooking with butter instead of oil. Far superior was French cookery, with its thousand sauces and flavourings, its appetising soups and pasties, its shoulder of mutton roast and garnished, which would tempt one away from the most delicate of other meats, the poultry, the rabbits, the pheasants, partridges and peacocks, the fattest venison that ever was seen, for it was forbidden to hunt wild creatures except in season.

From Cologne northwards the hitherto universal stove, prettily fitted with a tin washhand-stand, gave place to open fires. The change from the heated sitting-rooms to the bedrooms, where, in the coldest weather, one had to undress without either fire or stove, was extremely trying. Germans, however, did not mind it, for directly they were in their feather-beds they became as hot as fire. These beds, with *duvets* also made of feathers, were very big, and had the enormous pillows which travellers still have such difficulty in adjusting to their figures; the peculiar German bow seems traceable to the relation of these pillows to the back. The mattress was somewhat hardened by a certain mixture rubbed on either side as a specific against fleas and bugs. Antonio certainly was not bitten, but he sceptically ascribes his immunity to the cold climate. The feather-beds were the final cause of innumerable geese, sometimes four hundred in a flock. Comfortable as the beds were, the habit of putting as many in a room as it would hold was unpraiseworthy. In France they managed better, having two beds only, one for master and one for man. Readers of the *Sentimental Journey* will recognise this type of room. On the other hand, the simplest sanitary furniture was complete and clean, whereas in France the fireplace served all purposes, and that without any shame.

In the Netherlands high praise is given to cleanliness of person, dress and house. In every room there was a mat to wipe one's feet, and the floors were sprinkled with sand. Beds were smaller than in Germany, but framework and canopy were beautifully carved of oak imported from Russia, and quite unlike the Italian. This was also freely used in building. In large cities many houses were built of stone, but in those of brick faced with wood the tawny colour of the oak, its satin-like grain and its skilful carving, rather pleased than hurt the eye. The gardens too were very pleasant, full of roses, lavender and pinks; the pergolas were covered with vines, but the fruit ripened too late for use, and in consequence the wine made in Lower Germany was mere gooseberry.

In spite of superiority in cooking, France was inferior to her neighbours in general civilisation. Even in Paris, Rouen and Tours, houses were usually of wood, or lath and plaster, and could not compare with the stately mansions of Ghent and Bruges. Moreover, even the wooden houses of Upper Germany were commodious and very graceful, with richly carved projecting windows looking up and down the street, covered with tiles painted with the owner's arms and figures of saints, with iron bars of red, green, blue and yellow across the stout woodwork of the door. France had fine churches in her towns; but Antonio admired the steep German roofs and sharp steeples with the variegated lustrous tiles, the incomparable painted glass, and, in the Netherlands, the bizarre gargoyles and string-courses. The pulpits and lecterns were usually of brass imported from England; the chimes rang out to announce the approaching hour, and often even the half-hours were sounded. Each family had its appropriated pew, so that the churches were full of benches with a narrow passage up the middle, just like an Italian lecture-room; the choir alone was reserved for the priests.

Of the religious upheaval immediately at hand, Antonio gives no hint. The churches were always full, and both men and women attended frequently and devoutly, all saying their prayers upon their knees. They did not stroll about, or talk business, or flirt, as was common in Italy. Giuliano de' Medici, it may be remembered, was murdered while walking about during mass; and San Bernardino had denounced the use of church for conveniences of flirtation. Near every town and village were high crucifixes with the thieves hanging on either side, a sight conducive not only to religion but to wholesome fear. Very frequent too were the little shrines with crucifixes, the two Marys and emblems of the Passion; other saints, indeed, were rarely represented in German art without some such symbol. Of French religion little is said, save that in the larger churches there was fine concerted music, and that the six or eight choristers had their heads shaved like friars, and wore copes of red cloth with hoods, like so many Italian canons. The French method of burial was indecent, for even noble and wealthy people were buried outside the churches, and not even in enclosed graveyards, just as if they were Jews. In Germany only the rich, it is true, were buried in church, but other folk were laid in closed cemeteries and had crosses or slabs with inscriptions or coats of arms in bronze and buckets for holy water attacked.

Moral character naturally followed the religious lines. If all the gold of the world were thrown about a Netherlands inn, nobody would touch it; when visitors left valuables in their rooms, they were voluntarily restored. But at Gaillon Antonio's own purse was stolen from his saddle-bag; and so he feels compelled to speak the truth about these wretched French who had played him such a trick. More than once he notices the contrast between gentry and people. The former were well made and handsome, but the common sort were of mean appearance, and as cowardly and vicious as could be imagined. There was this excuse that, whereas the gentry were free from every impost, the peasantry were treated like dogs or slaves, and taxed to the uttermost. Very pleasant was a French noble's life, for in his turn he spent four months at Court, receiving pay; for the rest he could live in his castle among the woods, hunting and spending little, having no occasion to "fray his velvet", as the saying went. French nobles had, indeed, cause to thank God more heartily than any others, for, once born a gentleman, there was no chance of starving or of plying degrading trades, whereas few Italian nobles lived like real gentlemen, even if they had the means.

Love of pleasure infected Frenchmen of all conditions. They thought of nothing but living cheerfully, and were so much given to eating, drinking and love-making that it was hard to imagine how they could do any work. The lower classes pitiably lacked the military training which Antonio, like Machiavelli and Vettori, so greatly admired in Germany. From childhood Germans were trained to arms; and in every city and village there was a ground for matches with crossbow and fire-arms on holidays, and for drill with pikes and other weapons. Antonio had not only seen Maximilian's fine artillery at Trent and Innsbruck, but had visited the magnificent armoury at Nuremberg, with its big guns and small, its curious equivalent for *mitrailleuses*, its stores of ammunition, even its horses ready for the guns. There, too, he saw the great magazines of fuel and grain, maintained so that even during a lengthy siege the iron industries would not suffer.

Germany had her moral scourge in the brigand nobles, whose numerous castles gave shelter to malefactors of all classes; and life would be impossible unless justice were severe. Everywhere could be seen wheels and gallows, the latter sumptuously ornamented not only with carving, but with hanging men and women. Justice was also laudably active in France, where the innumerable gallows were always found "well furnished". There was, perhaps, not much to choose between the two countries. Brigands ensconced upon the high-road had forced the travellers to take a circuitous route to Ulm, under an Augsburg escort; and they were detained at Avignon for fear of Gascon mercenaries returning from Leo X's campaign against Urbino. On other dark sides of German life, such as the drinking, of which Aeneas Silvius gives such terrible pictures, Antonio does not touch. Nor does he mention the mixed bathing described by Rozmital's companions and Tafur. This was one of the sights of Bâle, where the respectable Tafur visited the baths with a pious baroness on a pilgrimage. He threw in coins for which her damsels dived. "Men and women", he concludes, "think no more of bathing together, stripped to the skin, than they do in Spain of going to church."

The Ritter, Arnold von Harff, had found women prettiest in Milan, noblest in Cologne, most extravagant in Venice, and blackest in the kingdom of Moab.[1] Antonio also, for a chaplain, took an intelligent interest in women and their dress. He says that in Upper Germany they kept their crockery cleaner than their persons, and wore the commonest clothes, too short and skimpy to hide their legs. They went barefooted, or, if they had shoes, were stockingless. The girls on feast-days wore crowns of flowers; but their elders, fearing cold, had quilted caps over their braided hair. They were pretty and pleasant, by temperament cold, but in practice somewhat wanton—at least so Antonio's more adventurous comrades told him. The ladies were elegantly dressed; and their spotless veils, drawn up into high peaks, or, in mourning, hanging like weepers down their backs, gave a very dignified appearance. Skirts were usually of black serge, rarely of silk. These ladies were particularly polite to foreigners of position, rising and curtseying as they passed. How different it was in Genoa, where young girls stood in groups till quite late, chattering to their friends and taking no notice of distinguished passers-by! Constance bore off the palm for pretty women, and here, curiously enough, Tafur had met the loveliest girl that he had ever seen, or could hope to see, loveliness that he had thought impossible in a human form; if only she were as good as she was beautiful she would have a large share in paradise.

In the Netherlands women were finely made, and had pink and white complexions, innocent of rouge or other artifice. Their teeth were, however, as in Germany, undeniably bad, which is ascribed to immoderate use of beer or butter. Butter and milk were also held responsible for the prevalence of leprosy. In this respect Tafur is more modern, for, like Dr. Williamson, he believed that leprosy was caused by improperly cured fish.

French women were unquestionably plain, and in Picardy downright ugly. A passing commendation is given to the

---

[1] Arnold von Harff, *Pilgerfahrt in den Jahren 1496–1497*, ed. E. von Groote (Köln, 1860).

now notorious beauties of Arles; but at Lyons, for a French town, the ladies were most beautiful. "Lyons itself, its men and its women, have some indescribable touch of lovely Italy, so that I judge it to be the handsomest town in France." Dress was singularly uniform, except that in the Île de France it was of finer material and superior cut. In the colder districts petticoats were quilted with lamb's-wool, and close caps, tied under the chin, were worn beneath the hats, and, in rainy weather, hoods covering the head and back. In Court circles ladies danced divinely and in the most perfect time with the music. Women were more employed abroad than in Italy. It was scarcely laudable that, as in the Netherlands, they should have charge of the altar and the relics; but then they were so pious and so honest! They sold in the markets, worked in shops like men, and in inns kept the accounts and managed everything. In France, also, they plied all kinds of trades, and even shaved gentlemen with much delicacy and dexterity.

For travellers the etiquette of the embrace was an essential study. In France it was correct to kiss the chambermaid as a token of courtesy and esteem. Not so in Germany with the three or four young and pretty maids besides the hostess and her daughters. Here politeness required the visitor to shake hands and then take them round the waist, giving indeed a hug. It was customary, too, to invite them to drink; but here propriety must intervene. Ignorance of etiquette led occasionally to lamentable consequences. During the Wars of Religion a young French officer, crossing the German frontier, was nearly beaten to death for kissing his hostess, doubtless as a mark of courtesy and esteem. Yet in Switzerland, writes Felix Faber, handsome girls with pretty figures were kissed by all and sundry. North of the Channel kissing was universal. Aeneas Silvius appreciated this pretty habit of the Scottish women, who, indeed, took the initiative. In Rozmital's travels we read that an English hostess and her daughters always kissed their guests instead of shaking hands.

Many hints on manufactures may be gleaned from

z

Antonio's journals; and the information on smaller local specialities is often fresh. Thus at Brixen the Cardinal bought an organ, at Waldsee flutes and all manner of wind instruments. Malines was famous for archery outfits; Genoa, not only for the finest velvet, but for coral ornaments. At Saint-Antoine de Bienne were purchased the best boxwood combs and little images of bad silver, with the saint's bell, his "Tau", and the notorious pig. Every pilgrim to Mont Saint-Michel carried home a coloured scarf, with shells stitched thereon, and a copper horn, which he blew all the way. Paris was chiefly remarkable for the infinity of minor trades carried on by both sexes in open shops. Antonio was unlucky in visiting Antwerp just as the Dutch traders had left the fair. For this, and for that of Bruges in its palmy days, recourse must be had to the admirable description of Tafur, who says that Antwerp surpassed Genoa, Frankfurt and Medina all combined. Antonio describes at length the processes of pickling hemp and flax in Holland, in course of which the girl picklers would tie the legs of passers-by to the frames on which the hemp was laid, and so exact contributions for their annual feast.

Cultivation also attracted the diarist's roving eye. He admired the Netherland hops, trained on poles like vines in Italy, and the pear and apple orchards of Normandy. Perry and cider he thought pleasanter than beer, though not so wholesome; while hops, in spite of bitterness, made beer most refreshing. In northern France oil was made from walnuts, as there were no olives. Mention is made of the Bon-chrétien pear (Buon Cristiano), and of the winter Bergamot (Bergamuto) found at Genoa. The muscatel grape was cultivated at Antibes, and black figs and raisins were as delicious at Avignon as at Naples. Antonio noticed the practice of chalking fields in northern France, and the plantations of tall, straight oak near Bourges, grown clear of underwood on approved modern principles. Near Montélimar could be seen fields of lavender for the supply of lavender-water for France and Germany. Nor are more ordinary crops forgotten, nor sheep and cattle, the small red cows of Germany and the

familiar black and white herds of Holland, the dappled sort
being the prettiest beasts a man could wish to see.

England is represented in the diary by Calais only. Most
impressive were its huge walls, its deep ditch and counter-
ditch, its canals regulated by locks, which could flood the
country four miles round. The solitary gate was open only
during day; if the King himself arrived after supper he must
sleep outside; the Governor must never leave the walls. The
garrison were the tallest, best-proportioned and handsomest
of mankind; and flattering conclusions are drawn as to English physique in general. Their practice with the bow was
marvellous; and one of the King's archers could pierce a pipe
full of wine from rim to rim. Sir Richard Wingfield, a gentlemanly man who knew Italy, was Governor; and the Cardinal
stood godfather to his child. A passage was taken for England,
but Wingfield dissuaded it, as the sweating sickness was
killing five hundred people a day in London.

Antonio's views on England would have been welcome.
We should have known whether the ladies still wore, as in
Rozmital's time, the longest tails in Europe; and whether the
men continued to be faithless, astute and ever compassing
the death of the foreigners. He could have remarked on the
novel sight of fields surrounded by hedges and ditches,
whereon none might trespass, on the strings of pack-horses
instead of carts, on the wealth in sheep, and the astounding
quantity of hares and rabbits around Salisbury, on the pheno-
menal skill of English sailors in climbing masts. Sandwich,
in Rozmital's time, must have tried the powers of the Seven
Sleepers, for all night long watchmen with fifes and trumpets
shouted the direction of the wind, so that traders might leave
their beds, board their ships, and steer for their respective
fatherlands. The feelings of Rozmital's suite towards England
were doubtless tempered by misfortunes. On their first
attempt they were all but wrecked, and on their final return
to Guernsey had a terribly rough passage. English men-of-
war, moreover, had the nervous or impulsive habits of more
modern navies, for two galleons, mistaking their vessels for
enemies, *tormenta explodere coeperunt.*

INDEX

THE END

Printed in Great Britain by R. & R. Clark, Limited, Edinburgh.

NEW MACMILLAN BOOKS

EGYPT SINCE CROMER. By the Right Hon. Lord
Lloyd of Dolobran, G.C.S.I., formerly High Com-
missioner for Egypt and the Sudan. Vol. II. With
Maps. 8vo. 21s. net.
Previously published: Vol. I. 21s. net.

NAPOLEON AND HIS MARSHALS. By A. G.
Macdonell, author of "England, their England."
Crown 8vo. 7s. 6d. net.

THE RISE AND FULFILMENT OF BRITISH
RULE IN INDIA. By G. T. Garratt and Edward
Thompson. 8vo.

THE JEWS IN THE MODERN WORLD. By Dr.
Arthur Ruppin, Lecturer in Sociology at the Hebrew
University of Jerusalem. With a Preface by L. B.
Namier. 8vo. 15s. net.

MAXIMILIEN ROBESPIERRE: A Study in Deterioration. By Rev. R. Somerset Ward. 8vo.

THE RUSSIAN JOURNALS OF MARTHA AND
CATHERINE WILMOT. Edited, with an Introduction and Notes, by the Marchioness of London-
derry and H. Montgomery Hyde. Illustrated. 8vo.
A fascinating picture of travel and Society in Tsarist Russia at
the beginning of the nineteenth century.

FRIEDRICH VON GENTZ' RELATIONS WITH THE
BRITISH GOVERNMENT FROM 1809 to 1812.
By C. S. B. Buckland, author of "Metternich and
the British Government." 8vo. 5s. net.

MACMILLAN AND CO. LTD., LONDON

7 35